SOCIAL WORK ISSUES IN HEALTH CARE

CONTRIBUTORS

Barbara Berkman
Bess Dana
Rosalind S. Miller
Helen Rehr
Gary Rosenberg
Andrew Weissman

SOCIAL WORK ISSUES IN HEALTH CARE

EDITED BY
ROSALIND S. MILLER
HELEN REHR

Prentice-Hall, Inc., Englewood Cliffs, New Jersey 07632

Library of Congress Cataloging in Publication Data

Main entry under title:

Social work issues in health care.

  Bibliography: p.
  Includes index.
  1. Medical social work—United States. I. Miller,
Rosalind S. II. Rehr, Helen. [DNLM: 1. Social work.
2. Sociology, Medical. 3. Delivery of health care.
W 322 S674]
HV687.5.U5S645 1982   362.1'0425   82-12294
ISBN 0-13-819532-3

Production Editor: Dee Amir Josephson
Manufacturing Buyer: John Hall
Cover Design: Ray Lundgren

Printed in the United States of America

10 9 8 7 6 5 4 3 2 1

ISBN 0-13-819532-3

Prentice-Hall International, Inc., *London*
Prentice-Hall of Australia Pty. Limited, *Sydney*
Prentice-Hall Canada, Inc., *Toronto*
Prentice-Hall of India Private Limited, *New Delhi*
Prentice-Hall of Japan, Inc., *Tokyo*
Prentice-Hall of Southeast Asia Pte. Ltd., *Singapore*
Whitehall Books Limited, *Wellington, New Zealand*

CONTENTS

PREFACE

Of all fields of practice in which social workers help their clients with psychosocial problems, the field of health and mental health is the largest. Problems of physical complaint, disease, substance abuse, emotional turmoil, or mental illness are among the conditions that bring the consumer to the physician's office or clinical setting. While many physical and psychological problems are biological or genetic in origin, factors of environmental stress, occupational hazards, and pollutants also have negative impact on the quality of life. Throughout the life span, every individual in the society, irrespective of age, income, or class, is at one time or another a recipient of health or medical care. In this country, health care has become the second largest "industry," representing about 10 percent of the GNP, with a projected expenditure for 1983 of $320 billion.

The decision to write this book was based upon the editors' belief that a text was needed for social work students that addressed the basic issues for social work practice in health care. The book may also be used by the practitioner or supervisor as a basic reference, as well as a source for updating knowledge about current practice concerns. The content covers the structure and organization of health care settings, the consumers of services, the health policies and legislation that regulate the way services are delivered, the knowledge base for practice, including models for intervention and the collaborative arrangements among a host of disciplines involved in the helping process, and the implications of practice for purposes of evaluation and research. And, finally, an attempt is made to forecast future directions for social work in health care in the coming years.

Regardless of the issues presented in this overview of the social worker's role and function in the health field, the content in each chapter is developed to show the integration of theoretical understanding to practice considerations. Attempting to achieve this integrative approach became the challenge—the unifying underpinning—for the contributors to this volume. In this endeavor, we hope we have met with some degree of success. Second, we have conceptualized practice for a health social worker (or a health-care social worker) without the labels, medical or psychiatric. There are two reasons: Social work is unique in its contribution, as other health professions are; and the ability of the social worker to enunciate that contribution dissipates the "hand-maiden" designation, particularly in an era that focuses on a holistic approach to health care.

We gratefully acknowledge our fellow contributors, each of whom has made significant contributions to social work in health as practitioners, researchers, and educators.

R. S. M.
H. R.

CONTRIBUTORS

Barbara Berkman, D.S.W., Professor and Director, Social Work in Health Care Program, Massachusetts General Hospital Institute of Health Professions

Bess Dana, M.S.S.A., Professor of Community Medicine; Director, Education Unit, Mount Sinai School of Medicine, City University of New York

Rosalind S. Miller, M.A., M.S., Associate Professor, Columbia University School of Social Work

Helen Rehr, D.S.W., Edith F. Baerwald Professor of Community Medicine (Social Work), Mount Sinai School of Medicine, City University of New York

Gary Rosenberg, Ph.D., Director, Department of Social Work Services, The Mount Sinai Hospital; Associate Professor, Department of Community Medicine (Social Work), Mount Sinai School of Medicine, City University of New York

L. Andrew Weissman, D.S.W., Senior Associate Director of Social Work Services, The Mount Sinai Hospital, Assistant Professor, Department of Community Medicine (Social Work), Mount Sinai School of Medicine, City University of New York

CHAPTER ONE
HEALTH SETTINGS
AND HEALTH PROVIDERS

Rosalind S. Miller and Helen Rehr

SOCIAL WORK IN HEALTH SETTINGS

Some 45,000 social workers practice in the health field today. They are practitioners who work collaboratively with other health providers in voluntary and municipal hospitals, in ambulatory care, community mental health clinics and psychiatric and state mental institutions. In large teaching hospitals, social service departments may employ a hundred or more workers while only one or two social workers will be found in a small general hospital. They are found also in prepaid group practices, Health Maintenance Organizations, as well as in industry and labor unions where they offer psychosocial services and also act as consultants to employees in substance abuse and preventive health care programs. They work for the U.S. Public Health Service, the Veterans' Administration, municipal, state, and federal health agencies. They are practitioners who meet the psychosocial needs of the physically and mentally ill; they are administrators, health planners, and policy makers. The National Association of Social Workers (NASW) reports that for 1981, out of a total membership of 85,000, 60 percent of the members practice in health and/or mental health.[1]

For nearly 80 years social workers have had formal sanction to practice in health, a sanction initially provided in 1906 by Dr. Richard C. Cabot when he

[1] Approximately 50 percent practice in health and/or mental health organizational settings; approximately 8 to 10 percent are in private practice. Informal communication from Maryanne Keenan, Senior Staff Associate–Health Policy, National Association of Social Workers, Washingtion, D.C.

established social services at Massachusetts General Hospital.[2] He assigned a small group of social workers to the outpatient department to work primarily with mothers and children. During the last decades of the nineteenth century, Boston and other urban areas saw large population shifts, the result of the wave of immigration, particularly from Ireland, Germany, and Eastern Europe. Crowded housing, inadequate nutrition, poor hygenic facilities, and economic plight were social problems that Cabot perceived as indivisible from the physical complaints and illnesses presented by the poor in his clinics.

It is a rare historical social work perspective that does not enunciate Cabot's seminal role in the development of medical social work. What makes the event noteworthy is not so much the involvement of social workers in health care, but rather the legitimism of social work within the hospital system. Prior to that point, first in England and then in the United States, the nineteenth-century settlement movement launched numerous programs and advocated innovative health policies to combat the danger of pollutants and dirt in the environment. Impure water, vermin, accumulated garbage, poorly ventilated houses, windowless rooms, and negligent reporting or no quarantine for cases of communicable disease were all problems attacked by health reformers and settlement leaders. Jane Addams, Lillian Wald, Edward Devine, and scores of other citizens, all of whom were devoted to the improvement of the health and welfare of the tenement people, are well-known names in the history of the movement. In large measure their initiatives and zeal were responsible for the establishment and growth of neighborhood health centers, baby clinics, diagnostic centers, first-aid rooms, open-air camps, and sanitaria.[3] Health reform during the era of the early days of the settlement movement is an exciting chapter in the history of social work, particularly medical social work. In the view of hospital administrators and physicians, it was one thing to be a health reformer as part of a "do-good" movement; but it was something else again to bring nonmedical personnel who were not even nurses into the hospital. By sanctioning the social worker, Cabot opened the door, so to speak, to a broader view of patient care. Just two years after social work was introduced at Massachusetts General Hospital, Jane Addams addressed the American Hospital Association, the first time a social worker appeared before that organization of hospital administrators. In a paper entitled, "The Layman's View of Hospital Work Among the Poor," Addams detailed for her audience the "failure of hospital personnel to see the patient as a person." Ida Cannon, who subsequently became the first director of social services at Massachusetts General, recorded some 35 years later that historic occasion and commented, "Her [Addams] characteristi-

---

[2] See Harriett Bartlett, *Social Work Practice in the Health Field* (New York: National Association of Social Workers, 1961), p. 24: "Sanction denotes the authority for carrying on practice. Social work practice is sponsored by the agencies—governmental and voluntary agencies—within which social work positions have been established. Sanction is also derived from the organized profession itself, which defines educational and other standards, and the conditions under which practice can be undertaken."

[3] See, for example, Robert A. Woods and Albert F. Kennedy, *The Settlement Horizon* (New York: Russell Sage Foundation, 1922) and Edward T. Devine, *When Social Work was Young* (New York: Macmillan, 1939).

cally courageous frankness must have created quite an ordeal for the hospital administrators. . . ."[4]

Within a few years, first at Bellevue and then at Johns Hopkins, other hospitals began to include social workers whose chief role was that of interpreter between patient and physician, patient and hospital. Hospital social service departments have flourished since their initial beginnings, so that today some 75 percent of the hospitals with more than 200 beds have social service departments.[5] Their growth and the leadership provided by their directors are still another fascinating chapter in the history of medical social services. Although it is beyond the scope of this chapter to detail that history, the social worker in health care should be familiar with the leaders who helped to shape medical social work: Ida M. Cannon, Mary Antoinette Cannon, Edith Baker, Janet Thornton, Eleanor Cockrell, Elizabeth Rice, and for conceptualizing medical social work practice, Gordon Hamilton and Harriett M. Barlett.[6]

Paralleling the development of medical social work, psychiatry turned to social workers for help in understanding the relationship between emotional factors and the individual problems in coping with the environment, problems that resulted in difficulties on the job, discontent within the family, and dissatisfactions with interpersonal relationships. As early as 1910, two years before they opened the doors to the first patients, Boston Psychopathic Hospital included social service as part of the initial plan. When the hospital opened in 1912 under the directorship of Dr. E. E. Southard, Mary C. Jarrett was appointed director of social service. Miss Jarrett developed the first in-service program for special social work training, introducing a new term—psychiatric social work. Quoting from *The Kingdom of Evils*, coauthored with Dr. Southard, Miss Jarrett said

> We claim no novelty or originality for the social work of the Psychopathic Hospital, but rather, we would claim to have created the part that the social worker is to play in the mental hygiene movement and to have given it a name—psychiatric social work. The bases of this new division of social work are the principles common to all forms of social case work. It is the application of old methods in a new field. It will, we expect, develop some new methods, which will in time be applied in the older fields.[7]

Her definition of the functions of the psychiatric social worker still have relevance for practice today. Had her vision of social work function been adhered to, subsequent narrowing of the worker's perception of role in psychiatric settings and with

[4] Ida Cannon, "Lay Participation in Hospital Service from the Point of View of a Medical Social Worker" in *Readings in the Theory and Practice of Medical Social Work*, ed. Dora Goldstine (Chicago: University of Chicago Press, 1954), p. 57.

[5] *Encyclopedia of Social Work* (Washington, D.C.: *National Association of Social Workers*, 1977), p. 616.

[6] Gordon Hamilton, *A Medical Social Terminology* (New York: Social Services Department of the Presbyterian Hospital, 1930) and Bartlett, *Social Work Practice in the Health Field*.

[7] Lois M. French, *Psychiatric Social Work* (New York: Commonwealth Fund, 1940), pp. 37-8.

it the cleavage that followed between the medical and psychiatric social worker might not have occurred. Jarrett emphasized

1. dealing with social problems,
2. working with the patient for return to community and normal living,
3. assuming executive duties for the purpose of efficient management,
4. educative functions in the community, including the promoting of an understanding of mental illness,
5. research.[8]

It was Jarrett's early training of social workers at Boston Psychopathic Hospital that paved the way for the introduction of the first course in psychiatric social work at Smith College in 1918. However, even before formal courses were introduced into schools of social work, psychiatric social service departments were formed in state hospitals and psychiatric clinics. Within a few years the child guidance movement was under way. The impetus behind the movement was Dr. William Healy's early research (1902) in Chicago with delinquents at the juvenile court. Then, in 1917, Dr. Healy and Dr. Augusta Bronner started a children's clinic in Boston under the name of the Judge Baker Foundation, the name to be changed in 1933 to the Judge Baker Guidance Center.[9]

Following World War I, the Surgeon General of the United States Public Health Service asked the Red Cross to assume responsibility for organizing social service departments in federal hospitals.[10] Later, the Veterans' Administration assumed responsibility for the veterans' hospitals.

During World War II, "a psychiatric social work consultant service was established for the military through the efforts of Maida Solomon and the American Association of Psychiatric social workers."[11] Today, thousands of social workers are employed in VA hospitals, performing services in all the medical and psychiatric specialties.

Since 1963, with the passage of the Mental Retardation Facilities and Community Mental Health Centers Construction Act (see Chapter Three), social workers, and to a lesser extent psychologists, have been the primary providers of mental health services in community mental health centers. More recently, we have seen an emphasis on primary health care—a holistic approach to patient care, one in which the physician or health team assesses not only the physical but the psychosocial needs of the patient. With the social worker as a member of the team, the model blurs the strong demarcation between medical and psychiatric social work functions and calls for a health social worker. Such a worker has knowledge about physical illness and

[8]*Ibid.*, p. 40.

[9]William Healy and Augusta Bronner, "The Child Guidance Clinic: Birth and Growth of an Idea" in *Orthopsychiatry, 1923-1948: Retrospect and Prospect*, ed. Lawson Lowrey and Victoria Sloane (Menasha, Wi.: American Orthopsychiatric Association, 1948), pp. 14-35.

[10]French, *Psychiatric Social Work*, p. 51.

[11]*Encyclopedia of Social Work*, p. 900.

emotional stress and can address the social components of the patient's problem as they affect the patient's medical and/or psychiatric complaints.

Over a span of eight decades, if we assess the roles and functions of both medical and psychiatric social workers, the commonalities and differences are quite clear. As a generalization, the "marriage" between psychiatry and psychiatric social work has been less fraught with problems of status and function than that between medicine and medical social work. Harriett Bartlett has observed

> While both medical and psychiatric social work function within medicine, psychiatric social work and psychiatry seem to be largely within the same framework, whereas medical social work and medicine (in spite of overlapping in the social area) seem to be operating in different frameworks. It has not been sufficiently recognized how greatly the problem of integration of service is increased by the degree of such difference; and, at the same time, how much greater is the opportunity to make a significant contribution of something new because of this very difference.[12]

Although Bartlett's observation was written 20 years ago it contains the essential message for the profession today. As a profession, we are able to demonstrate the effectiveness of our services to patients in more ways than at any previous time in the profession's history. And we can do so within the unique contribution that social work has to make. Our skills and knowledge address the primary function of helping patients negotiate the health care system. Through fast but accurate assessment, we can specify as we work collaboratively with the patient what are the social problems and environmental stressors, and the interpersonal and familial dysfunctions that impinge upon physical or emotional illness and impede recovery. And we can individualize our interventions, based upon our knowledge of physical, emotional, and environmental factors. This methodological approach as applied to the helping process with the individuals, families, and groups we serve is not new; over the years additional knowledge has helped to refine our skills, to select appropriate interventive modalities, to enunciate with good accuracy a rationale for appropriate case focus on the target problem, and with good accuracy to predict case outcome. As Jarrett wisely said, the methods and principles of social work are common to all forms of social work practice. The point is basic, then as now: the sanction for the roles and functions social workers perform in health settings remains secure as long as we maintain our social orientation to patient care. No other health provider circumscribes practice from this perspective; it is our domain.

The social worker's effectiveness to help the patient move through the health care system is also determined by the worker's understanding of organizational structures and administrative arrangements in the particular setting, along with a knowledge of the support system necessary to maintain the patient in the community. For practice in hospitals, this knowledge base is translated into action skills that (1) dictate early case finding to identify stressful patient situations and prob-

---

[12] Bartlett, *Social Work Practice in the Health Field*, p. 131.

lems; (2) specify early discharge plans to insure another appropriate level of patient care; and (3) meet the utilization requirements for reimbursement purposes. Similar skills are applied to the helping process with patients in ambulatory settings, psychiatric clinics, and community mental health centers. The vast majority of patients want help with the amelioration of tensions and dysfunctional coping that arise from present environmental stresses and current interpersonal and familial conflicts. To be of greatest help to the patient, the social worker is attuned not only to the selection of the most effective interventions in delivering direct services that accurately respond to the patient's need, but is also ever vigilant of the congruence between the policies and organizational structure of the agency and the services delivered to the consumer.

Whether the work is carried out with inpatients in hospitals or out patients in clinics, the activity is a collaborative one. Medicine, psychiatry, and administrators determine the inclusion and the numbers of social workers into the system. Therefore, as Barlett suggests, "It is important for social work to be aware of, and to maintain, its own position and framework."[13] Only then can our special contribution to patient care enhance our relevance and increase our job satisfaction. Within such a context social workers have greater opportunities to pursue social work objectives in the interest of the patient; to participate in effective interdisciplinary collaboration; to widen organizational sanction that legitimates social work as an integral part of the health setting; and to participate in shaping and changing health care policies to improve delivery systems.[14]

Hospitals

Of all health structures, the general hospital is the most complex. It is the "hub" of the health care system. Since World War II its services cross both medical and psychiatric illness, both for inpatient as well as ambulatory patient care. As an organization, it sets up its own tension with a dual structural arrangement: an administrative arm concerned with fiscal accountability, bookkeeping mechanisms, plant management, housekeeping activities, security procedures, labor policies, and public relations; a clinical arm concerned with service delivery by a host of professions and disciplines—physicians, nurses, social workers, psychologists, technicians, and researchers, the numbers and selection of each determined by the size of the setting. Whether administrative or clinical, each department, and within it, each division or service is a subsystem of the whole, with personnel stratified by position and rank, always in hierarchical arrangements. By its very structure, each subsystem is unitized; given its overall purpose, the hospital is a unified "whole." As has frequently been pointed out, the hospital is greater than its parts. Each employee negotiates the system, accountable both to the subsystem and the institution at large; and all, in one way or another, execute their functions in collaborative arrangements that secure the safety of the patient and insure quality of care.

[13] Bartlett, *Social Work Practice in the Health Field*, p. 131.

[14] We acknowledge our gratitude to the late Dr. Hyman Weiner, for our discussions of this content with him.

With emphasis only on the social worker, the greater the understanding brought to the system, the more effective the execution of practice objectives.

This point is obviously applicable to the hospital social worker, but it has equal relevance for all health social workers who are community based and who frequently refer their patients for tertiary care. In addition, while emphasis has been placed on the general hospital, the structural and organizational complexities are similar in state mental hospitals and psychiatric institutions. But whatever the institutional setting, an integral part of practice for the social worker includes the ability to recognize viable entry points for negotiating and modifying the system; to discern collaborative arrangements; to advocate for the patient with appropriate others; and to perform these myriad activities at a level that reflects the ethics and values of the profession.

The health care system in this country has changed over the last thirty years, due to the advances in medical technology. Diagnostic and therapeutic services, because of their sophistication, complexity, and costliness have moved from traditional office procedures by the private physician to the general acute care hospital. The growth of and expansion in hospitals and beds in the United States reflect also the increased number and kinds of specialized services offered by hospitals. Programs such as cardiac and other intensive care units, renal dialysis and transplant units, and a host of other specialized services have proliferated so that 54 are identified for special annual reporting to the American Hospital Association.[15] The impact is on the growth in facilities, specialists, and technicians with their own goals and priorities, expectations, rules, and regulations, compartmentalizing programs into small autonomous divisions, which must operate with interdependent practices in order to serve a patient among them. Also advanced technology has made testing procedures readily available and a virtual aid to doctors. The media-informed patient demands them as well. Between 1965 and 1970, laboratory tests and costs increased more than twice that of the overall increase in hospital costs. Such tests, often abused, may not even affect the health care status of a patient, but it does affect him in social and economic costs.[16]

Short-term medical institutions either make provision for these advanced medical technologies on their own or have merged with other medical institutions within a region so as to provide comprehensive services by a division of specialties among them. The merged or affiliated institution with a major university teaching hospital is becoming commonplace, and is seen as offering many advantages to patients, physicians, and other health care professionals in joining educational, research, as well as capital equipment resources.[17]

It is interesting to note that half of the over 7,000 hospitals in this country

[15] American Hospital Association, *Hospital Statistics* (Chicago: American Hospital Association, 1975), p. 187.

[16] Stephen J. Durnic and others, "The Physician's Role in the Cost-Containment Problem," *JAMA*, 24, no. 15 (April 15, 1979), pp. 1608-11.

[17] See Cecil G. Sheps, "Trends in Hospital Care" in *Health Care Administration: A Managerial Perspective*, ed. Samuel Levey and N. Paul Loomba (Philadelphia: Lippincott, 1973), pp. 21-3.

have less than 125 beds. These facilities are usually in small communities or in rural areas. In general the staff is said to know their patients, and usually know each other. Administrators of small institutions, while as concerned about the cost of giving care as their urban medical center counterparts, tend to be closer to their staff, doctors, and even to patients. These administrators can respond quicker to problems than the larger decentralized programs in urban medical care systems. On the other hand, doctors and their hospitals in the small communities sometimes hold decision-making as a solo responsibility, without involving others, even their patients, except in the expectation of compliance with recommendations.

The academic health center under the aegis of the university has a profound influence on the operational services of its teaching hospitals. They control more than 25 percent of the beds in this country. They also have been the beneficiaries of a great deal of medical research and education monies. Although the academic medical center's major concentration is on quality of care, this concentration is largely biomedical. Factors such as access, effectiveness, economy, and equity of services arise more out of social and community pressures to examine them, than as fundamentals to the delivery of medical services. Individuals suffering from the newly recognized social ailments of substance abuse, child, wife, and parent abuse enter the academic medical center's emergency rooms but in the context of a physical disorder. Although such problems are a major public concern, they are not within the purview of the biologically trained physician. The causes relevant to the before and after situations are not usually addressed. Although medicine has accepted the responsibility for the care of patients suffering from such problems, it has not been educated to deal with the complex social problems of today. These social problems call for knowledge from the range of social and behavioral sciences, and for treatments and programs with both a psychosocial and medical emphasis as mutually inseparable in the care of these sufferers. Within recent years, in order to rectify the biomedical focus, both social workers and psychiatrists have been assigned to emergency rooms.

In spite of the preponderance of social problems that can be witnessed in any emergency room, social service directors are just beginning to give priority to programming at this entry point into the health care system while they attempt to maintain an optimal level of social work assignments for inpatient services. The decision of where and how to deploy workers is a very complicated one, especially since discharge planning from inpatient services is a crucial hospital priority, and one that requires the major portion of a social work department's manpower. At the same time, hospital administrators are concerned about utilization patterns of emergency room services, particularly by consumers who present nonmedical problems or present social problems that a health care system is incapable of either modifying or ameliorating. A concomitant with these problems is the fiscal drain that all hospitals are now experiencing in their emergency and ambulatory services. The costs must be passed on. The patient requiring tertiary care is the one who finds the costs of ambulatory services reflected in his bill. There is an urgent need for social work administrators in hospital settings to continue to plan for creative ambulatory programs, including consortium arrangements with community social agencies, to address their consumers' needs as well as the hospitals' fiscal crisis.

The academic center is primarily concerned with teaching-learning processes. The relationship to service is more in the context of its contributions to the educational process.[18] Although it is said that hospitals with medical and psychiatric educational programs are ones with greater quality of care than those without, because of their proximity to the teachers in the halls of learning, they may not have the sensitivity to care and service that can be found in community hospitals. The university medical school controls the current organization of care, and there is comparatively little evidence of its wish to shift from traditional ways of delivering care and in programming its education in the existing medical care system. There is also the problem resulting from the wide range of technologies developing in the schools, with their application frequently related to educational demands rather than general cost-effective and ethical concerns. The result is usually a more indiscriminate use of tests and laboratory investigation, emphasizing the study needs, which can be very costly. The academic world has a responsibility to publish on its experimental programs and technological advances; it does so liberally, resulting in the public's demand for more. The current trend in medical technological advances is geared more toward the problems of the very sick than toward more common ailments. This is equally true for the psychiatric teaching hospitals that carry on elaborate studies such as the effect of lithium on the manic depressive patient or research into anorexia nervosa. Also, sophisticated technology such as dialysis and transplants are available for the few at very costly expenditures, which are borne by the public at large.

The academic model of medical care delivery has had a profound effect not only on the medical institution but on its professional and paraprofessional personnel as well. The administration of hospitals is usually directed to maintaining open service doors, relevant to the programs available with little emphasis on the why and how in relation to the needs of those served. The concentration has been on admitting and discharging patients, keeping the users comfortable, but also keeping the beds full.[19] There is some change in regard to the nature of admissions as a result of the federal government's 1974 intervention via its Professional Standard Review Organization (PSRO) regulations governing cost containment. This limitation of what is reimbursable and what has become an acceptable length of stay is discussed in Chapter Three.

Depersonalization tends to surface more in the larger institutions: the larger the hospital the less individualization. The rationale is lodged in a bureaucracy governed by rules, regulations, procedures, and priorities promulgated to secure efficiency and uniformity. Frequently, the results are routinized, mechanized responses

[18]Cecil G. Sheps, "The Role of the Academic Health Center," presentation, Conference Series, Issues in Health Care Policy, Department of Community Medicine, Mount Sinai School of Medicine, CUNY, September 30, 1977.

[19]Kerr L. White, "Health Care Arrangements in the United States: A.D. 1972," *The Milbank Memorial Fund Quarterly*, L, no. 4 (October 1972), p. 22.

to patients. It has been suggested that technological advancement adds to dehumanization. However, if one has entered a Coronary Intensive Care Unit (CICU) in a medical center, one perceives in spite of the equipment, more often than not, very close interpersonal communication. Technology in itself does not need to create dehumanized services. It will do so under conditions that foster a lack of communication between patients and staff. Inadequate communication exaggerates the medical mystique. In addition, it gives the impression that patients are put upon with unnecessary procedures, denied choices limiting self-autonomy, and restricted in their role of shared decision-making.

In the more complex institution the very skilled jobs go to specialists and the less prestigious tasks are assumed by caretakers where most of the contacts with patients occur, by housekeepers, dietary aides, nurses' aides, and volunteers. It is these staff who listen and comfort, when a humanized professional exchange is what the patient is seeking. Communication at this level may not always be informed or even helpful, unless there is sensitive interaction between professional and nonprofessional staff about the patient.

The Professionals

If one looks at the social health care professionals either as a collective health care body or in their separate professions, limiting them to physicians, nurses or social workers, they represent special interest groups. In the former they are providers of care in the human services arena; and in the latter they are an entity with all the privileges and protections that fall to a given profession. In the social health care field where medicine is the dominant profession, we see its influence on the basic philosophy and administration of care within medical institutions and also on the practice of both nursing and social work. Although there is some current struggle in both nursing and social work to assert their independence from medicine, the legal, institutional, and traditional ties and constraints make independence difficult to achieve.

The practice arenas, whether institutionally governed or governed by a private or group practice model, are set by academic indoctrination and by personal or clinical determinants. Medical and psychiatric services are modeled on the needs and expectations of those who practice in the system, whatever form it may take, to deliver their services in styles which they have learned in these very same settings. The services are not organized around consumer expectations and needs. The underlying assumption of these models is that the expert in medicine knows what sick people need, and the medical practitioner and the institutional interests are consonant with the best interests of the consumer as well.[20]

Physicians, nurses, and social workers do bring special knowledge to health care. Their professional ethics call for a commitment to the public trust and public good, as foremost in the performance of their services. In return, the public assigns

---

[20]Helen Rehr and Samuel J. Bosch, "A Professional Search into Values and Ethics in Health Care Delivery" in *Ethical Dilemmas in Health Care*, ed. Helen Rehr (New York: Prodist, 1978), pp. 37-8.

the professional practitioner special privileges and protections. The most critical of these are the profession's right to determine who will be admitted to its inner circle, as well as the right to self-monitor the profession's delivery of care. The interpretation of these tenets in the "social contract" granted by the consumer and accepted by the provider, is usually subjectively perceived by each. Thus, the individual biases of consumer or provider contribute to the differences that occur between them.

Medicine, nursing, and social work see themselves as experts, each with its own specialty. Theirs is an intensive knowledge-based position, and having achieved that status, each wishes to be perceived as a "specialist." In that context, not infrequently, their loyalty is to the specialization from which they gain personal and professional recognition. Each of these health care professions has been trained to believe that the "cure" of an ailment, or the "change" in personality are the basic goals of practice. Dealing with the etiology of the illness is frequently the professionally rewarding goal while reduction in symptoms is seen as routine. Doctors, social workers, and nurses do better with individuals as patients in the "therapist-patient relationship" than any of them do in relation to dealing with the broad health care system. Their orientations are less toward prevention or toward social-health maintenance, and more with uncovering illness and disorders, focused on the symptoms and problems already in evidence.

The education of doctors and nurses—less so for social workers who have had a community orientation—has separated them from the public health model since World War I. Although there was a renaissance with the birth of community medicine and community health programs during the 1960s, in the last half of the 1970s, these programs have receded in medical schools. They have surfaced in baccalaureate degree nursing schools, resulting in some conflict with the community-focused teachings in schools of social work. There has been some introduction of behavioral and social sciences, along with ethics, in medical education. However, their integration into practice still needs to be demonstrated. Perhaps as the old guard in academic medical settings is replaced by new physicians, their practice may demonstrate the concepts of biopsychosocial assessments and treatments which include the qualitative use and integration of the services of other health care professions.

At the present, there is a growing threat to medicine's perception of its own autonomy as a result of the newly emerging professions and in the new roles and responsibilities sought by nonmedical professions such as social work, nursing, and midwifery. These professions are moving more and more into primary caretaking roles to care for common ailments, conditions, and stress which constitute a very large segment of the practice arena of physicians. To offset this trend among nurses and social workers, medicine has claimed its legal responsibility for patient care through the newly created specialty of family medicine. Both medicine and psychiatry seek coordinating and supervisory roles over all nonmedical health care professions. The pattern of team care, which has its historical background in psychiatric and in rehabilitation programs has been largely hierarchical rather than collegial, more cooperative than collaborative in nature. The team model which has been claimed by social workers, nurses, and others as the collaborative design by which comprehensive care for the patient has been safeguarded, has not demonstrated that it is more effective in the care of a patient, and has proved more costly, more confusing for patients to relate to many and probably even fragmentizing.[21] The concern is whether interprofessional collaboration is more myth than it is reality. Medical autonomy still dominates multiprofessional care.[22]

Today's disorders, falling to medical care, as has been noted earlier, are more frequently social health problems rather than disease-specific, and not limited to the purview of a single profession for both diagnostic and therapeutic projections. They are problems that warrant an integrated assessment of biopsychosocial factors, that emphasize the impact of and on the individual, the family, the neighborhood, and the social environment in the fullest sense.

Specialization according to programs and services creates problems for the consumer who may not describe his needs in terms that open the right door. Consumers unwittingly enter doorways that tend to revolve, thereby excluding them unless the gatekeeper is informed and responsive to make a referral to an appropriate source. The revolving doors occur more frequently in social agencies, where specialization of services requires the client to identify his problem in a language acceptable to the agency.[23] They occur also in medical settings, at the emergency or specialized clinical departmental levels. It is doubtful that any social service or health setting could provide a full range of services to deal with any problem. Specialization has made for fragmentation of services. The burden has fallen on the consumer to find the right path and to coordinate his own care. Within specialization, there is also the problem that professionals attempt to mold the consumer to the particularized treatment, rather than exercise an openness that permits referral elsewhere.[24] Under circumstances of such misfit, it is usually the consumer who removes himself from care, but frequently at a price to his motivation to seek other assistance.

Social workers in health and mental health settings have carried the role of mediating the differences and problems that can occur between the service system and the consumer. Social work has served in two primary ways: (1) working with the patient and the practitioner in the milieu to mediate and coordinate the medical care projections; and (2) working for social-environmental changes within the milieu so as to safeguard the continuation of needed services to the consumer. The nurse has been struggling to break away from the solo role of transplanting medical or psychiatric recommendations into nursing tasks, in an attempt to find independent and autonomous functions in social health care.

The roles of social worker become clear as one works among hospitalized patients. Careful and selective interpretation of patients' needs to other hospital personnel is most important. This occurs by involving the ancillary staff in conferences

[21] Jeanette Regensberg, "The Working Parties" in *Medicine and Social Work*, ed. Helen Rehr (New York: Prodist, 1974), pp. 35-73.

[22] Bess Dana, "The School of Social Work—School of Medicine Connection," *Geriatric Education*, ed. Knight Steel (Lexington, Mass: Heath, 1981), pp. 193-9.

[23] See Alfred J. Kahn, *Neighborhood Information Centers*, Columbia University Press, New York, 1966, in re discussion of the problems of access in relation to provider selectivity patterns as to who shall receive services.

[24] Robert Perlman, *Consumer and Social Service* (New York: John Wiley, 1975), pp. 65-9.

and team meetings in which patients are discussed and their needs understood, while given assignments and tasks are made appropriately. Frequently, nurse-social worker patient care rounds are the means by which related staff become more qualitatively involved in patient needs. Treating the patient in a unit which safeguards continuity of care, where specialists come to the patients, while staff remains relatively constant, may open communication more and perhaps reduce the problems of depersonalization so frequently seen on the larger units of service. As reflected in numerous studies, it is also true that an informed patient who is prepared for what is to come makes fewer demands on a staff, and is more responsive to medical recommendations.

Social support of patients and families cannot be limited to social worker activity, but needs to be part of the care offered by other health professionals as well. Social workers can influence others. In particular they can communicate the meaning of sharing information with patients and their families for decision-making as a first step in a communication partnership which has listening as its primary component. Using patients and families as a resource with others in like situations in group orientation or preparatory sessions is another approach. Even where social workers are few in number in a small institution, their primary function may be influencing the social support structure of the hospital to secure more patient-focused services. Another function is accepting referrals of situations for which other health care professionals need expert consultation.

Problems in staff behavior and attitudes may not be lodged in indifference or in technological concentration but may be a product of emotional exhaustion or self-depreciation resulting from work-related stress, or "burnout." Personnel working in areas with the critically ill and their families who require intensive and constant contact under circumstances of high stress, are subject to reaction over time. Programs such as hospices, intensive care units, renal dialysis units, services dealing with acutely psychotic or regressed patients, tend to make the most demands on staff. The symptoms that staff members may evidence reflect changes in their behavior and attitudes from those they demonstrated in the past. Most institutional administrators have little experience in recognizing "burnout." Unless detected early, preventive steps cannot be taken, and frequently good staff members terminate rather than urge the institution to redress the problems. An exceedingly fine social worker we knew had three consecutive years on an oncology service witnessing terminal illness and offering social supports, without self-controlled time constraints. One day she indicated she had to "get away from it" and she left. Early awareness, and then drawing on staff "gut" sessions, along with flexible handling, could have meant a reassignment to a service where the pressures were more health-oriented than terminal, thus safeguarding a good staff member to a wider experience.

The Paraprofessionals

The creation of paraprofessional (subprofessional or nonprofessional) personnel in the fields of health and social sciences is lodged in a complex background involving a range of interdependent factors. In both fields, this new and expanding personnel has been helpful to the professionals while at the same time creating many problems. As the number of paraprofessionals has increased—in some instances becoming greater than the professional number—the concerns are with who carries what task and function, and who carries the responsibility and accountability for services rendered in the social and health services.

Although the movement to draw on a nonprofessional personnel has been with us since the Depression of the 1930s and through World War II, it accelerated in the 1960s, which opened a decade of great social ferment in the country. The identification of the social and health needs of the public also brought forth the identification of the need for an expanded manpower[25] to effectively serve those seeking care. The shortage in professional social work personnel to meet the demand was already recognized[26] and the push toward the creation of a large body of new manpower was well underway by the mid-1960s. The projections for increased demands for services in both the health and social work fields were seen as a result of the community mental health movement, Medicare, Medicaid, and a host of other socially oriented programs developed in that period. One outcome of the shortage of professionally trained personnel was the development of occupations to free the professional from exercising functions and tasks requiring less skill and knowledge which could be performed by others with less formal education. The field of social welfare, which consisted of approximately 76 percent nonmaster's degree personnel[27] prior to the 1960s, proliferated its own "assistants" and "advocates" as either subprofessionals or as indigenous nonprofessionals drawing on the untrained and frequently on former clients to serve their own group.[28]

At the same time, there was the growing complexity and the diversity of American health care. In this pluralistic system, operating in a wide range of media, the professionals, encountering more demands on them, moved to define what they do and to identify tasks and assignments which they believed could be carried by special ancillary personnel. The creation of paraprofessional groups such as the physician's assistant to the physician, the nurse's aide to the registered nurse (or the licensed practical nurse), and the social work technician, advocate or assistant to the master's degree social worker has been a mixed blessing.

Where the paraprofessional such as the physician's assistant to the physician functions under the eyes of the professional himself, then the professional accepts the benefits therefrom and the clients can identify the primary source of the service. However, where task and function have not been clearly defined, as frequently exists in settings that employ both a social worker and the social services paraprofessional,

[25] *Action for Mental Health*, report to the U.S. Congress of the Joint Commission on Mental Illness and Mental Health, 1961, and subsequently published (New York: Basic Books, 1961).

[26] "Expansion and Development of Social Work Manpower Training," *Congressional Record*, 19th Congress, 1st Session, 113, no. 33, (1967), p. 52495 (Bill No. 1150).

[27] Robert L. Barker and Thomas L. Briggs, *Differential Use of Social Work Manpower* (New York: National Association of Social Workers, 1968), p. 28.

[28] Arthur Pearl and Frank Riessman, eds., *New Careers for the Poor: The Non-Professional in Human Services* (New York: Free Press, 1965), pp. 187-207.

then the professional and the clientele are unclear about the value and source of the service.

On occasion, a paraprofession is created, answering to one of a number of professions such as nursing, social work, health care administration, and others, because each may have identified a series of deficiencies in the delivery of care. Such a paraprofessional is the patient representative, described in detail because the authors believe that it illustrates one of the newest of the paraprofessional groups in health care.

There are many problems a consumer of hospital care can face in the process of securing the service. The service may be inappropriate for his needs or there may be an obstacle in achieving the initiation and the continuation of needed care. The complexities of medical care institutions and the specialization of social and health agencies tend to cause the compartmentalization or the fragmentation of care. The patient and or consumer who has to cope with size, multiservices and a specialized personnel organization usually faces them with confusion and dismay, during a time of personal stress. In most institutions, it is generally left to the patient to find the right pathways and to negotiate his own care. Departments and programs within medical institutions tend to be specialized, with their own policies, procedures, and scheduling. In order to deal with these complexities before they create conflict and negative reactions, the patient may require a service that helps him or her reach and use the appropriate care. The "service" may be information and or appropriate referral. It may be a simple courtesy in directly assisting him to reach the program and the professional caretaker. All that may be essential is an explanation of rules and procedures. The patient may have a complaint or a grievance he wants redressed. He or she may need someone to speak for him or intercede with some member of the institution. To overcome these typical problems which arise in multiservice complex organizations, some of the institutions have developed patient advocate or representative programs. Although these are not advocacy systems as is sometimes found among community or special interest groups, they do offer services on behalf of a "stranded" individual. Patient representatives serve as liaison between the institution and the patient. In some instances the representative may also be the institutional or patient liaison with the community. The patient representative service, a program developed in medical institutions to overcome the problems noted, had its roots in a social work program which needed to find a way to deal with the organizational obstacles to individualized care, which social workers were observing.[29] In most programs, the representative acts on behalf of the patient and the family to secure resolution to difficulties arising out of encounters with any member of the institution. The representative is an employee of the institution and is dependent on the internal resources of the hospital to carry out his responsibilities. The concept of representative derives from two sources: the "ombudsman," a public program in Sweden, in which the citizen has his complaints against government bureaucracy dealt with,[30] and from the British Citizens' Advice Bureaus (CAB), a multineigh-

---

[29] Ruth Ravich, Helen Rehr, and Charles Goodrich, "Hospital Ombudsman Smooths the Flow of Services and Communication," *Hospital, JAHA*, 43 (March 1969), pp. 56–60.

[30] James E. Payne, "Ombudsman Roles for Social Work," *Social Work*, 17, no. 1 (January 1972), pp. 95–7.

borhood program created during World War II to meet citizens' needs.[31] The CAB offered advice, information and referral, personal and supportive services, advocacy, and introduced coordination of services for individuals when necessary.

The patient representative performs an information and steering function. In its most efficient form, the program will staff key areas so as to uncover persons who are "lost" in the institutions and need help to reach another area. Visibility is an important attribute in the utility of patient representatives. The advocacy function, well known to social workers, calls for assistance to the disadvantaged individual or groups who are powerless in their dealings with an institution. The patient representative, serving as an advocate for a patient, utilizes the major techniques of communication, data gathering, education, persuasion, and negotiation. It is nonproductive for the representative to employ coercive or adversary modes of intervention on behalf of a patient.[32] The institutionally based patient representative has to reconcile the consumer want or need with the hospital's capabilities.

There is an emerging new role for patient representatives in which the objective is to assist the patient and the family to set aside intentions to sue the institution for assumed personal damage as a result of care. Malpractice suits against medical institutions are growing steadily in number. This role has been identified by the American Hospital Association as "risk management." Frequently, patient representatives can sense the litigious intention of the consumer when he has been dealing with him as an aggrieved patient. Patient representatives can deal with the anger and dismay of a patient who perceives his problem as caused by the institutional staff. In dealing with both patient and staff, the representative sometimes removes the stress that otherwise could lead to a malpractice suit.

The functions carried by patient representatives in medical institutions derive from the many potential impediments to care that patients can face. In essence they are the institutional and personnel induced problems that surface in any complex organization. If a means exists to allow problems to be openly discussed by patients and to be corrected individually, the range of problems can then be reviewed for their commonality and a "feedback" system can be developed to find ways to modify or eliminate difficulties. Hospital administrators have trouble seeing the breakdown in selected areas because of their commitments to the wide range of operations. However, their concern with problems that patients encounter is a primary one. Here, they must also rely on their staff. Not only patient representatives but also social workers, nurses, and program administrators in any institution should be alert to problems so that consumers feel comfortable and secure in continuing their care. The provision of information and referral, steering, advocacy, negotiation, coordination, and whatever else it takes to overcome impediments a patient may face needs to be built into the operation of the system.

Within medical institutions, the question arises as to whose responsibilities

[31] Alfred J. Kahn, *Neighborhood Information Centers* (New York: Columbia University Press, 1966), pp. 33–5.

[32] Mildred Mailick and Helen Rehr, eds., *In the Patient's Interest* (New York: Prodist, 1981).

these functions will be. Where patient representative programs have developed, they may fall under the aegis of different organizational subsystems administratively determined. The quality of the program is predicated on the level of power assigned to it. A key issue to be faced by each of the health care professions is this: If a patient representative program exists, does that fact relieve the different professional groups or departments from the responsibility of conducting services relevant to dealing with the impediments in their own programs? Each department, each professional group, and each program needs to carry within it the responsibilities for adequately informing people, and for assuring their initiation into and continuation of care in a responsible way. This requires an internal "review" and "feedback" system to deal with problems and to safeguard needed change.

CONCLUSION

These are extraordinary times for what has come to be known as the "health industry." Hundreds of thousands of patients, representing millions of patient visits a year, enter this system through the doorways of private physicians or psychiatrists, group practices, health centers, extended-care facilities, acute-care hospitals, psychiatric clinics, or mental institutions. As subsequent chapters will attempt to illustrate, all of these settings and the vast manpower that provides myriad services do so through elaborate reimbursement mechanisms emanating from multiple funding sources. The organizational structures are inextricably tied to the fiscal dollar and both influence the service delivery system in more complicated patterns than ever before.

This means that social worker students planning to practice in the field of health or mental health, need a curriculum that provides content beyond the theories of direct practice and the skills acquired in field work settings. For in actual practice, social work knowledge and professional skill are shaped, if not dictated, by organizational arrangements and economic viability. How successfully the social worker negotiates the system on behalf of his client, interacts with other health providers and agency staff, sets work priorities from day to day, and executes multiple functions will depend upon how well the worker understands the setting. Such first-hand knowledge includes theoretical content about funding sources that flow into the institution, accountability mechanisms that insure reimbursement for services, utilization patterns that enhance quality care, structural arrangements among various services, and planning approaches for the introduction of new service delivery models or for the modification of existing programs. Of equal importance for the social worker is knowledge about organizational behavior as it relates to staff functioning, morale, motivational factors, leadership, and productivity. The social worker who is attuned to the structural arrangements of the setting as well as to the elements of organizational behavior of employees is more apt to identify "problems" as endemic to the system for which correction is indicated rather than to chalk up a "tension" or obstacle to incompatability with or personality factors in others. We suggest, as we have earlier in this chapter, that there are reality circumstances that are tension-producing for the worker and that may account for "burnout." But it is important to emphasize that "burnout" may be a concomitant with work-produced frustration that emanates from a lack of understanding about the structural arrangements of the setting.

In the interest of patient care and ultimately patient satisfaction, the worker's knowledge of the setting is crucial. What one patient accepts as normal procedure, another will perceive as an irritant. For example, the young patient may not think twice about the referral by the hospital-based physician to a hospital outpatient service for a urine analysis or a blood work-up; whereas an older patient, accustomed to an earlier time when physicians took urine and blood samples in the office, may perceive the new procedure as a rejection or—as it may well be—an additional expense the patient can little afford. The worker has an obligation, first to know why this change has occurred, and second, to interpret to the patient the reason for the change. The point is not to placate the patient but to lend an ear and to support or to help the patient ventilate feelings, and if necessary to negotiate with the business office for the patient who may need to pay for the tests over time. Let us remember that the reasons for patient noncompliance stem from many sources. For our older patient, the source of concern could be financial. The worker, unaware of the reason for a structural change within the setting, is unprepared to help the patient and unwittingly may be a reenforcing agent for the patient's noncompliance.

Not everything a worker needs to know about a setting will be learned at once. That is not the point. Rather, the worker who appreciates the need to understand the structural and organizational arrangements of the setting will be more attuned to the patient's need and, therefore, will be a better practitioner.

REFERENCES

Action for Mental Health.   Report of the Joint Commission Mental Illness and Mental Health to Congress in 1961. New York: Basic Books, 1961.

American Hospital Association.   *Hospital statistics.* Chicago: American Hospital Association, 1975.

BARKER, ROBERT L., & BRIGGS, THOMAS L.   *Differential use of social work manpower.* New York: National Association of Social Workers, 1968.

BARTLETT, HARRIETT.   *Social work practice in the health field.* New York: National Association of Social Workers, 1961.

CANNON, IDA.   Lay participation in hospital service from the point of view of a medical social worker. In Dora Goldstine (Ed.) *Readings in the theory and practice of medical social work.* Chicago: University of Chicago Press, 1954.

DANA, BESS.   The school of social work—school of medicine connection. In Knight Steel (Ed.) *Geriatric education.* Lexington, Mass: Callomore Press, D. C. Heath and Co., 1981.

DEVINE, EDWARD T.   *When social work was young.* New York. Macmillan, 1939.

DURNIC, STEPHEN J., ROTH, WILLIAM I., LINN, BERNARD S., PRATT, THEODORE, & BLUM, ALAN.   The physician s role in the cost-containment problem. *JAMA,* April 15, 1979, *24* (15).

Encyclopedia of Social Work. Washington, D.C.: National Association of Social Workers, 1977.

Expansion and Development of Social Work Manpower Training. *Congressional Record*, Ninetieth Congress, First Session, 1967, *113* (33).

FRENCH, LOIS, M. *Psychiatric social work*. New York: The Commonwealth Fund, 1940.

HAMILTON, GORDON. *A medical social terminology*. New York: The Social Services Department of the Presbyterian Hospital, 1930.

HEALY, WILLIAM & BRONNER, AUGUSTA. The child guidance clinic: Birth and growth of an idea. In Lawson Lowrey and Victoria Sloane (Eds.) *Orthopsychiatry, 1923–1948: Retrospect and Prospect*. Menasha, Wi.: American Orthopsychiatric Association, 1948.

KAHN, ALFRED J. *Neighborhood information centers*. New York: Columbia University Press, 1966.

MAILICK, MILDRED D. & REHR, HELEN (EDS.) *In the patient's interest*. New York: Prodist, 1981.

PAYNE, JAMES E. Ombudsman roles for social work. *Social Work*, January 1972, *17* (1).

PEARL, ARTHUR & RIESSMAN, FRANK (EDS.) *New careers for the poor: The non-professional in human services*. New York: Free Press, 1965.

PERLMAN, ROBERT. *Consumer and social service*. New York: John Wiley, 1975.

RAVICH, RUTH, REHR, HELEN, & GOODRICH, CHARLES. Hospital ombudsman smooths the flow of services and communication. *Hospital, JAHA*, March 1969 (43).

REGENSBERG, JEANETTE. The working parties. In Helen Rehr (Ed.) *Medicine and Social Work*. New York: Prodist, 1974.

REHR, HELEN & BOSCH, SAMUEL J. A professional search into values and ethics in health care delivery. In Helen Rehr (Ed.) *Ethical dilemmas in health care*. New York: Prodist, 1978.

SHEPS, CECIL G. The role of the academic health center. Presentation, Conference Series, Issues in Health Care Policy. New York, Department of Community Medicine, Mount Sinai School of Medicine, September 30, 1977.

SHEPS, CECIL G. Trends in hospital care. Samuel Levey and N. Paul Loomba (Eds.) *Health care administration: A Managerial Perspective*. Philadelphia: Lippincott, 1973.

STEEL, KNIGHT. *Geriatric education*. Lexington, Mass.: Collamore Press, Heath 1981.

WHITE, KERR L. Health care arrangements in the United States: A.D. 1972. *Medical cure and medical care. The Milbank Memorial Fund Quarterly*, October 1972, *L* (4).

WOODS, ROBERT A. & KENNEDY, ALBERT F. *The settlement horizon*. New York: Russell Sage Foundation, 1922.

CHAPTER TWO
THE CONSUMER AND CONSUMERISM

Helen Rehr

INTRODUCTION

When a consumer seeks professional care, the questions raised are Will it be helpful? Will it be good care? and Will it be attentive and personalized? The consumer in seeking care is responding to symptoms and illness, and very rarely reaches out for routine health maintenance. On the other side of the doctor-patient relationship, the professional is concerned more with "curing," and with the patient's health status primarily in relation to the illness that is being treated. At the planning and policy level, the roles consumers should and will play in regard to American health care still remain to be defined. What is in evidence currently is a growing willingness of providers to listen to their patients, so that an element of sharing in the delivery of care process may occur in the near future.

The consumer as an active partner in the patient-therapist relationship is a comparatively new idea in medical care. This type of relationship has, however, had some expression in social work in the last decade.[1] The consumer role in the consumer movement (consumerism) on the other hand, has a long history but it, too, has had more and more stirrings over the last 25–35 years. In either instance, the patterns drawn upon are multiple and too diversely structured for there to be any specific framework from which to draw. There are however, some guidelines based on experience. In order to develop principles, relevant to the consumer of direct ser-

---

[1] See Anthony N. Maluccio, *Learning from Clients* (New York: Free Press, 1979); Robert Perlman, *Consumers and Social Services* (New York: John Wiley, 1975); and John E. Mayer and Noel Timms, *The Client Speaks* (New York: Atherton Press, 1970) in regard to their analyses of the clients' part in the professional-consumer relationship.

vices, and to the consumer in the consumer movement, substantial review and assessment in each area will need to be undertaken. At the present, studies are still in their embryonic stage.

As the user, the consumer is the most critical component in the health care system. As taxpayer, insuree, or direct payee, the consumer supports its operation and holds the key to utilization. The consumer has opinions of what he gets in the way of services, of what he sees being delivered to others, and of what he reads or hears about medical care. These perceptions, though subjective and frequently without technical knowledge, are important factors relevant to the quality of care given. It is with these opinions that the consumer functions in a range of roles in a personal health care system and in that of consumerism.

This chapter offers a brief overview of the consumer in relation to direct service and the consumer movement, so as to give the social worker some perspective of the dynamics involved in the caring process and in health care delivery planning. What needs to be known? How does the consumer choose his medical care? What is available? Are "at-risk" patients guaranteed needed care? How can motivation to take care and to comply with recommendations be safeguarded? What is the nature of the relationship between consumer and providers? These questions are dealt with in the first part of the chapter so as to give the reader an understanding of what the consumer encounters when ill and reaching out for assistance. Next, we will examine not only the misgivings but also the endorsement by patients as consumers of the medical system. Some of the attempts to learn of consumer perception of and satisfaction with care are illustrated. Their place in social work services is discussed.

Consumerism as a movement in the health care field is addressed in the subsequent section. The patient's rights in a hospital have been a major achievement by consumers and are explored here, as are some of the developments of patient advocacy and patient representative (ombudsman) programs. Social work's contribution to these areas are described and illustrated. The final material covers the major area of promoting health on behalf of consumers. The development of self-help and patient groups, as well as special interest groups is described. They seem to have evolved as a result of the difficulty of the social and health care professions in meeting the consumers' social-psychological and health maintenance needs due to medical problems. Health education for consumers—a new tool—is examined. The chapter's conclusion tries to enhance the roles of medicine and social work in relation to the consumers of their services, and as advocates of new social-health programs.

THE CONSUMER AND THE PROVIDER:
DYNAMICS IN CARE

Consumers are concerned with what is available to them and what they get in both cost and quality terms. Although availability and access are the two most critical concerns, economic factors and the behavioral dimensions follow in importance. The ways in which consumers reach out for and use health care services are meaningful determinants for social workers in health settings.

Choosing Care

The phenomenon of choosing care in the first place and the nature of the care in the second place are complex dynamics for both the consumer and the provider as individuals, and in the doctor-patient relationship. Consumers have reacted at a personal level finding medical and psychiatric care increasingly unsatisfactory and less compassionate, as each of these provider groups have become more sophistocated, technological, and expensive. Although severity of illness and the nature of reactions to illness are important components affecting the response to care, the economic and the behavioral quality dimensions are most signficant in how consumers perceive care at the different levels.

1. Economic quality dimensions include a range of structural, access, and cost factors which affect the choice and use of services.[2]
   a. Cost: The consumer is interested in whether the specific service he or she seeks is "fair" priced. Cost is a key determinant in choice and use. In general, the consumer is without the technical knowledge to judge whether the utility of the service or product is sound. Frequently, illness, because it can influence the patient and the family as crisis, may also be a factor in their inability to seek out "fair" priced quality service. When ill, the consumer is dependent on a range of influences affecting the selection of services needed (see pp. 24-30). There is practically no organized means by which consumers seeking specialized services can find them except by word of mouth or through provider-system information. It is only recently that consumers have organized to offer a listing of a number of consumer-supported programs in health care, some of which may even be sponsored by consumer groups (see pp. 50-66). The present practice is for individuals to tend to reach out to on-going consumer-supported programs when they are not sick or facing a crisis. Choice under crisis may involve less rationale behavior than when a crisis does not exist, and time is available for thoughtful sorting out of choices.
   b. Accessibility: The consumer wants and expects care to be readily available. This includes the range of technology that has been publicized by physicians and scientists as advances in the care of certain disorders. A common phenomenon of illness in an individual is that his needs become subjective at the time of crisis, and also, he has little concern for cost effectiveness. Travel and waiting time are factors in accessibility. Studies have found these two variables are most critical in the way a consumer expresses his satisfaction with care. It is interesting that the shift in the pattern from home visits in the past to their present unavailability has been accepted by the public. This change in the delivery of medical care by physicians has imposed a major change on the emergency room demands of medical establishments. Those who are sick, the homeless, deinstitutionalized, substance abusers, and the socially dysfunctional, along with true emergencies, tend to make the most use of emergency services. Institutions have responded to this use and the cost of their emergency

---

[2] The following discussion is partially drawn from Nancy Wint Mitry and Howard L. Smith, "Consumer Satisfaction: A Model for Health Services Administrators," *Health Care Management Review* (Summer 1979), pp. 7-14.

rooms in a wide variety of ways. Some have closed them down. Some have instituted fee-for-service physicians on the premises. Where institutional emergency rooms are offering 24-hour service, they have become the primary source of care for many irrespective of social class.

c. Choice: The consumer finds the making of choices of medical care services most difficult. Although choice is considered a major factor in a free market, it is important to recognize that the American health care system is not a free market. It is controlled essentially by what the providers offer and their availability, not by consumers' free choice. Where a physician practices, and where the medical institution is located, what is available, when, and to whom are provider determinants. From the array of what is available, the questions arise as to whether consumers can become knowledgeable in making choices. In order to make effective decisions about what one needs, knowledge is required about one's illness and its possible course. It becomes apparent that consumers need the professionals to assist them in facilitating choices. The myths and the mystery that continue to surround medicine will need to be removed, and an openness between professional and consumers will insure that information is shared.

d. Medicial technology versus services: The consumer is exposed to the media's descriptions of the way physicians see the benefits from technological advances. The nature of the exposure leads him to place greater emphasis on technology, to value pacemakers, transplants, and dialysis techniques, and less on the professional judgment required for sound diagnosis and treating. To the consumer, costs for tangible items, those of which he has heard or read, may be more acceptable than the high costs of the intangibles of time, skill, concern, and resources, which make for good diagnosis.

e. Medical research: The consumer knows what can be made available to him through the public media or through those personal contacts of "someone who knows someone who-." It is from these sources that wants and expectations are determined. As a patient, the consumer believes he or she should have the same "right" to the new technology as someone else has.

f. Ethical issues: Every medical institution and provider is governed by a set of values and the consumer is subject to that given moral stance. Although one assumes a patient may be free to "take it or leave it," in reality, crisis does not usually allow the patient to practice self-determination. On critical questions governing life and death, medical "heroics" remain the choice of most institutions and their providers. Who receives dialysis and specialized rehabilitative services is frequently governed by availability and the source of payment. Abortion, euthanasia, and genetic counseling can be the choices of consumers only if available, financed, believed in, and practiced by available practitioners and their institutions.

g. Equity: The consumer's "right to health care" is considered an American democratic provision. Since the mid-1960s, the public health sector has argued the issue of the "right to health" versus the "right to care." The "right to health" as a public policy has been passed over as too complex and too expensive to be achievable, so that currently, it is the "right to care" that has become public expectation. However, while the "right to care" is accepted as a principle in equity, its implementation is complicated by the factors mentioned and by those described later in this and other chapters.

2. Behavioral dimensions include a range of subjective values and attitudes that affect how an individual will act.[3]
   a. Autonomy: Consumer participation in his own care is essential. Most patients want to know what is "wrong" and "why," so they can effectively participate. When a patient remains ignorant of his or her medical or mental health problems, the physician retains the advantage in the relationship. If not fully involved, the patient's dignity and self-worth are abused. Among too many physicians, the sense of professional superiority mitigates against the patient's need to be invested in the decisions about medical care. The physician believes the passive patient is easier to deal with, and in any event, the doctor's professional knowledge should be acceptable to the patient. Passivity can be inimical to improvement in a patient's condition because it does not enlist self-help. There is a growing recognition of the importance of the patient as a partner in care.
   b. Personalized attention: Does the consumer's expectation of the doctor or of any other health professional make an equilibrium in relationship possible? Professionals are trained to maintain an emotional distance and detachment from their patients. On the other hand, the consumer is fearful of depersonalization and the loss of individualization when under the care of a professional. The patient sees "detachment" as disinterest. In all surveys of the doctor-patient relationship, depersonalization is the most often expressed fear of the consumer of the quality of health care available.
   c. Communication: The degree of personalized professional attention and of participation in care that the practitioner gives to the patient can be found in the quality of communication that takes place between the parties. Communication calls for understanding and recognition of the individual in care. If decision-making participation is to take place, it means two-way communication will occur in which the patient can talk freely and ask questions of the practitioner. The practitioner has the responsibility to test for whether the social health care message is received by the patient. Whether the patient can and is participating in self-care must also be determined by the practitioner.

Access to Care

Access to health care is the most critical determinant in whether an individual reaches and complies with the care needed and prescribed. Access means the initiation of care and its continuation.[4] As a happening it "involves the prospective user, the prospective provider and a range of socio-political, economic, psychological, cultural and organizational dimensions which affect the behaviors and attitudes of both." In order to reach professional service, an individual needs to pass through a social or health services doorway. To do so requires a perception of need and some identification of the type of services that may be required and is provided by the medical establishment. The perception of illness, except the emergencies or accidents, and the courses people take before they turn to experts can be many. They may ignore symptoms, hoping they will go away. They may self-administer drugs or

[3]The following discussion is partially drawn from Mitry and Smith, "Consumer Satisfaction," pp. 11-14.

[4]Helen Rehr, "Access to Services: A Complex Dimension" in *In the Patient's Interest*, ed. Mildred Mailick and Helen Rehr (New York: Prodist, 1981), pp. 1-16.

remedies suggested by family, friends, or even a local pharmacist. If the signs of illness continue, the prospective consumer of medical services must decide they are necessary.

There are many barriers to access. Resources need to be available. They are not always easily available for a range of reasons. The primary barrier can be economic. Although a significant portion of the population is covered for some aspects of service through insurances, either publicly or privately maintained, the extent of coverage varies. Financial problems can cause people to postpone needed care or to draw from what is available to them within the limitations imposed. Other barriers can be organizational whereby the services are more often set to meet institutional rather than consumer needs—such as in the hours available, the geographic location, and in the services provided. It is well known that the so-called abuse of emergency room services is due largely to those who cannot readily use daytime services during typical business hours. Also the availability of private medical services is a doctor determination. A doctor is free to set up a practice wherever possible, to practice the kind of medicine, allocate the resources, and charge the fee as so desired. A typical example is the proliferation of specialists rather than primary care physicians when it is known the latter are more greatly needed by the general public.

Figure 2-1 depicts the general course individuals go through in seeking help. However, having arrived at the medical doorway, the prospective consumer must initiate entry and then continue in its care if it is recommended.[5] Both initiation and continuation of care are now mainly lodged in the receptivity, understanding, and skill of the gatekeepers and providers in helping the consumer to cross the medical threshhold and to stay in care if needed. The nature of that first encounter with the medical establishment, with the private practitioner, or with the institutional gatekeeper is critical. Most professionals believe they make the first contact with the prospective consumer. However, there are many different types of personnel who usually intervene before the practitioner does. In forgetting this the professional sometimes faces consumer behaviors not fully understood. Professionals need to be acutely tuned to the gatekeeping, entry processes that are a forerunner to the client-provider interaction. One way is for a provider to question a consumer about who was met and what happened before the doctor was seen. Another is to learn who did not reach the service and why. In the mental health arenas if the "password" to the particular program is not spoken, a consumer may face a "revolving door." That "password" may be provider imposed governing who to treat, or it may be a gatekeeper's translation of policy. The obstacles to service encountered by a consumer at the entryway are invariably provider induced. Professionals claim that persons who "cross the threshold" have demonstrated their motivation to utilize the help. However, what is unknown is who has been "persuaded" to turn away, and those who have withstood the pressure but are left with reactions to the care they will receive.

[5] Avedis Donabedian, "Models for Organizing the Delivery of Personal Health Services and Criteria for Evaluating Them" in *Organizational Issues in the Delivery of Health Services*, ed. I. Zola and J. B. McKinley (New York: Prodist, 1974), p. 135.

FIGURE 2-1   A Model of the Medical Care Process*

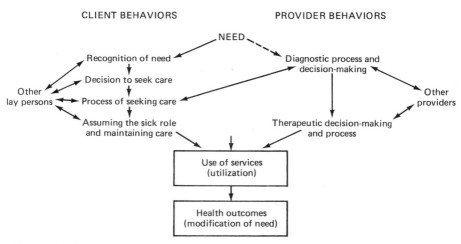

*From: Avedis Donabedian, "The Assessment of Need," in *Aspect of Medical Care Administration* (Cambridge, Mass.: Harvard University Press, 1973), p. 59.

The gateway to service cannot be a barrier that the sick must overcome or a knot that they must untie to reach appropriate needed care. What is needed is a single doorway through which all consumers can pass readily, regardless of the individual presenting problems. If an institution has multiple doorways, then channeling of individuals must be easily and prompty achieved. Screening and triaging of the patient and his problem are provider responsibilities, to be followed by ready channeling to appropriate resources. Such channeling would require a centralized information and referral system in proximity to the entryways and the screening devices. If the needed resources do not exist within the institution, then referral, if it is to be responsible, requires that the consumer understand why and what the appropriate resource is. This should be followed by a contact with the resource, a clearly understood referral, and follow-up to ascertain that the referral has taken place.

Once the consumer has entered the system, "the proof of access is use of service."[6] The complexities of the medical establishment have been described elsewhere. However, to place the medical center into context, it is important to indicate that it is a multidepartment, labor intensive with a range of professionals and paraprofessionals interacting with the consumer. All are governed by rules and regulations for the performance of tasks and services, and not for the facilitation of the patient encounter. These relatively independent departments are autonomies of care which lead to fragmentation and depersonalization of services.

One of the most problematic concerns for consumers of health care is the growing loss of both individualization and of personalization of services. Although hospitals, in the main, are admittedly remarkable for their scientific and technological accomplishments, it may well be that these advances have diminished the human-

[6]*Ibid.*

ism of their care. To perform in a humanized way enhances the commitment of both patients and practitioners. The requirements for such an environment call for perceiving individuals as whole persons, worthy and irreplaceable; sharing in decisions that affect their care, in a relationship that has reciprocity and egalitarianism in it; functioning with self-autonomy within the limitations imposed by illness and society; and being treated with empathy and warmth.[7] Since the inception of social services in health care, social workers have attempted to personalize and individualize the care of those served by health care establishments and to reintroduce these tenets into services given by primary health care practitioners. They have supported the principles of consumer self-determination and autonomy, which involve the right to make a decision from an informed set of choices. The consumer, in selecting the over-the-counter method of care before seeking other expertise, has made a self-help determination within keeping of self-autonomy. That same right to choice needs to be available within the medical establishment and requires a personnel oriented to the consumer, his needs, and responses.

Personalization and continuity of care are what most consumers seek. Continuation of care requires sensitive linkages within the institution, as well as in the community. Constancy of staff, periodic work-ups, and assessments openly discussed between provider and consumer help to keep a patient informed. Clearly written records and their ready availability serve as a tool in communication.

Guaranteed Access and Casefinding

As professional accountability has come to the foreground again, one recognizes the commitment to those who for whatever reason do not have care available or accessible to them. It is essential that "casefinding" of those "at risk" be introduced into the medical care system. Guaranteed access has been mandated for the poor. Those institutions that have benefitted from the Hill-Burton Act, from Medicaid, and from Medicare, are required to make their services available to the poor and to the elderly, as a component of provider accountability.

We have already seen that people in need may not reach care required, whereas those who do not need care may seek it out. Schweitzer's conception of those who seek care is shown in Table 2-1.

TABLE 2-1   Disease-Perception States[a]

		DISEASE STATE	
		WELL	SICK
PERCEPTION	WELL	(a)	(b_1)
	SICK	(b)	(a_1)

[a]Stuart O. Schweitzer, "Incentives and the Consumption of Preventive Health Care Services" in *Consumer Incentives for Health Care*, ed. Selma J. Mushkin (New York: Prodist, 1974), p. 37.

[7] Jan Howard and Robert A. Derzon, "Prospects for Humane Care Are Hopeful," *Hospitals, JAHA*, 53, no. 22 (November 16, 1979), p. 76.

The (a) and (a$_1$) diagonals could be considered so-called true states. They depict those who perceive themselves as well, and indeed are well (a), and those who perceive themselves as sick and are sick (a$_1$). The (b) and (b$_1$) diagonal could indicate false states depicting errors in perception; those who perceive themselves as well and are really sick (b$_1$), while those whose self-perception is that they are sick but are really well (b). When translated, the "worried" well who seek medical care, and the sick who do not seek medical care for whatever reason, are two major concerns in health care. The first group has a massive impact on the medical provider system and the second has a deleterious effect on the consumer himself and in time in the demand made in the health care system at a late stage of disease.

The worried well are those who see themselves as having symptoms which warrant medical attention. The stabilized sick are those whose conditions are medically under control but who seek medical support either under their own or their doctor's urgings. When the worried well and the stabilized sick are added together, it has been found that over 75 percent of all visits to private medical care are for supportive, counseling, or caring needs rather than for critical medical intervention.[8] The impact on a medical care system that is sickness and disability oriented can be overwhelming. In addition, there is the question as to whether medical education has prepared the physician for this type of care.

Individuals who do not reach services and who are "at risk" can be seriously vulnerable to permanent disability and even to life or death status, when their illness and diseases reach crisis or emergency states. Social health care institutions and agencies are usually slow to reach out to "at-risk" populations for a range of reasons. The philosophy predominant among providers is that their primary objective is to provide services to those who cross the threshhold, seeking out care. Underlying the principle is the belief that motivation is more than suggestive for those individuals who reach out for help, and those persons will deal with recommendations with more self-investment than those who do not. However, one of the major reasons for the lack of outreach or case-finding programs on the part of the institution is a result of their preoccupation with costs. In limiting utilization or in curbing excess use of ambulatory or emergency services, institutions can control costs by limiting their allocation of personnel and materials for those areas. Ambulatory services in hospitals have remained unprofitable, as well as unchanged in their delivery styles—generally archaic. As long as reimbursement costs remain at "cost plus" rates for in-patient services, medical institutions will continue to concentrate on keeping the bed occupancy rate as high as possible.

However, this may prove to be a narrow vision. An active ambulatory and emergency service when properly utilized are feeders for inpatient services. Impediments to access and to the use of services require special approaches and periodic interventive forays into those communities where high physical and social risk are suspected. "Outreach" programs that have been most frequently lodged in public schools or sometimes as public health case-finding programs of given community

[8] Lewis Thomas, "On the Science and Technology of Medicine," *Daedalus* 6, no. 1 (Winter 1977), p. 42.

social agencies are needed as structured responsibilities of regionalized social and medical care programs. These case-finding programs tend to be successful when designed for a local geographic area and "done in partnership between lay community people and specialists. The most important factor is not only the screening and case-finding but the follow-through to motivate the individuals to use available services."[9] Social workers, whether staffed in the community or in a medical institution can play key roles in assisting community residents to develop "outreach" programs based on needs that have been found to exist in the region.

There is in development a number of innovative plans by social workers, hospital administrators, and physicians to deal with the different needs hospitalized patients may face. The Veterans' Administration[10] has experimented in a program to deal with the different levels of care that patients may need. Based on qualitative assessment by health care professionals, in conjunction with the patient, a program of multilevel care is introduced. Even though these programs have been promulgated as a cost control in health services, multilevel care attempts to differentiate what is needed by the patient and what should be offered, rather than allowing each service to be an equal component in the care. Multilevel care is an advance on progressive care, the type of earlier programs utilized in hospitals. It perceives team care along a continuum in which the patient is identified by his condition and his response to it from very sick through the convalescent stage and into the posthospital period. As care is offered it is in services appropriate to need as evidenced over time. This is very different from the customary pattern of care that is structured into a medically oriented acute sick period (essentially diagnostic), followed by a treatment period and then convalescence within the institution and in postinstitutional care. In the traditional approach, the social services generally focus on the discharge plan alone.

Social workers will and do have a major role in determining where they can make significant input for services to patients and families within the new Veterans' Administration design of care as described. Since care inputs are determined by the specificity of need at points in the continuum, it is done by the determination of the relevant caretakers. The continuum care concept if it is to be comprehensive calls for a reordering of strategy requiring linkages among the within-the-institutional resources, and then among those outside the institution. The continued linkage between the institution and the community is imperative if the posthospital care is to be soundly addressed. This will require a great deal of social health planning to cover classification of social and health needs in relation to patients, their families, and the nature of the disorders. It also calls for an inventory of the existing and needed resources in the community. Triage, quality assessment, multilevel care, periodic review of care, and evaluation at both consumer and provider levels will have to be developed, if a comprehensive continuum of care is to be safeguarded.

[9] Helen Rehr and Mildred Mailick, "Dilemmas, Conclusions and Recommendations," ed. Mildred Mailick and Helen Rehr, *In the Patient's Interest* (New York: Prodist, 1981), pp. 145–171.

[10] "Multi-Level Care Program (Interim Report), Summer 1979," Veterans Administration, October 1979, Washington, D.C., 20420, pp. 1–37.

Another development by social workers in the health care system is one which addresses finding people with needs that impede both their using care and their maximization of getting well. This calls for methods by which social workers can identify persons at "high social risk." Indicators of vulnerability derive from the premise that social and physical dysfunctioning may be associated with chronic illnesses or disabilities. In addition external and internal factors such as job, environment, marital, and emotional problems may also put a person at risk and affect the way he responds to a medical regimen. Individuals and families who may be at high social and physical risk need to be found as early as possible.[11] A byproduct of developing a case-finding instrument is to allow personnel other than professional social workers to become knowledgable about the social, economic, and cultural factors which may be impediments to care. Sensitivity to personal and social determinants in health care personnel can influence the outcome of service.

Motivation and Compliance

When an individual reaches a service, the first stage of initiation of care has been taken. To continue in care requires a similar set of dynamics on the part of the consumer and provider as initiation did. What lies in each and what occurs between consumer and provider are the factors that make for motivation. Continuing care, being motivated or in medical parlance, "compliance," has been a subject of extensive study. When one reviews the studies of "drop-outs" or those who do not "comply" with recommendations, one finds a wide divergence of findings. Clients who do not keep their appointments nor follow recommendations are a key concern in social agencies[12] and an even greater concern in medical and psychiatric institutions.[13]

We have indicated earlier that consumers have to act in their own interest in staying well and in continuing care. "The health of human beings is determined by their behavior, their food and the nature of their environment."[14] This is not per-

---

[11] B. Berkman, H. Rehr, and G. Rosenberg, "A Social Work Department Creates and Tests a Screening Mechanism to Identify High Social Risk," *Social Work in Health Care*, 5, no. 4 (Summer 1980), pp. 373–85.

[12] For reports of studies dealing with drop-out clients, see L. S. Kogan, 'The Short-Term Care in a Family Agency–Parts I, II and III," *Social Casework*, 38 (May, June, July 1957), pp. 231–7, 296–302, 366–74; P. R. Silverman, "The Clients Who Drop Out: A Study of Spoiled Helping Relationships" (unpublished Doctoral Dissertation, Brandeis University, 1969); Mayer and Timms, *The Client Speaks*; Perlman, *Consumers and Social Services*; and Maluccio, *Learning from Clients*.

[13] For studies reported on medical compliance, see Milton S. Davis in *Journal of Medical Education*, 41, no. 11 (November 1966), 1037–48; Milton S. Davis in *American Journal of Public Health*, 6, no. 2 (March-April 1968), 115–22; Julia D. Watkins and others, *American Journal of Public Health*, 57, no. 3 (March 1967), 452–9; Leon Gordis and others in *Medical Care*, 7, no. 2 (January-February 1969), 49–54; and Rona Levy, "Facilitating Patient Compliance with Medical Programs," in *Social Work in Health Care*, ed. Neil F. Bracht (New York: Haworth Press, 1978), pp. 281–9.

[14] John H. Knowles, "The Responsibility of the Individual," *Daedalus*, 6, no. 1 (Winter 1977), p. 57.

ceived in terms of consumerism and patients' rights but rather in terms of the individual's responsibility for his own health.

The most critical concern providers hold is that the consumer who reaches the service does not follow recommendations. A consumer-patient or client is seen as in noncompliance with medical advice or recommendations when he or she (1) accepts treatment and does not follow recommendations; (2) drops out of care; or (3) remains in treatment, but selectively complies from within the total package of recommendations. Individuals need to take some action on their own behalf regardless of the source of their care. How and to what degree individuals assume responsibility for such self-invested actions in a social health context varies in accordance with a range of psychosocial and environmental factors, in addition to the organizational barriers already discussed. Although it is not known whether a high correlation exists between following advice for given conditions and maintaining health, it is known that compliance with recommendations can mitigate symptoms, discomfort, and even in the extreme, the avoidance of death. The logic that faces provider and consumer alike is that "following advice" can mean improvement in the sick state. Then why do such large numbers fail to continue with care, as recommended?

It has been demonstrated in the medical field that the pattern of compliance is generally one-third who comply completely, one-third who sometimes comply, and a third who seldom or never do. What is most interesting is that physicians express a belief that their patients are doing what has been advised. Studies reveal that as many as half may not be.[15] Consumers who do not comply do not usually voluntarily tell that to their physicians, and particularly so if physicians do not pose the question.

Most studies have demonstrated that no definite link exists between sociodemographic variables and compliance or motivation for care.[16] Prior to Medicare and Medicaid, there was indication that the poor and minority groups, the latter also poverty-related, did underutilize health care facilities.

Consumers frequently seek advice from their caretakers. However, if it is not compatible with an individual's habits or lifestyle it can be the deterrent to its pursuit. Also, deleterious encounters with members of the health care system, complex instructions or regimens, limited or unsatisfactory communication, and lack of clarity as to goals and expectations can also contribute to failure to follow through. A study by Cauffman and associates[17] of consumer referrals and their outcomes found

---

[15] See Milton S. Davis, "Variations in Patients' Compliance with Doctors' Advice," *American Journal of Public Health*, 58, no. 2 (February 1965), pp. 274–88; Milton S. Davis, "Physiologic, Psychological and Demographic Factors in Patient Compliance with Doctors' Orders," *Medical Care*, 6, no. 2 (March-April 1968), pp. 115–22; and Milton S. Davis, "Variations in Patients' Compliance with Doctors' Orders: Analysis of Congruence Between Survey Responses and Results of Empirical Investigators," *Journal of Medical Education*, 41, no. 11 (November 1966), pp. 1037–48.

[16] *Ibid.*

[17] For discussion of health referral patterns and their "take," see Joy G. Cauffman, "A Study of Health Referral Patterns: Parts I through IV," *American Journal of Public Health*, 64, no. 4 (April 1974), pp. 331–56 and Joy G. Cauffman, *Search Community Blueprint, Human Problems and Services (Medical and Social)* Vol. 1, 4th ed. (Los Angeles: Caligraphics, 1980).

that if they showed up for care, they would receive care. In seeking answers to what motivated people to follow through on a referral from one setting to another, the researchers looked at a range of factors. As in other studies, sociodemographic factors were not significant in whether an individual pursued the recommendation. In addition, factors long considered major social and environmental deterrents to pursuing services, such as inconvenient scheduling, poor transportation, excessive waiting, no baby-sitting services, financial deprivation, and poor English turned out to be without significance. Consumers showed up for care in spite of the existence of these problems. The most significant factors associated with showing (and staying) for health care were when appointments with providers had been personalized by having the name of the person to be seen, along with a confirmed time. The significance of these findings for all providers is that individualization and personalization of care appear to be the key in people's following a recommendation.

The Relationship:
A Dynamic in Personal Care

The relationship between the patient-client and the provider has been seen by both the consumer of the care and the provider alike as the most important phenomenon that exists in achieving the objectives of treatment. Although the relationship in the sense of the interaction between the parties is the most critical factor, it can also be the most vulnerable. The relationship has been extolled, written about, and supported by every type of human service profession. To many therapists, it is the sine qua non without which there is neither motivation, self-investment, self-help, or relevant outcomes. We will not deal with the significance of the relationship as a critical therapeutic tool here (see Chapter Four). Rather, our discussion will be more relevant to the value implications in relationship, and provider and consumer obligations therein.

The relationship between client and therapist, consumer and provider has been surrounded with many protective devices lodged in professional values and ethics, social contract, in law, and in usage. There are values that govern the nature of the relationship and as such govern the behavior of the professional.[18] Inherent in the relationship is the respect for one another. This calls for allowing the client autonomy to be a key component in the relationship. Pellegrino suggests that the recognition of the autonomy of the individual served, is the primary value in the caring relationship. To support this primary value, other values must be integrated into a professional stance. These include values of "freedom of action," "freedom of choice," "freedom from the power of others," and freedom from "threats to personal self-image." These become the basic armamentarium of a humanistic basis of professional ethics.[19] These are the humanistic ethics that derive from experience after experi-

---

[18] Avedis Donabedian, "Models for Organizing The Delivery of Personal Health Services and Criteria for Evaluating Them," *The Milbank Memorial Fund Quarterly*, L, no. 4 (October 1972), part 2, pp. 116–7.

[19] Edmund D. Pellegrino, "Humanistic Base for Professional Ethics in Medicine," *New York State Journal of Medicine* (August 1977), pp. 1460–61.

ence relevant to the commitment to the individual and which serve as the "social contract" of the professional.

One of the primary values brought to the relationship is that of individualization. For those who deal primarily in direct services, the decision is based on the participatory contributions of each party. It is possible to address the concept of the social good or those general values relevant to the public, as an overall social health concept, but the therapist must individualize his patient when it comes to direct care. As illustration of the societal good versus the individual need, it is possible to arrive at a definition of death in relation to life-saving equipment, but the decision to cut-off or to continue life-saving appliance has to be individualized to that patient-family's social environment. Such knowledge can more readily be secured through the intervention of other health care professionals. Critical decisions such as in life or death situations will rest on the interpretation which multiple professionals and patient and family bring to them. Thus, values that may be set at the level of the society good, that is to make life-saving equipment available, can be different from those values at the level of the individual good which require ethical behaviors relevant to the patient and family's wishes and needs.

The client-therapist relationship, a very potent force for helping can be very susceptible to manipulation and tampering. The "valued" aspects of the relationship have been seen to rest along many dimensions:

1. Congruence between the therapist and the client is essential as to expectations, and orientations as well;
2. Adaptation and flexibility need to be evidenced in the therapist so that he can adapt the clinical demands and the client's expectation;
3. Mutuality needs to occur in the sense of a working partnership toward a mutually agreed-upon achievable objective or contract, and from which each perceives gain;
4. Stability is essential to safeguard continuity; it takes constancy as well as reaching out;
5. Maintenance of client autonomy in allowing for choice and self-determination;
6. An egalitarian relationship between client and therapist, as much as possible;
7. Safeguard the client's participation through sharing knowledge and information, so that decision-making can be a mutual effort, and participation in carrying out therapy is seen as a part of self-help;
8. Maintenance of empathy and rapport without undue personal involvement of the therapist with the client is generally supportive to the relationship;
9. Maintenance of such a supportive relationship should be conducted without encouraging dependency;
10. Keep the interaction between the two parties within the boundaries dictated by legitimate medical and social functions;
11. Communication between the client and his family, and relevant others must be open; the therapist may need to be an active participant in essential communication;
12. Avoidance of exploitation of the client, and of the therapist either economically, socially, sexually, et al.;
13. Maintenance of the dignity and the individuality of each of the partners;

14. Maintenance of the privacy of the consumer;
15. Maintenance of the confidentiality of the relationship and the nature of the experience.[20]

The implementation of these dimensions noted require concurrent incentive from the provider and from the consumer. Relationship if it is successful places a complex demand on each to respond consciously to each expectation. It is also based on "a mutual need model,"[21] which means that each party will reach out to the other based on a need for each other.

Unfortunately, there is still too little known about what keeps people in continuing care. We have seen that factors related to age, sex, educational or income statuses, and social background do not seem to be very significant. If one looks at the personality factors of consumers, the findings are also inconclusive. One would think that a person who has understood what his illness or problem is, how to deal with it, and why and how it can be controlled, will be motivated to participate in his own care. Studies along these lines are also inconclusive showing that being informed does not correlate with positive actions. What seems to have the most meaning in holding people in care are a mosaic of factors that can enhance motivation:

1. Continuing expression of interest by the provider in the client; even exhortation is seen as a sign of positive interest.
2. Mutually arrived at agreements for objectives, preferably one but no more than two sets at a time, in which the consumer and the provider openly clarify each one's part in the expectations.
3. Such mutually agreed to contracts should be translated into simplified steps, whether dietary, personal habits, and so on, and will need to be compatible with the individual's lifestyle.
4. Secure family support for the goal, seeking their meaningful participation in the process.
5. Use a trade-off approach rather than an all-or-nothing style, such as taking medication as the first step, to be followed later by following a salt-free diet, and still later, giving up smoking, so that goals are limited and staggered over time.
6. If things need to be remembered or done repeatedly, explicit and written instructions should be proffered and tested for clarity with the consumer.
7. If scheduling of actions is required, link them to commonplace events such as medication before or after meals, so as to make them part of routine and therefore, simple to follow.
8. Short-term successful results should be recognized since they give a sense of achievement, and support the adding of new mutually agreed upon goals.
9. Continued interest in what is happening is an essential component of the caring process no matter what form it takes.

These are a few suggestions which can enhance the relationship between con-

[20] Donabedian, *The Milbank Memorial Fund Quarterly*, pp. 140–1.
[21] Anthony F. Panzetta, *Community Mental Health: Myth and Reality* (Philadelphia: Lea & Febiger, 1971), p. 99.

sumer and provider. They reflect the investment of the health care professional in his client. Personalization and individualization occur. In addition to the provider-consumer partnership in the contracting of and the pursuit of objectives, the family has a key place in supporting the patient in his continuation of care. This cannot be a one-time and spontaneous agreement to be helpful, but requires communication between the key actors with understanding of who is involved and what is required. It is difficult to be the lone person in a household of others, sick and having to follow a regimen of imposed limitations. The environment in which one lives, occupationally and neighborhood-wise, is also critical as a supportive measure. What is being worked on needs to be feasible and compatible with the environment one has, and expectations need to be consonant with the opportunities available and possible for the individual. Although an individual has to be self-invested, and acting in his own interest, the evidence is that he or she will be a fuller participant when there is a partnership with the provider that is open, supportive, personalized, and with understanding.

THE VOICE OF THE CONSUMER

The consumer can speak in many ways regarding what has happened to him personally and in relation to the process of seeking and receiving care. There are those who speak out freely and from a depth of feeling, and there are those who respond to questions asked them by administrators and providers of care, through their emissaries or through social researchers. There are also those who speak out as citizens with a cause and a message. We shall now examine the consumer-patient's view of his own care and the degree of satisfaction sought and described by consumers of care. The voice of the consumer group or special interest will be discussed under consumerism.

The Patient and or Family Talk
About Illness and Care

The patient or family member talking about what happened to him in the health care system at the hands of providers is commonplace. When one examines the voiced experience in economic-theory terms, it becomes clear that "word-of-mouth" is one of the most powerful factors operative in the so-called open market of health care. Illness and its care when openly discussed serve many purposes, not the least is the relief from anxiety and the tensions from the experience.

What is different from the past when it was not unusual for one individual to tell another about his illness, his doctor, and the outcome, is that the experience has now been viewed by the public in the media. Over the last decade the public has been exposed to a plethora of views from the consumer or a family member about the illness or disability suffered, the nature of care received, the interrelationship between physician and the consumer or relevant other, and the outcome. These have appeared in all forms—articles in popular magazines, books, television, and radio, as well as in movies or as theatre drama. The pattern that has been emerging from this range of viewing or reading materials has included the decrying of care received from either or both doctor and hospital, the story of an illness and its impact on the patient and the family, and an outcome which may be recovery, full or partial, or death. More recently a self-help focus has surfaced dealing with the sharing of responsibilities in care, those that fall to an individual as a patient, and make a strong case for the right of self-determination, and those that fall to the doctor.

"Who's Life Is It Anyway?" a recent Broadway hit and movie, depicted the conflict between the patient and his determination to choose between life and death while the medical staff remained determined to keep him alive. The conflict while depicted in the most extreme of situations—the patient was totally helpless and bed-ridden—is not an unusual one between physician and patient. The physician has been educated to see himself as a healer and a life-saver. The impact that this type of medical education has on the physician is that it carries an expectation that the patient should be willing to submit to medical judgment. This means that cure is always the first objective, followed in order by sustaining a patient at the best physical level possible, and in extreme circumstances "heroic ' medicine will be employed to keep one's patient alive. This objective of doing what's considered best for the patient is standard among all health care professionals. There is comparatively little philosophical difference among the medical and the social-psychological therapists, in which the latter seek changes in the client himself or in his situation as the most meaningful goals.

Norman Cousins, the journalist, expressed his view[22] of his illness and care in a book, *Anatomy of an Illness*, one chapter of which appeared as an article in the *New England Journal of Medicine*, a most unusual circumstance.[23] Cousins' message is one subscribed to by all physicians intellectually, and by a number in practice. He believes the individual as patient needs to assume responsibility for the processes of getting well and staying well. Although staying well and living long require genetic resources, they are both related to one's lifestyle. Cousins joins a number of physicians and social scientists who suggest that moderation in our social and physical way of life, including a well-balanced diet, continued physical activity, and involvement in community affairs or special interests right through to the end of life can contribute to its quality and its longevity. We have already learned that most illnesses are self-terminating. The genetic and healing processes of the individual facilitate getting well. Medical care can contribute to the process and even to the quality of getting well. However, recovery, according to Cousins, is dependent on one's own resources in terms of motivation and in coping capacities. Counsins notes the incredible numbers of nonmedical healers in the American culture who claim success. There are an infinite variety of modalities open to the seeking public such as biofeedback, laying on of hands, hypnosis, meditation, acupuncture, Zen or Yoga, and faith in drugs or religion. By and large, these are helping processes that rest on commu-

---

[22] Norman Cousins, *Anatomy of an Illness* (New York: W. W. Norton & Co., Inc. 1979).

[23] Norman Cousins, "Anatomy of an Illness (As Perceived by the Patient)," *New England Journal of Medicine*, 295, no. 26 (December 23, 1976), pp. 1458-63.

nication and the quality of interaction between a consumer and a helper. People believe something will happen and thus they can make it happen through their own will or with the support of another in whom they believe. So many people have turned to nonmedical sources of help because they have not found the medical care system helpful enough or responsive quickly enough to their needs.

Cousins writes of his illness and of his hospitalization. He is struck by the ineptitude, promiscuous use of equipment, the confusion, lack of cleanliness, indiscriminate use of tests, and of tranquilizers. When he is able to observe the care, he remarks on its significance in supporting helplessness and dependency. At this point he turns to his own resources in order to restore functioning again. It is his belief that "the most valuable service a physician can provide to a patient is helping him to maximize his own recuperative and healing potentialities."[24] Cousins turns around what appeared to have been a fatal illness to recovery. He does this by his own active intervention including projecting his own therapy in drugs and direct care. However his therapeutic design had the support of his physician.

For those who become seriously ill, there are things they can talk about and understand together which those who are not ill do not readily understand. There is a state of being relevant to illness, which Cousins identifies as happening to him while he was sick, and which may be familiar to many who have been seriously ill:

> . . . he finds the feeling of helplessness serves as a serious disease in itself; with it is a fear that one would never function normally again, which makes one shut out the world of activity; not wanting to be a complainer; wanting to protect one's family from extensive worry, which makes one even more isolated; the conflict between the terror of loneliness and the desire to be left alone; the illness was a result of something in one's self; dreading to know and fearing that things were being withheld; the fear of all the technology and being done to and being moved to one hospital area after another; the hunger for human interaction warm and friendly; with all this Cousins finds that compassion could be more helpful than technology and continuity of the same people in one's case was as important.[25]

A book by Martha Weinman Lear is that of a wife relating the happenings of her husband's massive coronary attack and its sequelae.[26] Mrs. Lear relives the experience of her physician-husband, not only with his illness and hospitalizations, but also the interrelationships with his medical peers and with a range of health care professionals. She portrays how these encounters resulted in his sense of powerlessness and rage, and how his illness affected their own interrelationship. The medical tragedy of such magnitude affected on every part of the marital relationship, as well as on their family lifestyle, affecting each as an individual and their actions together. The medical establishment and its human failings surface in Mrs. Lear's story. She describes some of the nonmedical helpers in the hospital who, in her opinion, reflect a more compassionate concern than the medical staff.

[24] Cousins, *Anatomy of an Illness*, p. 130.

[25] *Ibid.*, pp. 153–4.

[26] Martha Weinman Lear, *Heartsounds* (New York: Simon & Schuster, 1980).

The consumer and his family are voicing their experiences. There are many messages. Writing about oneself as a patient can be helpful to oneself and to others. Writing about someone close who has encountered severe pains helps one to relieve his or her grief and pain. In these writings about the medical care system there is invariably a message behind the tale of what happened, in a cry for change, or an alert to others to be aware of what care may be like in comparable circumstances. The major message is that one should be prepared to mobilize one's own resources in one's own behalf.

Consumer Satisfaction Serves to Evaluate Care

The voices of consumers regarding their view of care has been examined in a formal context by some researchers for almost two decades. Donabedian considered the consumer's perception of medical care an essential component in the evaluation of quality and urged its study.[27] Overton wanted social workers to turn to their clients to learn what they had to say about what was beneficial and what was not.[28] She believed that what was learned might induce change in methods of service delivery.

In general, assessment of care has been perceived as a basic responsibility of professionals in the context that their knowledge and skills are the monopoly of the given discipline. A tenet of "social contract" is the profession's commitment to monitor and review the care offered by peers so that it is in the public's good. Most of the helping professions have established standards to govern their practices. In addition they have reviewing bodies to examine the complaints of patients-clients who wish to call on the profession for redress of a "wrong" before seeking a legal course. The Joint Commission on Accreditation of Hospitals, created in 1957 by the American Medical Association, the American Hospital Association, and the American College of Physicians, was given the responsibility, as an independent body to establish accreditation standards for hospitals in the United States and to review them. Review of hospitals remained a voluntary function until it became a required activity with the passage of the Social Security amendments of 1965.

The assessment and judgment of the provider, practitioner, or hospital, have been seen along three dimensions: structural or administrative, process, and the outcome of care. The structural standards deal with the effective use of the organization (institutional, agency, or private practice) in serving the consumer. If one assumes that "good" structure facilitates a "good" process, and thus a "good" outcome occurs, then structure becomes an important dimension in evaluation. At this time there is no demonstrated linear relationship between structure and outcome.[29] However, studies do demonstrate that individuals respond to organizational factors

[27] Avedis Donabedian, "Evaluating the Quality of Medical Care," *The Milbank Memorial Fund Quarterly*, 44 (July 1966), part 2, pp. 166-203.

[28] Alice Overton, "Taking Help From Our Clients," *Social Work*, 5, no. 2 (April 1960), pp. 42-50.

[29] Helen Rehr, "Quality Assurance: Implications for Social Work" in *Professional Accountability for Social Work Practice*, ed. Helen Rehr (New York: Prodist, 1979), p. 21.

in terms of personal convenience and cost. Such items as admitting procedures, appointments and scheduling, waiting time, food service, housekeeping, and laboratory and x-ray equipment are extremely critical to consumers of social and health services and appear to have some effect on how they respond to services. The factor of process—the elements of practice, remedies, and interventions—deals with the translation of judgments emanating from diagnosis of the client's situation and problems. What is to be done to and for the patient have been the elements for evaluation of process as viewed by the professional. Often missing in these reviews is the consumer himself and what he has to take on as his part of the contract of care.

The early emphasis in assessing outcome of care concentrated on the consumer and what he did. His or her responsiveness was felt to be the primary ingredient in the way the services were utilized and the recommendations made. *Compliance* and *noncompliance*, terms used by physicians, which are compatible with *continuance* and *discontinuance*, terms used by social workers, have been studied over the last three decades in relation to a range of client characteristics. It was interesting that none of the studies revealed that patients' readiness to comply with recommendations seemed to correlate with any sociodemographic characteristic introduced.[30]

Outcomes, the third dimension used by providers to assess care is considered the sine qua non of indicators. Outcome is the result of what has been done to, for, and with the consumer, and is the most difficult to measure. The intervening variables that occur from the time the consumer enters a system of care to his departure are many and complex. Controlled studies that would be utilized to study cause and effect are extremely difficult to mount in clinical situations.

Evaluation of patient care is a complex dynamic involving multiple variables and is extremely difficult to achieve in the human services field. Studying the process of care in relation to outcome is subject to the development of criteria and standards. This requires dealing with multi-factor involvement rather than unidimensional approaches. Social and physical functioning and dysfunctioning, if they are to be clinically judged, require more than physiological factors alone; they also need to include social, cultural, and psychological factors. There is no means to evaluate such a mosaic of variables in a cause and effect relationship as yet.

Then what is it that providers evaluate at this time. One method is to enter into a peer review, that is, judgment by a group of professionals of another member's documented process and outcome in regard to a given patient's care. Another means is an audit of a given program for its structural and administrative functions in regard to achieving its objectives. How the arrangements affect the processes and outcomes of care in a cluster of cases is reviewed. This is usually done through a review of the records of cases, which have been selected for their common social problems, common illnesses or disorders, or any other agreed-to grouping.

There is no question that the responsibility for evaluation of the quality of care falls on all providers, on reimbursement agencies, on insurance companies, and

---

[30]Milton Davis, "Variations in Patients' Compliance with Doctors' Advice: An Empirical Analysis of Patterns of Communication," *American Journal of Public Health*, 58 (January 1968), pp. 274–88.

on the government, which is a primary reimbursing agent. The consumer is pivotal in all of these reimbursing sources as a user of services—as the payer, in a direct or indirect way, and as a taxpayer. When the practitioners and their professional societies exercise their reviewing function in implementing evaluation and assessments, they will need to draw on selected experts for technical assistance rather than to rely on subjective means alone. The essential objective of evaluation is the translation of findings into application and in change so that benefits fall to the individuals who require the service.

Should professionals dominate the assessment of quality of care? Can a consumer be involved in a review in a way that would prove meaningful to providers? There are many who question the contribution that consumers can make, believing that assessment is in the purview of the experts alone. To stress that the consumer's point of view in assessment should be recognized does not mean it should stand alone as a judgment of the professional service rendered. It is a recommendation that he or she, the recipient of services, should be included along with others. This is predicated on the assumption that the consumer-patient is as much a chief actor as is the professional in the interactive process between them. Both have critical parts to play and tasks to perform. The consumer is key in the process whereas the provider has the responsibility to provide the conditions that the consumer can draw on in helping himself.[31] There may be conditions deemed important to the process that are not in the purview of either the provider or the consumer. These will have to be openly acknowledged and recognized as being outside of the process.

What criteria would consumers of care use to judge their helpers. In using the basic framework of a "profession," Segal and Burnett suggest that there are four areas that could be considered for evaluation:

1. Theoretical components of basic concepts, theories, and abstract knowledge;
2. The theory of developmental normality relevant to optimal social and health performance;
3. Knowledge relevant to tested physical and chemical characteristics of and the remedies for those entities defined as illness;
4. The technique and skills relevant to putting knowledge to use.[32]

If we examine these components that give a professional the privilege to practice, it may be noted that (1) and (3) legitimate the professional content whereas (2) and (4) appear to be a moral and social phenomena where judgment employed is less scientific than it is creative art. In the latter two blurred areas, the laymen may be as equipped to have an opinion as the professional. The second area deals essentially with assumptions about what is normative behavior in regard to social and health factors. This area is still without scientific basis, and when introduced into practice tends to be very individualized. Techniques and skills, the fourth area, are

[31] Maluccio, *Learning from Clients*, p. 15.
[32] Material derived from Alexander Segal and Margaret Burnett, "Patient Evaluation of Physician Role Performance," *Social Science and Medicine*, 14A (January-June 1980), p. 269.

couched in affective or expressed behaviors of the professional and these then are observed and responded to by the consumer. It is in the areas of behaviors and performance that consumers have expectations, and on which they form opinions. Indeed studies demonstrate that consumer judgments about care are made on the affective responses of providers relevant to expectations they hold, rather than on any content or technical competencies.[33] Ben-Sera in his studies in Israel of general practitioners and their patients' response to care, examined content and mode of care, and found that affective behavior related to the mode of care is a decisive factor in the layman's satisfaction. The behavior that included characteristics as "devotion," "time," and "interest" was found more meaningful to patients, than either technical or even administrative procedures, such as waiting time.[34] DiMatteo and his colleagues found "caring and expenses" plus accessibility to doctors were more important factors in their continuance with care than either content or competence, which they believe to be too difficult to judge by patients. The primary reason for terminating with the practitioner, was poor interpersonal rapport or inadequate social-emotional responsiveness of the physician in his relationship to the patient.[35]

In involving the consumer in the evaluation of his care, the emphasis is then placed on his values, understanding, expectations, and preferences, his role in the process (the contract agreed upon), as well as his perception of the outcome and what he believes has been helpful or not helpful. The nature of the interaction between consumer and provider is the area to which the consumer is most sensitive, most observant, and most responsive. He or she unquestionably responds to that relationship in the perception of the quality of "doctoring" which in his lay interpretation is that of the "caring" level of the therapist. In most instances, it is whether the expectations he has of how the therapist will behave are realized that determine how he judges "good care."

There is frequently a great difference in the perception of expectations held by the therapist and those held by the consumer. This derives from the fact that each profession holds content and competence as the most significant areas of expertise. Diagnosing and remedying are key physician- or social-therapist-held attributes. Diagnostic acumen and therapy that aids the client to understand the reality of his situation and deal with it in his private interest are social work held values. Similarly, nurses judged their technical competence as most important.[36]

Most studies to date show that while consumers want solutions to their problems, it is the "mode" of delivery that they find most meaningful and related to the outcome of services. The "mode" is not a simple concept. It requires not only looking at the providers' performance but also that of the consumer, and the role comple-

[33] *Ibid.*, pp. 268–78.

[34] Zeer Ben-Sera, "The Function of the Professional's Affective Behavior in Client Satisfaction," *Journal of Health and Social Behavior*, 17 (March 1976), pp. 3–11.

[35] M. R. DiMatteo, L. M. Prince, and A. Taranta, "Patients' Perception of Physicians' Behavior," *Journal of Community Health*, 4, no. 4 (Summer 1979), pp. 280–90.

[36] Gwen D. Marram, "Patients' Evaluation of Nursing Performance," *Nursing Research* (March-April 1978), pp. 153–7.

mentarity achieved between them. Role complementarity is seen as "the interlocking set of expectations and behaviors in interpersonal systems."[37] The possible causes of failure in role complementarity between parties, whether they are family members, doctor-patient, or social worker-client relationships, may be lodged in

1. "cognitive discrepancy," which relates to the lack of awareness regarding what the roles require in a given system;
2. "discrepancy of goals," which involves different perception of goal expectations on the part of partners due to any type of reason, such as socio-cultural differences, attitudinal differences, stress, et al.;
3. "allocative discrepancy," which relates to differences between the partners in regard to the person's rights to the role he wants to occupy;
4. "instrumental discrepancy," which relates to the inability to enter role transactions due to technical reasons such as skill, adequate equipment, specialized theoretical formulations, et al.[38]

A breakdown in one area can cause discontinuance, or noncompliance in relation to care, resulting in a lack of satisfaction on the part of both consumer and provider. When mutual agreements or contracts are formulated in which each of the partners defines and redefines the goals, the expectations, and tasks, each partner is expected to carry the interaction with responsibilities agreed upon for in-between the interactions. When these terms are set by the partners, there is greater clarity regarding what is to happen.

The contract is an ongoing process between the parties. The functions therein are

1. clarifying the reciprocal expectations and enhancing the mutuality between client and practitioner;
2. resolving issues and overcoming blocks that arise in the client-worker interaction;
3. engaging the client's cognitive powers;
4. speeding up the helping process in cases in which the service is appropriate;
5. helping to terminate as early and as positively as possible.[39]

Unless these areas are openly identified, it is extremely difficult to qualitatively assess the judgements brought by the parties in regard to what is happening and has happened. The judgments or opinions of the service, without early definition and on-going contracting, are then usually made on expectations which have not been expressed. Congruence needs to be achieved between consumer and provider as to contract, and to determine role responsibilities of each. It is within the context that the process and the outcome can be assessed by both provider and consumer.

The studies done of consumer satisfaction with care received show results

[37] Maluccio, *Learning from Clients*, p. 9.

[38] The discussion of discrepancies in role complementarity derived from Maluccio, *ibid.*, pp. 9–10.

[39] *Ibid.*, p. 187.

which are essentially positive about services received. There is a predominantly high level of satisfaction reported. These are surveys of clients of social agencies,[40] as well as patients in hospitals[41] and in other health settings.[42] In general, consumers find both the delivery of services and the professionals helpful. The questions that hospitals have asked their discharged patients are generally simple ones such as "Would you again use or recommend the use of the service to others?" They usually tend to seek reactions to the administrative areas that govern admitting, food service, housekeeping, laboratory and x-ray services, nursing, and the discharging process. These are generally under the jurisdiction of hospital administration and nonmedical personnel. Medical institutions have been slow to draw on their consumers for their comments on doctoring leaving those areas to professional assessment. Social agencies have begun to turn to their consumers for their response to care, but both administrators and their professional staff have been slow to respond to the client's voice. As far as other health agencies' response to consumers, there have been studies, often one-shot affairs, where findings are usually returned to administrators who then decide whether to act on them.

Panzetta offers a paradigm for evaluation of care involving both provider and consumer (Figure 2-2.) He also reflects on the compatability of goals between the partners. Although each may start with different perceptions, they will need to be reconciled in order to initiate treatment. Panzetta makes the point that it is the consumer's reason for coming in the first place which must be addressed, and not what the therapist has to offer.[43] His paradigm reflects that while each may start from a different position and set of expectations, they must come together on treatment objectives and the means to achieve them.

There will be problems in seeking consumer satisfaction, as opinions are sought about client continuance, or discontinuance, compliance or noncompliance, contracts, interventions, role complementarity, and outcomes. However unless we ask our consumers of services a range of questions dealing with their expectations, perceptions of services, and what was helpful and what was not, we have only the providers' view of care without the voice of the consumer.

---

[40] See Maluccio, *Learning from Clients*; Perlman, *Consumers and Social Services*; and Mayer and Timms, *The Client Speaks*.

[41] See S. Kurella, "The Social Needs of Patients and Their Satisfaction with Medical Care," *Social Science and Medicine*, 13A (January-June 1979), pp. 737-42; M. J. Kupst, J. L. Schulman, and J. Dowding, "Evaluation: Attitudes Toward Patient Care and Work Satisfaction," *Hospital and Health Services Administration* (Winter 1979), pp. 78-92.

[42] See Ben-Sera, "The Function of the Professional's Affective Behavior in Client Satisfaction"; DiMatteo and others, "Patients' Perception of Physicians' Behavior"; J. H. Mitchell, K. Hardwick, and B. Beck, "Telephone Follow-up for E. R. Audits," *Quality Review Bulletin*, Special Edition, *Journal of Quality Assurance*, JCAH (1979), pp. 50-52; B. S. Hulka, S. J. Zyzanski, J. C. Cassell, and S. J. Thompson, "Satisfaction with Medical Care in a Low Income Population," *Journal of Chronic Disease*, 24 (1974), pp. 661-73; J. Kasteler, R. L. Kane, D. M. Olsen, and C. Thetford, "Issues Underlying Prevalence of 'Doctor-Shopping' Behavior," *Journal of Health and Social Behavior*, 17 (December 1976), pp. 328-39; M. E. Reid and G. M. McIlwaine, "Consumer Opinion of a Hospital Antenatal Clinic," *Social Science and Medicine*, 14A (January-June 1980), pp. 363-8.

[43] Panzetta, *Community Mental Health*, pp. 92-5.

FIGURE 2-2 Quality Control[a]

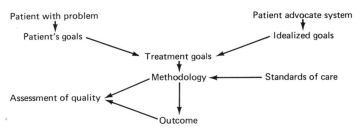

QUALITY CONTROL

Patient with problem

Patient's goals

Patient advocate system

Idealized goals

Treatment goals

Methodology ◄——— Standards of care

Assessment of quality

Outcome

[a]Anthony F. Panzetta, *Community Mental Health, Myth and Reality*, (Philadelphia: Lea & Febiger, 1971), p. 93.

CONSUMERISM IN HEALTH

The informed consumer with knowledge and motivation to act in his own and in behalf of other consumers is the goal of all consumer movements. The informed consumer is also a goal of health care systems that believe in seeking consumer response to care at both the individual and general level. When personal investment is a critical factor in treatment and in convalescence, a consumer must be informed in order for his motivation to be at the peak of responsiveness. Recently, there has been a growing concern regarding (1) the protection of the consumer in his transactions with providers, in particular with institutions and organizations, and (2) the advancement of the consumer's interests in the nature and the quality of services offered. Consumers have banded together in different types of organizations, and have drawn on a wide range of means in order to safeguard their health care interests. Although the consumer movement has taken many forms such as in lobbying groups for special interests, in the use of legal intervention, in tackling of goliath corporations, we will deal with a few of the measures affecting patient rights, advocacy on behalf of those rights, consumer advisory groups, special interest groups, consumer health education, and self-help programs. These movements can be either provider or consumer organized, and have some effect on the direction of social and health care services.

Dissatisfaction with the human condition, social and economic conditions, and with the institutions which serve people has surfaced at different times and under different circumstances. Efforts to improve social conditions or institutions within specific regions have been attempted from early times. Each change achieved would be more or less effective, until new breakdowns brought forth new social actions by the people and the next move toward seeking change was instituted. The first recorded instance of securing patient's rights in hospitals was in France in 1793 when the Council of the French Revolution decreed that only one patient should occupy a bed as opposed to the usual practice of from two to eight persons. Also, beds were to be spaced a minimum of three feet apart. The concept of hospitals as we know them developed approximately 80 years ago, having changed from social service custodial institutions to working laboratories for physicians just after the turn of the century. Quality control in hospitals was instituted in the United States in 1918 when the American College of Surgeons drew up a one-page list of standards. However, even 50 years ago, only 89 out of 700 hospitals agreed to follow the standards promulgated and the College was forced to remove them because of the 611 hospitals that failed to pass on them.[44]

In the twentieth century, major dissatisfactions began to erupt on a massive scale with the health care system following World War II. However, the Depression first and the war that followed caused concentrations on a range of other serious social problems so that even the early efforts of the New Deal to seek solutions to the medical care system in this country were not given any priority until the mid-1950s. The breakdown in health care was evidenced in inequities, fragmentation, lack of available services, and inaccessibility that affected large numbers of people. The public concern was generated into a series of political efforts resulting in the construction and expansion of hospitals through the Hill-Burton Act and in the infusion of federal monies into biomedical research to deal with strokes, coronary disease, and cancer—the three major causes of death and disability. Later, federal monies were made available for securing more advanced technology in medical care, and to increase health care personnel by supporting the education of students in the medical, nursing, and social work professions. In 1966 Medicare and Medicaid legislation was instituted to cover the medical costs of care of the elderly and the needy (see Chapter Three). In most instances federal and voluntary financed support over the last 30 years has been directed toward biomedical and scientific research with the notion that such advances could change the health status of the people in the course of time. The scientific advances were effective in broad areas such as in the virtual elimination of infantile paralysis and in rendering pneumonia harmless. It did not however do much for the quality of individual care. In the 1970s, there was a growing dissatisfaction with medical care as emphasized in the media, and as evidenced in the growth of consumer movements. The focus of these concerns was on the problems in the health care systems and organizations, and in the ways they delivered care and services. Pressure grew for an accountability of the quality of care. Although there was some self-regulation of hospitals by the Joint Commission on Accreditation of Hospitals, the responsibility for quality review was assigned to the professionals and to their institutions, by federal regulations promulgated under Professional Standard Review Organization. In all of these reviews there was very little turning to consumers for their perception or response to what they were receiving and the degree to which they benefitted from care, until PL 93–641. This law created the Health Systems Agency, a consumer majority program with some responsibilities for regional review of health care provisions and expansions.

[44] Margaret E. Walsh, "Nursing's Responsibility for Patients' Rights" in *Consumerism and Health Care*, National League of Nursing, Publ. no. 52–1717, 1978, pp. 19–27.

Health consumerism as we know it today had its beginnings in the 1930s. It started when fraternal orders such as the Workmen's Circle established health insurance and or health service cooperatives. In the service area, they employed their own physicians and designated the programs that they supported. As consumers of the services, members of the cooperatives exercised control over both program and benefits. Labor unions have played and continue to play a large role in bargaining for benefits and in opening access pathways to alternative health plans for their members. Some unions developed centralized ambulatory care programs.[45] The International Ladies Garment Workers Union established the Sidney Hillman Health Center in New York to serve its members. Although the federal government attempted to give consumers a voice in their own services within the 1960s with the Great Society programs of Presidents Kennedy and Johnson, the efforts come with greater frequency as the soundings of consumers and of the media becomes louder.

In the 1960s we see the first acknowledgment of the patient as a "consumer" of health services. It is in this period that we see the designation "patient" changed to "consumer." The difference is that the patient is seen not only as a recipient of care but as one who is a purchaser of services, directly or indirectly. This concept of "consumer" establishes him in roles that carry greater independence and decision-making responsibility than what he carried either as patient or as client.[46] The consumer movement begins to take off with government endorsement and with some financial underpinning.

As stated earlier, the major impetus to consumer involvement came in the promulgation of PL 93-641 in 1974 under government auspices, establishing Health Systems Agencies throughout the country. However, HSAs have had slow beginnings and have encountered serious difficulty in making any impactful headway on health care systems in this country. There is indication HSAs may have a major setback under the Reagan administration. Voluntary-organized consumerism has also been of minor consequence in its impact on hospitals and other aspects of the health and mental health fields.[47] However, there are some signs that it is growing not only at both the local and regional level,[48] but also at the national level as demonstrated by Nader's Health Raiders.[49]

Patients' Rights

The American Hospital Association, the organization of the hospital industry, introduced the Patient's Bill of Rights as a standard of hospital care in 1973. The American Hospital Association based its "rights" statement on the 1962 Statement

---

[45] Lester Breslow, "Consumer-Defined Goals for the Health Care Systems of the 1980's," in *Technology and Health Care Systems of the 1980's*, ed. Morris Collen (Washington, D. C.: U.S. DHEW, Health Services & Mental Health Administration, 1972), p. 115.

[46] Leo G. Reeder, "The Patient-Client as a Consumer: Some Observations on the Patient-Client Relationship," *Journal of Health & Social Behavior*, 13, no. 4 (December 1972), pp. 409-10.

[47] Breslow, "Consumer-Defined Goals," pp. 116-22.

[48] Barbara Ehrenreich and John Ehrenreich, *The American Health Empire: Power, Profits and Politics* (New York: Vintage Books, Random House, 1971), pp. 268-79.

[49] Margaret W. Sparrow, "Consumerism: Its Impact on America's Health Professionals," *Consumerism and Health Care*, National League of Nursing, Publ. no. 52-1717, 1978, pp. 7-17.

of Consumer Rights, a consumer pressured mandate, promulgated under the Kennedy administration. The 1962 statement supported the consumer in the right to be informed and to be protected against fraudulent, deceitful, or grossly misleading information. The consumer had a right to be given the facts needed in order to make an informed choice. The right to choose was to be assured, whenever possible, of access to a variety of products and services, of satisfactory quality at fair prices. In addition the consumer had the right to be heard and to be assured that his or her interests would receive full and sympathetic consideration in the formulation of any relevant government policy.[50] In citing the President's message, Monk notes that as far as the "frail elderly" or those in need of institutional care are concerned none of these rights exist as yet.[51] Even in hospital-based care, except where mandated by state codes governing hospitals, the Patient's Bill of Rights remains a determinant of an institution's board of directors. The intent of the 1962 statement has served as the forerunner for the 1980 Patient's Bill of Rights. Each hospital seeking JCAH accreditation is required to have a written statement and procedures by which it informs its patients of their entitlements at admission. Procedures are required to inform the staff of the promulgation of the Bill of Rights. Consumer groups have advocated for these rights all these years and the Health Care and Financing Administration now concurs in its benefits. Such Patient's Bill of Rights are now a monitored standard of the Joint Commission on Accreditation of Hospitals.[52] It is also expected that such statements will become a requirement of hospitals receiving federal reimbursement for services.[53] The standard covers such rights and responsibilities as access to care regardless of race, creed, or religion; the right to respect and dignity, privacy, and confidentiality; to know each provider of direct care by name and status; to be informed regarding condition including the right to refuse treatment, and to expect personal safety. The patient when informed of the rules and regulations of the institution is expected to comply with them, while also to be considerate of others. In addition he is expected to give information regarding his condition and to comply with recommended treatment. If he refuses what is being recommended, he assumes responsibility for his actions, and relationships between consumer and provider may be terminated without damage to either party. The right to informed consent is stipulated along with the patient's right of access to his records.

The individual's access to his own government-based records guaranteed by the Freedom of Information Act of 1974, has also enhanced the consumer's rights in health care. The Freedom of Information Act was intended to restore the confidence of the American people in government (and in bureaucracy) by ridding politicians

[50] Derived from the article by Abraham Monk, "Accountability Criteria and Policy Strategies in Direct Service Provision for the Aged," *Journal of Gerontology and Social Work*, 1, no. 2 (Winter 1978), p. 151, in which he makes reference to "Message from the President relative to consumer protection," Document No. 364, U.S. House of Representatives, 87th Congress, 2nd session, March 15, 1962.

[51] *Ibid*, p. 151.

[52] "Rights and Responsibilities of Patients," *Accreditation Manual for Hospitals*, Joint Commission on Accreditation of Hospitals, 1981 (see Appendix I).

[53] Federal Register, "Conditions Governing Hospitals," June 20, 1980.

of their practice of secrecy. Access to one's records in the health care system are privileged to the patient and to whomever he designates, so the patient is protected. There has been a recent innovative technique that opens the patient record to him and makes directly available diagnostic and therapeutic notations. There is evidence that this type of open communication in which formal medical chart entries are shared by physician with the consumer of services has enhanced the relationship between them.[54] The use of medical chart notations is an innovative means to keep the patient informed and under the circumstances of knowledge to secure the patient's investment in self-care. It has similarities to the method of securing mutually agreed-to contracts in which both consumer and provider have indicated their responsibilities toward achieving the agreed upon objective in care.

Patient Advocacy
and Ombudsman Programs

The complexity, the specializations, and the high degree of stratification of medical care institutions and their growing trends toward depersonalization and fragmentation of services have created special problems for the consumer. Even the most knowledgeable and sophisticated individuals in health care can find themselves at a loss, stranded in the complex maze of hospitals, and unable to deal with the impersonal behaviors of the staff. This bewilderment has registered itself within political arenas in growing complaints against the medical settings. Legal suits against providers accelerated in number. However, as the pressures began to get out-of-hand, an innovative approach developed to deal with the problem: patient representatives within institutions and ombudsmen or advocates in community based organizations.[55]

The concept of advocating for citizens is not new. Ombudsman derives from the Swedish system that adjudicates grievances of bureaucratic services on behalf of aggrieved citizen-consumers. The focus of ombudsman intervention, usually a government network, is to protect John Q. Public in his individual citizen status from official injustices. Although the courts, the legislature, and regulatory agencies responsible for given functions, are the usual means to hold government, commercial, and voluntary bureaucrats in check, the government ombudsman addresses each grievance on its own merits, from an unbiased and neutral position.

Redressing wrongs through the ombudsman is an "after the fact" method, done without the extensive machinery of a court inquiry. The advantage of the ombudsman system in dealing with the individual's grievance with the bureaucracy is that it provides an expert who can review policy, procedures, law, and regulation that consumers cannot deal with on their own behalf. In general practice, an ombudsman is appointed whose objectivity is ensured in that there is no relationship to other official bodies. In addition, the role is a highly visible one. The review service is readily accessible to all those affected. Impartiality and neutrality are the key char-

---

[54] David L. Bronson, Alan S. Rubin, and Henry M. Tufo, "Patient Education Through Record Sharing," *Quality Review Bulletin*, 4, no. 12 (December 1978), pp. 2–4.

[55] Mailick and Rehr, *In the Patient's Interest*.

acteristics of the function and a thorough investigation of a complaint is the typical practice. The findings and judgment are followed by a recommendation relevant to the situation. Occasionally the recommendations may address policy as well. The position of ombudsman carries its power and prestige from the status given the position by government at the highest level. Ombudsman programs in some form are more typical in European countries, and there is also a mechanism in Japan that deals with administrative oversights. In the United States, there is no such formal post at a national level. However, informal programs exist out of every congressman's office in which individual case redress is investigated by the legislator's staff. There are advocacy services offered at other levels of government: state and local. Again, many of the bureaucratic complaints of individuals are handled at the level of the constituency representative to the level of government involved.

The ombudsman function placed at the state level has been sought by citizens and their representatives in over half of the states; currently only the state of Hawaii has created a state ombudsman position. Most legislators have questions regarding the feasibility of ombudsmen at the state, and even at the national level. They have seen its value for small countries, but given the complexities of urban centers and the legislative structure in this country, they tend to believe it would create more bureaucracy and less individualization in the handling of complaints than their offices can provide.[56] In addition, there are others who believe that ombudsman functions will not address grievances of all Americans on an equitable basis.[57]

However, the problems brought to public attention in the mental health arena, in nursing homes, and in institutions in the profit and non-profit areas have forced the beginnings of public-advocacy programs in the nursing-home field, which have taken different forms in this country. The Nursing Home Ombudsman concept was supported by federal funds in 1973 under the jurisdiction of the then Department of Health, Education and Welfare. Seven states have created such posts in order to investigate complaints against institutions, usually of mistreatment of individuals.[58] Office public advocacy programs are being set up to deal with these types of citizen complaints and requests from legislators and public interest groups with regard to bureaucratic problems.[59] At least 28 states currently provide advocacy services as a component of state administered programs of mental health.[60] This advocacy is in addition to patient advocacy at the level internal to the system.

[56] See Jessie Unruh, "The Ombudsman in the States," *Annals of the American Academy of Political and Social Science*, 363 (January 1966), pp. 111–210 and Frank Zeidler, "An Ombudsman for Cities," *Annals of the American Academy of Political and Social Science*, 337 (May 1968), pp. 122–7.

[57] Richard Cloward and Richard Elman, "An Ombudsman for Whom?" *Social Work*, 2, no. 2 (April 1967), pp. 117–8.

[58] Patrick D. Linnane, "Ombudsman for Nursing Homes: Structure and Process," U.S. Dept. of Health, Education and Welfare, Office of Human Development Administration on Aging, n.d.

[59] "Public Advocacy Pioneers in N.J. and Seems to Work," *The New York Times*, January 14, 1979, p. E 7.

[60] See Angela McGuire and Lee Tracy, "Mental Health Consumer Complaints: Insights on Unmet Needs in Hospitals and Communities," mimeographed paper, April 1980; and Herbert Rusalem, "Ombudsman for Patients at a Mental Health Center," *Hospital and Community Psychiatry*, 24, no. 10 (1973), pp. 680–1.

At the voluntary level, consumer groups carrying advocacy functions on behalf of individuals have proliferated in various forms. There are some that carry a policy review and redress role in relation to government and even toward institutions. In the field of social work, advocacy as a function has a respectable history, long before the turn of the century. However, it took full shape again in the 1960s when the problems of the poor and powerless were of major significance. Social work assumed responsibility to help these individuals to deal with complex institutions, and the welfare system, in particular. Advocacy for the client's point of view as a formal role in community-based organizations began to flourish.[61] What was taken on were both case and class advocacy. Although social work continues to espouse the function, and it is still carried by some social work agencies, advocacy as such has moved into a more public arena and is carried by consumer groups that assume the function as a component of their objectives. An extremely active advocacy program is illustrated by F.R.I.A., the Friends and Relatives of the Institutionalized Aged, which as a citizens' group, using friends and family members, monitor programs, advocate on behalf of institutionalized individuals within New York State and have a record of securing improvements at both the institutional and state levels for the client's point of view.

It was this growing concern with breakdown in institutional services to its clients, that fostered the development of a patient representative program within a medical institution. In its beginning efforts a major function of patient representation was its advocacy on behalf of those who were disadvantaged, who had special difficulty in dealing with the institution. The program was initiated in a large medical center where complexity and multiple medical specialties made encountering personnel and traversing the institution very difficult.[62] (See Chapter One under Paraprofessionals.)

Consumer Advisory Groups and the Health Systems Agency

There are a number of consumer advisory mechanisms. Illustrative of consumer advisory programs are the development of an in-house advisory group of consumers representing a users' point of view and the consumer-provider Health Systems Agency with its involvements in the health care planning and delivery of services within a geographic region. The consumer advisory committee in health institutions has behind it the original support of a government mandate. The concept of "maximum feasible participation" of consumers emanated out of the Johnson Administration in its Comprehensive Health Planning legislation and which has gone through a number of transformations since its promulgation. PL 93–641 (1974), The National Health Planning and Development Act, has prompted major renewal of interest in consumer participation in the way health care is delivered. The law mandated the establishment of the Health Systems Agency, with a constituency of a majority of local consumers and representation from regional providers. The Health Systems

[61] Charles Grosser, *New Directions in Community Organizing: From Enabling to Advocacy* (New York: Prager, 1973), p. 18.

[62] Helen Rehr and Ruth Ravich, "An Ombudsman in a Hospital: The Patient Representative," in *In the Patient's Interest*.

Agencies (HSAs) function at regional, local, and state levels. (There is also a national advisory body.) They carry responsibilities for planning of health care, along multiple dimensions, and for the implementation of plans over time. In addition, they carry the function of review of local institutional projections for change in and development of their facilities, services, and manpower relevant to the needs of a region's (district) population. Although there is serious question as to the continuance of HSAs in the country as a result of the Reagan administration's projected curtailments, the principles and problems relevant to a publicly supported form of consumer-provider organization are significant to social-health planners.

On local levels there are some 9,000 volunteers who serve in actual health systems agencies. There are 2,000 more in the State Health Coordinating Agencies (SHCAs) and about 40,000 serving on various committees, task forces, and advisory groups. These consumer volunteers in HSAs give over one million hours of their time.[63]

The assumption in the development of the HSA programs was that consumers, because of their greater than 51 percent representation and their role in project review would have the balance of power at both state and local levels. In reality consumers have shown far less power than their functions imply. In New York State, where the review responsibility has now been set at projects projecting a $100,000 or more for new capital expense, only very large expenditures come in for local review. Multiple projects under $100,000 can bypass the process entirely. When reviews are made, they are always provider requested. Thus, the institution sets the pattern for the justification for its own project. The greatest contribution of the local HSAs to date is that they have identified the prevailing problems in the health care system and have identified the population groups who are not getting care.[64] They have no power to secure provider conformity with regional health planning projections.

The HSA is set up at local and state levels as a consumer-provider partnership to address regional concerns. However, it is interesting to note that the problems they face organizationally are common across the country. At the overall level the issues that must be addressed in order to help HSAs become functional are

1. the lack of clear national purpose and direction; and inconsistent guidelines from the Department of Health and Human Services;
2. unusually high turnover of staff at central and regional offices;
3. lack of access to timely data and poor data management;
4. arbitrary restrictions placed on medical institutions without awareness of regional needs;
5. finding consumers for board membership who can be informed and responsive;
6. inadequate funding to regional and local HSAs;
7. HSAs have not demonstrated effective planning or control of programs, either to its own constituencies, to the public or to the Congress.[65]

[63] Sally Berger, "Local Health Planning Must Be Revitalized," Hospitals, *JAHA*, 54, no. 13 (July 1, 1980), pp. 54–6.

[64] *Ibid*.

[65] *Ibid*., p. 55.

At the consumer level it is assumed that each member comes to the board with comparable knowledge of health matters, ability to understand and analyze data, and facility for working with groups. Also it is assumed that each HSA board member has an outside system such as an agency or organization for support and assistance. None of these expectations hold true. By and large, most consumers on HSAs do not have any health care backgrounds, except perhaps in personal experience. In addition, they have to participate in their spare time and are not adequately trained by HSA staff in content or in group participation. In contrast, the providers are informed and have organizational support. So to assume that "equality" exists among participants is a myth.[66] A critical problem is that consumers have in their personal culture and in societal expectation deferred to physicians. They rarely initiate ideas and tend to follow the providers' judgment. In a recent study, Grossman found that when consumers and providers are together, they tend to vote alike in either accepting or rejecting projects proposed for review. They do not seem to separate into special interest groups as one would expect. Under particular conditions it would be possible for special interest groups to dominate decision-making.[67]

Although consumer participation in HSAs is considered "a cost-free process to which all citizens have access,"[68] in actuality, participation takes the time, money, and efforts of consumers when serving at meetings and hearings. As more demands are made on individuals, more of them exclude themselves from the process. Cooper claims the costs to participants are great and are not sufficiently recognized by the HSA staff. The organizational components and the demands of implementation affecting participation in HSA activities by consumers are

1. its complexity, which deals with the extent of bureaucratization, rules, complications, by-laws, and the investment they call for from consumers;
2. its scale, which covers the size of the geographic district, and its distances which are significant to the consumer in terms of personal investment and knowledge;
3. the lack of availability of information and the frustrations in regard to its dissemination as well as its quality;
4. the sites where meetings are held, which are usually in community facilities generally not used in the evenings and with little parking facilities and poor public transportation available;
5. the meeting format and agenda, which are usually excessive, and generally formal presentations from experts, which leave little time for public participation;
6. the interaction among participants, which can be a problem because there is no common language to enhance communication between consumers and the providers;

[66] Shelley B. Frost, "Consumers' Impact on the Diffusion of Medical Technology," *Consumer Health Perspectives*, Consumer Commission on the Accreditation of Health Services, VII, no. III (June 1980), pp. 4–7.

[67] Rudolph M. Grossman, "Voting Behavior of HSA Interest Groups: A Case Study," *American Journal of Public Health*, 68, no. 12 (December 1978), pp. 1191–4.

[68] Terry L. Cooper, "The Hidden Price Tag: Participation Costs and Health Planning," *American Journal of Public Health*, 69, no. 4 (April 1979), p. 370.

7. the processing of membership which tends to be quite restrictive and geared toward known persons thus excluding many potentially capable individuals;
8. the elections, which when held are usually done without a quorum because of the limited attendance of consumer members.[69]

In addition to the costs cited, consumers identify other problems that make participation difficult. These problems are lodged in the HSAs structure and function. Staffing is usually inadequate or unavailable to consumers to provide technical assistance. Issues tend to be presented in a jargonese that require a special orientation, and in general, such training is usually not available. HSA tends to have an excess of emphasis on the regulatory functions imposed by federal mandate and much less time is available for planning of care in the region. Also, the review and comment processes that deal with the "condition of need" (CON) of institutions, are hurried and do not have adequate preparation. Therefore, the consumers' questions and views are frequently glossed over.[70] The provider members also express their dissatisfaction with HSAs. They feel they must comply with national guidelines regardless of local needs and that institutional and regional health care plans are not integrated. They see the "condition of need" process as excessively slow and imposing costly delays on them. They also do not see HSA dealing with what they believe are the current most serious health care problems, such as nursing-staff shortages and inadequate reimbursements to institutions. It is interesting to note that physicians who are eligible for provider membership tend not to participate because of the excess time demands and their belief that too little results from HSA activities. Business and labor tend to favor local planning but are frustrated by the HSA process. Business, in general, has sidestepped the HSA by setting up its own programs such as "The Business Round Table" or "The Washington Business Group on Health," which tend to reach politicians more readily than the HSA.

The current evaluation of PL 93-641 is that there has been little achievement of a satisfactory cost-benefit from health care planning and review under HSA. HSAs themselves have begun to find fault with the demand to concentrate on regulations in solving complex problems. There is a beginning shift from regulatory control toward the introduction of competitive market forces as the incentive to constrain costs. However, means by which the competition is being viewed as a force are not clear. Congress passed PL 96-79 in 1979 which revised its earlier Health Planning and Development Act. Its intent is to seek improvements in facilities, by attempting to have the institutions assure access, promote quality services, and contain costs by promoting efficiencies and by eliminating duplication and unneeded services.

As long as consumers are expected to participate in reviewing the project needs of institutions, and the new law continues that function, they will need to recognize that "condition of need ' projects are social policy issues and not solely technical ones. Except for replacement needs, institutions affect the social-health care structure in their regions when they project new capital and program investments.

[69] The discussion derived from Cooper, *ibid*., pp. 371-2.
[70] Berger, "Local Health Planning," pp. 54-6.

Decisions on CONs should not be left to the judgment of providers who invariably present their requests with an institutional self-interest. Decisions need to reflect value judgments governed by social policy arrived at by the citizenry with the advice and comment of the experts. Consumers need to learn to work with and to treat experts as resource persons in securing information and data essential in the decision-making process. These are some of the factors that should be considered:

1. "Need": What does the project deal with? How many people will be affected and or benefitted? What does it replace? Why? How does it help?
2. "Safety": What are the risks and potential harms, and what safety benefits accrue? What standards of safety govern use?
3. "Effectiveness": How well will it work? Over time, and under normal conditions? Its efficiency, that is, how well it does what it is supposed to do? What results can be expected from its use? What conditions are required for application? Can its effectiveness be measured? What measures will be introduced to assure its efficiency? Will the project make a difference in the care of people?
4. "Cost": What is the real cost in terms of manpower, environment and space needs, operations and maintenance? What are the actual purchase costs including installation? How do these costs compare with existing technology that addresses the same medical problem? Will the project pay for itself over time? Will it affect reimbursement rates? What is the future cost of care to the user?
5. "Regional impact": Is the project needed in the community, that is, its requirement is more than the institution's needs? Are there other ways to deal with the need? Does a service already exist and meet needs? What is the nature of demand? Can arrangements be made for the service elsewhere, conveniently, cost-effectively, and without deprivation to consumers?
6. "Consistency with the Health System Plan": Does the project fit in with regional goals set by the Health Systems Agency plans for the social health program of the future?[71]

It has been suggested that consumers may need an independent consultant as a resource available exclusively to them in order to help with data gathering, posing the right questions, searching for answers, and developing consumer-oriented, regionally sound social-health policies. At present, however, it is generally recognized that an effective consumer voice has not yet been achieved in the Health Systems Agency programs across the country. A great deal needs to be invested in order to prepare and to aid consumers in having a meaningful role in regional health planning. In addition to the education of consumers in the functions of HSA as an ongoing program, the agency structure will need to be reorganized in such ways so that consumers can readily recognize the benefits of their participation. It has been suggested that consumers, like providers, should derive personal and or occupational benefits from their participation in HSA activities. These benefits would be in the form of upward mobility position, time-off, and other "incentives" for participa-

[71] The discussion based on the projections made by Frost, "Consumers' Impact on the Diffusion of Medical Technology," pp. 4-7.

tion.[72] In many ways, the incentives that fall to the trustees of hospital boards for their participation in hospital affairs should be considered for consumers in advisory and participatory groups of similar expectations. Hospital trustees as lay participants are openly recognized by their own occupational, political, or social class constituencies for these activities. On the other hand, when one examines the impediments to conducting health care planning in a knowledgeable way, these lay trustees face the same uninformed states regarding their own hospital plans and deliberations and need education in the delivery of care in the same way that local consumers in HSA or community health groups do.

Even if the HSAs should become defunct by virtue of curtailment of funds by the federal government, a means to secure an organized response to care by consumers will continue to be generated.

PROMOTING HEALTH:
SELF-HELF AND PATIENT GROUPS,
CONSUMER HEALTH EDUCATION,
AND SPECIAL INTEREST GROUPS

There is a growing demand from the public to deal with how to stay healthy and to keep well. As a result consumers have turned to organizing themselves into self-help groups and to special interests' groups. In addition, the traditional institutions have started to expand their functions from the provision of services to the sick to that of health promotion for the population in general. The National Health Consumer Information and Health Promotion Act (PL 93-317) of 1976, in placing emphasis on consumer health education, introduced health maintenance into the national health policy. The medical institutions are beginning to emphasize "prevention" in different ways in addition to serving the ill. The American Hospital Association, in affirming a health promotions policy for its members, sees the hospitals' role

> to work with others in the community, to assess the health status of the community, identify target health areas and population groups for hospital-based and cooperative health promotion programs, develop programs to help upgrade the health in those target areas, ensure that persons who are apparently healthy have access to information about how to stay well and prevent disease, provide appropriate health education programs to aid those persons who choose to alter their personal health behavior or develop a more healthful life-style, and establish the hospital within the community as the institution which is concerned about good health as well as one concerned with treating illness.[73]

[72] Warren R. Papp, "Consumer-Based Boards of Health Centers: Structural Problems in Achieving Control," *American Journal of Public Health*, 68, no. 6 (June 1978), pp. 578-82.

[73] "AHA policy affirms hospitals' role in community health," *Promoting Health*, AHA (1979), p. 1.

Even a superficial review of the new policy suggests that the parent organization of hospitals will encourage its hospitals to enter the health maintenance field, in addition to maintaining its sick-care programs. It would seem that the policy could be interpreted to allow for any and all forms of programs, projects, modalities, and approaches that foster the "stay-healthy" or "good-health" concepts. It can be noted that AHA sees its members entering into a wide range of roles, into the communities reaching unknown persons—not necessarily their patients as yet—to help them stay out of their institutions as in-patients by becoming and being informed about a "healthful life-style," which serves as a preventive against disability or illness.

In general, consumers have already started in this direction by a range of self-directed and self-invested programs. Self-help, education, self-improvement, mutual-aid programs and special-interest groups have been some of the ways the public has responded to its concerns with the existing service arena. Impersonal care, unresponsive to the individual together with the dependency-encouraging attitudes of professionals have both served to arouse the public to react with a sense of independence and to draw on community informal social supports; both of these have been somewhat untapped human resources since the end of World War II.

Self-Help and Patient Groups

Self-help groups have emerged almost as a movement in itself during the 1970s. "Hundreds of thousands of self-help groups exist across the country."[74] What is self-help? It is the means by which people join together in groups to deal with common and identified needs. In the health arena self-help groups are organized for various reasons:

1. To deal with problematic behavior that individuals are unable to control, such as smoking, overeating, child abuse, substance abuse such as alcohol, or to deal with common problems resulting from a chronic illness or a physical disability,
2. To fight for a cause as in discrimination or in the stigmatization felt relevant to a disease or a handicap, while working to strengthen the image and position of those suffering from the "stigma."

Mutual aid from peers with the same or similar identifiable problem has been the means by which individuals have been helped. The goal is to enhance the individual's ability to cope with his problems resulting from the ailment or the problem. Mutual aid is not new. It is as old as people gathering together for a special concern. In this country self-help in the service arena arose in the Depression era. Although public programs were growing as a result of the federal and state investments of the 1930s and 1940s, largely supported by social welfare public health professionals, there was that somewhat independent wish, which survived the Depression, to achieve

---

[74] Ann Withorn, "Helping Ourselves: The Limits and Potential of Self-Help," *Social Policy* (November/December 1980), pp. 20-7.

for oneself without undergoing bureaucratic difficulties.[75] It was that drive that fostered a host of mutual-aid societies. Some of the earliest were for group welfare and burial insurance, which were invariably family focused. Food, clothing, and housing exchange efforts came out of the movement. One of the earliest self-help models is Alcoholics Anonymous founded in 1935 in reaction to the lack of help received from professionals. Alcoholics Anonymous, a behavior-focused program with a touch of religious support, utilized the principle that admitting to drinking was critical to securing support and help from others who had endured the consequences of the problem, and had licked it. Each day as a day of abstinence, that is, getting through "one day at a time," was the key support mechanism. A network of local groups of A.A.s across the country grew up.[76] Each local group is an independent clustering of peers ready to be at hand for the individual who has signed up and who may falter at any time. It is important to be aware that motivation, at least to join the group, must be in evidence for an individual to achieve membership.

It has been indicated that self-help groups have grown in such numbers either because of the lack of availability, accessibility, or even helpfulness of the traditional caring systems, or because the resources for the need just had not been developed by professionals. In most instances they have grown spontaneously, drawing on the value of individual and personal participation and are action-oriented.[77] In the fullest sense, the self-help group is a support system that in a nonprofessional way offers friendship to each other.[78]

With more of these self-help groups, professionals tend to carry referring roles, occasionally facilitating care to an individual and even consultation to the group, but rarely if ever leadership. Such self-help groups can be extremely helpful to the individuals involved in them, but they are not a 100 percent sure thing. Gartner and Riessman have noted that there is no scientific data to suggest that problems are resolved.[79] There are those people who seem to require more than a sharing, supportive friendship in dealing with their problems. For these, professional services may be required.

The mutual-aid group of peers described is different from those patient or family-member groups that have been formed at the instigation of professionals who have recognized not only the common problems and needs, but also the value of the shared experience to secure problem resolution, under expert guidance. In a special sense, these patient or family-member groups have the primary purpose of using education and counseling in order to achieve some change in the individual, which in its way is not different from self-help groups. The change sought is either attitudinal or behavioral. Invariably the change to be realized is from what is believed

[75] *Ibid*, p. 22.

[76] *Ibid*.

[77] Alan Gartner and Frank Riessman, *Self-Help in the Human Services* (San Francisco: Jossey-Bass, 1977), pp. 31–57.

[78] Carol H. Meyer, "Social Work Purpose: Status by Choice or Coercion?" *Social Work*, 26, no. 1 (January 1981), p. 73.

[79] Allan Gartner and Frank Riessman, "Potentials and Limitations of Self-Help," in *Self-Help in the Human Services*, pp. 119–45.

to be a "negative" to a "positive" point of view or action. The intent is to secure a cognitive or coping stance different from the one currently held by the individual. In drawing on the group process, the professional social worker recognizes that a patient and his or her family need, not only each other, but others to help them make sound adaptations to the impact of the illness or disability. In utilizing the interpersonal relationships in defined ways specific to the psychosocial needs of the individual, the social worker attempts to catalyze the group interaction to the individual. In addition, the socialization phenomena of the group itself is drawn upon in a constructive way. Being accepted by others, not only the therapist, but those who are in the group, tends to lead to self-acceptance, even self-esteem. The conscious use of the dynamics of the interrelationships often allows for reality testing in which group members react to an individual's expressed feelings and opinions. The professional direction is to oversee that the content and communication are sound, not detrimental or excessively anxiety-provoking, and to encourage, even challenge, through the peer process, the individual's motivation to deal with and to work on the problem. Although this process is comparable to that of the mutual-aid peer group in that a give-and-take, a learning from and responding to others, tends to occur, it differs in that a conscious professional overseeing occurs wherein planned direction rather than "spontaneous" help takes place. In their ways, both are self-help or peer groups, completely, consumer-oriented but under different auspices. Both can be helping and valuable processes. Health settings are particularly well suited for provider-founded groups because they are places where people with common problems, illnesses, disabilities, and needs can be readily identified and brought together.

When social workers in health settings are involved with groups, they are usually in favor of "orienting" or "educating" targeted persons about what to anticipate, or how to counsel in relation to specific needs or problems. Social workers in medical settings initiate "orientation" groups that allow newcomers to a service-program to learn what to expect and what is expected of them. Frequently "orientation" groups serve to uncover or find individuals with social problems that warrant further services. In this way an educational group can serve as a casefinding mechanism. There are other types of health education programs that will be addressed. Although some social workers perceive ongoing counseling groups particularly in disease-specific areas such as a Terminally Ill Group or a Myasthenia Gravis Group as having educational components, they are usually biopsychosocially oriented. To be truly effective, educational and informational content is an invariable component of the process. In health care settings, such groups may be co-led by social worker and doctor, or with a nurse. They have the advantage of both biological and psychological expert underpinning on behalf of patients.[80]

---

[80] Rosalie A. Kane, "Thoughts on Patient Education," Editorial, *Health and Social Work*, 6, no. 1 (February 1981), pp. 2–4.

Consumer Health Education

AHA has encouraged its member hospitals to introduce consumer health education programs with regard to specific diseases and ways to maintain the care of oneself, following discharge from the hospital, or a clinic program. These are usually general care projects requiring personalization and individualization if they are to be effective. In general, consumer health education has been initiated by a growing number of health care professionals who have seen health education as a must in their relationships with their clients. Many have begun to recognize that individuals need to be informed and educated to what is essential if they are to be invested in their own care.

When a patient has suffered illness, disease, or disability no matter how efficient and qualitative the diagnosis and the treatment plans are, unless the patient is involved in that plan and its outcome, benefits will be difficult to realize. Patient education is a sine qua non of the doctor-patient relationship, as it is of any therapeutic partnership, including that of the social worker and client. To secure the patient's involvement requires an informed, understanding, and motivated individual. Education, however it is addressed, is a requirement of the care process. It is predicated on the quality of communication that can exist between the partners. Neither the physician nor the patient start out as easy communicators. Social workers and nurses have an edge on doctors in this regard. In general, the factor that permits the ability to question, disagree, even challenge what has been said to one is not a ready component of the interrelationship between a provider and client.

Hospital-based patient education programs are being initiated in a wide range of areas. An extremely interesting program is described by a gynecologist-obstetrician on her use of the patient's medical record as an educational device.[81] She cites her belief that the patient's chart should be open and the content shared with the patient. Dr. Storch is convinced that knowing improves the quality of the care. Record sharing is seen as a major dynamic in enhancing a patient's understanding of his or her condition and increases motivation to follow the treatment plans.[82] This approach in medical care planning is akin to contracting between a social worker and the client. It is predicated not only on a qualitative assessment of the client's situation, but also on the patient's participation as essential in establishing the objectives for his own care. Setting the goals is done in conjunction with the parts that provider and client will play in the process. If the client is an understanding participant initially, there is likelihood that he or she will continue. As the client has added understanding of the problems that required medical care and of the plans for dealing with them, the partners find their roles more clearly determined, and increased responsibility for self-care and management of problems fall to the client.

[81] Marcia L. Storch and Barbara Wendorf, "Storch on Storks," *Quality Review Bulletin*, 4, no. 9 (September 1978), pp. 4-6.

[82] David L. Bronson, Alan S. Rubin, and Henry M. Tufo, "Patient Education Through Record Sharing," *Quality Review Bulletin*, 4, no. 12 (December 1978), pp. 2-4.

Every individual should have access to information about the range of social health care services available. In addition, one needs to learn what a healthy environment is in the full range of positive and negative factors. Both require information to be imparted in some form so that the individual can deal with his own social-health needs, as well as with environmental hazards. Education for health should be a community endeavor and education per se is fundamental to health maintenance at every age level. However, motivation of the individual to assume responsibility for his own health status is not achieved by education alone. Resources and opportunity to achieve given objectives need to be available. In addition, to stimulate motivation in some can also require a considerable degree of professional investment, and programs to encourage compliance will need to be available alongside of health education endeavors.

Health education is not a function limited to social work. Nor is it a function exclusively a public health, family, or school responsibility. It can be provided anywhere in a wide range of forms and media, by many and varying sources. The physician, the parent, the teacher, the public-health practitioner, special interest groups, and voluntary social and health agencies are some of the forces from which education is a constant expectation. The arenas in which health education can take place are at home, in the school, in the workplace, in the community, and certainly in the health care facility, public, private, or voluntary.

The objectives of health education are to reach each individual so that each one is interested in personal health maintenance, in how to achieve or to improve it, to learn when to seek care for oneself and immediate kin, where and how to seek it, and to understand the difference between good care and quackery. Motivating to use services or to be interested in health maintenance may be accomplished by the educational process, but frequently will require a range of other services, counseling, in particular. In order to be an active participant in his own health maintenance and care, the consumer needs to overcome his ignorance, in general, and to acquire specific social-health information, in particular. Information, therefore, becomes the primary component, but information to be meaningful to the consumer needs to be relevant, timely, in the individual's own interest and should allow him to draw on inner as well as external resources to achieve the objective. There are those who claim the individual has the solo responsibility for his health status. In this writer's opinion, that places a blame or a responsibility on the individual beyond his exclusive due. For an individual to become or to be informed requires the investment of a large number of others.

There are many health-education programs which assume that to be informed is all that is needed to secure an individual's response and action. In these instances, logic, understanding of self-destructive or external destructive forces, or fear are believed to be important incentives for securing action. However, the evidence is that punishment or exhortation tends not to be very effective educational approaches. When massive health-education programs that involve large audiences are attempted, problems frequently arise. The primary criticism of large-scale programs is that there is no way to differentiate people in the audience as to who they are, their specific needs, or their response potential.

When health-education programs are contemplated, a mosaic of factors are worth considering:

1. The targeted group should be known;
2. The objective and the goal should be realistic, limited, and within a time set frame of reference;
3. The strategy can involve multiple methods, but should include some trial and error before putting a large scheme into place;
4. Study of the results should be included in every health-education program, so that outcome data are understood.

When health education is introduced, its expectation should be for partial gain and not for total change. There is growing indication that educational programs that can reach targeted groups are somewhat effective in achieving their objectives, particularly when limited. However, the most serious concern in the field is that most programs studied reflect the short-term gain,[83] and there have been few programs that have been able to demonstrate long-term achievement.[84]

> With only few exceptions, the efforts in research, demonstration, teaching and service are at an embryonic stage of development, inadequately funded and minimally staffed. Research design lags behind the sophistication of those associated with biomedical investigations. Many times, health education projects are more descriptive than evaluative, confined to populations too small to establish statistical significance (too big so as to invite failure), and lack the use of control groups that would make their findings more persuasive. Demonstration projects in health education often suffer from the lack of clearly articulated goals. This fact, compounded by their short life span under existing grant and contract mechanisms, militates against the capacity to measure outcomes.[85]

The opportunity to overcome these difficulties has been instituted into law by President Ford in PL 94-317, the National Health Consumer Information and Health Promotion Act. Will this commitment to consumer health education survive? There is no question that when consumers or providers are asked they endorse the need. The complexities in the expectation are enormous.[86]

---

[83] Cherye Perry, Joel Killem, Michael Telch, Lee Ann Slinkard, and Brian G. Danaher, "Modifying Behavior of Teenagers: A School-Board Intervention," *American Journal of Public Health*, 70, no. 7 (July 1980), pp. 722-5.

[84] David Evans and Dorothy S. Lane, "Long-Term Outcome of Smoking Cessation Workshops," *American Journal of Public Health*, 70, no. 7 (July 1980), pp. 725-7.

[85] Bess Dana, "Consumer Health Education" in "Health Services: The Local Perspective," *Proceedings of the Academy of Political Science*, 32, no. 3 (1977), p. 191.

[86] *Ibid*, p. 192.

Special Interests

There is no single national organization that represents consumers in regard to health policy or health care delivery in the same way that the American Medical Association represents the physicians, or the American Hospital Association represents the hospital and health care provider industry. There are as we have noted earlier under Self-Help Groups an incredibly large number of programs created by persons with special needs requiring and giving assistance to individuals. When one addresses the issue of health advocacy or social health policy reform, even though there are consumers invested in many of the organizations, the majority of them have been provider dominated. These special interests in the health field are in large measure focused on a single disorder or a system of disorders, such as the American Cancer Society, the National Diabetes Association, American Heart Association, or American Lung Association. These are fund-raising organizations, with multiple purposes including the support of specialized programs, of research, but most frequently with the primary interest in lobbying on behalf of their constituencies. They compete with each other for funds from the public, at both the national and local levels. These special-interests groups differ from self-help groups in many ways, but the major difference is the latter are invested totally in direct help to its constituency. The former are concerned with the legislative and public policy changes that will affect their constituencies. There are groups that exercise both direct service and advocacy such as veterans' groups and even those mentioned occasionally offer a direct service. Most special-interest and self-help groups are also invested in some aspect of health education.

However, special-interests groups, and they are numerous, see their primary role as advocating for their concerns. The advocacy is done on behalf of a group encountering an injustice, a dissatisfaction, or anticipating one. The advocacy is done not only for the group, but by and with the members of the groups. As indicated in the health field, these can be both a lay and professional constituency. There are people who think of special interests groups as very powerful forces fighting for a single issue. Such advocacy is as old as society, and in America it may be the cornerstone of democracy. The fact that there can be such expression of diverse interests is part of the American democratic system. The concern with power becomes critical when its exercise by a group or a coalition of special-interest groups is such that its control excludes others from being heard.

Advocacy[87] can be expressed in many forms: by an individual or by a coalition of individuals. It can be undertaken by lobbying so as to influence the political process in regard to public policy, by administrative or regulatory processes so as to influence the implementation of a policy, a law or a regulation.

Making complaints, making requests for hearings or appeals when one believes

[87]Discussion on advocacy derives from William J. Hanna, "Advocacy and the Elderly," in *Aging: Prospects and Issues*, ed. Richard H. Davis (Los Angeles: University of Southern California Press, 3rd ed., 1981), pp. 297–317.

something unfair has occurred can be perceived as advocating on behalf of an issue. Advocacy requires some skills and certain characteristics. In addition to being an expression of social justice, advocacy requires energy and will. These skills can be considered to involve the following:

1. Personal commitment in the form of persistence, willingness to undertake risks, a modicum of savvy, and a degree of resiliency or flexibility;
2. The ability to plan, which includes listening to others, in particular, the opposition;
3. Concentration or single-mindedness in that the issue should be single, felt to be most urgent; the issue should be feasible so that something can be done about it in a realistic and achievable sense and within a reasonable period of time.

    Advocacy steps to be undertaken are

1. documenting the issue; identify it clearly and gather sound data to make the points intended;
2. bringing the appropriate parties together so that a coalition is achieved, allowing the constituency to decide what to do, what can be done, what will be done;
3. doing an analysis of what is required to be done including a review of the resources available and needed;
4. planning strategy, including a course of action that allows for review and the opportunity to shift in midstream, if necessary;
5. implementing the strategy, safeguarding the objective with adequate manpower;
6. assessing the outcome and undertaking recommendations;
7. making new plans based on the evaluation.

In one way or another special-interests groups tend to function drawing on the advocacy principles as outlined. To keep a special-interest group active requires an action program, and these invariably involve lobbying—keeping the public informed via a wide range of media of the issue at hand, and activating regional or local enterprises to keep the concern an ongoing one. As we have noted, professionals have as much interest in these single issues as do consumers. Some stay with a special interest; others may move from issue to issue. It is not uncommon for this concentration on a special issue to create fragmentation in the overall health care field. The most critical example was the successful lobbying by the National Kidney Disease Association in achieving insured coverage by the government under its Medicare program for a special group requiring renal dialysis and transplants. What started out as a comparatively small federal commitment has now turned into a singularly large one, enough to have turned off the financial spigot in regard to support of any other special illness.

CONCLUSION

Consumers of health care services are demanding greater participation in their own care and will be more invested in the delivery of that care at both the personal social health services level and at the organizational levels in the future. Having crossed the thresholds of the social and medical care systems, a conscious awareness of the quality and of the effectiveness of the care has become a concern for most consumers. The assessment of care by consumers is based on two major components: technological excellence and perceptions of the human interpersonal factors between consumer and provider. In the sphere of technological excellence, the consumer, at the present time, is neither very much involved in nor equipped to bring qualitative judgment to these aspects of care. On interactions, consumers bring personal and subjective assessments that are extremely important and, as we have noted, can be instrumental in their reactions. There is the growing awareness among a number of professionals that consumers are judging the outcome of care received and, therefore, should be exposed to a greater understanding of the potentialities and limitations of the technological components of care available and on the drawing board. What professionals are more reluctant to have consumers judge is the process of care.[88] On the other hand, it is the process to which consumers bring subjective judgments and see personal communication and professional investment as critical components of it.

We have attempted to document the imbalance in the present system, describing the need for a partnership between the consumer and his caretaker, and among consumers, health care providers, and politicians. At the personal health care level, the consumer's right to an open and shared service, which includes information and understanding of the situation and the implications of care, is now moving to the forefront of the relationship between consumer and provider.

At the planning and the self-help levels, consumers have begun to organize in a wide range of ways so as to affect what they get, and to influence the political process as it deals with health programs, and the planning process at the regional and even institutional levels. Codetermination will require a partnership among consumers, health care professionals, politicians, and office holders who are instrumental in health care planning. Although consumers are already invested in the process to a degree, the problems faced in being active in such coalitions are myriad. Consumers have understandable difficulty in sustaining ongoing commitment to the process of planning, in contrast to providers whose job usually calls for the effort. The rising influence of special-interests groups, whether at the consumer or provider level, and of self-help groups that are competitive with professional services is a strong pull in the direction of forming coalitions. However, to have the consumer a knowledgeable participant in such coalitions will take a special investment from the professionals.

[88] Steven Jonas, "The Role of Consumers in Health Care Delivery Systems," in a letter to Feedback, *Hospitals* (April 1, 1981), pp. 57-8.

If one were to project an outline of steps to enhance consumer investment, one could begin with the following:

1. An information service affording reliable and relevant data is important. Such information needs to be regularly available, and periodically reported. If decisions on special issues must be arrived at, they will require special preparation and opportunities for consumers to hear different points of view. Types of services, professionals, costs, availability, utilization patterns, state of technology, and more will assist the consumer in becoming an informed partner. The system of information needs to be so structured as to give consumers the opportunity to inform providers of the needs and wants of the constituency they represent. Case finding and referral concerns will be some of the issues raised by consumers, as will access and availability. Providers do need to inform consumers of pending plans and policy considerations until consumers can be true partners in making such projections on their own.

2. There will need to be training of consumers for effective participation in the planning process and in what is needed to arrive at sound decision-making. At the present time there is very little opportunity for consumers to be knowledgeable. It is most likely that consumers will have to seek out professional consultation in their own interests for the time being, until the investment of consumer and provider can be trusted.

3. Consumer participation in decision-making processes will occur. Initially consumers will have to place their energies in arenas where they can be heard. At the local and regional levels one can expect consumers to be found as representatives on the advisory boards of the different health care programs such as hospitals, health-maintenance organizations, community boards, and professional-review systems. Their interests will be consumer oriented, a logical expectation. On the other hand, the quality, efficacy, and cost-effectiveness of care are both consumer and provider shared interests.

4. A grievance and complaint mechanism to deal with individual problems and their redress will need to be formally structured within institutions, together with an external system that permits consumer assessment alongside that of providers. It is most likely that the external program may need to be supported by governmental enterprise, since solo professional-review mechanisms to date have not heard the consumers' review of care.

5. Health education at a range of levels will be addressed by consumers and providers alike. Such programs will include prevention at the primary level that is directed at avoiding disease or disability of the individual in order to enhance the health status of targeted populations and individuals. Preventive care will be extended far beyond the present enterprises at the secondary and tertiary care levels. It will include consumers in self-help groups as well as care by providers in a range of personal social health care programs at educational, orientation, and counseling levels.

6. Quality assurance and accountability programs within provider systems will need to include consumer involvement. To be soundly involved, professionals will need to share with consumers to make them as fully informed as possible of the provider investment and components of care. Standards essential for quality and efficiency, which safeguard privacy, confidentiality, rights, and conduct for both consumers and providers, will be addressed by consumers and providers.

7. A consumer council of advisory groups covering a region of social health services could serve in the interests of consumers. Even though the regional, state, and federal health-system-agency concept created by the federal government appears to be under fiscal constraints, consumers at the local levels seem to be rallying into new coalitions to safeguard some of the participation and recommendation rights they had won. A council or coalition of consumers, including local providers and industrial interests with their investment in health programs, is a likely development of the future.

The consumer in personal social and health care and the social and health care consumerism movement have a long haul before full partnership with providers in either sense can be arrived at. The professional will recognize the value of the client as a full partner in direct care. Making the helping process work rests on the availability of care and its accessibility. It also requires a knowledgeable joint investment by both professional and consumer.

APPENDIX: RIGHTS AND RESPONSIBILITIES OF PATIENTS[89]

The basic rights of human beings for independence of expression, decision, and action, and concern for personal dignity and human relationships are always of great importance. During sickness, however, their presence or absence become vital, deciding factors in survival and recovery. Thus it becomes a prime responsibility for hospitals to assure that these rights are preserved for their patients.

In providing care, hospitals have the right to expect behavior on the part of patients, their relatives and friends, which, considering the nature of their illness, is reasonable and responsible.

This statement does not presume to be all-inclusive. It is intended to convey the Joint Commission's concern about the relationship between hospitals and patients, and to emphasize the need for the observance of the rights and responsibilities of patients.

The following basic rights and responsibilities of patients are considered reasonably applicable to all hospitals.

Patient Rights

Access to care.   Individuals shall be accorded impartial access to treatment or accommodations that are available or medically indicated, regardless of race, creed, sex, national origin, religion, or sources of payment for care.

Respect and dignity.   The patient has the right to considerate, respectful care at all times and under all circumstances, with recognition of his personal dignity.

[89] Reprinted from *Accreditation for Hospitals* (Chicago: Joint Commission on Accreditation of Hospitals, 1981), pp. xiii–xvi.

Privacy and confidentiality.   The patient has the right, within the law, to personal and informational privacy, as manifested by the right to

1. refuse to talk with or see anyone not officially connected with the hospital, including visitors, or persons officially connected with the hospital but who are not directly involved in his care;
2. wear appropriate personal clothing and religious or other symbolic items, as long as they do not interfere with diagnostic procedures or treatment;
3. be interviewed and examined in surroundings designed to assure reasonable audiovisual privacy. This includes the right to have a person of one's own sex present during certain parts of a physical examination, treatment, or procedure performed by a health professional of the opposite sex; and the right not to remain disrobed any longer than is required for accomplishing the medical purpose for which the patient was asked to disrobe;
4. expect that any discussion or consultation involving his case will be conducted discretely, and that individuals not directly involved in his care will not be present without his permission;
5. have his medical record read only by individuals directly involved in his treatment or the monitoring of its quality, and by other individuals only on his written authorization or that of his legally authorized representative;
6. expect all communications and other records pertaining to his care, including the source of payment for treatment, to be treated as confidential;
7. request a transfer to another room if another patient or visitors in that room are unreasonably disturbing him by smoking or other actions;
8. be placed in protective privacy when considered necessary for personal safety;

Personal safety.   The patient has the right to expect reasonable safety insofar as the hospital practices and environment are concerned.

Identity.   The patient has the right to know the identity and professional status of individuals providing service to him, and to know which physician or other practitioner is primarily responsible for his care. This includes the patient's right to know of the existence of any professional relationship among individuals who are treating him, as well as the relationship to any other health care or educational institutions involved in his care. Participation by patients in clinical training programs or in the gathering of data for research purposes should be voluntary.

Information.   The patient has the right to obtain from the practitioner responsible for coordinating his care, complete and current information concerning his diagnosis (to the degree known), treatment, and any known prognosis. This information should be communicated in terms the patient can reasonably be expected to understand. When it is not medically advisable to give such information to the patient, the information should be made available to a legally authorized individual.

Communication.   The patient has the right of access to people outside the hospital by means of visitors, and by verbal and written communication.
When the patient does not speak or understand the predominant language of

the community, he should have access to an interpreter. This is particularly true where language barriers are a continuing problem.

Consent. The patient has the right to reasonably informed participation in decisions involving his health care. To the degree possible, this should be based on a clear, concise explanation of his condition and of all proposed technical procedures, including the possibilities of any risk of mortality or serious side effects, problems related to recuperation, and probability of success. The patient should not be subjected to any procedure without his voluntary, competent, and understanding consent, or that of his legally authorized representative. Where medically significant alternatives for care or treatment exist, the patient shall be so informed.

The patient has the right to know who is responsible for authorizing and performing the procedures or treatment.

The patient shall be informed if the hospital proposes to engage in or perform human experimentation or other research/educational projects affecting his care or treatment, and the patient has the right to refuse to participate in any such activity.

Consultation. The patient, at his own request and expense, has the right to consult with a specialist.

Refusal of treatment. The patient may refuse treatment to the extent permitted by law. When refusal of treatment by the patient or his legally authorized representative prevents the provision of appropriate care in accordance with ethical and professional standards, the relationship with the patient may be terminated upon reasonable notice.

Transfer and continuity of care. A patient may not be transferred to another facility unless he has received a complete explanation of the need for the transfer and the alternatives to such a transfer, and unless the transfer is acceptable to the other facility. The patient has the right to be informed by the responsible practitioner or his delegate of any continuing health care requirements following discharge from the hospital.

Hospital charges. Regardless of the source of payment for his care, the patient has the right to request and receive an itemized and detailed explanation of his total bill for services rendered in the hospital. The patient has the right to timely notice prior to termination of his eligibility for reimbursement by any third-party payer for the cost of his care.

Hospital rules and regulations. The patient should be informed of the hospital rules and regulations applicable to his conduct, as a patient. Patients are entitled to information about the hospital's mechanism for the initiation, review, and resolution of patient complaints.

Patient Responsibilities

Provision of information. A patient has the responsibility to provide, to the best of his knowledge, accurate and complete information about present complaints, past illnesses, hospitalizations, medications, and other matters relating to his health. He has the responsibility to report unexpected changes in his condition to the responsible practitioner. A patient is responsible for making it known whether he clearly comprehends a contemplated course of action and what is expected of him.

Compliance with instructions. A patient is responsible for following the treatment plan recommended by the practitioner primarily responsible for his care. This may include following the instructions of nurses and allied health personnel as they carry out the coordinated plan of care and implement the responsible practitioner's orders, and as they enforce the applicable hospital rules and regulations. The patient is responsible for keeping appointments and, when he is unable to do so for any reason, for notifying the responsible practitioner or the hospital.

Refusal of treatment. The patient is responsible for his actions if he refuses treatment or does not follow the practitioner's instructions.

Hospital charges. The patient is responsible for assuring that the financial obligations of his health care are fulfilled as promptly as possible.

Hospital rules and regulations. The patient is responsible for following hospital rules and regulations affecting patient care and conduct.

Respect and consideration. The patient is responsible for being considerate of the rights of other patients and hospital personnel, and for assisting in the control of noise, smoking, and the number of visitors. The patient is responsible for being respectful of the property of other persons and of the hospital.

REFERENCES

AHA policy affirms hospitals role in community health. *Promoting Health, American Hospital Association,* 1979.

BEN-SERA, ZEER. The function of the professional's affective behavior in client satisfaction. *Journal of Health and Social Behavior,* March 1976, *17.*

BERGER, SALLY. Local health planning must be revitalized. *Hospitals, JAHA,* July 1980, *54* (13).

BERKMAN, B., REHR, H., & ROSENBERG, G. A social work department creates and tests a screening mechanism to identify high social risk. *Social Work in Health Care,* Summer 1980, *5* (4).

BRESLOW, LESTER. Consumer-defined goals for the health care systems of the 1980's. In Morris Collen (Ed.) *Technology and health care systems of the*

1980's. Washington, D.C.: Health Services & Mental Health Administration, U.S. Department HEW, 1972.

BRONSON, DAVID L., RUBIN, A. S., & TUFO, H. M.   Patient education through record sharing. *Quality Review Bulletin*, December 1978, *4* (12).

CAUFFMAN, JOY G.   A study of health referral patterns: Parts I through IV. *American Journal of Public Health*, April 1974, *64* (4).

CAUFFMAN, JOY G.   *Search community blueprint, human problems and services (Medical and Social)*. Vol. 1. (4th ed.) Los Angeles: Caligraphics, 1980.

CLOWARD, RICHARD & ELMAN, R.   An ombudsman for whom? *Social Work*, April 1967. *2* (2).

Conditions governing hospitals,   *Federal Register*, June 20, 1980.

COOPER, TERRY L.   The hidden price tag: Participation costs and health planning. *American Journal of Public Health*, April 1979, *69* (4).

COUSINS, NORMAN.   *Anatomy of an illness*.   New York: W. W. Norton & Co., Inc., 1979.

COUSINS, NORMAN.   Anatomy of an illness (as perceived by the patient). *New England Journal of Medicine*, December 23, 1976, *295* (26).

Doing better, feeling worse.   *Daedalus*, entire issue, Winter 1977.

DANA, BESS.   Consumer health education. *Proceedings of the Academy of Political Science*, 1977, *32* (3).

DAVIS, MILTON S.   Variations in patients' compliance with doctors' advice. *American Journal of Public Health*, February 1965, *58* (2).

DAVIS, MILTON S.   Variations in patients' compliance with doctors' orders: Analysis of congruence between survey responses and results of empirical investigators. *Journal of Medical Education*, November 1966, *41* (11).

DAVIS, MILTON S.   Physiologic, psychological and demographic factors in patient compliance with doctors' orders. *Medical Care*, March-April 1968, *6* (2).

DiMATTEO, M. R., PRINCE, L. M. & TARANTA, A.   Patients' perception of physicians' behavior. *Journal of Community Health*, Summer 1979, *4* (4).

DONABEDIAN, AVEDIS.   Evaluating the quality of medical care. *Milbank Memorial Fund Quarterly*, 1966, *44* part 2.

DONABEDIAN, AVEDIS.   *Aspect of medical care administration*. Cambridge, Mass.: Harvard University Press, 1973.

DONABEDIAN, AVEDIS.   Models for organizing the delivery of personal health services and criteria for evaluating them. In I. Zola and J. B. McKinley, Eds. *Organizational issues in the delivery of health services*. New York: Prodist, 1974.

EVANS, DAVID & LANE, D. S.   Long-term outcome of smoking cessation workshops. *American Journal of Public Health*, July 1980, *70* (7).

EHRENREICH, BARBARA & EHRENREICH, J.   *The American health empire; Power, profits and politics*. New York: Vintage Books, Random House, 1971.

FROST, SHELLEY B.   Consumers' impact on the diffusion of medical technology. *Consumer Health Perspectives*. Consumer Commission on the Accreditation of Health Services, June 1980 *VII* (III).

GARTNER, ALAN & REISSMAN F   *Self-help in the human services*. San Francisco: Jossey Bass, 1977.

GORDIS, LEON, MARKOWITZ M. & LILIENFIELD, A.   The inaccuracy in using interviews to estimate patient reliability in taking medications at home. *Medical Care*, January-February 1969, *7* (2).

GROSSER, CHARLES.   *New directions in community organizing: From enabling to advocacy*. New York: Prager, 1973.

GROSSMAN, RUDOLPH M.   Voting behavior of HSA interest groups: A case study. *American Journal of Public Health*, December 1978, *68* (12).

HANNA, WILLIAM J.   Advocacy and the elderly. In Richard H. Davis (Ed.) *Aging: Prospects and issues*. (3rd ed.) Los Angeles: University of Southern California Press, 1981.

HOWARD, JAN & DERZON, R. A.   Prospects for humane care are hopeful. *Hospitals, JAHA*, November 16, 1979, *53* (22).

HULKA, B. S., ZYZANSKI, S. J., CASSELL, J. C., & THOMPSON, S. J.   Satisfaction with medical care in a low income population. *Journal of Chronic Disease*, 1974, *24*.

JONAS, STEVEN.   The role of consumers in health care delivery systems. Letter to Feedback. *Hospitals*, April 1, 1981.

KANE, ROSALIE A.   Thoughts on patient education. Editorial. *Health and Social Work*, February 1981, *6* (1).

KASTELER, J., KANE, R. L., OLSEN, D. M. & THETFORD, C.   Issues underlying prevalence of doctor-shopping behavior. *Journal of Health and Social Behavior*, December 1976, *17*.

KOGAN, L. S.   The short-term care in a family agency—Parts I, II and III. *Social Casework*, May, June, July 1957, *38*.

KNOWLES, JOHN H.   The responsibility of the individual. In John H. Knowles (Ed.) *Doing better, feeling worse: Health in the United States*. New York: W. W. Norton and Co., Inc., 1977.

KUPST, M. J., SCHULMAN, J. L., & DOWDING, J.   Evaluation: Attitudes toward patient care and work satisfaction. *Hospital and Health Services Administration*, Winter 1979.

KURELLA, S.   The social needs of patients and their satisfaction with medical care. *Social Science and Medicine*, 1979, *13A*.

LEAR, MARTHA WEINMAN.   *Heartsounds*. New York: Simon & Schuster, 1980.

LEVY, RONA.   Facilitating patient compliance with medical programs. In Neil Bracht (Ed.) *Social work in health care*. New York: Haworth Press, 1978.

LINNANE, PATRICK D.   Ombudsman for nursing homes: Structure and process. Washington, D.C.: U.S. Department of Health, Education and Welfare, Office of Human Development Administration on Aging, n.d.

McGUIRE, ANGELA & TRACY, L.   Mental health consumer complaints: Insights on unmet needs in hospitals and communities. April 1980, mimeographed.

MAILICK, MILDRED D. & REHR, H.   *In the patient's interest*. New York: Prodist, 1981.

MALUCCIO, ANTHONY N.   *Learning from clients*. New York: Free Press, 1979.

MITCHELL, J. H., HARDWICK, K., & BECK, B.   Telephone follow-up for E.R. audits. *Quality Review Bulletin, Journal of Quality Assurance*, special edition, 1979.

MARRAM, GWEN D.   Patients' evaluation of nursing performance. *Nursing Research*, March-April 1978.

MAYER, JOHN E. & TIMMS, N.   *The client speaks*. New York: Atherton Press, 1970.

MEYER, CAROL H.   Social work purpose: Status by choice or coercion? *Social Work*, January 1981, *26* (1).

MITRY, NANCY WINT & SMITH, H. L.   Consumer satisfaction: A model for health services administrators. *Health Care Management Review*, Summer 1979.

MONK, ABRAHAM.   Accountability criteria and policy strategies in direct service provision for the aged. *Journal of Gerontology and Social Work*, Winter 1978, *1* (2).

OVERTON, ALICE. Taking help from our clients. *Social Work*, April 1960, *5* (2).
PANZETTA, ANTHONY F. *Community mental health, myth and reality*. Phila-delphia: Lea & Febiger, 1971.
PAPP, WARREN R. Consumer-based boards of health centers: Structural problems in achieving control. *American Journal of Public Health*, June 1978, *68* (6).
PELLEGRINO, EDMUND D. Humanistic base for professional ethics in medicine. *New York State Journal of Medicine*, August 1977.
PERLMAN, ROBERT. *Consumers and social services*. New York: John Wiley, 1975.
PERRY, CHERYL, KILLEN, J., TELCH, M., SLINKARD, L. A., & DANAHER, B. G. Modifying behavior of teenagers: A school-board intervention. *American Journal of Public Health*, July 1980, *70* (7).
Public advocacy pioneers in N. J. and seems to work. *The New York Times*, Janu-ary 14, 1979.
REEDER, LEO G. The patient-client as a consumer: Some observations on the pa-tient-client relationship. *Journal of Health & Social Behavior*, December 1972, *13* (4).
REHR, HELEN. Quality assurance: Implications for social work. In Helen Rehr (Ed.) *Professional accountability for social work practice*. New York: Prodist, 1979.
REHR, HELEN. Access to services: A complex dimension. In Mildred D. Mailick and Helen Rehr (Eds.) *In the patient's interest*. New York: Prodist, 1981.
REHR, HELEN & MAILICK, MILDRED D. Dilemmas, conclusions and recom-mendations. In Mildred D. Mailick and Helen Rehr (Eds.) *In the patient's in-terest*. New York: Prodist, 1981.
REHR, HELEN & RAVICH, RUTH. An ombudsman in a hospital: The patient representative. In Mildred D. Mailick and Helen Rehr (Eds.) *In the patient's interest*. New York: Prodist, 1981.
REID, M. E. and McILWAINE, G. M. Consumer opinion of a hospital antenatal clinic. *Social Science and Medicine*, 1980, *14A*.
Rights and responsibilities of patients. *Accreditation manual for hospitals*. Chicago: Joint Commission on Accreditation of Hospitals, 1981.
RUSALEM, HERBERT. Ombudsman for patients at a mental health center. *Hos-pital and Community Psychiatry*, 1973, *24* (10).
SCHWEITZER, STUART O. Incentives and the consumption of preventive health care services. In Selma J. Mushkin (Ed.) *Consumer incentives for health care*. New York: Prodist, 1974.
SEGAL, ALEXANDER & BURNETT, M. Patient evaluation of physician role per-formance. *Social Science and Medicine*, 1980, *14A*.
SILVERMAN, P. R. The clients who drop out: A study of spoiled helping rela-tionships. Unpublished doctoral dissertation, Brandeis University, 1969.
SPARROW, MARGARET W. Consumerism: Its impact on America's health pro-fessionals. *Consumerism and Health Care*. National League of Nursing, 1978.
STORCH, MARCIA L. & WENDORF, B. Storch on storks. *Quality Review Bulle-tin*, September 1978, *4* (9).
THOMAS, LEWIS. On the science and technology of medicine. *Daedalus*, Winter 1977.
UNRUH, JESSIE. The ombudsman in the states. *Annals of the American Academy of Political Science*, January 1966.
WALSH, MARGARET E. Nursing's responsibility for patients' rights. *Consumer-ism and Health Care*. National League of Nursing, No. 52–1717, 1978.
WATKINS, JULIA D. A study of diabetic patients at home. *American Journal of Public Health*, March 1967, *57* (3).

WITHORN, ANN. Helping ourselves: The limits and potential of self-help. *Social Policy*, November-December 1980.
ZEIDLER, FRANK. An ombudsman for cities. *Annals of the American Academy of Political and Social Science*, May 1968.

CHAPTER THREE
LEGISLATION
AND HEALTH POLICIES

Rosalind S. Miller

INTRODUCTION

The year 1965 saw a dramatic change in the reimbursement patterns in health care delivery, which has since affected access and consumer choice in this country. With the passage of Medicaid (Title 19), federal funding made possible greater access to medical services to the poor. Medicare (Title 18) legislation, passed the same year, considerably increased the amount of medical care utilized by and partially paid for through a federally sponsored insurance program. However, since the mid-1960s, there have been many modifications in the way health care is paid for, or reimbursed, resulting in changes in how services are delivered by health providers—physicians, nurses, and others—and how hospitals and medical facilities are organized to meet health care needs. With the passage of Titles 18 and 19, as well as subsequent legislation and federally sponsored health policies and regulations, it is essential that social workers in the health field, along with other health practitioners, know not only what services their patients are entitled to receive but under what time limitations for each level of care.

Prior to the mid-1960s, a social worker's knowledge about the basic principles of casework practice and an understanding of the significance of multiple psychosocial factors that impact upon illness generally provided a working base on which social workers delivered services to patients. The settings where social workers were employed served to orient them to the implications for care. This orientation is no longer sufficient. Today the sanction for social work practice in both medical and psychiatric settings is circumscribed by health policies and legislation emanating from all levels of government, as well as by systems of care which vary according to whether they are private, voluntary, or governmental institutions and who and how they serve the ill and disabled. The federal government in its arrangements with the states and local communities assumes a major role, very different from its previous stance, in the sponsorship of health care, particularly to the aged, the poor, the mentally ill, the handicapped or developmentally impaired, and to women and children. Such matters as who is entitled to these services, for what length of time, and how health services are financed are determined by regulations and periodic federal, state, and local review mechanisms for which health providers and institutions are held accountable.

And so it is not enough that the health social worker brings good diagnostic or assessment skills to treatment or interventive planning with his or her patients. The worker must be sure that patients are either receiving all services to which they are entitled or are offered explanation as to why some services are denied or are time limited. Protecting service entitlements, particularly of the poor and the aged— the population health social workers primarily see—require the same professional vigilance and skill that are brought to assessment and treatment. In this multidimensional health care system, programs and personnel must assist in safeguarding what the patient requires.

In this chapter we shall highlight some of the historical background and circumstances that shaped the way health care has been organized and services delivered in the past. A brief historical overview should help us to understand how medical care developed, so that we may look at the current health care system and address ourselves to such questions as: How does present health policy and regulation affect social work practice? How do social services get organized? What social work service delivery patterns best meet the needs of patients? What are the fiscal implications for the social work profession in the health field? What are the ethical and value conflicts for social workers, given present legislation?

As we shall attempt to show in this chapter, the health social worker must be knowledgable about major provisions in health legislation that provide for medical services on the one hand and limit and restrict such care on the other. Familiarization with policy issues has importance for the social worker regardless of setting, whether in general hospitals, mental institutions, neighborhood health centers or psychiatric clinics, or even in the private practice of social work.

Social workers primarily see a constituency of at-risk population who, along with physical and or emotional symptoms which bring them to health facilities, may frequently present economic and social stress factors that compound their illnesses. Hence multiple problems further complicate the social worker's responsibility for the provision of a range of services. From an organizational point of view, health and social welfare services, at best, parallel rather than intersect each other, so that problem solution to client need frequently depends upon the way the social worker negotiates a fractionated system in an attempt to coordinate services in the interest of the client. Hence the woman who is being treated under Medicaid in an outpatient medical setting for hypertension and high cholesterol count may be unable to meet her dietary needs under her restricted AFDC budget established by the social welfare agency. Or the 70-year-old man, covered by Medicare for the treatment of a myocardial infarction and whose medical condition necessitates a change in living arrangements, may not be a candidate for public housing because his income falls slightly above eligible range.

Until the mid-1960s, social workers in health settings were relatively free from any concerns about cost to determine social work treatment modalities as well as the length of time in which they saw patients. Patients paid for their health care (now called out of pocket), had insurance that covered medical expenses, were seen in outpatient clinics free of charge, or paid on a sliding scale, based upon income.[1] Charity cases, known as "city cases" were also carried on large many-bedded wards in hospitals.[2] Charity cases or "without charge" arrangements no longer pertain. One way or another, everyone who seeks health care today pays: the physician, hospital, clinic, or nursing home are reimbursed, either by the patient, by a third party (insurance company), under Titles 18 or 19, or through other government entitlement programs. For some individuals, who, as a result of age (under 65), income level (above the poverty line), or citizen status (illegal alien), medical and psychiatric services may be beyond their reach. Who the social worker sees in the health setting, and under what time constraints, are actually all dictated by the factor of cost or what we have come to call reimbursement mechanisms. Today, the social worker, or any health provider, is not only accountable for the quality of service rendered to the patient, but the accountability extends to the length of time, given an episode of illness in which the service is performed. As we shall see, the organizational mechanism for accountability rests within a structure called a utilization review committee.

Health practitioners are performing services and offering medical and psychiatric care to more people than at any other time in our history, largely because of legislation that has increased the access to medical care. The federal government has assumed leadership for setting regulations for institutional health care providers, but standards for practice are established at state and local levels, while the professional practitioners are required to monitor the quality of care. In addition, we have in this country a mix of public, private, and voluntary structures that formerly catered to discrete populations according to their ability to pay, but who now compete among themselves for patients and the ever-escalating reimbursement dollar. In spite of regulations and standards setting, many problems remain. Chief among them is that we are a country without a national health policy that would help to shape a national health care system. As Mechanic points out, the physician is still in control of the marketplace so that "both planners and federal administrators have moved cau-

---

[1] In addition, specific populations had their health care met by some government sponsored programs, including, for example, Maternal and Child Health programs, health services under the Veterans' Administration, health care for American Indians living on reservations, American seamen, and so on.

[2] For many decades, the concept of 'free of charge" carried with it philanthropic endeavors by civic-minded, wealthy, and influential citizens, who provided not only financial backing of hospitals but served as members of Boards of Trustees and Ladies' Auxiliaries, dictating policies and services.

tiously in attempts to structure medical care, and when they have moved, they have worked primarily at the margins."[3] Over time, bits and pieces of health legislation have been passed by the Congress to meet the needs of various groups. As we shall detail later, many health programs emanated from a variety of bureaucratic structures within different parts of the federal government, each program setting its own criteria. But we need to ask why the United States, the wealthiest country in the world, instead of enunciating a national health policy, has promulgated legislation that results in inequities for the rich as well as the poor. Using Medicare and Medicaid, by example, Wildavsky states the following.

> The wealthier aged, who can afford to pay, receive not merely the same benefits as the aged poor, but even more, because they are better able to negotiate the system. Class tells. Inequalities are immediately created within the same category. Worse still is the "notch effect" under Medicaid, through which those just above the eligibles in income may be worse off than those below. Whatever the cutoff point, there must always be a "near poor" who are made more unequal. And so is everybody else who pays twice, first in taxes to support care for others and again in increased costs for themselves. Moreover, with increased utilization of medicine, the system becomes crowded; medical care is not only more costly but harder to get. So there we have the paradox of time—as things get better, they get worse.[4]

To suggest the notion that we have only to look at our past in order to understand the present is an oversimplification. Nevertheless, there are social, economic, political, and class-dictated forces that together have been threaded into an American woven fabric, distinct and unique from those forces that have formed national policies—in health, for example—in other countries around the world. A society that has valued individualism, separation of state and federal responsibilities, a pay-as-you-go philosophy, and has held to a Puritanical work code from which flow material rewards, moves slowly and cautiously to a health system sponsored by a national health policy and financed by a national insurance plan for all. Robert Blendon states that Americans believe that there is a national problem in the way health services are delivered in this country, just as they agree that our unemployed and our poor have problems in our educational system.

> The reasons for this are straightforward. The numbers of persons suffering from each of these problems is very large when viewed absolutely—usually millions of our citizens. However, the percent of our population so suffering is relatively small—usually less than 15 percent of the entire population. The majority of people do not suffer directly enough from these problems to provide the intense attention required in a society such as ours to bring about a swift change in policy or sharp break with our nation's established traditions. It is for these reasons that Charles Lindbloom of Yale in his essay, "The

[3] David Mechanic, *Future Issues in Health Care* (New York: Free Press, 1979), p. 5.

[4] Aaron Wildavsky, "Doing Better and Feeling Worse: The Political Pathology of Health Policy," *Doing Better and Feeling Worse: Health in the United States*, ed. John H. Knowles (New York: W. W. Norton & Co., Inc., 1977), p. 110.

Science of Muddling Through" held that "democracies change their policies almost entirely through incremental adjustments. Policy does not move in leaps and bounds."[5]

We need to look briefly at those forces, embedded in our tradition, in order to better understand the current issues and dilemmas, particularly acute in the present Reagan administration, as they affect the health care of the entire population.

AN HISTORICAL PERSPECTIVE

How long we shall continue to deliver health care in this country under a fragmented health policy—if, indeed, this nation has a health policy at all—depends upon how we resolve the question of whether health care is a right to which all people are entitled, or whether it is a privilege, some getting more and some less. Although the question is greatly complicated by economic issues—costs, reimbursement mechanisms for health providers and institutions, and vendorship (national auspices or private insurers)—as well as by ideological stance and political preference, in the long run, our society's vision about the physical and emotional well being of its population has been reflected in its moral stance and ethical values, deeply rooted in our historical development. To read about the growth and development of health care in America reinforces the fact that regardless of the technological gains and the increased access to health care for more and more people, our delivery system has been erected on a commitment to a two-class health care structure.

There has been one system of care for the privileged rich and the prospering middle class, and another for the needy and underprivileged poor. To trace this history far exceeds the scope or purpose of this chapter, but the reader is urged to become acquainted with the historical background of the development of health services in this country, for which only a brief overview can be given here in order to understand why down to the present decade the issue of privilege versus need remains paramount.

From the earliest period in the seventeenth century when the settlers formed their first communities in New England through Colonial times, citizens recognized that they had responsibility for those among them who were unable to work productively as a result of physical illness, lunacy, blindness, or other physical impairment. To this group were added the wanton, the drunken, and the paupers; all were considered public charges for whom help had to be given, particularly food and shelter. Since most of the colonists had come from England, the statutes upon which clarity for the needy was provided were based upon their knowledge of the Elizabethan Poor Law of 1601. Whether vagrant or ill, this needy group, with one exception, was not differentiated as to the reasons for their plight. They were the community's public charges for whom some provision had to be made. What the

---

[5] Robert Blendon, "The Prospects for State and Local Governments Playing a Broader Role in Health Care in the 1980's," *American Journal of Public Health*, 71, no. 1 (January 1981), supplement, p. 10.

provisions were and who was entitled to the largesse from the taxpayer's dollar were clearly enunciated. Based upon the moralistic code of the day, those who were deemed worthy or deserving poor received preferential treatment. Because there were very strict settlement requirements, only those who were part of the community were considered for help. Each individual or family was carefully evaluated in order to determine that an infirmity was not the result of sinful or wanton behavior.[6]

The well-to-do and the middle class, most of whom lived in tight family structures, cared for their own. As Demos and other social historians have pointed out, a perusal of family wills and court documents reveal that on the death of the head of the household, the oldest son assumed the care of the widowed mother. Arrangements were also made for the care of orphaned children by either other family members or family friends, and stipulations were included for basic schooling and apprenticeship in a trade. The emotionally and mentally ill were nurtured or "secreted" within the family; on occasion, a sick citizen would be treated and even cared for in the home of the local physician. The U.S. Congress passed legislation in 1798, based on a bill introduced by Alexander Hamilton, to establish hospitals for merchant seamen.[7] But direct government involvement occurred only for that part of the population for which there was federal responsibility.

From the eighteenth century down through the first decade of the twentieth, the sick and the poor were ministered to in public institutions. By whatever name—the almshouse, the county home, the hospital—these settings were filled with inmates, some of whom were sick, all of whom were needy. With little recognition of the multiple social, environmental, economic, or political forces that caused their impecunious or ill conditions, the poor and the ailing, as if inextricably tied to the other, were cared for together. As late as 1877, Massachusetts had a single agency called the State Board of Health, Lunacy and Charity. For the more fortunate in the society, family members were cared for by the women and wives who either depended heavily upon the household medical manual, the indispensable text that sat on the family bookshelf, or by the private physician. The doctor cared for his patient at the bedside or, in cases of surgery or bone setting, on the kitchen table. The physician went to his patient's home with no thought of hospital referral. Throughout much of the nineteenth century, hospitals were largely supported through philanthropic endeavor and served as institutions of social control, isolating those individuals deemed less desirable by the community. Vogel reports that lying-in hospitals cared primarily for women giving birth to illegitimate children, and careful screening procedures were followed for those who were thought to be deviant.[8] At the turn of the twentieth century when philanthropic endeavor at Brooklyn

[6] John Demos, *A Little Commonwealth* (New York: Oxford University Press, 1970), pp. 62–81.

[7] Milton Roemer, "The Foreign Experience in Health Service Policy," *Regulating Health Care*, ed. Arthur Levin (New York, The Academy of Political Science, 1980), p. 206.

[8] Morris Vogel, "The Transformation of the American Hospital, 1850–1920," *Health Care in America*, eds. Susan Reverby and David Rosner (Philadelphia: Temple University Press, 1979), p. 105–6.

Jewish Hospital could not keep up with increased costs of hospital care, administrators and trustees began to look for the paying patient. Technological and medical advance also dictated specialized care that could only be offered in a hospital setting. As the middle class and privileged began to use hospitals "instead of seeing the poorer patients as needy and consequently deserving of care, hospital administrators viewed neediness as a moral failing of the patient."[9]

By the midnineteenth century, physicians not only dispensed services to hospitalized patients in the name of charity, but also began to use the hospital as a place to teach their medical students first hand about patient care. In the famous Loomis trial of 1850, a physician, Dr. James Platt White, defended his decision to allow his medical students, whose primary learning about medical care came from textbooks and diagrams, to observe him while he cared for a woman about to give birth. The details of the trial as reported in Drachman's work make interesting reading, but the views about the virtue of women expressed by many of the physicians opposed to demonstration teaching are noteworthy.

> Yet the doctors also seemed to share the understanding that one could modify this principle of preserving female virtue. While they spoke about respecting the virtues of womanhood in general, it appears that they were most concerned about upholding the virtues of middle-class and upper-class women. They loosened their rigid standards when the woman in question was poor. White's patient, Mary Watson, for example, was a recent immigrant from Ireland, an unmarried woman living in the Erie County poorhouse . . . . One physician testified, for example, that he would "be fearful of introducing (demonstrative midwifery) into a private institution" and that in his "private practice he never expose[d] the female." Another stated that "there ought to be a difference made between medical instructions to a class and private practice," that he "considered them entirely different," and that he would not pretend to make ladies in private practice the means of instruction to classes.[10]

Beginning with the Civil War period, state and local governments began to assume responsibility for monitoring community health problems. With the coming of industrialism and the building of factories, which required unskilled labor, there was an ample employment market for immigrants from Ireland and Germany. As these groups tended to cluster and live in crowded urban centers, ill nourished and poorly paid, they were susceptible to infectious diseases. Problems of polluted water, spoiled food, and accumulated garbage necessitated the establishment of state boards of health. But as Victor and Ruth Sidel emphasize

> by the mid-nineteenth century it was recognized that epidemic diseases were promoted by adverse social conditions, particularly poverty and crowding,

---

[9] David Rosner, "Business at the Bedside: Health Care in Brooklyn, 1880–1915," *Health Care in America*, p. 125.

[10] Virginia G. Drachman, "The Loomis Trial: Social Mores and Obstetrics in the Mid-Nineteenth Century," *Health Care in America*, p. 73.

but that the wealthy were not immune to them. Thus a large part of the drive for public health measures arose not out of altruism or because people most afflicted were powerful enough to demand such measures, but because those who did have the power felt themselves endangered by the epidemics of communicable diseases.[11]

State responsibility for public health services then, did not grow out of any conviction for equal health care for all, but rather out of fear by the middle and upper middle classes who were affected by disease and, like the poor, could be victimized by it. The catalytic agent was a self-serving concern by a citizenry fearful of the dreadful epidemics of diseases such as tuberculosis that frequently resulted in chronic illness and death.

The growth of mental-health services for the emotionally ill parallels the history of services for the physically ill. The federal government played no immediate role in developing a national health policy for either the physically or emotionally ill, fearful that any activity would interfere with the rights of the states. As suggested earlier, the mentally ill were cared for in the home or, if impoverished, were sent to the alms houses. We do know that mentally ill patients were admitted to the Pennsylvania Hospital as early as 1756; and in 1773 a mental asylum was established under government auspices in Williamsburg, Virginia.[12] When in the 1850s, Dorothea Dix, the feminist social reformer, proposed that mental institutions be established under a system similar to the development of land grant colleges, whereby federally owned land was transferred to the states, enough support was found in the Congress to pass the necessary legislation. However, the bill was vetoed by President Pierce, who stated that the federal government could play no role in the care of the mentally ill, except for designated groups such as members of the armed forces and their dependents, Indians on reservations, and residents of Washington, D.C. Persistent and persuasive, Dix did get state legislatures to act to provide funds for the building of state mental institutions. Dorothea Dix was also responsible for subsequent congressional action that led to the establishment of St. Elizabeth's Hospital in Washington, D.C. Well into the twentieth century, the state hospital became the primary setting for the treatment and custodial care of the mentally ill. Many of these hospitals, built in isolated areas, separated patient from family, and served to reinforce the fact that while the states "cared" for their ill they also effectively "hid" them from the rest of the population.

At the same time the nineteenth century saw medical and psychiatric technological advance in the treatment of patients. In the early years of the state mental hospitals, while census figures were low, custodial care and treatment of the mentally ill was generally good. By the end of the nineteenth century and into the twentieth, state institutions became overcrowded; with too little money allocated by the

---

[11] Victor Sidel and Ruth Sidel, "Past and Present," *A Healthy State* (New York: Pantheon Books, 1978), p. 230.

[12] Lorrin Koran, "Mental Health Services," in *Health Care Delivery in the United States*, ed. Steven Jonas (New York: Springer, 1977), p. 211.

states, care deteriorated.[13] Private hospitals for both the physically and mentally ill were organized by physicians and psychiatrists in the vanguard of their profession, but these hospitals were primarily for private patients. In point of fact, until the Depression of the 1930s, the federal government assumed little leadership or responsibility for the health care of the nation. Beyond this brief historical review, it is unnecessary to belabor the point that the underpinning for health care in the United States rested on a two-class system. As we look at subsequent developments in health legislation at the federal level since 1935, it becomes clear that the struggles in the Congress, among the medical professionals, and within special interest groups, were related to a desire on the part of many to protect the status quo: easy access and ample health providers for those able to pay and means tests and limited services for the poor.

HEALTH LEGISLATION
(1935-1960)

Economic crisis, such as the Great Depression of the 1930s, can serve as an impetus for change. With the passage of the Social Security Act of 1935, social-welfare programs shifted from being solely the states' responsibility to a national concern.[14] The President's Committee on Economic Security recommended a health insurance program in their report, which served as a basis for The Social Security Act; but President Roosevelt, not wanting to jeopardize other parts of the legislation, which covered costs and benefits for the aged, unemployed, and children, did not recommend a health insurance program to the Congress. Throughout his terms of office, President Roosevelt in his annual State of the Union addresses referred to the "right for good medical care" but without specific recommendations to the Congress. One major health program, which did have a brief existence from 1921 to 1929—the Maternal and Infancy Act, administered by the Chilren's Bureau—was reestablished under the Social Security Act, and provided funds under a matching grant arrangement with the states for maternal and child health services and services for crippled children.

The issue of health and medical care began to gain prominence. Workman's compensation for job-related injuries was federally mandated; labor unions negotiated for health insurance protection; and increased hospital costs resulted in the development of Blue Cross and Blue Shield plans for those who could pay for them or for those employers who were able to support the costs. The "Blues" only covered hospital and surgical expenses, but not ambulatory care.[15] This meant that the

[13] Bernard Bloom, "Antecedents of the Community-Mental-Health Movement," *Community Mental Health* (Monterey, Calif.: Brooks/Cole, 1977), p. 13.

[14] For historical perspective, see Roy Lubone, *The Struggle for Social Security 1900–1935* (Cambridge, Mass: Harvard University Press, 1968); for a concise summary of health legislation, see Florence A. Wilson and Duncan Neuhauser, *Health Services in the United States* (Cambridge, Mass: Ballinger, 1976).

[15] Sidel and Sidel, *A Healthy State*, pp. 239–40.

poor and needy continued to receive care from public institutions. With the push for medical services from all classes in the society, the time seemed ripe for three Democratic congressmen—Senators Jay E. Murray (Montana), Robert F. Wagner (New York), and John D. Dingell (Illinois)—to introduce into Congress in 1943 the first bill that called for a national health insurance program to be financed through a payroll tax. Congress took no action and the bill died.

At the beginning of the Truman administration in 1945, the issue of national health insurance, vigorously recommended by the President to the Congress, was bitterly fought out between the executive and legislative bodies. Each year President Truman proposed that Congress act, but congressmen like Senator Robert Taft (Republican from Ohio) fought back on the grounds that national health insurance would lead the country to socialized medicine. The President was clear in enunciating the difference between his proposal, which left the consumer free to select his own physician and hospital for his care, and socialized medicine under which the government was the employer of the physician and hospitals were nationally controlled. For ideological and political reasons, this basic distinction between the two plans continued to be obscured by organizations like AMA and private insurance companies vehemently opposed to national health insurance. Congressman Taft felt that a counter-proposal was needed to offset a national plan, and so in 1946 he proposed that money be appropriated to the states to provide comprehensive medical care to the poor. The Taft bill, endorsed by AMA, did not come up for congressional action, but it represented a conservative approach, well grounded in a long tradition that found approval among those who supported medical care as a "welfare aid" to the poor.

Throughout the Eisenhower years (1953 to 1961) various health plans were proposed; each in turn was rejected. Although it was clear that the country was not ready for a national health insurance program, it was also clear in the post-World War II era through the 1960s that the retired elderly could not finance their medical care on income received from their social security check. The poor were also disadvantaged because there was a wide discrepancy from state to state as to the medical benefits for which each state was willing to pay. Although a plan to provide health services lagged, the postwar period saw a greater involvement on the part of the federal government in other areas of health need. The Department of Health, Education and Welfare was established in 1953, providing the administrative branch of the government with a structure to promote health programs.[16] As a result of curtailed spending during the Depression and then the war years, the country found itself with outmoded hospitals and too few beds. In 1946 Congress passed the Hill-Burton Act that allowed for federal spending for construction and renovation of hospital facilities.[17] Under the Veterans' Administration, VA hospitals were built to meet the medical and psychiatric needs of veterans.

In 1960 Senators Wilbur Mills (Democrat from Arkansas) and Robert S. Kerr (Democrat from Oklahoma) sponsored a bill, The Social Security Amendments of

[16] *Ibid*. p. 241.

[17] Eli Ginzberg, *The Limits of Health Reform* (New York: Basic Books, 1977), pp. 25–6.

1960, which increased the government's involvement in health care for the poor and the aged.[18] This piece of legislation expanded medical services for welfare clients who were Old Age Assistance (OAA) recipients. For those aged who were not eligible for OAA and could not afford to pay for their medical care, a program called Medical Assistance to the Aged (MAA) took care of the medical and hospital services of this group. Obviously this program did not answer the need for a national health plan. Furthermore, it was administered by the Bureau of Public Assistance; and the aged under MAA were unhappy because as recipients of medical service, they had to pass a means test. In summary, "Kerr-Mills was predicated on a welfare, means-oriented, not a social security insurance oriented theory."[19] Given this country's two-class orientation, it comes as no surprise that the Kerr-Mills Act won support in the Congress and was endorsed by the AMA. That the program fostered dependency, requiring the low income aged to deplete whatever resources they had before they were eligible for medical services, then leaving them with no recourse but public welfare assistance for the remainder of their lives, was a problem not forseen or if forseen not addressed, by legislators or health planners. Nor did they take into account that medical and health care were offered only after illness struck. There were no plans for preventive care. Nor had legislators thought about the affect on the aged of placing a health program within a public welfare structure, especially feelings of stigmatization by those who had maintained their independence until illness struck. For many of these aged, sickness and physical impairment were concomitants of advanced years, paid for out of savings, until there was no recourse but the welfare rolls. The Kerr-Mills Act was a response to a pressing national problem, and provisions under which it was administered delivered the age-old message that health care was a privilege, not a right. In hindsight, it is easy to look at health policies, in simplistic and negative terms; but from a balanced perspective it becomes important to reinforce our earlier point that national policies evolve and are modified and amended through a process over a period of time.

GOVERNMENT HEALTH INSURANCE

During his administration, John F. Kennedy called for a hospital insurance program, but the bill died in a House-Senate conference committee. In 1965, the era of the Great Society, President Johnson was successful in getting the Congress to pass two landmark pieces of health legislation: Medicare (Title 18), to meet the cost of medical services to the aged, and Medicaid (Title 19), to provide a health care program for the "medically indigent" or poor. In our discussion of the effect of these two significant programs upon the health industry and the recipients of care, it is not

[18] Karen Davis and Cathy Schoen, *Health and the War on Poverty: A Ten-Year Appraisal* (Washington, D.C.: The Brookings Institution, 1978), p. 51.

[19] Robert Stevens and Rosemary Stevens, *Welfare Medicine in America: A Case Study of Medicaid* (New York: Free Press, 1974), pp. 30–1.

our intention to review in detail the provisions of each act, or to summarize the ample literature available to the reader. As for all providers of health care, social workers need to be thoroughly familiar with the fiscal arrangements as well as the benefits provided for under each of these programs. Two basic points need emphasis. First, since what is paid for effects the range of services, it is important that social workers keep abreast of current regulations to insure that the patients with whom they are working receive all services to which they are entitled. Such responsibility entails more than a treatment role; in many instances it means interpreting to patients their entitlements, advocating for patients with physicians and administrators, and planning for adjunctive services through liaison activity with other social and health agencies in the community. Second, the provision for some social services with reimbursement has been written into the legislation.

Medicaid

In 1965 the Social Security Act of 1935 was amended, and Title 19, or Medicaid, became a landmark piece of legislation that addressed the health needs of the poor and the medically indigent. This program is not to be confused with Medicare (Title 18) legislation enacted at the same time; as we shall see, Medicare is administered differently, and it addresses the medical needs of the aged population, 65 and over.

Medicaid is the largest health program for the poor ever sponsored by the federal government. The program (fiscally organized in a joint arrangement with the states) is administered by the states under federal guidelines, with recipients required to pass a means test in order to establish their eligibility. Income level determines who is eligible for welfare assistance and also entitled to Medicaid. Since each state sets its own standards and eligibility requirements for welfare assistance, there is a broad variation from one part of the country to another concerning which families are entitled to health care under this program. For example, in 1976 the income level for a family of four entitled to public assistance and hence eligible for Medicaid in North Carolina was $1,400; in Wisconsin, $5,600,[20] while Arizona had no Title 19 program.[21] Since there are such divergent eligibility requirements, social workers need to know about entitlements in the states in which they are employed in order to interpret benefits to their clients and, when necessary, to advocate for them with the local welfare departments (see Chapters Two and Four for discussions on advocacy).

For states to be eligible for federal funding under Medicaid, services must include outpatient and in-patient care, laboratory tests and x-ray, and extended care, in a skilled nursing or health related institution. Recently, states have focused more on provision of services for the chronically ill as a way to cut costs including home care as an alternative to institutionalization. Some states also cover services

[20] Karen Davis and Cathy Schoen, "Medicaid: Successes and Problems," *Health and the War on Poverty*, p. 53.

[21] *Medicaid Statistics* (Washington, D.C.: U.S. Department of Health, Education and Welfare, No. (HCFA) 78–03150, June 1977), p. 5.

provided by dentists, optometrists, chiropractors, and other health professionals. Social workers can identify the Medicaid benefits available in their state to eligible recipients through their local social welfare agencies. All states must cover families who are recipients of Aid to Families of Dependent Children (AFDC). Of all persons served under Medicaid, AFDC is the largest group for whom vendor payments are made; in 1977 the figure was approximately 55 percent according to the 1977 Medicaid statistics. The aged, disabled, and blind are generally covered as recipients of supplemental security insurance (SSI), as are the medically indigent whose incomes are insufficient to cover their medical needs. This last group includes persons 65 years of age and older who are not on welfare assistance programs but who require assistance beyond the coverage provided by their Medicare benefits. The need for Medicaid supplementation becomes particularly acute for those aged who exceed the number of in-hospital days allotted under Medicare, or for those who cannot finance long-term extended care in a nursing home. According to the 1977 Medicaid statistics, this latter group represented payment under Title 19 nearly equal to those persons on maintenance assistance programs. For the medically indigent, then, costs are met by a combination of Medicare—Medicaid benefits.

There is rarely a day when the Medicaid program is not under attack, either by legislators appalled by increased costs of the program, or by the mass media in accounts of waste and abuse by health providers, institutions, and Medicaid recipients. The facts are that the initial estimate in 1966 for the cost to the federal government for Medicaid was $238 million dollars.[22] Within the first three years, federal and state expenditures increased to $3.45 billion for services to 11.5 million persons.[23] As of 1979, "Medicaid paid $21.7 billion in benefits . . . averaging $947 per person, on behalf of 22.9 million recipients."[24] Although it is true that there has been some abuse of the program by patients' overutilization of medical facilities, as well as a small group of health providers who have been reimbursed for unnecessary or unprovided services, these figures are small when compared with other overriding factors. We would include the growth in the nation's population over the past 15 years; the burgeoning of nursing homes and extended care facilities; salary increments for health professionals and supporting staff in a period of runaway inflation; and greater utilization of health facilities by the general population at all levels of health provision, including a psychiatric deinstitutionalized population now cared for at the community level. But federal reporting on health expenditures for the country at large reinforces the same factors that apply to the Medicaid program.

As had been the case since mid 1977, roughly two-thirds of the growth in personnel health care expenditures was attributable to inflation. . . . Just over a quarter of the growth of expenditures for the twelve months ending in Sep-

[22] This estimate proved to be correct, but only six states had programs that year. See Jo Ann Silverstein, "Medicaid, Problems and Prospects," *City Almanac*, Center for New York City Affairs of The New School of Social Research, 2, no. 5 (February 1977), p. 2.

[23] Davis and Schoen, *Health and the War on Poverty*, p. 56.

[24] *Health Care Financing Review* (Washington, D.C.: U.S. Department of Health and Human Services, No. 03054, Summer 1980), p. 7.

tember 1979 was due to increases in "intensity"—frequency of care, quality of care, and so on. Population growth accounted for the remainder of the growth in expenditures.[25]

For whatever reason, the high cost of health care is a major concern and source of dissatisfaction among poor and nonpoor alike. Discontent with medical care in this country is reinforced by the fact that between 24 and 30 million people have no financial means, either from earned income or federal-state subsidization, for their medical care. This is the group that "falls between the cracks." As Blendon observes, whether the problem is health care, poverty, unemployment or other social ills, the percentage of the population affected is only about 12 to 15 percent, but it represents some 24 million people.[26] According to Davis, the following individuals or groups are not eligible for health care under Medicaid:

1. widows and other single persons under 65 and childless couples;
2. most two-parent families (which constitute 70 percent of the rural poor and almost half the poor families in metropolitan areas);
3. families with a father working at a marginal, low-paying job;
4. families with an unemployed father in the 26 states that do not extend welfare payments to this group; and unemployed fathers receiving unemployment compensation in other states;
5. medically needy families in the 22 states that do not voluntarily provide this additional coverage;
6. single women pregnant with their first child in the 20 states that do not provide welfare aid or eligibility for the "unborn child";
7. children of poor families not receiving AFDC in the 33 states that do not take advantage of the optional Medicaid category called "all needy children under 21."[27]

For this group, medical care is either nonexistent or when offered by hospitals committed to take a small percentage of patients, these nonreimbursable services have cost them millions of dollars a year, bringing many hospitals to the brink of bankruptcy.

Medicare

Enacted at the same time as Medicaid, Medicare, or Title 18 amendment to the Social Security Act, is a medical insurance program for persons 65 years of age and older. All persons who receive monthly Social Security benefits or payments from the Railroad Retirement System are entitled to Medicare.

It is important to remember that there are two parts to this program: Part A

---

[25] *Health Care Financing Trends, Winter 1980* (Washington, D.C.: Compiled by Daniel R. Waldo, Division of National Cost Estimates, Health Care Financing Administration, Office of Research, Demonstrations, and Statistics, U.S. Department of Health, Education and Welfare, 1, no. 2), p. 1.

[26] Blendon, "The Prospects for State and Local Governments," p. 10.

[27] Davis and Schoen, *Health and the War on Poverty*, p. 53.

is a compulsory hospital insurance (HI) program financed by a payroll tax to which both employer and employee contribute. Short-term care (60 days) in a general, psychiatric, or tuberculosis hospital provides a broad range of services, including a semiprivate room, regular (not private) nursing services, drugs, laboratory tests, x-ray, appliances furnished by the hospital, and medical social services. Deductibles and coinsurance provisions are built into the plan. For example, when the program began in 1966, the deductible—the amount the beneficiary must pay each year before Medicare begins to pay for services—was $40 and over the years has increased appreciably, ($204 in 1981). After this initial payment, all hospital costs are picked up by Medicare through the sixtieth day. From the sixty-first through the nine-tieth the beneficiary pays one-quarter of the daily rate ($51 in 1981); and for the next 60 days one-half the daily rate ($102 in 1981). After 90 days insurance bene-fits cease. There is a lifetime reserve benefit of 60 additional days in a hospital, and a lifetime 190-day benefit in a psychiatric hospital.

For those patients who do not require all the services provided by a hospital but who need full-time nursing care in a protected setting, Medicare provides 20 days of free services in a skilled nursing facility. From the twenty-first through the one hundredth day, the copayment is one-eighth ($25.50 in 1981). A beneficiary must have been in a hospital for three consecutive days to be eligible for nursing home care. Although the law requires that a patient enter a nursing home, upon a physician's recommendation, within 14 days of discharge from hospital, the waiting period for an available bed may extend beyond the fourteenth day, since review committees (see under Review Organizations) stringently monitor cases for inap-propriate overutilization of hospital beds.

Home Health Agency (HHA) services are available under Part A.[28] A phy-sician must determine the need for home health services that may include skilled nursing care—usually visiting nurses (VNS), physical, occupational, speech therapy, home health aides, medical social services, all on a part-time or intermittent basis. Except for medical prescriptions (drugs), medical supplies and appliances are in-cluded. The other major specification for home health (in addition to the require-ment that the plan must be made by the patient's physician within fourteen days following discharge from a hospital or skilled nursing facility) is the patient must be confined to the home for the same condition for which services were rendered in the hospital or nursing facility.

Part B is a voluntary supplementary insurance program (SMI) that covers all the HHA services just described. The services are limited to 100 home health visits a year, whether or not the beneficiary was in either a hospital or skilled nursing facility. A 1972 amendment to Title 18 created incentives to maintain people in their homes as a way to decrease costs of institutional care.

Anyone 65 years or older may subscribe to Part B, whether or not the per-son has Part A. From an initial cost of $36 a year in 1967, periodic increases have

[28] *Medicare—Use of Home Health Services: 1976* (Baltimore, Md.: Health Care Financing Administration, Office of Research, Demonstrations, and Statistics, U.S. Department of Health, Education and Welfare, n.d.), p. 1.

brought the cost up to $123.60 (in July 1981). There is a deductible of $60 a year before SMI picks up the cost of services, in addition to which the beneficiary pays 20 percent on allowable charges for physician's services. In those cases where the physician's fee is above the allowable charge (reasonable costs), the patient must pay the difference plus the 20 percent.

Two 1972 amendments to Title 18 expanded coverage, beginning in July 1973, to two new groups: (1) disabled persons under 65 years of age who had received Social Security benefits for 24 consecutive months and who had been disabled for at least five months, and (2) persons insured or entitled to Social Security benefits, under 65 and to their spouses and dependent children who had end stage renal disease requiring either kidney transplant or renal dialysis.[29]

Some 28 million people are covered by Medicare. With the exception of 10 percent, they are all 65 years of age and older. For this group of citizens, Medicare has provided health care to many low income and near poor who without this legislation would not have had the financial means to meet their medical costs. Prior to 1965 many of our citizens went without care or, when acutely ill, were carried as charity patients, with costs picked up by private philanthropy, local government, or by physicians who rendered services without charge. With the advent of Title 18, the program relieved children and families from the financial burden of paying for their parents' health care. Illness is greater among the aged than any other group, and costs, particularly in an inflationary period, have increased at alarming rates. The current $200- to $400- (based on region and type of institution) a-day hospital bed could quickly result in a financial crisis for the average family if it had to assume responsibility for a parent's hospitalization. Although the majority of the aged live independently in the community, we are in an era where there is greater mobility, with individuals and families moving from one geographic area to another—for whatever reason. With the spiraling costs for housing, rather than have the aged depending upon extended family structures for support, we find more of the elderly in institutional settings—retirement homes, extended care facilities—than at any other time in our history. For skilled nursing home facilities alone—settings that offer nursing care and related services to posthospitalized patients—between 1975 and 1979 there has been an increase of 1,031 facilities, over 132,000 beds.[30] The aged who need extended care frequently use up their limited benefits under Medicare, plus whatever savings they may have before establishing eligibility for Medicaid.

Although Medicare has provided a security blanket for the over-65 population, particularly for those who remain physically and psychologically well, the program has not addressed some major problems for this population: Medicare does not

---

[29] Edye Peterson and Herbert A. Silberman, "Medicare: Persons Enrolled, 1978," *Health Care Financing Notes* (Baltimore, Md.: Health Care Financing Administration, Office of Research, Demonstrations, and Statistics, U.S. Department of Health and Human Services, n.d.), p. 2.

[30] "Medicare: Participating Health Facilities, 1979," *Health Care Financing Program Statistics* (Baltimore, Md.: Health Care Financing Administration, Office of Research, Demonstrations, and Statistics, U.S. Department of Health and Human Services, n.d.), p. 4.

meet total needs. In fact, given physician and hospital experiences, it is possible that out-of-pocket expenses can easily run 50 percent of costs. The program does not cover the costs for prescriptions, eye glasses, hearing aids, or total physician charges. Nor does the program address long-term care. There has been greater emphasis in recent years for keeping the aged in the community in their own homes as long as possible, yet services are provided only on a part-time basis. Where approval is given for round-the-clock nursing aide support, limited manpower frequently makes such planning impractical. Many of the aged who go to extended care facilities usually do so on a permanent basis. For those who need short stays but longer than Medicare reimbursement covers, the financial drain on personal savings can become so great that return to the community may not be possible. Finally, for those aged who have SMI, the premium, deductible, and physician fees above the 80 percent for allowed charges, may well represent out-of-pocket costs that many cannot pay from limited, fixed incomes. Although Medicare is not a program for the indigent, and while premiums may not be increased more than increases in retirement or survivor benefits from Social Security,[31] increased inflationary costs for food, clothing, and shelter may well limit the amount of money the aged feel they can spend on their health.

Cost Control and Quality Health Care

With the introduction of Medicare and Medicaid legislation, the nation's lawmakers were not only concerned with health care programs providing greater access for more people to medical care, but they also recognized the imperative to monitor services to insure quality care that was also economical. The 1965 Medicare legislation stipulated that hospitals and extended care facilities accepting Medicare patients had to have utilization review plans.[32] Hospitals quickly set up committees composed of physicians, and in some cases nonmedical personnel—nurses, admission officers, and social workers—to monitor patient admissions and length of stay to guard against inappropriate utilization of beds and hospital facilities. These early monitoring attempts did result in controlling costs and expediting patient discharge. The result was the introduction in 1972 of legislation that has had a profound affect on the consumer of health care as well as upon all health providers. It is the one piece of legislation that has dictated significant changes in the way social workers practice and deliver psychosocial care to patients.

Professional Standards Review
Organizations (PSRO)

As part of the Social Security Amendments of 1972, Professional Standards Review Organizations (PSRO) were established. This legislation required the Sec-

---

[31] Robert M. Gibson, "National Health Expenditures, 1979," *Health Care Financing Review, Summer 1980* (Baltimore, Md.: Health Care Financing Administration, Office of Research, Demonstrations, and Statistics, U.S. Department of Health and Human Services, n.d.), p. 7.

[32] Florence A. Wilson and Duncan Neuhauser, *Health Services in the United States*, p. 225.

retary of Health, Education and Welfare (now Health and Human Services) to designate some 200 geographical areas in which panels of physicians would monitor health services.

The *PSRO Program Manual* summarizes the function and responsibilities of the program.[33]

102   Information on the PSRO Program

The 1972 Amendments to the Social Security Act provide for the creation of Professional Standards Review Organizations (PSROs) designed to involve local practicing physicians in the ongoing review and evaluation of health care services covered under the Medicare, Medicaid and the Maternal and Child Health programs. The legislation is based on the concepts that health professionals are the most appropriate individuals to evaluate the quality of medical services and that effective peer review at the local level is the soundest method for assuring the appropriate use of health care resources and facilities. The PSRO is the means by which the legislation attempts to translate these concepts into practice.

106   Summary of PSRO Review Responsibilities

Professional Standards Review Organizations will review the health care provided under the Medicare, Medicaid and Maternal and Child Health programs and make judgments on the medical necessity and quality of the care. PSROs will determine whether care is proposed to be provided or has been provided at a level of care which is *most economical*, consistent with the patient's medical care needs.

PSROs are required over time, to perform review of the care provided in institutions (i.e. short-stay hospitals, tuberculosis hospitals, mental health hospitals, skilled nursing facilities and intermediate care facilities). A PSRO may review non-institutional care if it requests to do so and if the Secretary approves such a request.

Initial PSROs should, at a minimum, establish *a system for review of care (quality assurance, peer review, necessity and appropriateness of hospital stay, and effectiveness of discharge planning through medical care evaluation studies)* provided to inpatients in short-stay hospitals and develop a phased plan for the performance of review in long-term care facilities.[34]

197   Data Collection, Processing and Reporting

The data collection and processing system is structured in accordance with guidelines developed by the Secretary in consultation with the National PSR Council, with a view toward assuring maximum efficiency, economy, and coordination in all data-gathering efforts . . . The mechanics of the data processing system, e.g. coding of diagnostic and procedural data, integration of Medicare, Medicaid, and other data bases,

---

[33] *PSRO Program Manual* (Rockville, Md.: Public Health Services, Health Service Administration, Bureau of Quality Assurance, U.S. Department of Health, Education and Welfare, 1974).

[34] Italics added.

must be consistent with the policy and procedural guidelines issued by the Secretary.

In this brief summary of the legislation are multiple practice issues for all health providers, including social workers. For our purposes, we need to see the relevance of the legislation for social work.

First, both Medicare and Medicaid, as we have seen, reimburse services for both physical as well as psychiatric care, although provisions for the latter—both in-patient and outpatient—are much more limited. Nevertheless, reimbursement mechanisms, utilization patterns, and reporting procedures for recipients of all services are prescribed under Titles 18 and 19. A single funding stream for either physical and or psychiatric problems for the poor and the aged—two of the largest constituencies social workers help—means that reimbursement for health and mental health for these groups emanate from the same source. This is one reason why the social work profession generally perceives health to include not only physical and psychiatric problems, but also health provision at all levels of care: from prevention, to primary, secondary, tertiary care, to rehabilitative and extended care. Some models of health care (some primary health care settings, HMOs, prepaid family group practices, and so on) address the biopsychosocial—or comprehensive—problems of the patient; while other health structures—the psychiatric clinic, the community mental health clinic (CMHC), and the psychiatric hospital—focus exclusively on psychiatric care. But from a funding and accountability perspective, all health social workers, regardless of setting, must familiarize themselves with the federal legislation which establishes parameters not only for patient entitlements but also social work function.

Second, built in cost control factors consistent with the most economical way of caring for the patient mandates for the social worker treatment approaches congruent with short-stay hospitalizations. For the past decade, the open-ended case, one begun by the worker at some time during a patient's hospitalization and perhaps continued even after the patient s discharge, can no longer be considered cost effective. Planned short-term treatment, crisis intervention, and the brief contact or episode of service are the more cost effective interventive approaches. Casefinding at the point of patient admission, a procedure advocated by this author and others as early as the mid-1960s,[35] is essential, since it allows the worker the maximum amount of time to determine through quick assessment what services patients require. Although the casefinding procedure is no guarantee that discharge planning, particularly for those cases requiring referral to extended care facilities, will be easier, casefinding helps to eliminate many problems that accrue from late case referral by the physician, often when the patient is ready for discharge. With an average stay of nine days in short-stay hospitals and generally 30–60 days or fewer in psychiatric facilities, the social worker must be competent to perform fast psychosocial assessments, to determine accurate interventions that address and modify

[35] Rosalind S. Miller, "A Social Work Model for Servicing the Chronically Ill," in *Social Work Practice* (New York: Columbia University Press, 1966), pp. 145-57.

psychosocial problems. Then the social worker must develop discharge plans for another level of patient care either in health related or other facilities or in the patient's home, with the help of community support systems.

Third, recording for the medical or psychiatric chart needs to be current as well as concise, to meet the purpose of medical care evaluation studies required under PSRO, or medical audit as termed by the Joint Commission on Accreditation of Hospitals (JCAH). Hospital social service departments have experimented with a variety of recording models that attempt to meet PSRO requirements and provide the data for evaluation studies and quality assurance programs, such as described in Chapters Four and Six as well as in studies reported in the literature by Coulton, Rehr and Berkman, and others.[36]

Fourth, the social worker's recording for the chart or medical record provides the basis for medical audit through a peer review process that monitors the quality of the worker's professional practice. PSRO legislation mandates that the physician's delivery of medical care be evaluated by his peers. This is still an elective process for nonmedical providers. Many issues have been raised about peer review structures, including Freidson's observation related to "professional etiquette"— directly criticizing or calling into question a colleague's judgment, if not his or her competence.[37] Jonas and other physicians question if it is possible to engage in a quality control process "for which not all theoretical and technological problems have been solved."[38] From a social work perspective, Coulton questions "whether one can judge the quality of service by looking at what the worker did or whether it is necessary to look at what happened to the client as a result of the service."[39]

Fifth, by mandating a phased plan for patient discharge, the legislation has in effect delineated a major function for social workers who, historically, have been primarily responsible for discharge planning in hospitals. There is a growing awareness among hospital social workers that discharge planning is an integral part of the quality of care. In reality there is no more important function a hospital social worker can perform, no function that requires greater practice skill, fast assessment of patient need, knowledge of community resources, and formulation of a treatment plan, that will sustain and support the patient through posthospitalization.

[36] See, for example, Claudia J. Coulton, *Social Work Quality Assurance Programs: A Comparative Analysis* (Washington, D.C.: National Association of Social Workers, 1979); Barbara Berkman and Helen Rehr, "Social Work Undertakes Its Own Audit," *Social Work in Health Care*, 3 (Spring 1978), 275–86; Patricia Volland, "Social Work Information and Accountability Systems in a Hospital Setting," *Social Work in Health Care*, 1 (Spring 1976), 277–86; Roslyn Chernesky and Abraham Lurie, "Developing a Quality Assurance Program," *Health and Social Work*, 1 (February 1976), 117–30; and William Hall and Gerald St. Dennis, eds., *Quality Assurance in Social Service Programs for Mothers and Children* (Washington, D.C.: Bureau of Community Health Services, U.S. Department of Health, Education and Welfare, 1975).

[37] Eliot Freidson, "Speculations on the Social Psychology of Local PSRO Operations," *Conference of Professional Self-Regulation* (Washington, D.C.: Public Health Service, Health Resources Administration, U.S. Department of Health, Education and Welfare, June 1975), p. 36.

[38] Steven Jonas and others, "Measurement and Control of the Quality of Health Care," in *Health Care Delivery in the United States*, p. 399.

[39] Claudia Coulton, *Social Work Quality Assurance Programs*, p. 17.

Patients frequently come into the hospital with illnesses or disabilities involving social and psychological implications; and these the social worker addresses through casefinding, high-risk screening, and appropriate referral. In short, the social worker's most basic value to the hospital system rests in discharge planning activity. If social workers are not vigilant in their responsibility to move patients expeditiously out of hospitals, other health providers and hospital administrators are waiting in the wings or are, in fact, performing these tasks, and are all too eager to assume responsibility for discharge functions.

Sixth, quality assurance rests upon data collection, evaluation of services rendered, and outcome measures. Data about social epidemiological factors of the population served, the range of psychological stress and environmental strains, the development of a problem classification system, the computation of cost effective factors, and outcome measures related to patient satisfaction are but a few areas social work may pursue in order to meet the guidelines and standards set by the legislation. These are all activities that tend to promote high quality services in order to meet the needs of consumers—a topic discussed at length in Chapter Two.

In her study (1975) of the PSRO legislation, Gosfield observed that "balancing the needs for cost control with quality assurance of medical care has been one of the most difficult areas of health care policy."[40] And it remains so. An area of great concern for social workers in hospital settings is whether or not they can demonstrate cost effectiveness in their programs and services. Facilitating the flow of patients from hospital to community, concern about appropriate utilization of beds, and skillful case management that protects costs but strives for good patient care are the major social work functions most highly prized by hospital administrators. President Reagan's request of Congress to eliminate PSROs by 1983 as part of his budget cutting program suggests another area of concern to social work as well as advocates who maintain that the PSRO "program is the only one that looks after 'the poor, the sick and the elderly,' and that a 'competitive' (local control over the nation's health-care system) health care system 'won't give a damn for them.'"[41]

Whereas physicians were initially reluctant to endorse PSRO legislation, the peer review process now has wide support among doctors, many of whom are now protesting the Reagan administration's plan to eliminate the program. The estimate in savings was $3.7 million in 1980 for New York State alone because of the peer review process that helped to reduce hospital stay, unnecessary surgery, x-rays, and other hospital procedures.[42]

Even if Congress eliminates the program, monitoring patient care for quality assurance and cost control will in all probability continue under the jurisdictions of

[40] Alice Gosfield, *PSRO's: The Law and the Health Consumer* (Cambridge, Mass.: Ballinger, 1975), p. x.

[41] Ronald Sullivan, "Physician Review Program Seeks State Aid," *The New York Times*, March 29, 1981, p. 55.

[42] Bernard Weinraub, "Doctors Gain in Efforts to Retain Review Program," *The New York Times*, April 14, 1981, p. 17.

the states. Either for reasons of cost control or maintenance of quality care, professionals, providers, and the public will be vigilant and protect this piece of legislation from dismantlement.

MATERNAL AND CHILD HEALTH SERVICES

We alluded earlier in the chapter to the provisions of the Social Security Act of 1935 that addressed legislation providing old age benefits; federal assistance to the needy elderly, dependent children, and the blind; and fiscal incentives to establish unemployment compensation, as well as state and local public health programs. Although President Roosevelt, as we have seen, did not urge the Congress to include compulsory health insurance as part of the total legislative package, Title 5 of the Social Security Act

> Provided grants to the states for maternal and child health and child welfare services, and services to crippled children. Administration of the program was assigned to the Children's Bureau.[43]

Concern for the health and welfare of the nation's children predated by many years the Title 5 program. For the previous quarter of a century interested groups had attempted to develop a health policy that would assure medical, health, and welfare services to children. In 1909 a White House Conference on Children called for the creation of a federal children's bureau to monitor these activities.[44] But it was not until 1912 that the Children's Bureau was established, initially out of concern about child labor conditions and infant mortality rates. Early studies "named family income, housing, employment status of the mother, and early care of mothers and infants as crucial factors in determining whether babies and mothers lived or died."[45] In 1921 The Maternity and Infancy Act (Sheppard-Towner Act), provided grants-in-aid to the states for promotion of maternal and child health programs. But a short eight years later the act expired, because of the opposition of physicians and some religious groups.

The Great Depression of the 1930s again highlighted the health and welfare problems of needy children, and provided the impetus for the inclusion of Title 5 in the Social Security Act. Specifically, the act was to be administered by the Children's Bureau with emphasis on three major programs: (1) maternal and child health services, (2) child welfare services, and (3) health services to crippled children. Initial programming centered not on direct service delivery, but rather on preventive aspects of health care, training professional health manpower, and planning for

[43] Wilson and Neuhauser, *Health Services in the United States*, p. 250.

[44] Roger B. White, Donald A. Cornely, and Anita Gately, "Interdisciplinary Training for Child Welfare and Health," *Child Welfare*, LVII, no. 9 (1978), pp. 549–51.

[45] Davis and Schoen, *Health and the War on Poverty*, p. 122.

projects. The only direct medical services offered were to the wives and babies of men in the lower ranks of the armed forces in World War II.[46]

Title 5 was amended in 1963 because of President Kennedy's interest in mental retardation. Two amendments provided for maternal and infant care (M and I) followed by the development of Children and Youth (C and Y) projects for low income families, with comprehensive services offered in both public and private institutions as well as neighborhood health centers.[47] Virginia Insley, former Chief of the Social Work Section of the Division of Maternal and Child Health Care (initially placed in the Children's Bureau but with the reorganization of HEW in 1969, MCH was placed within the Bureau of Public Health Service) commenting about the need for the added legislation in the 1960s, observed that there was

> . . . overcrowding of public hospitals and outpatient departments to the extent that it was becoming increasingly difficult to provide medical care of acceptable quality, particularly for those women with complications of pregnancy. Adverse influences of social factors which deterred women from using these hospitals and clinics were well documented. Financial eligibility, residence requirements, necessity to travel long distances, delays of days or weeks before service could be given, long waiting periods in clinics, requirements for blood donations, and lack of common courtesy in the handling of patients were some of the reasons known to be deterrents to use of prenatal clinics. Many women who had not had prenatal care came to hospitals in labor, and with some exceptions, hospitals had to accept them regardless of eligibility factors. Women were often admitted and then in forty-eight hours or less after delivery discharged to make room for new admissions.[48]

MCH programs, including C and Y and M and I projects have attempted to rectify these problems. C and Y projects are designed to offer to high-need urban and rural areas comprehensive services, including screening, diagnostic treatment, nutritional, dental, eye and ear, and social services. M and I projects have been successful in attracting "many unmarried women who would otherwise have received little or no care.[49] Although theoretically included as an essential component of comprehensive care, to allow for outreach and network activity to schools and community, preventive programming is frequently curtailed. Direct patient contact rather than community outreach has funding priority because community activity defies cost benefit and accountability measurements. Emphasis primarily on direct services is a problem that results in weakening C and Y and M and I programs and draws justified sharp criticism from social workers. Probably for this very reason, Hartman takes an adversary position to that part of PSRO that requires quality assurance programs, when she comments

[46] *Ibid.*, p. 123.

[47] Wilson and Neuhauser, *Health Services and the United States*, p. 147.

[48] Virginia Insley, "Some Implications of Recent Legislation for Social Work," *Mothers-At-Risk: The Role of Social Work in Prevention of Morbidity in Infants of Socially Disadvantaged Mothers*, ed. Florence Haselkorn (New York: Adelphi University School of Social Work Publications, 1966), 1, no. 1, pp. 49–50.

[49] Davis and Schoen, *Health and the War on Poverty*, p. 139.

... in agencies where production is measured by in-person client contact, all other activities do not "count" and thus the most rewarding model of practice is typified by scheduled, in-office, face-to-face interviews with clients who keep appointments. Home visits, collaterals, the development of resources, efforts to intervene in the environment, all become activities which, rather than being rewarded, detract from the worker's productivity.[50]

Health data from numerous sources, including the 1980 Surgeon General's Report on Health Promotion and Disease Prevention, indicate that dramatic gains have been made over the past several decades in the health of the American people. Yet the problems enunciated by Insley in her discussions of the MCH programs of the 1960s remain to be faced in the 1980s. Social workers assigned to medical clinics and emergency rooms in hospitals as well as social workers and administrators responsible for Medicaid programs at the local social welfare agency level are conversant with a range of child and adolescent health problems that continue to place these groups at high risk. The 1980 Surgeon General's Report clearly highlights these concerns:

1. Teenage pregnancies frequently result in premature and low birth weight infants (545,000 babies were born in 1978 to unmarried American women and almost half of these were teenagers).
2. Unmarried mothers tend to receive their prenatal care late in pregnancy, while some wait until just before confinement to come to the hospital.
3. Unplanned births are greater among the poor population.
4. The teenage population accounts for approximately one-third of the more than a million American women each year who terminate their pregnancies by abortion.
5. Maternal mortality in 1978 was 9.6 per 100,000 live births, but the rate for blacks was almost four times that for whites.
6. In 1978 infant mortality rate was 13.8 per 1,000 live births, but for black babies the rate was 92 percent higher than for whites.
7. Nearly two-thirds of the infants who die are low birth weight.[51]

Late prenatal care, substance abuse, inadequate education about nutrition, family planning, health, contraception, and access to information and medical care remain problems that must be addressed by legislators as well as all citizens, for physically and mentally sound infants are this nation's most important asset and insurance for our country's growth and greatness.

In 1977 Senator Jacob Javits (Republican from New York) and Representative James Scheuer (Democrat from New York) proposed a National Health Insurance

[50] Ann Hartman, "Quality Assurance in Social Services," *Proceedings: Quality Assurance in Social Services in Health Programs for Mothers and Children*, eds. William T. Hall and Gerald C. St. Denis, March 31–April 4, 1975 (Pittsburgh, Pennsylvania: An institute sponsored by The Bureau of Community Health Services Administration, Department of Health, Education and Welfare and the University Graduate School of Public Health, Public Health Social Work Program) p. 13.

[51] *Promoting Health/Preventing Disease, Objectives for the Nation, Fall 1980* (Washington, D.C.: Public Health Service, U.S. Department of Health and Human Services), pp. 1–15.

for Mothers and Children Act (better known as the Kiddicare Bill). It called for entitlements for all mothers and children up to age 18, comprehensive health care, including preventive, primary, secondary, tertiary, rehabilitative, and extended care,
and also included x-rays, laboratory, drugs, and social services. Home, psychiatric,
and dental services were limited to the first four years. All health services were to
be covered for women during pregnancy and for three months postpartum. The bill
was to be financed by a payroll tax; a 10 percent copayment by the patient was also
proposed (except for the poor) and preventive services to children were recommended.[52]

As Eli Ginzberg points out, the bill was attractive because it added still another constituency, along with the aged and poor, to a guaranteed health care program, a more viable alternative to national health insurance (NHI). Nevertheless, the
bill died in Congress. With a shrinking health dollar and the current administration's
recommendation in 1981, that the states assume responsibility for health programs
financed through block grants of money from the federal government to the states,
there appears to be little chance over the next several years for the passage of legislation that offers mothers and children such broad health provisions as recommended
under Kiddicare. It seems ironic that in 1980, designated "The International Year of
the Child," no new legislation for child health care was forthcoming. Rather than a
national health policy for children, we have fragmented programs, diverse health
services for children that vary from state to state. Programs addressing maternal and
child health needs also emanate from a variety of different federal legislation.

The nation's lawmakers, aware and concerned about the current health care
needs of mothers and children commissioned a panel of child health experts to prepare a report to the Congress delineating the major concerns and offering recommendations for a national health policy to improve the health care of pregnant women and children, particularly those at high risk. The breadth of problems—economic, housing, environmental, nutritional—that impact on health, the health and
mental health service arrangements, and the recommendations for change are com-
prehensively described in a four-volume report to the Congress, entitled *Better
Health for Our Children: A National Strategy.*[53]

Direct services by social workers to mothers and children cut across many
fields of practice and include assessment and intervention at multiple levels for both
health and welfare care. Given the fact that it is not possible to separate health and
social welfare factors, that "health can no longer be viewed as the absence of disease
or disability, but must be perceived in the more positive terms of physical well-
being, mental and emotional adjustment, and social satisfaction and functioning,[54]
social workers must address preventive as well as ameliorating programs. In addition
to supportive (counseling) services and meeting a specific concrete need for the

[52] Ginzberg, *The Limits of Health Reform*, pp. 173-6.
[53] *Better Health for Our Children: A National Strategy* (Washington, D.C.: The Report
of the Select Panel for the Promotion of Child Health, 1980, U.S. Department of Health and
Human Services, No. 79-55071).
[54] White, Cornely, and Gately, "Interdisciplinary Training for Child Welfare and Health, '
p. 551.

client, interventive strategies must include educational programming, identification of high-risk clients through outreach and primary prevention models (services that prevent symptoms and or problems before they begin), and network activity for procurement of personal social services. These may include social welfare assistance, genetic counseling, infant and child care education, physical fitness activities, and prenatal education.

PSYCHIATRIC CARE (1940 to 1963)

Just as we "discovered" poverty in the 1960s, with the outbreak of World War II, the American people "discovered" mental illness. No other event provided an impetus for developing a national mental health policy and legislation than the statistics of American young men who were rejected by selective service boards from entering the armed services. About 1.8 million men were rejected for service, diagnosed as having either emotional or psychiatric problems. Given a limited psychiatric manpower and short assessment interviews, some draftees entered service who were not identified as having emotional problems; others under the stresses of war had to be separated from the service, either sent to psychiatric stations or returned to the states. Of all reasons for discharge from the armed forces, a large proportion of the men had neuropsychiatric problems.[55]

Until World War II the federal government did not actively support mental health services, except for a narcotic department and some psychiatric hospitals under the Public Health Service, and a few psychiatric hospitals administered by the Veterans' Administration.[56] For inpatient care there were two resources. First, there was the state mental hospital providing more custodial care than active treatment for a population that was primarily from the lower socioeconomic class, frequently homeless or abandoned in fact or in effect by their families. With few full-time psychiatrists on staff, patients were cared for primarily by untrained attendants, while the back wards housed patients, who sometimes had been hospitalized 20 and 30 years. Some of these state facilities had been built in the late nineteenth and early twentieth century, institutions frequently situated in isolated locations, the more invisible to the community the better. In the post-World War II era this author paid a first visit, as a social work student, to a state mental hospital. All wards were locked, access was gained by the insertion of a large key into a fortresslike door that provided entrance into a bare, square unfurnished room in which unkempt, ragged inmates either lay on the floor or crouched against the wall, arms crossed on their knees and heads bent against their chests. A series of small rooms lined one side of the corridor for patients requiring solitary confinement, each a small cubicle containing a mattress on the floor. Beyond was a large ward with iron cots lined up on either side of the room. The windows were covered with metal mesh; the walls

[55] David Mechanic, "The Development of Mental Health Policy in the United States," in *Mental Health and Social Policy* (Englewood Cliffs, N.J.: Prentice-Hall, 1969), pp. 55–64.

[56] Bloom, "Antecedents of the Community-Mental-Health Movement," p. 14.

were bare—not a poster nor a picture. In these deteriorated institutions, miserable, unhappy, forgotten people spent their undifferentiated days. Much needed improvements had been postponed, since the war years had precluded renovation of new construction of these antiquated facilities.

It would be misleading to suggest that every state hospital was poorly staffed or did not strive to offer good care; but the fact remains that the best psychiatric care was available either in private psychiatric hospitals or in what were termed *psychopathic hospitals*, some of which were started early in the century.

> The rationale for the psychopathic hospital was based on a set of what were then quite radical ideas. First, it was believed that patients should be identified and treated soon after the onset of their disorder. Second, it was believed that patients should not be isolated from their families, friends, and other sources of support. Third, it was believed that patients' families could provide very useful information to those persons responsible for the patients' treatment and that such information would be easier to obtain if the treatment facility were in the community. Finally, the psychopathic hospital was designed to stimulate in local physicians an increased interest in the problem of mental illness.[57]

For outpatient care, there were child guidance clinics, community clinics, and outpatient psychiatric clinics in general hospitals. Most psychiatrists were deeply committed to psychoanalysis as the treatment for their private patients and brought their theoretical understanding to treatment of clinic patients, modifying interventions with psychotherapy within a traditional medical model. The late 1930s and the decades of the 1940s and 1950s found social workers borrowing heavily from psychoanalytic psychology in their treatment of clients and patients. It was an era when the open-ended, usually long-term (a year or more) case was the primary interventive approach. The main focus was on interpsychic processes, with little emphasis on social and environmental stress factors.

Experiences that psychiatrists and social workers had in the armed services during World War II resulted in some dramatic changes in the treatment of the emotionally and mentally ill in the postwar years. At the front, psychiatrists saw servicemen soon after acute psychiatric symptoms were identified. For many men functioning under crisis conditions and situational stresses created by war and combat, early psychiatric intervention, with a treatment focus on reality events, sometimes including a short hospitalization or a few weeks in a rehabilitative setting, was sufficient support to enable these servicemen to return to the front. Two of the early social work articles, based on the army experience of social workers, Milton Wittman and Albert Lehman, report on brief treatment as a viable alternative to long-term intervention.[58] Interestingly enough, it would take many years before social

[57]*Ibid.*, p. 19.

[58]Milton Wittman, "Casework in a Military Setting," *The Family. Journal of Social Casework*, XXV, no. 4 (June 1944), pp. 123–7; and Albert Lehman, "Short Term Therapy in a Military Setting," *The Family: Journal of Social Casework*, XXV, no. 6 (October 1944), pp. 223–8.

work conceptualized brief service interventions as preferred modes of treatment.[59]

The Public Health Service in 1930 had as part of its responsibility a Division of Mental Health, but organized medicine opposed the development of increased health services under federal auspices, so that on a federal level little was accomplished during those years.[60] But new approaches to psychiatric care during World War II, reinforced by vocal psychiatrists who wished to pursue new ways of caring for the mentally ill after the war resulted in the passage of a National Mental Health Act in 1946 and provided for the organization of the National Institute of Mental Health (NIMH). This agency was responsible for reviewing applications for training grants for psychiatric personnel (psychiatrists, psychologists, and social workers) as well as supporting research grants in the field of mental health. Dr. Robert H. Felix, who had been with the Division of Mental Health of the U.S. Public Health Service since 1933, became the first NIMH director. As Foley reports

> Felix developed an awareness strategy which resulted in the nearly seven fold expansion of Federal financing of research on mental illness in the NIMH between 1953 and 1960. . . . [In addition] every major medical school's department of psychology, graduate schools of social work, and graduate schools of nursing received some training grant support from NIMH. The resulting collaborative efforts both in research and in the application of research knowledge resulted in the emergence of an improved technology in the mental health field.[61]

In retrospect the 1950s were important and exciting years for all practitioners in the mental health field. It was a period marked by changes in the care of the mentally ill. The mental hospital offered not only custodial care for those patients who needed an institutional setting, but introduced the idea of a day hospital and a night hospital, originally experimented with and developed in England. Some patients who no longer needed hospitalization but continuing therapeutic support to reinforce the gains they had made were discharged to live at home and attended hospital programs during the day. Others left the institution during the day for gradual reentry into the community, and returned to the hospital at night. Ward life, within the institutional setting, became less custodial and more "community-oriented" in what has come to be identified as the therapeutic milieu model. Half-way houses, established sometimes on the grounds of the hospital or in the community, provided residences for groups of patients to live together, preparatory to the return to their families and or neighborhoods. In addition, after-care agencies provided daytime

[59] William Reid and Ann W. Shyne, *Brief and Extended Casework* (New York: Columbia University Press, 1969); Howard J. Parad, ed., *Crisis Intervention: Selected Readings* (New York: Family Service Association of America, 1965); and Robert J. Barker and Thomas L. Briggs, *Differential Use of Social Work Manpower* (New York: National Association of Social Workers, 1968) are early texts on brief interventions.

[60] David Musto, "Whatever Happened to Community Mental Health?" *Psychiatric Annals*, 7, no. 10 (October 1977), p. 512.

[61] Henry A. Foley, "Community Mental Health Programming," *Regionalization and Health Policy*, ed. Eli Ginzberg (Washington, D.C.: Public Health Association, U.S. Department of Health, Education and Welfare, 1977), p. 38.

activities such as the example of Fountain House in New York City, with programs of daily living—food management, menu planning, cooking, and serving responsibilities—as well as social activities and agency controlled job opportunities in the community.

Most important of all, the decade saw the introduction of psychotherapeutic drugs, a pharmacological approach to patient care that dramatically changed psychotic patient behavior on the wards. These tranquilizing drugs had a far-reaching effect on inpatient management and care. In many institutions the locked ward was to become an anachronism with the introduction of an open-door policy. All of these changes represented the beginning—later to be called "deinstitutionalization"—of the return of the mentally or emotionally ill to the community and required an increase in the number of psychiatric clinics to treat patients on an ambulatory basis.

But the postwar decade also saw the number of patients in state hospitals increased to over 500,000. By 1955 Congress appointed a Joint Commission on Mental Health, and following four years of investigation, the Commission made a series of recommendations in their 1960 report, *Action for Mental Health*:

1. Acute disturbed mental patients should be cared for in community mental health clinics, one such clinic per 50,000 population;
2. There should be a psychiatric inpatient unit in every general hospital with 100 or more beds;
3. There should be intensive care facilities of no more than 1,000 beds;
4. There should be expanded after-care facilities;
5. A mental-health education program should be developed to increase the public's understanding about and acceptance of mental illness.[62]

Mental Retardation Facilities and Community Mental Health Centers Construction Act (1963)

Overcrowded mental hospitals, increased costs in care, new treatment techniques, and the dramatic changes brought about by the introduction of psychotropic drugs were all important factors that prepared the way for the most important and all-encompassing piece of mental health legislation passed by the Congress up to that time, The Mental Retardation Facilities and Community Mental Health Centers Construction Act of 1963. President Kennedy in his message to the Congress on February 5, 1963, stated that

> Mental illness and mental retardation are among our most critical health problems. They occur more frequently, affect more people, require more prolonged treatment, cause more suffering by the families of the afflicted, waste more of our human resources, and constitute more financial drain upon both

[62] Bloom, *Community Mental Health*, p. 25.

the Public Treasury and the personal finances of the individual families than any other single condition.[63]

This was "the first presidential message Congress had ever received on behalf of the mentally ill and mentally retarded.[64]

Eight months later, in October 1963, the legislation was enacted into law by the Congress, but not without a fight.

> There were fears that Federal financing, although presented as temporary state aid, might become permanent. Chief critic of Federal payments to center staffs was the American Medical Association (AMA). On the recommendation of the House and Senate committees, which introduced the Centers legislation, the staffing provision was dropped. The possible loss of the entire legislative package was not worth that one provision.[65]

Grants providing for start-up costs for personnel were not available until the Act was amended in 1965, during the Johnson administration.

In summary, the act sought to establish Community Mental Health Centers (CMHCs) in geographical locations known as *catchment* areas to cover the needs of no fewer than 75,000 and no more than 200,000 people. Hence, accessibility to care for all, regardless of diagnosis, was a primary criterion. There was no longer to be a sharp division between inpatient and outpatient care, thus assuring *continuity* of service, with all facilities and agencies, federal, state, local—public and voluntary—involved to *coordinate* services that were *comprehensive* and met the needs of each individual. The centers were to offer services, including *preventive* programming as well as primary, secondary, and tertiary care: the model emphasized mental health not mental illness.

Under the legislation centers were required to offer five essential services: inpatient, outpatient, emergency care, partial hospitalization, and consultation and educative programs to the community. Recommended but not required were specialized diagnostic services, rehabilitation, preadmission and postdischarge service for state hospital patients, research and evaluation programs, and training and education. Appropriations were authorized through grants-in-aid for the construction of centers and the remodelling of existing structures. The allocation of federal funds to the states was determined by the resources of each state, with the smaller, poorer states receiving a greater percentage of the federal appropriation. Although the federal government's role was primarily one of regulation and standard setting, each state was responsible for creating a state agency charged with reviewing all CMHC proposals before recommending them to the federal government. The federal goal was the establishment of 2,000 centers by 1980.

---

[63] "A Message from the President of the United States Relative to Mental Illness and Mental Retardation," reprinted in Bloom, *Community Mental Health*, p. 263.

[64] Koran, "Mental Health Services," p. 214.

[65] Foley, "Community Mental Health Programming," p. 40.

The act was subsequently amended in 1967 to extend grants for construction, and to authorize the expenditures of federal monies for construction of facilities and services for substance (alcohol and drug) abusers. Amendments in 1970 made possible additional grant support for mental health services to children and additional financial support for CMHCs; and in 1972 a new amendment required the centers to expand their programs to include treatment and rehabilitative services to drug abusers. In 1975, legislation expanded the required services to include specialized programs for children and the aged and provisions for the composition of advisory committees among local residents. The number of required services was expanded from the original five to twelve at the CMHC or through any number of arrangements between and among the mental health facilities serving the catchment area. The additional requirements included services to children, services to the elderly, screening services, follow-up care, transitional services, alcohol abuse services, and drug abuse services—all requirements to be met by the centers within two years. In 1977 the CMHC program was authorized for another year; and the 1978 amendments reauthorized the center program through 1980, with additional mandated services, to be phased-in over three years, to include day care and partial hospitalization, specialized services including transitional half-way houses, specialized services for children and the aged, and substance abuse programs. Also added was a provision for cross-catchment sharing of services including emergency, inpatient, and half-way houses.[66]

Impact of CMHC Legislation on Mental Health

The CMHC legislation and the subsequent amendments, as briefly summarized, indicate an intent by the federal government, in collaborative arrangements with the states, local psychiatric facilities as well as general hospitals and social service agencies, to offer comprehensive and coordinated care to the emotionally and mentally ill. The program was enhanced by provision for citizen participation on local advisory boards, since it was thought that they were best able to identify the social and mental health needs of their community. The stigma attached to mental illness—the notion of crazy people who should be "put away"—was addressed by reconceptualizing the problem, emphasizing mental health and preventive aspects of care and services. The program accomplishments and data are impressive when we address the question, What difference did this mental health policy make to the health care system and the people it served? The decline of patients in state mental hospitals has continued from an all-time high of approximately 600,000 in 1956 to approximately 160,000 in 1978.

Since the historic plea for those suffering from mental disabilities, the CMHC Program has reached 105 million persons with a Federal investment of $2.232

[66] "History of the Existing Community Mental Health Centers Program and the Need for New Legislation," *The Mental Health Systems Act* (Washington, D.C.: U.S. Government Printing Office, Report No. 96–712, May 15, 1980), pp. 13–20.

million. There is now an extensive network of CMHCs covering approximately half of the nation.

Since the beginning of the program in 1963, the National Institute of Mental Health has funded a total of 163 centers; 95 with construction grants only, 281 with staffing or operations grants, and 387 with both construction and staffing or operations grants.

To date (1978), 744 centers are fully operational, providing the required services and, in many cases, additional programs designed to meet the special needs of their communities.[67]

To summarize other data developed by NIMH (1977-78), an estimated 834,000 persons were in treatment in CMHCs at the beginning of 1977 to which an additional 1.05 million were added during the year; 81 percent were white, 19 percent all other races; 49 percent male, 51 percent female; children (under 15 years of age) comprised 15 percent of the additions, and 4 percent were 65 years and over. Utilization indices for the same period include 269,000 episodes of inpatient care; 140,000, partial care, and 1.7 million, outpatient care. With total receipts from all sources per center averaging about $1.7 million, 61 percent was from government funds, 36 percent from earned revenues from delivery of direct services, and 3 percent from other sources. Less than one-third of all receipts came from third-party reimbursements.[68]

But however impressive these figures may be, a vast literature, available since the mid-1960s enumerating the myriad problems with our present mental health arrangements, has attacked the CMHC legislation and, in turn, has forced the Congress to recommend new legislation (the Mental Health Systems Act of 1980) for revising funding and programs, beginning in 1982. With the change of administrations, it appears unlikely that the Mental Health Systems Act will receive Executive support as the Reagan administration pushes for fiscal arrangements with the states through block grant proposals for social welfare and health programs.

Social, ideological, fiscal, and organizational problems impeded the intent as well as the extent and kind of care originally envisioned under the CMHC legislation. Since the need for CMHCs was greatest in those underserved communities with the largest number of at-risk citizens, many community leaders who were influential and actively involved in the planning phase of the centers felt that in order to promote mental health it was important to address the social problems, possible concomitants of emotional stress, deviant behavior, and psychological disorders among the citizenry. Some psychiatrists and professional personnel, initially enthusiastic about the CMHC movement, attempted to work with the community but quickly became embroiled in definitions of mental health services. Some communities questioned the effectiveness of psychiatric treatment, and preferred to address issues of education, housing, and employment. The struggles between professionals and community members weakened the development and operational programs of some CMHCs. In two communities "local mental health workers, acting in the name

[67] *The Mental Health Systems Act*, p. 20.
[68] *Ibid.*, pp. 9-25.

of the community, seized the Lincoln Hospital Mental Health Center in New York and the Temple University Mental Health Center in Philadelphia."[69] Other CMHCs gave lip service to the inclusion of citizens on their community advisory committees, and consumers frequently dropped out because their opinions were neither valued nor requested.[70] In retrospect while the CMHC developed programs and services during the 1960s—that era of the Great Society when anything seemed possible—it is now clear that the CMHCs were not going to be nor could they be "agents" of social change. Furthermore, neighborhood councils or advisory boards, in order to function in behalf of the community, had to delineate the roles and functions of the professional and lay members if they were to carry out their mandates in good faith and respect for what each could contribute.

Depending upon geographical location and the availability of health resources, the structuring of mental health services varies considerably.

> Though commonly thought of as a "building," a community mental health center is best described as a *system* for the delivery of mental health services, involving the coordination of mental health services with other human services in the catchment area. Some 93 percent of all CMHCs actually represent a formal affiliation of two or more existing community agencies which together provide a coordinated program. In some instances, as many as 18 different agencies have organized to form a "community mental health center."[71]

The advantages of "linkage" or coordination among health and or mental health and social welfare agencies represent a highly desirable model, reinforcing the notion of multiple access, appropriate referral, continuity of care—a comprehensive approach, given a vast array of resources. The model also addresses agency function, sets realistic parameters for service delivery, circumscribed by program development that reflects provider competence. Yet implementation of this model has been extremely difficult, as a review of the literature illustrates.[72] Major problems include too few community resources resulting in limited housing for patients discharged from institutional care; reluctance on the part of communities to endorse and support group living arrangements for the mentally ill and mentally retarded; referral of patients from one community agency to another without follow-up procedures to insure that a needed service is provided; lack of resources for vocational counsel-

[69] Foley, "Community Mental Health Programming," p. 43.

[70] Franklin Chu and Sharland Trotter, "The Fires of Irrelevancy," *Mental Health in America: The Years of Crisis*, ed. Richard C. Allen (Chicago: Maquis Academic Media, 1979), p. 338.

[71] Foley, "Community Mental Health Programming," p. 42.

[72] See, for example, F. Arnhoff, "Social Consequences of Policy Toward Mental Illness," *Science*, 188 (June 1975), pp. 1277–81; E. L. Bassuk and S. Gerson, "Deinstitutionalization and Mental Health Services," *Scientific American*, 238 (Feb. 1978), pp. 46–53; The President's Commission on Mental Health, *Report to the President from the President's Commission on Mental Health*, 4 vols. (Washington, D.C.: U.S. Government Printing Office, 1978); and W. A. O'Connor, "Ecosystems Theory and Clinical Mental Health," *Psychiatric Annals*, 7, no. 7 (1977), pp. 363–71.

ing, employment, or social programs; cuts in federal appropriations which result in limiting services and curtailing manpower; below standard placements in boarding facilities, single room occupancy (SRO) buildings, and foster group homes; and inappropriate placement of discharged patients from mental institutions to nursing homes.

Similarly, there are problems for patients utilizing psychiatric outpatient and CMHC clinics. Many psychiatric services are rendered in general hospitals (Foley reports "85 percent of all Federally-funded CMHCs are affiliated with general hospitals");[73] and for those hospitals that are, in turn, medical-school affiliated, it is not uncommon to find intake procedures and case disposition criteria based upon the "interesting" case that enhances the intern's or resident s learning experience rather than selection based upon patient need. Although models that insure early services to patients—"the 24 hour walk-in clinic, the crisis clinic, the hot-line—are well known,"[74] there is still much evidence that the "preferred" patient has easier access to care.

The legislation provides that the CMHC must be under the administrative responsibility of the physician (psychiatrist). Since the inception of the program, psychiatrists have generally been directors of service, with fewer offering direct services to patients. Most direct services to patients, the majority of whom have low incomes,[75] are provided by nonmedical personnel, particularly psychologists and social workers.[76] Reporting on the role and function of the social worker in CMHCs, Magner saw in this new mental health movement an exciting model in which social workers who had been primarily focused on offering services reflecting a narrow clinical approach, now have an opportunity to broaden their interventions to include not only services to the individual but also to families and groups, as well as consultative services to agencies, schools, and community boards.[77] Although there is no question that such programming has been done, social work activity has too frequently been limited to the office interview, rather than preventive, consultative interventions in the community, because the reimbursement dollar which keeps CMHCs alive is still primarily geared to psychiatric nosology, the diagnostic classification currently established in the Diagnostic and Statistical Manual of Mental Disorders (DSM III). Since treatment in CMHCs is offered in large measure by nonmedical personnel generally under the supervision of a psychiatrist, we continue to find that social workers adhere to the so-called medical model, with less emphasis

[73] Foley, "Community Mental Health Programming," p. 43.

[74] See, for example, Allan Beigel and Alan I. Levenson, eds., *The Community Mental Health Center* (New York: Basic Books, 1972); and Donald G. Langsley and David S. Kaplan, *The Treatment of Families in Crisis* (New York: Grune & Stratton, 1968).

[75] Foley, "Community Mental Health Programming," p. 42.

[76] P. J. Fink and S. P. Weinstein, "Whatever Happened to Psychiatry? The Deprofessionalization of Community Mental Health Centers," *American Journal of Psychiatry*, 136, no. 4A (April 1979), pp. 406–9.

[77] George W. Magner, "Trends: Social Work Practice in Mental Health" (Washington, D.C.) *Abstracts for Social Workers*, National Association of Social Workers, 6, no. 3 (Fall 1970), pp. 3–14.

on important, if not seminal, sociocultural factors that impact on the problems of patients and their ability to cope in their environment. Much research is currently needed if we are to understand the reasons for the high no-show and discontinuance from treatment rates, which run as high as 45 percent in many psychiatric clinics. A study of intake procedures, waiting lists, and case disposition criteria would undoubtedly reveal an incongruence between the service delivery patterns and the populations being served. Lengthy intake procedures which delay the delivery of services to patients, particularly in an era of "dehospitalization" when clinics are seeing increasing numbers of severely mentally disturbed patients, impede comprehensive care, or continuity of care, with easy access to all.

Another problem area is related to psychiatric care that focuses primarily on seeing patients for purposes of prescribing and monitoring psychotropic drugs. As reported by Miller, Wiedeman, and Linn, while psychiatrists perform administrative clinic functions and assume responsibility for diagnosis, more and more nonmedical personnel monitor the functioning of psychotropic drugs.[78] This includes evaluating side effects, determining patient referral to psychiatrist for periodic evaluation, writing prescriptions for physician signature, and even counting and placing drugs in containers. These activities raise a host of ethical and professional questions which the medical as well as psychological and social work professions must address, particularly since there is evidence that, in general, insufficient training about psychopharmaceuticals is offered either by way of in-service training or as part of graduate school curricula. For many of these patients, few services are offered beyond drug-maintenance—a far cry from the initial legislative mandate. Borus makes the following comment about the limited range of services that a CMHC can offer.

> ... A CMHC that offers just support, just medication, just crisis intervention, or even just psychoanalysis to all of its patients is inherently providing second-class treatment. All treatment alternatives do not have to be available in one setting; a coordinated network of services ... can be established in which different therapeutic services are provided in different locations. CMH professionals should alert citizens' groups and politicians to the possible conflicts between quality and quantity care, i.e. the provision of a large quantity of inappropriate therapies is not helpful to patients and a smaller volume of service may be necessary to foster a higher quality and broader spectrum of treatment alternatives that promote appropriate problem-treatment fit.[79]

Drawing upon the work of several investigators interested in the psychiatric care that patients receive in nonspecialty mental health settings (general practitioners, outpatient hospital departments, industrial clinical settings) Regier, Goldberg, and Taube estimate that in 1975, 60 percent of all persons seen in these health sectors, or 19,218,000 persons, had mental disorders. Although treatment by general practitioners for identified mental illness varies considerably, some studies "found psy-

---

[78] Rosalind S. Miller, Louis Linn and George Wiedeman, "Prescribing Psychotropic Drugs: Whose Responsibility?" *Social Work in Health Care*, 6, no. 1 (Fall 1980) pp. 51–61.

[79] Jonathan Borus, "Issues Critical to the Survival of Community Mental Health," *American Journal of Psychiatry*, 135, no. 9 (September 1978), p. 1030.

chotropic drugs prescribed for 60% to 80% and 'supportive therapy' provided in up to 96% of those identified with mental disorders."[80]

Many persons referred to CMHCs are in need of additional and/or other social services; yet in 1977, "only 24 percent of the persons discontinued from services in the CMHC program . . . were referred to other service providers or community care-takers. Of those that were not referred, 36 percent dropped out of the program and 25 percent were reported to be no longer in need of further treatment."[81]

Foley summed it up well when he observed several years ago

> The CMHC program came about as a result of a strong centralized initiative that was not characteristic of our American political process. The initial pol-icy-making was not incremental, distributive, and pluralistic. These basic political processes are now being played out at the local and state levels, while the authority and moral suasion of the NIMH and the rest of the central-ized mental health establishment is falling apart. Under the influence of shift-ing political winds, the redistribution of resources is generally pluralistic. That trend raises new questions about regionalization and community mental health programming.[82]

A reorganization of our mental health services, one that will more realistically delineate the parameters of services that can be offered by a CMHC to a highly di-verse population, is needed. Concurrently we must develop at the states' level new structures to meet the needs of the seriously mentally handicapped, the aged, racial and ethnic minorities, women, and others in a more coordinated program that ad-dresses health and mental health and social needs of the population as was the in-tent of The Mental Health Systems Act slated to begin in 1982. Since the bill was introduced in 1980, we have had a change in administration, committed, as noted, to the distribution of federal funds through the block grant. Although there is little hope for this new legislation to be enacted, the states must address the problems of human services for the mentally and emotionally ill.

THE ISSUES AHEAD

As events on the national level suggest, the 1980s—certainly during the Reagan ad-ministration—will find the United States and other countries around the world tackling the problems of an inflationary economy, unemployment, increased costs of services and goods, and unstable trade conditions. In this country fiscal con-straint and a curtailed participation in health and social programs at the federal level indicate that we will not see an elaborate expansion of health and human ser-vices. Nor will the predictions of the 1970s for the passage of National Health Insurance Act be realized.

[80] Daniel A. Regier, Irving D. Goldberg, and Carl A. Taube, "The De Facto US Mental Health Services System," *Archives of General Psychiatry*, 35 (June 1978), p. 692.

[81] *The Mental Health Systems Act*, p. 24.

[82] Foley, "Community Mental Health Programming," p. 46.

Nevertheless, the states and local regions are immediately faced with addressing the problems of a health care system that is presently too costly and too inefficient. Among the many issues that could be enumerated, four appear to be of immediate import: the reorganization and restructuring of services, cost containment, consumer expectations, and deployment of manpower.

Reorganization and Restructuring of Services

At all levels of government, the unwieldy bureaucratic structures responsible for regulating health and social services have made it difficult to implement, oversee, and conceptualize health and welfare policies in the interest of the consumer. This is particularly true in the instance of the Medicaid program which, in spite of its size, mission, and cost, continues to be part of the welfare structure rather than part of a total health care system. The regulatory functions for which the states will carry ultimate responsibility through the regionalization of health services need to emanate from one health structure.

Ambulatory services require restructuring, and the groundwork has been laid in recent years through the development of a variety of primary health care models—Health Maintenance Organizations (HMOs), prepaid group practices, family care clinics, satellite health centers linked to general hospitals, and so on. Services are designed to meet the comprehensive health needs of the consumer. These models enhance multidisciplinary arrangements and require greater collaborative activity among health providers to identify through early diagnosis and assessment both the physical as well as the psychosocial complaints and problems of patients. So organized, primary health care becomes the first entry for the consumer into the system. This model does not eliminate the need for specialized physical or mental health services. Yet at the first entry of care it serves two purposes: (1) to treat acute physical and or emotional and mental illness problems at the earliest point possible, and (2) to provide, when necessary, for referral and follow through to a specialized setting or another level of care.

Coordination between health and social agencies, particularly when consumer problems are related to environmental and social stress factors would relieve the pressure on CMHCs and other health agencies to restrict their functions to areas of service that are specifically health related. In addition to controlling costs, limiting the functions of health agencies also requires the revitalization of family agencies. Over the past decade the latter have been competing for the mental health dollar, while curtailing extremely important functions they once performed—working with the "worried well," the frail elderly, marital problems, parent-child difficulties, transitional life stresses, homemaker functions, developmental-age specific crises, community social stress factors, and the like. Such reorganization of services between the health sector and human services requires that block grant monies be authorized to cover both types of services. A classification of services provided by each of these human service sectors would also go a long way toward the elimination of "turfdom" issues, "client-grabbing," and consumer-shopping problems that result in the duplication of services and fiscal waste. An incentive system is urgently needed to reward agencies for provision of early access to patients and clients, preventive programming, and interventions that impede or retard more extended and costly care.

Such reorganization requires the regions and communities to negotiate with their states, which under block grants will determine fiscal allocation to the local communities. Providers will be competing for funds from state legislators. Urban centers as well as poor rural sections, both with the largest number of at-risk, low income groups, will be at a disadvantage, as opposed to relatively stable, middle income suburban groups requiring less fiscal help or having the capability of financing health and human services with less deprivation to their population. In this regard, block grants to the states are highly precarious for what monies get doled out to whom through a political process rather than because of a human need may well retard any move toward the development of human services so organized as to meet basic requirements of the citizenry. Therefore, the reorganization and restructuring of health and human services are a first-level priority, for no social agency or clinic no matter how comprehensive its service can meet all the needs of a diverse population.

In our present system, emergency rooms have become centers for the homeless, the addicted, and the mentally ill. Psychiatric clinics and CMHCs feel they carry a mandate to treat the mentally ill as well as to offer preventive and consultative services that reflect a mental health model; state mental institutions discharge patients to communities that are unable and frequently unwilling to provide for them. Depending upon a public health policy at any one point in time, the federally appropriated dollar—whether for cancer research, drug addiction, family planning, or mental health programs—has determined what the marketplace offers, with too little regard for the parameters within which clinics, hospitals, and social service agencies can realistically offer help. Hence family service agencies that once offered homemaker and home care services now compete with psychiatric clinics for the Medicaid dollar, and psychiatric clinics have still to assess the differences between meeting the needs of that part of the population that is chronically mentally ill or acutely psychotic and of another population for whom preventive and educational services enhance the goals of a mental health model. Public health policies, whether rooted in ideological stance, fiscal necessity, or social movements, have had enough impact to effect health delivery priorities and programs, but there has been little evaluative research to substantiate the reason for the shifts. In the field of mental health, Arnhoff concludes that there is little evidence that keeping mentally ill patients in the home, "at least during the initial, acute illness phase" is therapeutically more effective than hospitalization and that the social cost to families can be harmful as well as a financial burden.[83] For both health and mental health settings, HHS at the federal level has supported primary prevention, programming involving tasks well known to social workers who have long been involved in community organization and environmental work. As Matus and Nuehring show in their study,

[83] Arnhoff, "Social Consequences of Policy Toward Mental Illness," p. 1280.

while social workers do more primary prevention than their other health colleagues, "they do not, however, conceptualize these activities as preventive, and moreover, do not particularly embrace a preventive ideology."[84] The need to restructure services is easier said than done, but service delivery in the 1980s at the state and local levels will require attention to issues of coordinated efforts as well as clarity about roles and functions of the health providers in the delivery of health care.

Cost Containment

PSRO structures and quality control measures have enhanced efforts to impede the spiraling costs of health care. But monitoring programs to help eliminate waste, inappropriate utilization, and duplication of services—even imposing financial penalties on hospitals where abuses have been identified—has somewhat curtailed but not retarded health costs. As inflation spirals costs, the present organization of services militates against cost containment. The issues related to cost containment are multiple and difficult; no one cost-control measure is a panacea for solving health care expenditures. The answer does not lie in addressing just capitation, a fixed payment to the physician, regardless of the number of patients he sees; or in cost sharing, which requires the patient to pay for part of his care through coinsurance or deductibles; or only in utilization rates, or in organizational arrangements. All of us need to look at a broad variety of cost-control approaches in order to provide incentives attractive to health providers and at the same time to insure the maintenance of quality services. Our experience from the 1960s, particularly with Medicare and Medicaid, shows that the infusion of federal dollars into health care resulted in tremendous gains for the population, including dramatic changes in morbidity and mortality rates, developing medical technology, and increasing health manpower. Now the job is to find ways to augment these gains while containing costs.

The strategic placement of maternal and child health centers, family group care clinics, and primary health care practices close to stable population groups enhances patient access to care and provides for better monitoring of services. A highly mobile and transient population, particularly in urban centers, makes continuity of care extremely difficult, sometimes resulting in consumer utilization of multiple health facilities with duplication of diagnostic and treatment procedures inevitable. These situations escalate costs. Some communities have developed innovative approaches to monitor patient appointments, by using facilities for multiple purposes and by monitoring patients through quick retrieval and exchange of medical data through computer tracking. In one South Carolina community computerized records were "used originally as an administrative tool to track broken appointments and monitor service loads of various providers and clinics; it has provided quick ex-

---

[84] Richard Matus and Elane M. Nuehring, "Social Workers in Primary Prevention," *Community Mental Health Journal*, 15, no. 1 (1979) p. 39. See also Andrea M. Vayda and Felice D. Perlmutter, "Primary Prevention in Community Mental Health Centers," *Community Mental Health Journal*, 13, no. 4 (1977) and Milton Wittman, "Application of Knowledge About Prevention in Social Work Education and Practice," *Social Work in Health Care*, 3, no. 1 (Fall 1977).

change of information when a client has appeared at a satellite clinic different from the one he/she usually attended."[85]

The placement of health facilities near or in housing projects, elementary and secondary schools, welfare centers, retirement homes, and social centers permits large groups of people to familiarize themselves with the availability of local human resources and to receive primary care and preventive health care programming without the expense and burden of travel. The current trend of shifting ambulatory care out of hospitals into the community, with each satellite clinic, preferably under hospital auspices, has cost effective potentials. The community clinics are the channeling agents for patients requiring secondary and tertiary care as inpatients; further, the hospital is the setting for high technology procedures, thereby guarding against expense from duplication of equipment in other community health settings. Cross networking among health and human services provides for easier referral to the appropriate agency. Such models are currently in operation, but research is very much needed to determine their replicability.

> In Memphis-Shelby County a maternal and child health clinic shares a building with a day care center, a branch library, a program providing hot lunches for senior citizens, a social center, and a recreation program which includes bus tours to recreational and educational facilities. Most of these services are sponsored by the Community Action Program which works in close collaboration with the health department. Similarly, in Denver, one of the full service satellite health centers is located across the street from a center of the Community Action Program which provides day care and many other support services.[86]

Other models bringing services and consumers together need to be tried, each design dependent upon geographical location, resources, and population characteristics of the locale. These programs reflect community efforts at the public sector level, primarily addressing the health and psychosocial needs of the lower socioeconomic groups. In this respect they foster a two-level system of health care, but there is little indication for the 1980s that we shall have a National Health Insurance (NHI) plan in place for all Americans. As noted earlier, we are farther away from NHI than we were during the past decade when a variety of health insurance bills were introduced in the Congress. Hence it is realistic—if not ideal—to look for health care arrangements that protect the needs of the poor.

Other measures for containing costs include the utilization of excess beds in hospitals for establishing extended care facilities, instead of constructing new nursing homes. Extended care within hospitals requires nurses, social workers, and paraprofessional personnel, with physicians available only as needed. Utilizing hospital space in this fashion is less expensive than new construction and would also provide

---

[85] Arden C. Miller, Merry-K Moose, Jonathan B. Kotch, Marie L. Brown, and Maureen P. Brainard, "Role of Local Health Departments in the Delivery of Ambulatory Care," *American Journal of Public Health*, 71, no. 1 (January 1981), supplement, p. 24.

[86] *Ibid.*

for easier access to medical care when necessary. With an increase over the next few decades in the number of the aged, not only will extended care facilities be needed but also programs and services to provide more home care for the elderly. As Ginzberg and others point out

> The number of older and disabled persons who need long-term care will inevitably grow. Currently, individuals and their families carry the major responsibility of paying for this care. An approach aimed at broadening entitlements to long-term care for these groups would prove expensive. On the other hand, unless the present system is modified and strengthened, increasing numbers will not receive the care they need.[87]

Consumer Expectations

As noted earlier in this chapter, the vast majority of consumers of health care in this country report that they are satisfied with the health care they receive.[88]

> Most people (about 90 percent) have a regular source of medical care, and for most people that source is a privately practicing physician or group (80–90 percent). Poor people and especially poor Blacks have reduced likelihood of having a regular source of care (about 80 percent) and reduced likelihood that the source is a private practicing physician or group (55–60 percent).[89]

Since Chapter Two was devoted to the consumer's role in health care, only the economic factors will be discussed here. In terms of health policy, one major issue for the 1980s is how the cost factor will affect consumer use of health services and, which consumers are most likely to be cut off as health services are curtailed. There is little doubt, for example, that we shall see changes in coinsurance and deductibles in Medicare. With increased out-of-pocket expenditures for physician fees and hospital costs, the elderly must dig deeper into their pockets to meet costs. One concern is that more of the aged will postpone treatment until their problems become chronic or more serious. In the long run, postponement of care increases costs. For the larger Medicaid population now utilizing outpatient facilities and Medicaid mills, there is little chance that they will have a single physician who knows their medical problems. This factor, combined with long waiting periods for appointments and impersonal approaches by Medicaid physicians militates against continuity and comprehensive care, and provides for a major source of client discontent. The Reagan administration's proposal to consolidate health services, while eliminating some of the present health programs (mental health, maternal and child health services, substance abuse programs, primary health care centers, and so on), through block grants to the states will deny medical care to over a million people who now are entitled to a broad array of health services. Under the "New Federal-

---

[87] Ginzberg, p. 173.

[88] *Special Report*, The Robert Wood Johnson Foundation, no. 1 (1978), p. 10.

[89] Miller and others, "Role of Local Health Departments in the Delivery of Ambulatory Care," p. 26.

ism" proposal, beginning in 1984, the federal government would assume fiscal responsibility for Medicaid. If new eligibility requirements are set that eliminate some recipients now covered by Medicaid, consumer satisfaction issues, until now defined as related to the quality of services rendered primarily by physicians, will be expanded to include issues of deprivation and denial of any health care. The states and, in turn, the local sector must address, then, not only the quality of care but the issue of deprivation of health care, particularly for the poor and the aged. Social interest groups, social agencies and communities need to be vigilant while legislators must apply stringent capacitation rates for health services delivered by community health clinics and outpatient hospital services.

Development of Manpower

Another major issue to be faced in the 1980s has to do with the distribution of manpower. During the past decade Congress passed two pieces of legislation to promote distribution of health providers to geographical areas in greatest need. The Comprehensive Health Manpower Training Act of 1971 provided for capitation grants to institutions for students enrolled in professional schools and the cancellation of loans, up to 85 percent, for those professionals willing to practice in localities of greatest need.[90] The Health Professions Education Assistance Act of 1976 was intended to increase the number of residency positions in primary health care as contrasted with specialty training. In addition, stipends and tuition expenses were paid for those students willing to serve a minimum of two years in a shortage area. For each year of service, a year of tuition was cancelled. Although the armed services have been able to attract young physicians under this arrangement, the development of health personnel to areas in greatest need has not been generally successful.[91]

At this time there is no way of knowing to what extent the federal government will continue to provide incentives to achieve distribution of manpower to shortage areas. Local sectors will need to accrue the most accurate data possible to determine the number and kinds of manpower they need. Providing incentives to physicians to encourage more of them to move into family medicine and primary care practice rather than specializations has already been tried with limited success. However, group practices that provide physicians with shorter work hours, profit sharing, and sabbaticals for study and research have attracted some physicians. Incentives to nurses, who have taken to the picket lines to reenforce their discontent with working conditions and low status, need to be created to include functions that mirror their competence and training. Some half a million trained nurses are not in the profession; they are urgently needed, particularly in municipal hospitals. Health institutions and administrators must not only urge their return but examine the reasons why such a large professional work force has abdicated what was initially their professional calling.

[90] Wilson and Neuhauser, *Health Services in the United States*, pp. 179–80.
[91] Ginsberg, *Limits of Health Reform*, p. 160.

Social workers have long been attracted to the health field: out of an estimated total of 205,000 social workers practicing in all types of settings in the United States in 1976, some 43,000 were employed in health and related programs. Whereas in 1950, when the total number in health was only 6,200, social workers were evenly divided between medical and psychiatric settings. By the mid-1960s there began a dramatic change that has continued with approximately three times as many social workers (31,200) going into psychiatric settings as into other medical settings (11,800).[92] As noted earlier, the figure now stands at about 45,000 social workers in health and mental health, and this may be a conservative estimate. As schools of social work continue to reorganize and change their curricula and as more health settings develop a comprehensive approach to health care, the profession of social work urgently needs to reconceptualize the historic division between the medical and psychiatric specialities. To more accurately characterize the functions of the worker, the role needs to be defined as a health (or health care) social worker who handles the psychosocial aspects of both physical and emotional illness, no matter what the practice setting.

In addition to the core function of delivering direct services to patients, the 1980s should see social workers placing increased emphasis on evaluative studies and research activities that provide data vital to the functioning of health organizations and health providers from other disciplines. Such activities not only expand the functions of social work but establish the profession as an essential component in the health field. Studies that illuminate priorities for programming, based upon social epidemiological data, quality control and cost accounting studies that address patient utilization patterns, research that helps refine the patient discharge process, and new approaches that enhance coordination of health services are all illustrative of high priority areas if social work is to remain an essential health discipline in an era of fiscal constraints.

Over the last two decades, federal legislation along with state and local regulations have circumscribed, in all the ways this chapter has attempted to show, how health practitioners, including social workers, must practice. For the 1980s the balance will shift from federal to state, but no matter what health policies are enunciated, health social workers will find that their service delivery goals for patient care are enunciated in large measure by legislative mandates emanating from federal, state, and or local government.

REFERENCES

ARNHOFF, F.   Social consequences of policy toward mental illness. *Science*, June 1975.
BARKER, ROBERT J. & BRIGGS, THOMAS L.   *Differential use of social work*

[92] *Health Resources Statistics: Health Manpower and Health Facilities*, 1966–77 Edition, U.S. Department of Health, Education, and Welfare, Public Health Service, Office of Health Research, Statistics, and Technology, National Center for Health Statistics, Hyattsville, Maryland, 1979, p. 249.

manpower. New York: National Association of Social Workers, 1968.

BASSUK, E. L. & GERSON, S. Deinstitutionalization and Mental Health Services. *Scientific American*, February 1978, *238* (2).

BEIGEL, ALLAN & LEVENSON, ALAN I. (Eds.) *The community mental health center*. New York: Basic Books, 1972.

BERKMAN, BARBARA & REHR, HELEN. Social work undertakes its own audit. *Social Work in Health Care*, Spring 1978, 3.

BETTER HEALTH FOR OUR CHILDREN: A NATIONAL STRATEGY. The report of the select panel for the promotion of child health: 1980. Washington, D.C.: U.S. Department of Health and Human Services, No. 79-55071.

BLENDON, ROBERT J. The prospects for state and local governments playing a broader role in health care in the 1980's. *American Journal of Public Health*, January 1981, *71*(1), supplement.

BLOOM, BERNARD. Antecedents of the community-mental-health movement. *Community Mental Health*. Monterey, Calif.: Brooks/Cole, 1977.

BLOOM, BERNARD. A message from the President of the United States relative to mental illness and mental retardation. *Community Mental Health*. Monterey, Calif.: Brooks/Cole, 1977.

BORUS, JONATHAN. Issues critical to the survival of community mental health. *American Journal of Psychiatry*, September 1978, *135*(9).

CHERNESKY, ROSLYN & LURIE, ABRAHAM. Developing a quality assurance program. *Health and Social Work*, February 1976, *1*.

CHU, FRANKLIN & TROTTER, SHARLAND. The fires of irrelevancy. In Richard C. Allen (Ed.) *Mental health in America: The years of crisis*. Chicago: Maquis Academic Media, 1979.

COULTON, CLAUDIA J. *Social work quality assurance programs: A comparative analysis*. Washington, D.C.: National Association of Social Workers, 1979.

DAVIS, KAREN & SCHOEN, CATHY. *Health and the war on poverty: A ten-year appraisal*. Washington, D.C.: The Brookings Institution, 1978.

DEMOS, JOHN. *A little commonwealth*. New York: Oxford University Press, 1970.

DRACHMAN, VIRGINIA G. The Loomis trial: Social mores and obstetrics in the mid-nineteenth century. In Susan Reverby and David Rosner (Eds.) *Health care in America*. Philadelphia: Temple University Press, 1979.

FINK, P. J. & WEINSTEIN, S. P. Whatever happened to psychiatry? The deprofessionalization of community mental health centers. *American Journal of Psychiatry*, April 1979, *136*(4A).

FOLEY, HENRY A. Community mental health programming. Eli Ginzberg (Ed.) *Regionalization and health policy*. Washington, D.C.: Public Health Association, U.S. Department of Health, Education and Welfare, 1977.

FREIDSON, ELIOT. Speculations on the social psychology of local PSRO operations. Conference of professional self-regulation. Washington, D.C.: Public Health Service, Health Resources Administration, U.S. Department of Health, Education and Welfare, June 1975.

GIBSON, ROBERT M. National health expenditures, 1979, *Health Care Financing Review, Summer 1980*. Washington, D.C.: Health Care Financing Administration, Office of Research, Demonstrations and Statistics, U.S. Department of Health, Education and Welfare, n.d.

GINZBERG, ELI. *The limits of health reform, The search for realism*. New York: Basic Books, 1977.

GOSFIELD, ALICE. *PSRO's: The law and the health consumer*. Cambridge, Mass.: Ballinger, 1975.

HALL, WILLIAM & ST. DENNIS, GERALD (Eds.). *Quality assurance in social service programs for mothers and children*. Washington, D.C.: Bureau of Community Health Services, U.S. Department of Health, Education and Welfare, 1975.

HARTMAN, ANN. Quality assurance in social services. In William T. Hall and Gerald St. Dennis (Eds.) *Proceedings: Quality assurance in social services in health programs for mothers and children.* Pittsburgh: Penn., March 31–April 4, 1975. An institute sponsored by the Bureau of Community Health Services Administration, Department of Health, Education and Welfare and The University Graduate School of Public Health, Public Health Social Work Program.

HEALTH CARE FINANCING REVIEW. Washington, D.C.: U.S. Department of Health and Human Services, Summer 1980, No. 03054.

HEALTH CARE FINANCING TRENDS, Winter 1980. Washington, D.C.: Compiled by Daniel R. Waldo, Division of National Cost Estimates, Health Care Financing Administration Office of Research, Demonstrations, and Statistics, *1*(2).

HEALTH RESOURCES STATISTICS: HEALTH MANPOWER AND HEALTH FACILITIES, 1966–77 edition. Hyattsville, Md.: Public Health Service, Office of Health Research, Statistics, and Technology, National Center for Health Statistics, U.S. Department of Health, Education and Welfare, 1979.

HISTORY OF THE EXISTING COMMUNITY MENTAL HEALTH CENTERS PROGRAM AND THE NEED FOR NEW LEGISLATION. *The mental health systems act,* Report No. 96–712. Washington, D.C.: U.S. Government Printing Office, May 15, 1980.

INSLEY, VIRGINIA. Some implications of recent legislation for social work. In Florence Haselkorn (Ed.) *Mothers-at-risk: The role of social work in prevention of morbidity in infants of socially disadvantaged mothers.* New York: Adelphi University School of Social Work Publications, 1966, *1*(1).

JONAS, STEVEN, & OTHERS. Measurement and control of the quality of health care. *Health care delivery in the United States.* New York: Springer, 1977.

KORAN, LORRIN M. Mental health services. In Steven Jonas (Ed.) *Health care delivery in the United States.* New York: Springer, 1977.

LANGSLEY, DONALD G. & KAPLAN, DAVID S. *The treatment of families in crisis.* New York: Grune & Stratton, 1968.

LEHMAN, ALBERT. Short term therapy in a military setting. *The Family: Journal of Social Casework,* October 1944, *XXV*(6).

MAGNER, GEORGE W. Trends: Social work practice in mental health. *Abstracts for Social Workers,* National Association of Social Workers, Fall 1970, *6*(3).

MATUS, RICHARD & NEUHRING. ELANE M. Social workers in primary prevention. *Community Mental Health Journal,* 1979, *15*(1).

MECHANIC, DAVID. The development of mental health policy in the United States. *Mental health and social policy.* Englewood Cliffs, N.J. Prentice-Hall, 1969.

MECHANIC, DAVID. *Future issues in health care.* New York: Free Press, 1979.

MEDICAID STATISTICS. Washington, D.C.: Department of Health, Education and Welfare, June 1977, No. (HCFA) 78–03150.

MEDICARE: PARTICIPATING HEALTH FACILITIES, 1979. *Health care financing program statistics.* Baltimore, Md.: Health Care Financing Administration, Office of Research, Demonstrations and Statistics, U.S. Department of Health and Human Services, n.d.

MEDICARE–USE OF HOME HEALTH SERVICES: 1976. Baltimore, Md.: Health Care Financing Administration, Office of Research, Demonstrations, and Statistics, U.S. Department of Health, Education and Welfare, n.d.

MILLER, C. ARDEN, MOOSE, MERRY-K., KOTCH, JONATHAN B., BROWN, MARIE L., & BRAINARD, MAUREEN P. Role of local health departments in the delivery of ambulatory care. *American Journal of Public Health*, January 1981, *71*(1), supplement.

MILLER, ROSALIND S. A social work model for servicing the chronically ill. *Social work practice*. New York: Columbia University Press, 1966.

MILLER, ROSALIND S., LINN, LOUIS, & WEIDEMAN, GEORGE. Prescribing psychotropic drugs: Whose responsibility? *Social Work in Health Care*, Fall 1980, *6*(1).

MUSTO, DAVID. Whatever happened to community mental health? *Psychiatric Annals*, October 1977, *7*(10).

O'CONNOR, W. A. Ecosystems theory and clinical mental health. *Psychiatric Annals*, 1977, *7*(7).

PARAD, HOWARD J. (Ed.) *Crisis interventions: Selected readings*. New York: Family Service Association of America, 1965.

PETERSON, EDYE & SILBERMAN, HERBERT A. Medicare Persons enrolled, 1978. *Health Care Financing Notes*. Baltimore, Md.: Health Care Financing Administration, Office of Research, Demonstrations, and Statistics, U.S. Department of Health and Human Services, n.d.

THE PRESIDENT'S COMMISSION ON MENTAL HEALTH. *Report to the President from the President's commission on mental health* (4 Vols.). Washington, D.C.: U.S. Government Printing Office, 1978.

PROMOTING HEALTH/PREVENTING DISEASE, OBJECTIVES FOR THE NATION. Washington, D.C.: Public Health Service, Department of Health and Human Services, Fall 1980.

PSRO PROGRAM MANUAL. Rockville, Md.: Public Health Services, Health Service Administration, Bureau of Quality Assurance, U.S. Department of Health, Education and Welfare, 1974.

REGIER, DANIEL A., GOLDBERG, IRVING D., & TAUBE, CARL A. The de facto U.S. mental health services system. *Archives of General Psychiatry*, June 1978, *35*.

REID, WILLIAM & SHYNE, ANN W. *Brief and extended casework*. New York: Columbia University Press, 1969.

ROEMER, MILTON. The foreign experience in health service policy. Arthur Levin (Ed.) *Regulating health care*. New York: The Academy of Political Science, 1980.

ROSNER, DAVID. Business at the bedside: Health care in Brooklyn, 1880–1915. Susan Reverby and David Rosner (Eds.) *Health Care in America*. Philadelphia: Temple University Press, 1979.

SIDEL, VICTOR & SIDEL, RUTH. Past and present. *A healthy statement*. New York: Pantheon Books, 1977.

STEVENS, ROBERT & STEVENS, ROSEMARY. *Welfare medicine in America: A case study of Medicaid*. New York: Free Press, 1974.

SULLIVAN, RONALD. Physician review program seeks state aid. *The New York Times*, March 29, 1981.

VAYDA, ANDREA M. & PERLMUTTER, FELICE D. Primary prevention in community mental health centers. *Community Mental Health Journal*, 1977, *13*(4).

VOGEL, MORRIS. The transformation of the American hospital, 1850–1920. In Susan Reverby and David Rosner (Eds.) *Health care in America*. Philadelphia: Temple University Press, 1979.

VOLLAND, PATRICIA. Social work information and accountability systems in a hospital setting. *Social Work in Health Care*, Spring 1976, *1*.

WEINTRAUB, BERNARD. Doctors gain in efforts to retain review program. *The New York Times*, April 14, 1981.

WHITE, ROGER B., CORNELY, DONALD A., & GATELY, ANITA. Interdisciplinary training for child welfare and health. *Child Welfare*, 1978, *LVII* (9).

WILDAVSKY, AARON. Doing better and feeling worse: The political pathology of health policy. *Doing better and feeling worse: Health in the United States.* (John H. Knowles (Ed.) New York: W. W. Norton & Co., Inc., 1977.

WILSON, FLORENCE A. & NEUHAUSER, DUNCAN. *Health services in the United States.* Cambridge, Mass.: Ballinger, 1976.

WITTMAN, MILTON. Application of knowledge about prevention in social work education and practice. *Social Work in Health Care*, Fall 1977, *3*(1).

WITTMAN, MILTON. Casework in a military setting. *The Family: Journal of Social Casework*, June 1944, *XXV*(4).

CHAPTER FOUR
PRACTICE ROLES AND FUNCTIONS OF THE HEALTH SOCIAL WORKER

Gary Rosenberg

INTRODUCTION

This chapter will delineate the major health care practice roles performed by social workers today. It rests on the premise that values are an important part of the professional's action system. Two categories of values are discussed. Values of the social work profession, in general, and specific values with regard to the health care field. The knowledge base of social work practice in health care is then examined. Knowledge about health and illness with specific reference to disease entities; the knowledge base of community medicine, a model of health-related problems; knowledge with respect to social ecology, stress, and coping; knowledge with regard to role theory, personality theories, developmental theories of individuals, families, and groups; and knowledge with respect to effective practice are seen as the key knowledge base of social work in health.

This chapter then describes the clinical process of care, beginning with entry and assessment skills, touching briefly on collaborative practice, and of contracting with clients. It is important to present a wide range of interventive skills, based on the idea that an eclectic approach to practice is crucial for the health care practitioner. Evaluation of outcomes and recording skills are also examined. Problem and service classification systems are offered, as are the screening and outcome measures of clinical practice. Individuals are viewed in their social context and the clinical use of individual, family, and group approaches are presented. Termination is discussed in the context of these concepts. The chapter ends with a brief discussion of some major innovations in health care in the 1980s, which will include social work in primary care settings, in health maintenance organizations, in the private office of physicians in mental health settings, and other innovative settings. A comprehensive reference list is offered to the reader. Clinical vignettes are utilized to give the reader a foundation in the actual practice of social work in health care settings.

VALUES

Values are part of every professional's action system. Social work has had continuous interest in explicating and scrutinizing its values. Our literature reflects concerns about values and includes discussions regarding the social work code of ethics, the bedrock value statement. "What social workers do is based on values—that is, on what social workers regard as preferably done. How it is done is also based on values—preferences concerning the way of doing what is done. . . . Ethics, in effect, is values in operation."[1] Part of the unique context of practice in health care is that it is multidisciplinary and that other professions have value systems that differ from social work. Bartlett suggests

> Thus, it is possible to perceive how differing value orientation may influence the relations of physicians and social workers to patients and each other. The emphasis on scientific knowledge increased the authoritative role of the physician and enables him to move more quickly in working with patients, as he often must do because of the urgency of illness. The social worker's emphasis on the patient's view point requires the development of a professional relationship which will permit the individual to express his feelings in a tempo generally keyed to the individual's readiness.[2]

Pincus and Minahan point out the need for identified fundamental values that establish the outer boundaries of the profession.[3] These values are essential given the ethical ambiguities of the change agent role. Inherent in our role is the need to maintain a balance among flexibility, integrity, self-awareness, and technical expertise as well as a tolerance for ambiguity. Values can help contain the anxiety that may arise as the social worker experiences the inherent dilemmas in the role of change agent.

The following are a list of primary values held by the profession and some special values unique or inherent to health care social work. Primary values include

1. The belief in the dignity and worth of the individual;
2. The belief that the individual can be aided to reach his fullest potential;
3. The belief that social work practice and organized systems of care should enhance and maximize self-determination.

[1] Charles S. Levy, "The Value Base of Social Work," *Journal of Education for Social Work*, 9, no. 1 (1973), pp. 34-42, and Charles S. Levy, *Social Work Ethics* (New York: Human Science Press, 1976), p. 14.

[2] Harriet M. Bartlett, *Social Work Practice in the Health Field* (Washington, D.C.: National Association of Social Workers, 1961), p. 102.

[3] Allen Pincus and Ann Minahan, *Social Work Practice: Model and Method* (Illinois: F. E. Peacock, 1973), pp. 37-52.

Pincus and Minahan suggest that the primary values of social work might be stated as follows.

1. Society has an obligation to insure that people have access to the resources, services and opportunities they need to meet various life tasks, alleviate distress and realize their aspirations and values.
2. In providing societal resources, the dignity and individuality of people should be respected.[4]

Another value explicated by social work is that of social justice. "Social justice embodies equity, fairness, impartiality and equality of opportunity. It is concerned with the needs of all the citizenry for the maximum development of all persons in our society and for the conservation and advancement of all human resources."[5]

In addition to these general social work values, there is also a distinct set of values held by social workers with regard to health care.

1. Total health care is a right;
2. Access to what is already in existence is a right;
3. Quality of life is to be striven for, as contrasted with an emphasis purely on the prolongation of life;
4. The concepts of caring and coping need to be stressed more than continued investments in already sophisticated technological systems;
5. Any new system must emphasize the positives of social health, rather than follow a disease focused model, for example, use people's strengths, educate for health maintenance, and prevent illness.

In a conference held on ethical dilemmas in health care, Drs. Bosch, Rehr, and Lewis identified a set of value guidelines for social health care services.

1. There should be universal access to health care based on basic population needs and on securing optimum social functioning.
2. There should be mutual participation of consumers and providers in policy making and in the operation of programs, with accountability of the provider to the consumer.
3. There should be an element of choice for consumers from among many care options.
4. Availability and comprehensiveness of care should be guaranteed within reasonable distances, timely and within community needs.
5. Human and material health resources should be reorganized in regionalized networks based on population needs.
6. There should be an element of predictability in program budgets.
7. Physicians should do doctoring at the primary, secondary and tertiary levels,

---

[4] Pincus and Minahan, *Social Work Practice*, pp. 37-52.

[5] Jeanette Regensburg, *Toward Education for Health Professions* (New York: Harper & Row, 1978), p. 5.

but in partnership with a broad range of manpower from other disciplines and with differential manpower overseen by professionals.

8. Preventive actions and health education both for individuals and populations should be given high priority. Prevention incentives should be incorporated.

9. All health care professionals should be educated to function in a social health care system.

10. Educational goals should address a concept of bio-social psychological care, health maintenance and prevention.

11. Education should be broadened to include the learning of interprofessional appreciation and collaboration.

12. Research cannot be limited to the basic sciences, but needs to include clinical and community health services as well.[6]

In operationalizing values in practice, "The crucial point is that the client's own values should be at the center of attention when change is under consideration and should be readily available as a criterion against which induced behavior can be measured."[7]

> All value dimensions influence treatment systems in one way or another. . . three such dimensions that concern the practitioner's position vis-à-vis his clients and relate specifically to values placed on: (1) the client's own expressed wishes; (2) the worker's notions of what the client "needs" or what is "good" for him; (3) the protection of the interests of others as the worker sees them—the community, the family or other individuals. Most value issues and premises concerning the caseworker's relations to his clients can be described along these dimensions or at points of conflict among them.[8]

The worker in health care as in other settings experiences value conflicts. Value conflicts arise between the worker and the client, the client and the care-giving system, and with the community at large. Clearly, self-awareness assists the worker in meeting his responsibility for explicating a value framework for practice. As Kelman says

> . . . from the point of view of reducing the manipulativeness of the situation; it would be important to encourage mutuality at least to the extent of acknowledging that what the therapist introduces into the situation is not entirely based on objective reality, but on an alternative set of values, which are open to question.[9]

Values and knowledge are related systems of thought and action. It is important for the social worker to distinguish when an interventive action is based on val-

[6] Helen Rehr, ed., *Ethical Dilemmas in Health Care: The Professional Search for Solutions* (New York: Prodist, 1978), p. 83.

[7] Herbert C. Kelman, "Manipulation of Human Behavior: An Ethical Dilemma for the Social Scientist," *Journal of Social Issues*, 21, no. 2 (1965), 43.

[8] William Reid and Laura Epstein, *Task-Centered Casework* (New York: Columbia University Press, 1972), p. 16.

[9] Herbert C. Kelman, "Manipulation of Human Behavior," p. 42.

ues or knowledge or a combination of the two, to avoid resulting actions which are ineffective, unpurposeful, or harmful.[10]

THE KNOWLEDGE BASE
FOR SOCIAL WORK PRACTICE
IN HEALTH CARE

Knowledge forms a core of the professional action system. Knowledge about an issue is not the same as knowledge of how it can be resolved. The social work literature is replete with references to concepts such as borrowed knowledge, core knowledge, and knowledge building. There is some concern about whether a core of knowledge exists in social work that would make it identifiable as a full profession. We agree with Gordon and Schutz, who have articulated broad guidelines for social work. These concepts set the parameters for social work knowledge building.

> . . . a social work specialization must be concerned with some interface between persons and their environments for the purpose of making people's transactions with their environments more conducive to their own development and to the amelioration of the environment for others. The immediate cause of the mismatch between coping capability and environment may lie primarily with a person's limited coping ability or with the unfavorableness of the impinging environment and interventive efforts may be more concerned with one side of the interface in question than with the other. But as long as a dual focus is used to achieve a better match between coping capabilities or the environment are not ignored, a social work specialization may be identified.[11]

Professional competence is rooted in knowledge and skill and is guided by the social purpose and values of social work. This combination of purpose, knowledge, and skill as the basis of competence helps in turn to create, sustain, and enhance a clear firm sense of social work entity. The commitment or social purpose of the profession and the definition of social work practice underscore the need for knowledge and theory about environments and about transactions between people and environments.[12] Knowledge, to be effective for practice, must meet the following criteria.

> It must lead to action which is researchable with outcome demonstrated as effective. Change may be brought about in two ways: (a) by altering the client's behavior or manners of responding, feelings and conditions, or all of these,

[10] William E. Gordon, "Knowledge and Value: Their Distinction and Relationship in Clarifying Social Work Practice," *Social Work*, 10, no. 1 (July 1965), pp. 32-9.

[11] William E. Gordon and Margaret L. Schutz, "A Natural Basis for Social Work Specializations," *Social Work*, 22, 4 (September 1977), p. 423.

[12] Carel B. Germain, "An Ecological Perspective on Social Work Practice in Health Care," *Social Work in Health Care*, 3, no. 1 (Fall 1977), pp. 67-76.

and (b) by altering any of the social systems or the environment in which the client functions.[13]

The theories upon which knowledge is based range from those that are formal and explicit to those that are less formal, personal and vague.[14] As Epstein states

> The test of a good theory is its usefulness. A theory is useful if it can generate predictions of propositions that turn out to be verified, that is, true. A theory is useful if it generates research or new forms of practice. A theory is useful if it has a reasonable degree of consistency with, or similarity to, known empirical findings (from research and observations). A theory is particularly useful to practitioners if it cuts down the strangeness and complexity of disconnected observations made in real life. Many behavioral events can be identified and described in a wide variety of ways. A useful theory should organize observations, instruct us about what to concentrate on and suggest what things hang together. In perceiving ourselves and other people, we always use a theory as a guide.[15]

There is no single theoretical perspective that deals with the total range of problems in which social workers are involved.

Social work practice in health care has an eclectic knowledge base. Within the limitations of personal bias, this author has selected key concepts that constitute baseline knowledge in social work practice.

KNOWLEDGE ABOUT HEALTH AND ILLNESS

Health is a difficult concept to define. The World Health Organization defines health as a state of complete physical, mental, and social well-being and not as the absence of disease or infirmity. This definition is a romanticized one and probably almost impossible to obtain. Thus, as suggested by Callahan, it is a dangerous definition and desperately needs a more modest replacement.[16] Its emphasis on complete physical, mental, and social well-being puts both medicine and society in the untenable position of being required to seek unattainable goals. Although a reasonable concept of health would be important for social policy development in social work as well as for other health care professions, a more operational understanding of how to achieve optimum health for the individual is important for social workers in terms of their practice roles and functions.

[13] Carel B. Germain, ed., *Social Work Practice: People and Environments* (New York: Columbia University Press, 1979), pp. 1-22.

[14] Joel Fisher, *Effective Casework Practice: An Eclectic Approach* (New York: McGraw-Hill, 1978), pp. 64-9. See also Calvin S. Hall and Gardner Lindzey, *Theories of Personality*, 3rd ed. (New York: John Wiley, 1978).

[15] Laura Epstein, *Helping People: A Task-Centered Approach* (St. Louis, Mo.: C. V. Mosby, 1980), p. 87.

[16] Daniel Callahan, "Health and Societies: Some Ethical Imperatives," in *Doing Better and Feeling Worse: Health in the United States*, ed. John H. Knowles (New York: W. W. Norton & Co., Inc., 1977), pp. 23-33.

The behaviors of individuals in obtaining optimum health have been studied by Breslow and Belock.[17] They suggest that life expectancy and health are significantly related to the following basic habits: three meals a day at regular times without snacking; breakfast every day; moderate exercise two to three times a week; adequate sleep—7 to 8 hours a night; no smoking; moderate weight; and no alcohol or only moderate amounts.

In addition, we are aware that some risk in certain populations may be at higher level than others for some diseases such as cancer. Risk of cancer is increased in the following populations: (1) those with known host factors (genetic and other congenital defects and immunological deficiency diseases); (2) those with exposure to environmental contaminants known to produce cancer; and (3) those with certain demographic characteristics, which reflect as yet unknown carcinogenic factors (place of residence or migration).

Prevention requires that the organization of personal health services be reinforced by environmental measures and mass education. In order to reach populations in potential need, social workers should locate in schools, hospital clinics, places of work, and doctors' offices as well as in hospitals, health care, and mental health clinics. Social work can contribute to preventive medicine by concentrating on people who are at high risk for specific diseases. Helping people who are at-risk for high blood pressure to attain routine screening and to follow through with treatment; helping women at-risk for breast cancer and cancer of the cervix and uterus to learn and use low-cost testing; promotion of multifacet screenings to detect serious and correctable defects; helping immunization against infectious disease and preventing the spread of venereal disease are important areas for social workers.

Activities to promote mental health should have the following general elements: (1) a target condition that can be observed and recorded in precise terms; (2) an identified population at-risk for that condition; (3) a measure of the incidence of that condition in the population; (4) a clearly defined plan for intervention applied to the identified population; and (5) the measurement of incidents following the intervention.[18]

Meyer has described social work's preventive role as being carried out through consultation to primary institutions in the society; family life education programs; and monitoring social policies and their impact on human functioning.[19]

Preventive programming has been described by Perlmutter[20] as activities that promote mental health and reduce the incidence of emotional disorder. Among these

[17] N. B. Belloch and L. Breslow, "The Relation of Physical Health Status and Health Practice," in *Preventive Medicine*, 1 (August 1972), pp. 409-21.

[18] Donald C. Klein and Steven E. Goldston, *"Preface"/Primary Prevention: An Idea Whose Time Has Come*, Donald C. Klein and Steven E. Goldston, eds. (Rockville, Md.: NIMH, 1977), p. VII.

[19] Carol Meyer, ed., "Preventive Intervention: A Goal in Search of a Method," in *Preventive Intervention in Social Work* (Washington, D.C.: National Association of Social Workers, 1974), pp. 1-12.

[20] Felice D. Perlmutter, "Prevention and Treatment: A Strategy for Survival," *Community Mental Health Journal*, 10 (Fall 1974), pp. 276-81.

programs are support groups, targeting services for groups at-risks, helping victims to cope with their problems, dealing with losses and situational crises, and strengthening natural and artificial support systems. These activities tend to be carried out through consultation, educational and community development programs, and specialized preventive mental health for minorities and other vulnerable groups.

Illness has been defined as an experience that connotes both physical and social states.[21] It is a person's reaction to a biological alteration and is perceived differently by different people, according to the individual's state of mind and cultural belief system. Therefore, illness is an extremely imprecise term and represents an individualized response to a set of physiological and psychosocial stimuli. Disease is a professional construct. It is perceived as being precise and reflects the state of professional knowledge, particularly that of the physician. Social workers need to know about specific medical illnesses. Even though knowledge may be imprecise as to cause and cure, social workers can help patients to understand the process of the illness, and can bring to bear knowledge about coping patterns necessary for patients to adjust to illness. These mechanisms should mesh with the patients' personal constructs of the meanings of illness with the particular illness that they are experiencing. Most of the appropriate material describing personal constructs of illness are available in the proper literature. Much of the "bio" of the biopsychosocial model is achieved for social work by collaborative effort with physicians and nurses.[22] However, knowledge about the specific process of an illness, as well as its physiology, can help social workers accurately empathize with their patients, as well as help them provide patients with information needed to cope with illness. Bracht offers a reference guide for social treatment interventions with selected illnesses.[23] A number of books have been written for social workers about understanding the biopsychosocial phenomena attached to illnesses. For example, Georgia Travis' book, provides information on chronic illness in children.[24] Written by a social worker for social workers, there is a body of literature that helps social workers understand biopsychosocial risk factors from perinatal care through aging. Much has been written about death, and bereavement in families who survived the death of loved ones.

Knowledge about mental illness is an important component for social workers. Social workers have always preferred descriptive or psychosocial assessments as compared to clinical diagnoses made by psychiatrists. However, knowledge of clinical diagnoses, psychopharmacological interventions, causative factors in mental illness, its distribution in the population, and associated risk factors are crucial components of social work knowledge. With the advent of the DSM-III,[25] the clinical and diag-

[21] Renee C. Fox, "The Medicalization and Demedicalization of American Society," in Knowles, *Doing Better and Feeling Worse*, pp. 9-22.

[22] Gary Rosenberg, *Social Work and Liaison Psychiatry*, presentation before the Society of Liaison Psychiatrists, March 1980, unpublished paper, p. 24.

[23] Neil Bracht, *Social Work in Health Care: A Guide to Professional Practice* (New York: Haworth Press, 1978), pp. 141-54.

[24] Georgia Travis, *Chronic Illness in Children* (California: Stanford University Press, 1976).

[25] *Diagnostic and Statistical Manual 3*, (Washington, D.C.: The American Psychiatric Association, 1980).

nostic manual for psychiatrists published by the American Psychiatric Association, we see a broadening of knowledge base of psychiatrists. This type of labeling is important for social workers to know and to use, so that a proper referral can be made where the diagnosis clearly indicates the need for psychopharmacological or other physical interventions. In the DSM-III system individuals are evaluated along three axes: (1) clinical syndromes, wherein conditions are attributed to a mental disorder— that are the focus of attention or treatment; (2) personality disorder or specific developmental disorder; and (3) physical disorder and condition. In addition, the DSM-III also looks at severity of psychosocial stressors and evaluates the highest level of adaptive functioning during the past year.

COMMUNITY MEDICINE
KNOWLEDGE BASE

Social work now has available new tools that better define incidence, prevalence, and risk factors in health care. The science of epidemiology helps identify these aforementioned factors. Community medicine is concerned with the identification and solution of health problems in population groups. Community medicine practice involves the use of epidemiology, behavioral and management sciences, knowledge of the organization and coordination of health services, and of primary, secondary, and tertiary levels of care. In its early development, social work helped people adapt to the psychosocial demands of illness and hospitalization. Social work has now moved to understanding the need for services which deal with prevented health care, and the primary, secondary, health care needs of populations. As Dana suggests, health care and medical care should be perceived as social utilities.[26] The spectrum includes the promotion and maintenance of health, prevention of disease, diagnosis and treatment of illness, the optimum rehabilitation of the sick and disabled, and the humane and compassionate care of the chronically and terminally ill. Dana suggests that as an ideology, science, and methodology, community medicine has the potential, not only to fortify social work, but also to provide it with numerator and denominator components of the professional equation in health as in disease.[27] The uses of epidemiology and biostatistics can assist in the assessment and resolution of problems in population groups. These concepts help us to identify the social and psychological characteristics of population at high risk for disease and disability, develop useful criteria for process and outcome assessments of our practice, and provide the social evidence now often missing, for the identification and solution of health problems in populations. Thus, community medicine offers an allied health science body of knowledge for use in the specificity of social work practice and in emphasizing the social nature of social work practice.

[26] Bess Dana, "New Directions in Community Medicine: Implications for Social Work Education and Practice," *The Community Medicine Contribution to Social Work*, delivered at the 75th Anniversary of the Mount Sinai Hospital Department of Social Work, New York, 1980.

[27] Numerator is the individual case, family, or group. Denominator is the collective population group.

A BASIC MODEL
OF HEALTH-RELATED PROBLEMS

Illness may be explained as a function of the interaction between a person's adaptive capacity and infectious agents, nonbiological toxins, and or safety hazards. Adaptive capacity refers to the person's ability to resist infectious agents, and to avoid nonbiological toxins and safety hazards. Adaptive capacity also includes genetic predispositions to certain syndromes as well as an assessment of social and emotional life space. Infectious agents include bacteria and viruses responsible for diseases such as smallpox, plague, polio, hepatitis, and diptheria. Nonbiological toxins that destroy tissue or disturb the systemic balance of the person occur in man-made phenomena. Such phenomena include natural and man-made radiation, ambient air and water pollutants, and harmful substances in the home and work environment. Safety hazards would include automobile, occupational and recreational aspects as well as physical processes of floods, tornadoes, earthquakes, and fires.[28]

Throughout its historical development, the public health sector has been concerned with each one of the aforementioned factors. At different times, however, the public health discipline focused primarily on one or another of the factors. The dominance of a single point of view downgraded the importance of the other factors. In the eighteenth century, the acceptance of the germ theory led to an underestimation of the importance of adaptive capacity, nonbiological toxins, and safety hazards. As major epidemic diseases came under control, emphasis shifted to toxic agents in the form of environmental pollutants. Most recently, ecological analyses of human communities appear to be leading to a renewed interest in the adaptive capacity factor. Thus, social work and public health are brought full circle back to an ecological paradigm which replaces the precocious but crude observations of the ancient Greeks.

It is within this framework that Neil Bracht states that it is extremely important for social workers to remember that no amount of behavioral change aimed at better personal health habits will offset the weight of long-standing social and economic dislocation which have contributed in a large part to the poor health of large segments of our country.[29] Renee Dubos emphasizes the notion that "theories of disease must account for the surprising fact that in any community a large percentage of healthy and normal individuals continually harbor potentially pathogenic microbes without suffering any symptoms."[30] Dubos also points out that the property of virulence was once regarded as lying solely within the microbes themselves, following the germ theory of disease. However, virulence is now coming to be thought of as an ecological component of illness. Whether a person lives in equilibrium with microbes or becomes their victim, depends in large part on the circum-

---

[28] See for example Daniel Callahan, "Health Societies: Some Ethical Imperatives" and John H. Knowles, "The Responsibility of the Individual" in *Doing Better and Feeling Worse*, pp. 23-34, pp. 57-80.

[29] Neil Bracht, "Health Care: Issues and Trends," in *Social Work in Health Care*, pp. 19-36.

[30] Renee Dubos, *Man Adapting*, (New Haven: Yale University Press, 1965), p. 65.

stances under which he encounters them (his ecological life space). This ecological concept is essential to a proper formulation of the problem of a disease, to its treatment, and to its control.[31]

SOCIAL ECOLOGY

"The ecological perspective rests on an evolutionary adaptive view of human beings in continuous transactions with the environment."[32]

As a metaphor for practice, the ecological perspective provides insights into the nature and consequences of such transactions both for human beings and for the physical and social environments in which they function. The perspective is concerned with the growth, development, and potentiality of human beings and with the properties of their environments that support or fail to support the expression of human potential by clarifying the structure of the environment and the nature of its influence on adaptation. This perspective appears to be admirably suited to the task of developing concepts and action principles for intervening in the environment. Stress, coping, adaptation, and the quality of physical environments, are major concepts of the ecological approach. The interaction among all these factors provides the sum total of the life space within which the ecological approach can be applied.[33]

STRESS

Stress is an upset in the interchange between people and environments. The stress of illness or disability represents a transactional process between inner and outer events that disturbs the goodness of fit between person and environment. Strain and Grossman identify eight categories of psychological stress experienced by all acutely ill hospitalized patients:

1. The basic threat to self-esteem and sense of intactness "narcissistic integrity";
2. Fear of strangers;
3. Separation anxiety;
4. Fear of loss of love and approval;
5. Fear of the loss of control of developmentally achieved functions;
6. Fear of loss or of injury to body parts;
7. Guilt and fear of retaliation;
8. Fear of pain.[34]

---

[31] Carel B. Germain and Alex Gitterman, *The Life Model of Social Work Practice* (New York: Columbia University Press, 1980), pp. 1-33.

[32] Germain and Gitterman, *ibid.*; p. 5 and Carel B., Social Work in Health Care.

[33] Carel B. Germain, ed., *Social Work Practice: People and Environments.*

[34] James J. Strain and Stanley Grossman, *Psychological Care of the Medically Ill: A Primer in Liaison Psychiatry* (New York: Appleton-Century-Crofts; 1975), pp. 24-30.

Stress response occurs when a stressor is experienced by the person. Mediating factors include inner resources and deficits, and external resources and deficits. The person may either have adaptive or maladaptive responses. Most research concludes that under certain sets of circumstances a pathogenic try-out of events involving physical illness or injury, other fateful loss events and events that disrupt the individual's usual social supports will override mediating factors and lead directly to maladaptive responses.[35]

For stress to be dealt with successfully, coping skills must be brought into play. Coping refers to capacities and skills people use to handle stress. Included are the individual's motivation, cognition, problem-solving ability, planning, judgment, anticipation, self-esteem, self-confidence, and defenses against anxiety and depression.[36] Coping can lead to either eradication or reduction of stress.

In a demonstration study of over 300 patients treated on an inpatient psychosomatic service, treatment was designed to involve the patient in self-care. Attempts were made to reduce symptomatology through behavior modification, social skills training, and family treatment. A follow-up one year later showed that most patients achieved self-set goals and patients who had returned to intact families showed continuing decreases in somatic symptoms and increases in achievement orientation. Treatment failures in this study who were characterized by a return to the medical care system often lacked an intact family.[37] Thus, the environment and the intact family as part of the environment have demonstrable evidence in the research literature as a coping support for individuals.

In a brilliant study entitled "The Structure of Coping," Perlin and Schooler report that coping behavior can be extended in three ways: (1) by eliminating or modifying conditions giving rise to problems; (2) by perceptually controlling the meaning of experience in a manner that neutralizes its problematic character; and (3) by keeping the emotional consequences of problems within manageable bounds.[38] It has been found that coping interventions are most effective when dealing with problems within the close interpersonal roles of marriage and child rearing and least effective when dealing with more impersonal problems such as those found in the occupational sphere. Effective coping modes are unequally distributed in society, with men, the educated, and the affluent making greater use of efficacious mechanisms.[39]

With regard to environmental fit, Germain states that the environmental nutri-

[35] George V. Coelho, David A. Hamburg, and John E. Adams, ed., *Coping and Adaptation* (New York: Basic Books, 1974).

[36] J. Adams and E. Lindeman, "Coping with Long-Term Disability," in Coelho, Hamburg, and Adams, *Coping and Adaptation*, pp. 127-38; and Rudolph H. Moos and Vivien D. Tsu, "The Crisis of Physical Illness: An Overview," ed., Rudolph Moos, *Coping with Physical Illness* (New York: Plenum, 1977), pp. 3-22.

[37] Susan C. Wooley, Barry Blackwell, and Carolyn Winget, "A Learning Theory Model of Chronic Illness Behavior: Theory, Treatment and Research," *Psychosomatic Medicine*, 40, no. 5 (August 1978), pp. 379-401.

[38] Leonard I. Pearlin and Carmi Schooler, "The Structure of Coping," *Journal of Health and Social Behavior*, 19 (March 1978), pp. 2-21.

[39] *Ibid.*

ents required by patients who are coping with the stress of illness and disability are

1. the opportunity for taking action, exercising judgment, making decisions to the degree allowed by the nature of the illness;
2. staff behaviors in patient services that support patient self-esteem and reward coping efforts;
3. organizational procedures and policies that respect patient's life-styles, cultural values, and social supports;
4. the provision of information, and by giving the appropriate amount at the appropriate time.[40]

Humanized health care thus emphasizes community social roles rather than "sick" roles.

In an excellent exploratory study of person-environment fit, Coulton found that patients were able to perceive discrepancies between themselves and their environment. These discrepancies fell into the following areas:

1. Having sufficient opportunity for social relationships;
2. Having sufficient opportunity to express feelings;
3. Having sufficient sources of emotional support;
4. Being able to fulfill responsibilities;
5. Meeting expectations of self and others;
6. Having opportunities to engage in interesting and productive activities and to achieve goals;
7. Fulfilling demands of certain situations such as jobs and social events;
8. Getting information to allow some certainty about the future;
9. Having knowledge about their physical condition, community resources, and so on;
10. Knowing where things are, what to expect, how to behave in new settings;
11. Having sufficient financial resources to meet demands and obligations;
12. Having help with physical and self-care needs;
13. Finding the means to move from place to place.[41]

Coulton's work operationalizes the concept of person-environment fit among the chronically ill.

COPING SKILLS

Moss and Tsu suggest seven adaptive tasks that affect patients dealing with discomfort, incapacity, or other illness-related problems. These adaptive tasks include three that are illness-specific: dealing with pain and incapacity; dealing with hospital

---

[40] Germain, "An Ecological Perspective on Social Work Practice in Health Care," pp. 69-74.

[41] Claudia Coulton, "A Study of Person Environment Fit Among the Chronically Ill," *Social Work in Health Care*, 5, no. 1 (Fall 1979), pp. 5-18.

environment and special treatment procedures; and developing adequate relationships with health care staff.

The following are four general tasks: (1) preserving a reasonable emotional balance; (2) preserving a satisfactory self-image; (3) preserving relationships with family and friends; and (4) preparing for an uncertain future.

These tasks are achieved by the following skills:

1. Denying or minimizing the seriousness of the crisis;
2. Seeking relevant information and using intellectual resources effectively;
3. Requesting reassurance and emotional support from concerned family, friends, and health care staff members;
4. Learning specific illness-related procedures, for example, feeding and caring of a premature baby, performing home dialysis, and so on;
5. Setting concrete, limited goals;
6. Rehearsing alternative outcomes;
7. Finding a general purpose or pattern of measuring, for example seeing some positive value to the experience, putting the experience into a long-term perspective to make the events more manageable.[42]

Social workers assist patients and or families to maximize their ability to cope by recognizing stress problems in person and or environment fit, humanizing health and mental health environments, assisting in problem solving, and supporting patients and families with positive adaptation behaviors. They may also help by providing environmental nutrients for growth development of the individual.

Different coping skills are needed at various stages of illness. "The Diagnostic, Chronic, and End-Stages of . . . Illness" pose special tasks and require different defenses and capacities from the patient, family, and health care personnel. During the diagnostic phase or an acute phase of a chronic illness, the right amount of information is needed by the patient and the family. Autonomy is an important aspect of this phase as is the overall maintenance of the internal organization of the patient and family. After the family and patient have dealt with the crisis of the diagnostic and acute phase, they must deal with the tasks of the chronic phase. This phase requires adaptation to discomfort, pain, and loss of physical control. The patient and family learn to make maximum use of the health care system and to adapt to necessary role shifts for the patient and family. In the ending stage, the family and patient work through the impending and the actual loss.[43] Remissions can occur during these stages and the family and patient need to make maximum use of these periods while maintaining the recognition that remissions do end. The process just described is applicable to medical and to psychiatric illness.

[42] Moos and Tsu, "The Crisis of Physical Illness," p. 3-22; Mildred M. Mailick, "The Impact of Severe Illness on the Individual and Family: An Overview," *Social Work in Health Care*, 5, no. 2 (Winter 1979), pp. 117-28; and Harriet M. Bartlett, *Social Work Practice in the Health Field*, pp. 130-37.

[43] Regensburg, *Toward Education for Health Professions*, pp. 1-44.

ROLE THEORY

Role theory offers a particularly viable construct to social workers in health care settings. Although initially a sociological concept, the notion of role has penetrated a wide range of disciplines.

Hare defined role as a "set of expectations of a person who occupies a given position in the social system." An equally valid perception is "an individual's definition of his situation with reference to his and other's social position."[44] Questions concerning, "How should I behave?" or "What is expected of me?" offer clues to individual problems of role definition.

As Northen states

> When a person enacts or performs a role, he is responding to a set of expectations that others have for his behavior, but he is also acting in accordance with his own expectations and motives. The expectations for behavior both affect and are affected by the individual in the role, by the social system and its component parts and by the expectations of the social "milieu."[45]

The hospital social worker utilizes role theory as a way of tuning in to the dynamic transactions that occur between the patient and the helping person, the patient and his family, and the patient and the institutional system. Loss of status and role confusion are problems for patients in hospitals. Role expectations and perceptions are affected by the illness entity itself, its implications for chronicity and the length of stay required for treatment in the hospital. Social work interventions are often directed towards helping the patient improve his role-taking aptitude. Social workers also assist the family system to negotiate the environment in accordance with the new role demands made upon both the family system and the patient.

PERSONALITY THEORIES

Personality theories offer numerous insights into understanding the individual. Psychoanalytic, behavioral, cognitive learning, Gestalt, and other theories enlighten our efforts to empathize appropriately with individual clients. However, no single theory offers a total understanding of human behavior. Furthermore, because social work is an action profession, personality theory may have little immediate use in practice, and techniques used by advocates of a single personality theory do not always lead to helpful outcomes.[46]

[44] Paul A. Hare, *Handbook of Small Group Research* (New York: Free Press, 1962), p. 27.

[45] Helen Northen, *Social Work with Groups* (New York: Columbia University Press: 1969), p. 29.

[46] Epstein, *Helping People*, pp. 86-8.

Although it has been suggested that ego psychology is the behavioral science to which social work should subscribe, psychoanalytic theory and particularly the techniques derived from that theory, provide only a small part of the knowledge necessary to do effective work. It does not serve well as the method of choice for people in states of crisis, some of whom may not have asked for social work services, and for whom service is time-limited. People who enter settings dealing with illness do not translate their physical pains into social-psychological terms. When social workers "find" their clients, they must "market" their services. This process frequently requires translating physical dysfunctioning into social functioning objectives. The social worker is rarely behind the desks waiting for the client who arrives identifying his problem for professional intervention. Most often he or she is "casefinding," developing motivation and translating resources into achievable contracts acceptable to both client and worker. Too frequently in social work, we perceive clinical practice narrowly. Overconcern with relationship and process is evident with less interest in the client's perception of the problem-at-hand and in developing a shared goal.

According to Reid and Epstein, it is clear that no one theory of practice or series of techniques answers all practicing social workers' needs.[47] The social worker should "take on" a position of theoretical pluralism that enables him to utilize whatever formal theories are relevant to his purposes. Although psychoanalytic theory has contributed much to our understanding of human behavior in health care settings, it is neither easily testable nor always useful in treating clients.

DEVELOPMENTAL THEORIES
OF THE FAMILY,
INDIVIDUAL, AND GROUP

Developmental theories are highly important in understanding the life cycle of individuals, families, and groups. Problem-solving social work takes place within the constraints of normal growth and development. Developmental theories enable the social worker and client to identify and resolve problems encountered in the life cycle. By identifying obstacles to the continuance of a person's life-cycle growth that come from within the person and from his environment, the social worker can apply developmental theories concerning individuals and families to practice. A staged model based on family developmental theory and Erikson's stages of individual development and associated nuclear tasks is in Table 4-1 and is offered as a framework for understanding the developmental approach.

Although developmental theory is important to all social workers, it has particular relevance for those in health care. The family is the basic unit of health management. As Kumabe and others state,

As the basic unit of health management, the family exhibits characteristic

[47] Reid and Epstein, *Task-Centered Casework.*

TABLE 4-1 A Developmental Framework[a]

FAMILY PHASE	AVERAGE NO. OF YEARS	FAMILY TASK	EGO TASKS OF ADULT MEMBERS OF FAMILY	EGO TASKS OF CHILDREN
I. Marriage Married couple with children	2	Intimacy vs idealization or disillusionment	Identity vs role diffusion—intimacy vs isolation	—
II. Childbearing family—oldest child up to 30 months	2.5	Replenishment vs turning inward	Identity vs role diffusion—intimacy vs isolation	Basic trusts vs mistrusts
III. Families with preschool children—oldest child 30 months to 6 years	3.5	Replenishment vs. turning inward	Generativity vs stagnation	Autonomy vs shame and doubt; initiative vs guilt
IV. Families with school children—oldest child 6-13	7	Individuation of family members vs pseudomutual organization	Generativity vs stagnation	Industry vs inferiority
V. Families with teen-agers—oldest child 13-20	7	Companionship vs isolation	Generativity vs stagnation	Identity vs identity confusion
VI. Families as launching centers—first child leaves—all leave	6.5	Regrouping vs binding or expulsion	Generativity vs stagnation	Intimacy vs isolation
VII. Families in the middle years—empty nest to retirement	15	Rediscovery vs despair	Ego integrity vs despair	Generativity vs stagnation
VIII. Aging families—retirement to death	16	Mutual aid vs uselessness	Ego integrity vs despair	Integrity vs despair

[a]Drawn from Erik H. Erikson, "Identity and the Life Cycle," *Psychological Issues*, 1, no. 1, Monograph 1 (New York International Universities Press, 1969); Sonya L. Rhodes, "A Developmental Approach to the Life Cycle of the Family," *Social Casework* (May 1977), pp. 301-11; and Ira Balick and David R. Kessler, *Marital and Family Therapy* (New York: Grune & Stratton, 1974).

patterns of health practices, definitions of illness and responses to symptoms, and the utilization of medical services. Its commitment to protect its members through stressful situations makes the management of illness more than an individual function and focuses on the family as a significant source of strength—or weakness—in the individual's coping process. The patient who appears at a health facility is seldom a single individual seeking help; rather, he is a member of a family which has exhausted its known internal and external resources to deal with the problem.[48]

Thus, a family-centered approach is crucial in dealing effectively with the health concerns of the patient.

In using developmental theory, we must be guided by Klein's cautions regarding its application to mental illness. Psychiatry, psychology, and social work in the United States have been dominated by theoreticians who singlemindedly emphasize and derogate the contributions of socioeconomic, physiological, and constitutional factors.[49]

Strain and Beallor have identified five parameters to be fulfilled if the family is to be of assistance to an ill family member:

1. The ability of the family to accept the fact that the patient may regress physically and mentally as a consequence of his illness;
2. Their ability to help him ward off the stresses evoked by his illness;
3. Their ability to tolerate the patient's expression of his fears and feelings, for example, that he is going to die, that he will never be the man he once was, that he will never recover, and so forth.
4. Their ability to enlist the patient's basic trust, that is, his confidence that they will not abandon him and at the same time to support his efforts to function as autonomously as possible;
5. Their ability to mobilize outside support on behalf of the patient when necessary.[50]

Group development theory is useful to the practitioner in working directly with formed groups and also in working with collaborative groups of health care professions.[51] Most formed groups move from a preaffiliation stage to establishing purposes, creating exchanges (the work), developing identification with the group,

---

[48]Kazuye Kumabe, Chikae Nishiba, David O'Hara, and Charlotte Woodruff, *A Handbook for Social Work Education and Practice in Community Mental Health Settings* (Hawaii: University of Hawaii School of Social Work, August 1977), p. 25.

[49]Donald F. Klein, Rachel Gittleman, Frederick Quitkin, and Arthur Rifkin, *Diagnosis and Drug Treatment of Psychiatric Disorders: Adults and Children*, 2nd ed. (Baltimore, Md.: Williams & Wilkins, 1980), p. 17.

[50]James J. Strain and Gerald Beallor quoted in James J. Strain (ed.), *Psychological Interventions in Medical Practice* (New York: Appleton-Century-Crofts, 1978), p. 166.

[51]See for example, Saul Bernstein, ed., *Explorations in Group Work* (Boston: School of Social Work of Boston University, 1965); Irving D. Yalom, *The Theory and Practice in Group Psychotherapy*, 2nd ed. (New York: Basic Books, 1975); and J. K. Wittaker, "Models of Group Development," *Social Service Review*, 44 (1970), pp. 308-22.

maturing the group, and terminating the group. Collaborative groups go through developmental stages as do other formed groups.[52] More than in other theoretical approaches, the field of developmental psychology is tied to facts and research. Its core is relevant to the major concerns of social workers; to helping people to become independent; to exercise restraint in actions; to be rational, organized, and planful.[53]

CONCEPTS REGARDING EFFECTIVE PRACTICE

Determining effective social work practice is a part of the knowledge base of social workers in health care settings. The roles and functions of social work are aimed at modifying the environment, as well as the transactions between people both on an individual and family level. Practice effectiveness must deal with a wide range of phenomenon; from policies and the effects of policies on health care delivery systems, families and or individuals, and health care practitioners to specific interventions directed towards ameliorating or resolving illness or the effects of illness on individuals, families, and groups. Bracht has identified five premises and has identified associated studies that support effective social work interventions:

1. Social, cultural, and economic conditions have a significant and measurable effect on both health status and illness prevention. A growing body of research suggests positive relationships between these variables and the development of illness conditions.
2. Illness-related behavior, whether perceived or actual, frequently disrupt personal or family equilibrium and coping abilities. Illness conditions, whether acute, chronic or terminal can be exacerbated by the effects of institutionalization.
3. Medical treatment alone is often incomplete and occasionally impossible to render, without accompanying social support and counseling services.
4. Problems of access to and appropriate utilization of health services are sufficiently endemic to our health care delivery system to require concerted community and institutional innovation.
5. Multiprofessional health team collaboration on selected individual and community health problems is an effective approach to solving complex sociomedical problems.[54]

Other social work practitioners have demonstrated effectiveness in both

[52] Jane Isaacs Lowe and Marjatta Herranen, "Conflict in Teamwork: Understanding Roles and Relationships," *Social Work in Health Care*, 3, no. 3 (Spring 1978), pp. 323-30.

[53] Epstein, *Helping People*, p. 90.

[54] Bracht, *Social Work in Health Care*, pp. 24-31.

medical and psychiatric health care.[56] Social workers need to be familiar with literature that shows treatment effectiveness as well as the literature that shows no difference or improvement. Sensitivity to the iatrogenic aspect of social work practice
needs to be focused on by researchers and practitioners alike. A number of authors
have examined what seem to be the components of effective practice. Epstein suggests
that the following general characteristics are likely to lead to good outcomes: struc·
ture, specificity, and practitioner and or client congruence.[57] She explains that
structure means the arrangements of a set of interventions according to the dominant goal. Specificity means exact and sharply defined goals. It implies that actions
taken by any or all participants are demonstrably connected to targeted problems
and goals. Practitioner and or client congruence means correspondence between
client and practitioner not only on the problems, but also on intervention necessary to reduce problems. Wood's review of casework effectiveness suggests six principles of quality practice that can be extracted from an analysis of 22 studies:

1. accurate definition of the problem;
2. analysis of the problem, factors creating or maintaining it and factors that
    can help resolve it;
3. assessment of the problem's workability and setting of goals;
4. negotiation of a contract with the client;
5. a planned strategy of intervention;
6. evaluation of the process and outcome of the effort.[58]

In the most extensive work on effectiveness of clinical intervention, Fisher
suggests that a set of core conditions including empathy, warmth, and genuineness
are particularly important at the beginning of the helping process. He cautions that
these conditions alone do not make for effective practice. Fisher suggests an eclectic
approach to practice effectiveness.

> The essence of eclectic practice involves technical flexibility; selecting inter-
> ventive procedures on the basis of the specific client/problem/situation con-
> figuration and, to the extent possible, on the basis of evidence of effective-

---

[56] See for example, Gerard E. Hogerty, Essie Goldberg, and N. R. Schooler, "Drug and
Sociotherapy in the Aftercare of Schizophrenic Patients III: Adjustment of Non-Relapsed Pa-
tients," *Archives of General Psychiatry*, 31 (1974), pp. 609-18; Eleanor Clark, "Post-Hospital
Care for Chronically Ill Elderly Patients," *Social Work*, 14, no. 1 (January 1969), pp. 62-7;
Myrna Weissman, Gerald L. Clurman, and B. A. Prusoff, and others, "Treatment Effects on the
Social Adjustment of Depressed Outpatients," *Archives of General Psychiatry*, 30 (1974), pp.
771-78; Barbara Berkman, "Psychosocial Problems and Outcome: An External Validity Study,"
Health and Social Work, 5, no. 3 (August 1980), pp. 5-21; Barbara Berkman and Helen Rehr,
"Social Work Undertakes Its Own Audit," *Social Work in Health Care*, 3, No. 3 (Spring 1978),
pp. 273-86; Barbara Berkman and Eleanor Clark, "Survey Offers Guidelines for Social Work,"
Hospitals, 54 (March 16, 1980), pp. 105-12; and Helen Rehr, ed., *Professional Accountability
for Social Work Practice: A Search for Concepts and Guidelines* (New York: Prodist, 1979).

[57] Epstein, *Helping People*, p. 53.

[58] Katherine M. Wood, "Casework Effectiveness: A New Look at the Research Evidence," *Social Work*, 23, no. 6 (November 1978), pp. 437-59.

ness. This is a highly prescriptive approach to casework practice, individually tailored to client needs with a client-specific prescription for dealing with the problems of each client. But above all, perhaps, eclecticism involves a way of thinking about practice: systematic, data based, cognizant of alternative approaches to dealing with problems and the literature and research on those alternatives, oriented to technical flexibility and to specific and often idiosyncratic client concerns, and all this grounded in humanistic values and the philosophy, traditions and breadth of vision of social work.[59]

Individual, group, family, behavioral, cognitive, crisis, and short-term approaches are among the interventive methods from which one can draw.

THE CLINICAL PROCESS

Social work practice in health care offers a wide range of approaches and techniques. The three most important approaches in health care social work are crisis theory (including situational and transitional crises) short-term treatment, episodic interventions, and long-term treatment (extending beyond a year). Such interventions describe secondary and tertiary prevention levels and do not address primary prevention roles that will be described later in this chapter.

The Process of Care

Following entry into the system, the patient-social worker collaborative team engage in a distinct set of behaviors and interactions. The social worker brings knowledge, values, and skills to a time-phased set of processes. A brief overview follows and is focused on the essential skills required for successful practice.

> *Entry and Assessment Skills* include developing a framework for making assessments and identifying key factors in the presenting situations of the patient/family; screening information in order to focus on problem formulation and resolution; selecting appropriate problems on which to work; assessing problems in relation to level of functioning, patterns of relationships, and strengths, as well as problem areas in the patient and his social system; assessing with whom to work and establishing measurements of success. Assessments must be framed with conceptual clarity and precision, must lead to problem formulation and must state the expected resolution.
> *Collaborative Practice* involves the recognition that while most social workers in health care, while functioning as autonomous professionals, independent from physicians, must develop collaborative skills in order to make a full assessment, as well as to contribute essential information to the health care team.
> *Contracting with the Client* describes the worker's ability to formulate problems and to develop initial and sequential contracts with the patient about identified problems. Time and participation of the patient in contracting, constitute major factors in determining success.

[59] Fisher, *Effective Casework Practice*, pp. 189-218.

Intervention Skills include selection of appropriate interventions to be used for the client at the proper moment and for a suitable period of time. Interventions flow from assessments, i.e., clearly formulated problems, collaborative practices, social contracts and established goals. Workers should be trained to direct interventions toward the social context of the patient, his family, or other social systems. It is the social worker's task to formulate a presenting problem clearly and to design an intervention, in the patient's social situation, to change it accordingly in order to make it resolvable.

Evaluation of Outcomes emphasizes teaching workers to evaluate outcome of treatment in simple terms: the types of intervention used; their appropriateness, the worker's satisfaction with outcome; the client's satisfaction with outcome; the possibility of handling the problem differently, and how that might be done.

Recording Skills include how to record clearly and concisely in the patient's chart the following information: entry and assessment; collaborative efforts; problems formulated, contracts, interventions, and the evaluation of treatment processes; outcomes. Good recording requires conceptual clarity in stating these phases of treatment.[60]

Entry Into the Social Work System of Care

Most health care social workers rely on referrals as the basis of client entry into the social work system of care. As Berkman and Rehr state

When the first medical social work department was established at Massachusetts General Hospital in Boston, Dr. Richard C. Cabot . . . recognized the need to understand more about the patient's social situation as it affected his total medical problem and to help the patient make the wisest use of his own and the community's resources. It was in this context that Dr. Cabot held the social worker to be an expert in his field and urged physicians to see him as a collaborator rather than as a subordinate. Ironically while emphasizing this collaborative relationship between the medical and social work staffs, Dr. Cabot was probably responsible for fostering a patient referral system that subordinated the social service casefinding procedures to the "good will" and decision-making of the physicians. At that time he stated that no attempt should be made to introduce social workers into any medical or surgical ward or any part of the outpatient department unless they were actually asked for by physicians.[61]

A referral is an exchange and a linkage between people and resources.[62] Most studies are of completed agency-to-agency referrals. Referrals are problematic because over 50 percent of the clients never receive the help they requested.[63] When a

[60] Gary Rosenberg, "Continuing Education and the Self-Directed Worker," in *Professional Accountability for Social Work Practice*, pp. 114-5.

[61] Barbara Berkman and Helen Rehr, "Anticipated Consequences of the Casefinding System in Hospital Social Service," *Social Work*, 15, no. 2 (April 1970), p. 63.

[62] Epstein, *Helping People*, p. 152.

[63] Andrew Weissman, *Environmental Intervention Referral Technology* (unpublished doctoral dissertation University of Maryland, School of Social Work and Community Planning, 1979).

referral system is operative in health care, it is necessary for the referrer to be specific about the problem or the patient's potential service need and to prepare the patient for referral. Even though referral systems can increase collaborative practice since physicians and nurses request social work assistance for clients, there are major drawbacks.

> It is evident that by failing to define its own casefinding systems social work relinquishes the right to set its own priorities. Efforts should be made to develop reliable casefinding procedures not dependent on referrals by members of other professions and free from biases within the social work profession so that unbiased doorways to social service can be achieved.[64]

Referrals by other professionals predetermine not only the timing of social work intervention but also often introduce obstacles to be overcome.[65] Social workers based in hospitals have been developing the means to make the services available without waiting for others to perceive social problems or to prescribe social work intervention. Social work utilization of independent screening mechanisms is one solution to the dilemma of late referrals and or misconceptions of patient's and family's social situation. By systematically identifying variables associated with high social risk, social workers should be able to predict which clients are in need. This procedure enables early identification of those patients either prior to or at the time of admission to the institution. Because it offers opportunity for more comprehensive and effective services, early intervention enhances social work's contribution to social health care.[66]

The concept of early identification and appropriate intervention through screening is neither new nor limited to social work. Historically, Jane Addams and others in social work used high social risk screening up to the time of World War I. They found malnourished poor, those suffering from tuberculosis, the mentally ill, and many others who had defined social problems. After the Milford Conference, however, social work adopted a guideline for mental health practice with a strengthening of the emphasis on referral or self-referral. This guideline was based on the prevailing assumption that motivation was a necessary part of the treatment process. Over the last decade, there have been studies of who receive services; how they reached the department of social work; the types of services received; the types, frequency, and time of interventions; and more recently the outcomes as perceived by both social workers and their clients.[67] Professional social workers have had major concerns about their lack of control over the people entering the system of care. This lack often resulted in aborted or pressured work with clients and concomitant frustration for the worker. Professionals outside the social work system of care

[64] Berkman and Rehr, "Anticipated Consequences," p. 68.

[65] Barbara Berkman and Helen Rehr, "The Sick Role Cycle and the Timing of Social Work Intervention," *Social Service Review*, 46, no. 4 (December 1972), pp. 567-80.

[66] Barbara Berkman and Helen Rehr, "Early Social Service Casefinding for Hospitalized Patients: An Experiment," *Social Service Review*, 47, no. 2 (June 1973), pp. 256-65.

[67] Berkman and Rehr, "The Sick Role Cycle," p. 570.

perceive psychosocial needs from their own professional perspective, and may not be familiar with the types of problems dealt with nor the range of services offered by social workers. In addition referral systems tend to lead to selection of those clients with easily visible needs and those who can mainly benefit from specific services. This same referral system fails to refer those patients and family members who could use help with a wide range of psychosocial stresses which accompany illness and hospitalization. Then, too, referrals are made late in the course of the patient's hospitalization and limit the services the patient and family can receive by imposing a time constraint which can adversely influence the outcome of the situation.[68]

Some departments of social work services utilize screening devices as a case-finding mechanism. In either situation, people invited to use social work services may or may not be experiencing stress in some areas of their lives. Services may be proferred to hospital patients screened by social workers or by other staff for special needs. The potential client may be interested, uninterested, or neutral in response to offered social work services.[69] There is a hypothesis on the part of the staff, family, or patient that a problem or resource need exists for the patient who

FIGURE 4-1 HSR Screening Form A

Category I.   Automatic Social Work Assistant Review—high social risk identified as:
_____ 1. Over 70 years, living alone, with eye surgery projected
_____ 2. Institutional transfers into the hospital

Category II.   Social Worker Review—high social risk identified as:
_____ 1. 80-year-old and over
_____ 2. 70-year-old and over, living alone
_____ 3. Emergency admission
         (except appendicitis, hernias, pneumonias)
_____ 4. Severity of illness—life threatening
         (i.e., metastatic or terminal CA and blood dyscrasias, all admissions
         to ND, CICU, Ames, CT, RT)
_____ 5. Severity of illness—physical dysfunctioning
         (i.e., organic and/or mental brain syndrome, encephalopathies;
         syrengo-myelia; CVA and stroke, aphasia, pathological fractures;
         carcinoma of the colon, rectum, pancreas, brain or masses leading
         to "ostomies", any limb surgery leading to amputation due to dia-
         betes, gangrene, circulatory diseases; carcinoma of the throat, vocal
         chord, larynx, tongue, airway obstructions leading to "ectomies";
         rental diseases leading to dialysis and/or transplant; multiple frac-
         tures; eye disorders, i.e., glaucoma, retinal detachment, conditions
         which are sight threatening.)
_____ 6. Chronic Diseases
         (i.e., lupus, Hodgkins, myasthenia gravis, ulcerative colitis, multiple
         sclerosis, cerebral palsy, hemophilia, sickle cell, muscular dystrophy,
         rheumatoid arthritis, liver diseases.)

[68] *Ibid.*, p. 572.
[69] Germain and Gitterman, *The Life Model of Social Work Practice*, p. 35.

is referred to or screened in by casefinding devices. This presumption is tested by the worker in face-to-face contact with the patient, in collaborative contacts with other health care personnel (physicians, nurses, and so on), by reading the patient's chart, or by means of a combination of these sources. Although referral systems continue to dominate in health care institutions, social work's quest for autonomy and for defining its own professional role as well as efforts to improve its services to patients by early intervention have lead to a movement away from referral towards social work's own casefinding.

One hospital has piloted a high social risk screening device which has reliability and validity (see Fig. 4-1).

When using a referral system, protocols are useful in reducing bias and increasing the likelihood that clients who need social work services will actually receive them (see Fig. 4-2).

Entry Skills

Entry skills fall into two classifications: preparatory and exploratory. "Entering into a person's life space and its field of forces requires delicacy, knowledge, compassion, careful planning, and skill."[70] There are two kinds of preparation. The social worker identifies whatever data are available. In screening, this may mean reading the chart. It may also mean talking with physicians and nurses to specify potential problems or to allow the social worker's concerns regarding presumed high social risk. Once the decision to enter the situation occurs, the social worker needs to review what he or she already knows about this patient. Is it a child fearful of the hospital? Is it someone suffering from schizophrenia who has had multiple hospital contacts? What is the meaning of another contact? Is it someone suffering from bipolar illness who is concerned about accepting the use of psychotropic medications? Is it an older person who may need to enter a nursing home? Is it a young person confronted with the possibility of a disabling or life-threatening disease? Thus, the social worker can begin to develop anticipatory empathy.[71] This anticipatory empathy needs to be formulated into tentative hypotheses, as in the following example.

A client, age 44, suffering from kelosis and an ulcerated toe, is approached by the social worker. She hypothesized that her patient has been beset by this serious illness for many years, that it is now in an exacerbated state, and that he is now beginning to experience some of the effects that may well lead to increasing disability. The worker needed to assess the patient's defenses that mashed his rage, fear, and unrealistic anxiety about his and his family's future.

---

[70] *Ibid.*

[71] *Ibid.* See also Fisher, *Effective Casework Practice: An Eclectic Approach* (New York: McGraw-Hill, 1978), p. 193.

FIGURE 4-2 Revised Protocol for Social Work Referral in OBS

The social worker can assist with any social and/or emotional problem presented by the patient/family or observed by the physician, nurse or other staff member. The Social Work Service involvement with the patient/family can be either individual or family treatment, either as short term crisis intervention or long-term counseling; direct assistance re practical concerns; referral to an appropriate community agency or other professional. Home visits for social evaluation or accompanying patient to agencies can be a part of the Social Work Treatment Plan. Assistance to patients may also take the form of consultation with other disciplines (i.e., physician, nurse) in reference to the patient or conferences with other disciplines and the patient. The Social Worker may also conduct ongoing or short-term groups of patients with common concerns when appropriate.

There are certain situations where a referral is always indicated and others where experience has shown that patients generally can use help. In the latter the physician/nurse judgment as to the patient's need for Social Service assistance should be used. The patients should always be advised of the referral to Social Service and the reasons for it. The reasons should be indicated in the medical chart. The team nurse doing the exit interview will then accompany patient to Social Work Service desk.

I. Reasons for Automatic Referral to Social Service
1. Drug abuse and/or methadone maintenance
2. Alcohol abuse
3. Child care problems
4. Patients 16 years old and under
5. Psychiatric consult (social service does screening and follow-up)
6. Request for sterilization (i.e., for discussion of nonmedical ramifications)
7. Adoption or foster care for child
8. Request for abortion
9. Patient request to see social service
10. Suspected child abuse, neglect
11. Battered women

II. Other Suggested Reasons for Referral to Social Service
1. Family problems
2. Marital problems
3. Recent loss of meaningful person
4. Sexual problems
5. Housing
6. Financial
7. Not responsive to medical reassurance
8. Constant physical complaints without medical basis
9. Inability to tolerate medical examination
10. Inability to follow medical direction
11. Emotional distress, i.e., depression, anxiety
12. Stillbirth or baby born with problems
13. Problems with pregnancy, i.e., death in utero, threatened abortion
14. Past history of repeated induced or spontaneous abortions

In developing anticipatory empathy, the worker draws upon the knowledge base of social work and identifies what the worker believes the patient may be thinking and feeling. The social worker also draws upon knowledge of other patients who have experienced similar difficulties and acknowledges the worker's own feelings with regard to people in this situation. An important preparation factor is the social worker's degree of comfort in having an offer of services accepted or turned down. In addition, the worker must consider what to do if the patient needs care but does not see a need at this time.[72]

When a patient is referred, the social worker should endeavor to obtain a specific reason for the referral. It is essential that the social worker identify the specific problems noted by the referring agent and discuss this information with the patient. If it is a self-referral, the social worker needs to be readily able to discuss why the patient thinks help is needed and what is the problem or resource need.

Exploratory skills are based on the aforementioned preparatory skills but are generally conducted by in-person interview with the patient and or family and collaborative contact with other health care staff. The purpose of the exploratory phase of the entry process is to ascertain what problems the patient has; how important they are; how the patient perceives them; in what systems they occur; whether the problems as currently conceptualized are resolvable through the problem-solving skills of the worker-patient relationship; and the available resources. If not, it is the responsibility of the worker to reframe the problems in a way that is more acceptable to the client so as to lead to a more positive resolution.[73]

If the client has sought service, the worker initially "establishes a welcoming climate of courtesy, support, acceptance, and communicates his interest and respect verbally and nonverbally."[74] The worker notes what concerns brought the client to seek help. He or she pays attention to the cognitive set in terms of how the client presents this problem, the affective mood, and the systems in which the behavior which typifies the problem exist. It is important to develop a mutual assessment of the problems. Issues of onset, duration, intensity, previous coping behaviors, and other avenues from which the patient has sought help are investigated.

When workers indicate contact they must define the reasons that they are entering and offering service and also clearly define the purpose of such contact and exploration. As Germain and Gitterman point out, "Exploration or the concern of an inquiring mind, together with the caring heart, marks the skilled and effective practitioner."[75] Exploration is a process that continues through the life of the case, with humility and recognition that one can never fully know another human being. However, it is crucial to arrive at accurate problem definition and that is the purpose of the initial exploration. It is important to define the problem as early as possible although premature problem definition and incorrect problem definition should be guarded against. Golan suggests that some workers are quite accurate, particularly in crisis interventions, in identifying problems but may "miss entirely the clues that other more lasting disruptions are taking place currently in life." She suggests that it is important to put crisis and services into two sets of mental maps:

[72] See Germain and Gitterman, *The Life Model of Social Work Practice*; Epstein, *Helping People*; and Fisher, *Effective Casework Practice*.

[73] Jay Haley, *Problem Solving Therapy* (San Francisco: Jossey Bass, 1976).

[74] Germain and Gitterman, *The Life Model of Social Work Practice*, p. 46.

[75] *Ibid.*

1. A thorough understanding of the age-stage phases and core issues involved in the maturational processes that individuals and families pass through in the course of their life cycles;
2. Cognizance of the sequences of both material-arrangemental and psycho-social tasks that must be dealt with during the period of disruptions.[76]

Accurate definition of problems also include the ecological set within which the problem of the patient takes place. Gitterman and Germain suggest that exploration, relevant salience, and individuation are the three major ways of looking at the ecological perspective and problem definition.[77] Clearly defined problems are the result of exploration and can be reduced to three or four basic issues.

Assessments

Although the assessment phase can begin as early as preentry, it is a continuing and ongoing part of social work. *Assessment* refers to all those activities involved in the selection of information or data for clinical practice, the actual data collection process, and the interpretation of these data in the early stages of intervention. Assessment is the procedure by which the clinician identifies and empirically characterizes the presenting problems and their related situational and social and/or psychological factors and the goals of interventions. Its aim is to help the client and clinician determine the target problems for intervention and delineate intervention goals.[78] Pincus and Minahan identify five factors that enter into problem assessment (1) identifying and stating the problem; (2) analyzing the dynamics of the social situation; (3) establishing goals and targets; (4) determining tasks and strategies; and (5) stabilizing the change effort.[79] Data for assessment may come from collateral sources such as physicians or nurses; from the patients through direct interviewing; from interviews with significant others in the patient's life; from personality or other research type inventories; from observations; and from supervision. The key outcome of the assessment phase is to clearly identify problems that need to be framed out in such a way that they can become resolved.

Early on, Bartlett identified a need for a problem classification system that would allow social workers to conceptualize problems and to measure the outcome of problem resolution.[80] Although numerous problem classification systems exist, Berkman and Rehr have validated their problem classification which they originally developed as a system applicable to elderly patients. This classification has been revised and applied to hospitalized patients regardless of age, physical disease, disorder,

[76] Naomi Golan, "Using Situational Crises to Ease Transitions in the Life Cycle," *American Journal of Orthopsychiatry*, 50, no. 3 (July 1980), p. 549.

[77] Germain and Gitterman, *The Life Model of Social Work Practice*, p. 52.

[78] Srinika Jayaratne and Rona L. Levy, *Empirical Clinical Practice* (New York: Columbia University Press, 1979), pp. 46-77.

[79] Pincus and Minahan, *Social Work Practice*, pp. 101-16.

[80] Bartlett, *Social Work Practice in the Health Field*, p. 135.

or disability.[81] It has then been tested in six hospitals across the U.S.[82] and with 4,000 cases in the New England region alone.[83] Although some conceptual problems remain, it is a usable system that can be modified to include prevalent problems within the client population served by the particular health care organization. The problem system is precise enough to differentiate among problems and general enough to be useful in client validation of social work contracts and assessments of outcome. Figure 4-3 is an example of this system. Major parts of the assessment phase include allowing the patient and or family to present their problem in such a way as to understand its beginning, intensity duration, their perception and experience, and what efforts they have made at resolution.

Assessment in mental health agencies has traditionally mirrored procedures in family service agencies. It has usually consisted of a presenting problem and a dynamic, genetic formulation focusing on the personality of the person and the social situation. In large measure, it has been based on the ideology of mental illness. Such lengthy assessments contribute to the inability to focus on specific problem resolution and create vague goals for the treatment process in social work. The social worker needs to gather as much relevant information as possible to understand the problem. He then must frame the problem so that it is resolvable and or should provide the resources necessary to resolve the problem. Problem resolution does not necessarily require a total understanding of the patient and his situation. By concentrating on the 4Rs of assessment, one gains specificity with regard to problem resolutions:

1. Assessing the patient's social roles—how they are affected by illness and what roles need to be maintained and strengthened as well as which will require adaptive behaviors on the part of the patient/family;
2. Assessing the patient's interpersonal relationships, sources of problems and potential support and solutions to the problems and resource needs;
3. Assessing the patient/family emotional reactions to the problems;
4. Assessing the patient/family available resources which can be involved for problem resolution.[84]

Collaborative Practice

Collaborative practice is a major dynamic of clinical practice in health care. This section will discuss the narrow application of collaborative practice to the

[81] Helen Rehr and Barbara Berkman "Patient Care Evaluations: Social Work Prerequisites and Current Approaches," *Professional Accountability for Social Work Practice*, ed. Helen Rehr (New York: Prodist, 1979), p. 110.

[82] Barbara Berkman, "Innovations for Social Services in Health Care," *Changing Roles in Social Work Practice*, ed. Francine Sobey (Philadelphia: Temple University Press, 1977), pp. 92-121.

[83] Barbara Berkman and Eleanor Clark, *Hospitals*, March 16, 1980, pp. 105-12.

[84] Bertha Doremus, "The Four R's: Social Diagnosis in Health Care," *Health and Social Work*, 1, no. 4 (November 1976), pp. 120-39.

Problem/Outcome on Closing

Patient's Name _____
(insert)

Worker's Name _____
(insert)

Unit Number [ ][ ][ ][ ][ ][ ][ ]
1 2 3 4 5 6 7

Worker's Number [ ][ ][ ]
(last 3 digits)
8 9 10

Service Location [ ]
11

Date (today) _____
(insert)

A. Medical, B. Obstetrics, C. Pediatrics, D. Psychiatry, E. Surgery, F. Adoles. Health Center,
G. Ambulatory Care, H. Other _____
(specify)

Instructions: Number the psychosocial "contracts" that you and the client *have dealt with* in order of their importance, e.g., 1, 2, 3, etc. to the left of the applicable listed problems. Then, for each problem (contract) you enter, tell what happened by circling *one and only one* Outcome in Part I (A, B, C or D), and circle *one and only one* factor in Part II, Resource Status (E, F, G, H, I, or J).

OUTCOME

I — Problem Status

II — Outside Resource Referral Source

	Resolved	Improved (but not resolved)	Situation Unchanged	Situation Worsened	Resource Not Needed	Adequate Resource Obtained	Inadequate Resource Obtained	No Resource Available	Patient and/or Family Refuses Resource	Resource No Longer Needed–Patient Died
__12 Concrete aids medically recommended (telephone, appliances, prosthesis, equipment, etc).	A	B	C	D	E	F	G	H	I	J
__13 Coping with grief reaction and bereavement.	A	B	C	D	E	F	G	H	I	J
__14 Coping with interpersonal relations (e.g. marital problems; school problems; care of children).	A	B	C	D	E	F	G	H	I	J
__15 Educational or vocational functioning problems.	A	B	C	D	E	F	G	H	I	J
__16 Family interrelationships adversely affect patient's condition and/or response to hospital.	A	B	C	D	E	F	G	H	I	J
__17 Family members need help in coping with patient's needs.	A	B	C	D	E	F	G	H	I	J
__18 Financial management/assistance/applications	A	B	C	D	E	F	G	H	I	J
__19 Health education needed (e.g. family planning)	A	B	C	D	E	F	G	H	I	J
__20 Home health supports needed (coordinated home care program).	A	B	C	D	E	F	G	H	I	J
__21 Home supports needed (eg: homemaker, homehealth aide, baby-sitter, day care).	A	B	C	D	E	F	G	H	I	J
__22 Hospital service complaints.	A	B	C	D	E	F	G	H	I	J
__23 Housing unsuitable for continuing needs (e.g. too many stairs, inadequate kitchen, security).	A	B	C	D	E	F	G	H	I	J
__24 Legal services needed.	A	B	C	D	E	F	G	H	I	J
__25 Letters or reports needed for other agencies.	A	B	C	D	E	F	G	H	I	J
__26 Long term ambulatory care needed (e.g. psychiatric OPD services; other social agencies; day hospital).	A	B	C	D	E	F	G	H	I	J
__27 Long term institutional care needed.	A	B	C	D	E	F	G	H	I	J
__28 Patient/family having role disorder problems as result of illness/disorder/pregnancy	A	B	C	D	E	F	G	H	I	J
__29 Patient/family problems with staff	A	B	C	D	E	F	G	H	I	J
__30 Patient/family anxiety stress or depressive reactions related to diagnosis, medical procedures, prognosis or treatment, dying, etc.	A	B	C	D	E	F	G	H	I	J
__31 Patient/family anxiety stress or depression (eg. thought and mood disturbance/psychomatization)	A	B	C	D	E	F	G	H	I	J
__32 Patient has problems in self-esteem; feelings of inadequacy; or in sexual functioning.	A	B	C	D	E	F	G	H	I	J
__33 Permanent placement required for child(ren) eg. adoption, foster home)	A	B	C	D	E	F	G	H	I	J
__34 Psychosocial evaluation only for assessment of ability to use treatment, or re, admission to hospital.	A	B	C	D	E	F	G	H	I	J
__35 Sheltered care needed (e.g. halfway house; foster home for adults).	A	B	C	D	E	F	G	H	I	J
__36 Social isolation/withdrawal	A	B	C	D	E	F	G	H	I	J
__37 Temporary care of dependent child(ren) during patient's hospitalization.	A	B	C	D	E	F	G	H	I	J
__38 Temporary institutional care away from home.	A	B	C	D	E	F	G	H	I	J
__39 Transportation services needed.	A	B	C	D	E	F	G	H	I	J
__40 Visiting nurses service needed.	A	B	C	D	E	F	G	H	I	J
__41 Other (write in).	A	B	C	D	E	F	G	H	I	J

150

clinical situation while Chapter Five describes the essential components of collaborative practice in broader perspective. The model of collaboration utilized in health care, reflects the cognitive stance of the organization with respect to non-physician roles.

In some organizations, there is a recognition that health care is controlled by physicians. Yet, each professional is seen as practicing independently within a collaborative framework and the fulcrum of such collaboration is the patient and or family. Each professional and nonprofessional contributes to the level of expertise based on a shared understanding of the problems to be addressed. In collaborative relationships, the autonomy of social work to enter biopsychosocial situations is not compromised by the physician. It is incumbent on the social worker, however, not only to let the physician know the worker has entered the case but also to obtain from the physician and from other health care professionals information relevant to identified problems, obstacles to resolution, and plans for resolution. Social work education has *not* provided for a significant biological knowledge base. It is only through the collaborative network with physicians and others that the biopsychosocial approach for social work is enacted.

Teamwork is another model of collaboration that has developed in the mental health field. Panzeta offers us two views of teamwork.[85] One view suggests that all mental health professionals are basically interchangeable with slight edges on expertise in particular areas. The other model suggests (and is more similar to the collaborative health care model), that many professionals, paraprofessionals, and nonprofessionals must work together in order to deal with the complexity of problem or illness situations. The assets and liabilities of each of these models affect the autonomy of social work practice as well as the roles that social work can perform in the particular service delivery system. Although conflict is an inherent part of either model, the automatic self-directed worker is more comfortable in the collaborative team than in the hierarchical team. From an historical standpoint, many social workers in mental health value the role of psychotherapist.

Although psychiatrists are more comfortable now with the notion that social workers practice psychotherapy, the problems of social workers in relation to psychiatrists remain unresolved. Some important psychiatrists continue to view social work as an adjunctive therapy, practiced only under medical supervision. Unfortunately, many social workers subscribe to such a point of view. What is clear, nonetheless, is that social workers need to be able to make a differential diagnosis with respect to the influence of biological factors in illness and in presenting symptomatology; they frequently need physician input in a collaborative framework to supply biological data.

Whatever the model of collaboration used, the key factors are attention to the patient and or family problems, concerns, and service needs. Conflict naturally

[85] Anthony F. Panzetta, *Community Mental Health: Myth and Reality* (Philadelphia: Lea & Febiger, 1971), pp. 43-61.

occurs among professionals working together and can be utilized to achieve patient and or family problem resolution.[86]

Contracts

Contracts have been identified in numerous studies as predictors of treatment success in social work practice. Contracting is an explicit agreement between worker and client on the work they are presently engaged in and their expectations of themselves and each other.[87] A contract is also defined as "the explicit agreement between the worker and the client concerning the target problems, goals and the strategies interventions and the roles and tasks of the participants".[88] Starting where the client is, letting the client know where you are, and where you are going, are important parts of contracting. The literature describes contracting as a dynamic, developing process.[89] A number of phases have been identified: (1) exploration or negotiation; (2) preliminary contract phase; (3) preliminary work or agreement, that is, mutual understanding of goals and procedures of the process, the development of secondary contract; and (4) the termination phase.

Different kinds of contracts are used in social work treatment. There are implicit and explicit contracts consisting of verbal and written contracts created by or edited by the client. Written contracts have a clear advantage in accountability, in that people can check out whether or not actions were agreed to and which actions were taken. One study reports that clients like the specificity of written contracts.[90] In some areas, contracts have not been proven to be useful, such as with involuntary clients or where the practitioner is acting as an agent of social control. Resistant clients may not be able to use contracts, neither may clients who do not specifically state what they mean when they make verbal agreements. Woods' research suggests that negotiations of contracts are one of the major components of quality practice.[91] Epstein suggests eight basic elements that should be included in the contract:

---

[86] Lowe and Herranen, "Conflict in Teamwork," pp. 323-330. See also Helen Rehr, ed., *Medicine and Social Work: An Exploration in Interprofessionalism* (New York: Prodist, 1974), and Rosalie A. Kane, "The Interprofessional Team as a Small Group," *Social Work in Health Care*, 1, no. 1 (Fall 1975), pp. 19-32. For an excellent article on enhancing relationships between physician and patient see Sandra Blatterbauer, Mary-Jo Kupst, and Jerome L. Shulman, "Enhancing the Relationship between Physician and Patient," *Health in Social Work*, 1, no. 1 (February 1976), 45-57.

[87] Sonia Rhodes, "Contract Negotiation and the Initial Stage of Casework Service," *Social Service Review*, 51, no. 1 (March 1977), pp. 124-40.

[88] Anthony N. Maluccio and Wilma Marlow, "The Case for the Contract," *Social Work*, 19, no. 1 (January 1974), pp. 28-36.

[89] See for example, Zane P. Nelson and Dwight P. Mowry, "Contracting in Crisis Intervention," *Community Mental Health Journal*, 12, no. 1 (1976), pp. 37-44; Richard S. Dies and Sue Henry, "The Therapeutic Contract in Work with Groups: A Formal Analysis," *Social Service Review*, 50, no. 4 (December 1976), pp. 611-22; James Strain, *Clinical Social Work: The Theory and Practice* (New York: Free Press, 1978), pp. 58-75; and Brett A. Seabury, "The Contract: Uses and Abuses of Limitations," *Social Work*, 21, no. 1. (January 1976), pp. 16-21.

[90] Maluccio and Marlow, *The Case for the Contract*.

[91] Katherine M. Wood, "Casework Effectiveness," pp. 437-59.

1. Specify the priority target problems (maximum 3);
2. State the specific client goals accepted by the practitioner;
3. State the client's general tasks;
4. State the practitioner's general tasks;
5. State the duration of intervention sequence, the calendar time to be used or the time limits;
6. State the schedules for interviews, dates, plans and location of the interviews;
7. State the expected schedule for intervention, their sequence and timing;
8. State the parties who are to participate in the intervention, names and relations to primary client.[92]

Contract Skills

Contracting skills require the ability to conceptualize a problem in resolvable terms. To create a contract the problem needs to be stated in terms understandable to and agreed upon by the client, and which can be moved towards resolution.

> Mrs. A.'s physical condition makes it impossible for her to continue to manage alone the upkeep of her apartment. The contract would be first to consider the alternatives and subsequently to help her achieve the one she selects.
>
> Mrs. B. is having a severe emotional reaction to learning about her husband's diagnosis but wishes to care for him at home. The contract would be to help her cope with her reaction to enable her to do so.
>
> A third example is that the X.s are being threatened with a court order of separation because of child abuse. The contract would be to help with identification of the precipitating factors, so that they may then work on changing the pattern.

These are all examples of how contracts and problems are interrelated. Research based practice requires an explicit statement of a problem and the ability to measure its outcome. Once that agreement is reached, tasks are assigned both to the worker and the client. There are two broad types of task conceptualizations: general tasks and operational tasks.[93] General tasks state the direction of an action but do not spell out exactly what is to be done. For example, Mr. X. needs to maintain living arrangements near the day hospital. Mrs. X. needs to find alternative care arrangements.

Operational tasks state the specific action the client is to undertake and are generally subtasks of a general task. For example, Mrs. A. needs to fill out a Medicaid form. Mr. A. needs to provide information to the worker so that the worker may fill out a form for referral to a nursing home.

Tasks for the client have both a general purpose and a general action. The purpose is to devise and organize actions to reduce the problem. The basic actions

[92] Epstein, *Helping People*, pp. 205-6.
[93] Reid and Epstein, *Task-Centered Casework*, and Epstein, *Helping People*.

come from exploring alternatives and contracting (that is, agreeing with the client on what tasks need to be performed, specifying the tasks for implementation, and summarizing the tasks).

Practitioner tasks emanating from the contract are "supplements to client actions for the purpose of facilitating the client's work." Epstein conceptualizes practitioner tasks as negotiating actions with agency and community officials, transferring resources such as services and or good will from the organization to the client, packaging or designing these resources, and establishing sequence and time limits.[94]

Sequencing is an essential element in contracting. Problems flow one from the other and client and worker can rank them with respect to which needs to be resolved first. At the same time one must fully recognize that many problems are interrelated and will affect each other. The issues of who to address in the intervention sequence also emanates from contracting skill. Is the problem to be addressed by interviews with individuals, with the family, with family therapy, with peers, through negotiating resources, or through group treatment approaches?

Contracting in mental health is exemplified by goal attainment scaling. Generally, goal attainment scaling has been used for long-term mental health problems. It has been adopted extensively in both short- and long-term mental health problems and is being used currently for social work health care quality assurance. Goal attainment scaling is a useful device which teaches problem formulation, contracting, and charting movement towards problem resolution.[95]

It is important to underscore that in contracting, the social worker approaches the client with empathy, warmth, and genuineness.[96] Accurate empathy is crucial in helping the client to define a problem, to accept the definition of the problem, and to work towards resolution. Whether interventions are directed towards cognitions, affects, or behaviors, accurate empathy will assist the social worker in contracting with the client and in moving the client toward problem resolution. It is a crucial part of a contracting skill as well as a more general component of the treatment process.

Interventions

Interventions are based on an assessment and definition of problems or resource needs in the client system, collaboration with key health care professionals involved in providing services, a contract with the client regarding the problems to be resolved, and specific tasks for each participant in the problem-solving process. Thus, interventions begin with the first face-to-face contact with the client system.

---

[94] Epstein, *Helping People*, p. 266.

[95] Thomas Kiresuk and Robert Sherman, "Goal Attainment Scaling: A General Method for Evaluating Comprehensive Community Mental Health Programs," *Community Mental Health Journal*, 5, no. 6 (1968), pp. 443-53, and Thomas Kiresuk and Robert Sherman, "Goal Attainment Scaling," *Evaluation*, special monograph, no. 1 (1973), pp. 12-18.

[96] See R. R. Carkhuff and R. Berenson, *Beyond Counseling and Therapy*, 2nd ed. (New York: Holt, Rinehart & Winston, 1977), and Fisher, *Effective Casework Practice*, pp. 189-218.

The goal of this first encounter is to set a structure for problem definition and resolution. Once this is accomplished interventions are directed towards final resolution
and may include more refined definitions of existing problems and the identifica-
tions of new problems relevant to the health status of the client.

Interventions are directed towards change in the client and or family system:
in affects, cognitions, obtaining resources, developmental issues, preparatory activities, and strengthening coping and adaptive behaviors.

Intervention involves three dimensions: (1) formulating an intervention strategy; (2) selecting specific intervention procedures; and (3) developing a method for
evaluating the impact of the program.[97]

Formulating an Intervention Strategy

The first decision to be made, with regard to intervention, is the size of the
action system. The social worker needs to decide whether to work on a one-to-one,
one-to-group, family-oriented treatment, or environmental resource provision. The
social worker chooses the primary interventive direction, taking into account (at
least cognitively) all systems. One can work with an individual fully aware of his
resource needs as well as his family needs. Fisher suggests three categories with respect to formulating an intervention strategy that include: (1) increasing desired
behaviors that are already a part of the client's system; (2) decreasing undesirable
behaviors; and (3) changing cognitive patterns.[98] We would add (1) setting tasks for
the client and worker; (2) dealing with affects which serve as obstacles to further
growth and development; (3) obtaining needed resource through a referral or other
mechanisms; and (4) creatively selecting combinations of the aforementioned to
move the clients towards achieving contracts and goals.

Selected Specific Intervention Procedures

Interventions in health care settings are influenced by the amount of autonomy granted to the social worker, the social worker's theoretical perspective, the
patient's problems (whether biopsychosocial or resource and environmental), the
range of worker techniques, the time frame for problem resolution, the amount of
stress and press experienced by the client, and the health care available with respect
to the identified problems. Thus, there are a variety of ways to resolve problems as
well as many theoretical systems and sets of techniques. The intervention of the social worker depends on his own creativity, knowledge, and ability to apply a set of
techniques acceptable to the client and effective in resolving the problems faced by
the client. All interventions with the client system will have more or less of the following prescriptions:

1. Providing opportunities for action and decision-making to confront the passivity inherent in the role of patient;

[97]Fisher, *Effective Casework Practice*, p. 261.
[98]*Ibid.*, p. 262.

2. Helping staff and the patient to reward the patient's coping efforts and support their sense of dignity;

3. Respect for the patient's life-style, culture values and social relationships, even when it confronts the dominance of organizational norms and patient care;

4. Assisting in providing necessary information on which successful coping often depends.[99]

Significant others in the patient's life space should be involved in the treatment process on an as-needed basis. It is the patient's right to determine who should be involved in the problem-solving effort, though this in no way detracts from the social worker's decision as to the context of treatment (individual, family, group, or resource utilization). The nature of the problem will affect the interventive scheme. An acute-crisis situation, a transitional situation, or a chronic illness will differentially affect the problem-solving system. A very useful notion for social workers is one borrowed from environmental medicine. It is called *clinical latency*. The concept can be explained by analogy. Frequently, patients and families cope well with problems of a chronic nature but the continuation of a problem over a period of time has a deleterious affect. As an analogy, the more one is exposed to even low doses of asbestos—a toxic substance, the more likely it is that difficulty will develop. Clinical latency should be kept in mind when intervening into problem situations which seem to have no precipitant and which in the past have been coped with rather well.

The following is a set of guidelines regarding interventions which can be applied equally well in health and mental health settings but need to be modified based on problem-client system and social worker sanction. These are drawn from the literature and from practice with respect to the conduct of problem resolution:

1. Avoid minimizing problems;

2. Attempt to avoid abstractions. Focusing on specific behaviors rather than larger issues is usually helpful;

3. Avoid being in coalitions with the health care team, the physician, or anyone in the family;

4. Avoid general philosophical debates;

5. Minimize past events by focusing on the present;

6. Avoid crystallizing power struggles—multiple helping persons can make the situation more difficult to change;

7. Avoid irreversible positions.[100]

In the treatment process, tasks should be assigned to the client and or client's family. Patient and social worker tasks should be explicitly understood by the work-

[99] Germain, "An Ecological Perspective on Social Work Practice," pp. 69-74.

[100] Jay Haley, *Problem Solving Therapy*. Reed and Epstein, *Task-Centered Casework*. Abraham Lurie and Gary Rosenberg, ed., *Social Work in Mental Health: A 25 Year Perspective* (New York: Long Island Jewish Medical Center, 1977).

er and the patient. Therapy is seen in this model as a source of influence. This type of influence has been termed by Haley as giving directives. Haley suggests that the purposes of directives is to get people to behave differently and to have different subjective experiences.[101] Directives are used to intensify the relationship with the social worker and to gather information. Directives include the entire repertoire of social worker behaviors, both verbal and nonverbal. When social workers smile or nod their head in an encouraging way or ask the patient to tell them more about the situation, they are also issuing directives. Haley offers two special types of directives: (1) telling people what to do when the social worker wants them to follow his instructions; and (2) telling people what to do when the social worker does not want his instructions followed and the worker wants them to change by rebelling.[102] The latter is a difficult type of intervention for social workers to pursue. It is considered manipulative and should only be used when the first type of directive fails. As an example,

---

A woman who had a laryngectomy and was angry for months continued to be incontinent though every sign suggested that she was capable of controlling her urinary and bowel functions. The nursing staff and physicians on the unit were furious with her. No amount of assistance seemed to help the woman change her behavior, vent her fury, or deal effectively with the anger she was feeling with regard to her situation. Whatever empathy existed slowly fell by the wayside. The social worker presented a plan to the team which called for giving a paradoxical directive to the patient. Team cooperation was necessary in order for this plan to work. The social worker told the patient that she thought that it was very good that the patient not control her bowel or urinary functions. She implied that this was an excellent way for her to express her anger and encouraged the patient to try and increase the number of times she asked the nurses to change her bedding. The patient did not respond to the social worker's intervention and for the first week she continued her incontinence. The social worker continued to praise the patient for her behavior. By the second week, the patient began to decrease this behavior. The social worker did not comment but continued to encourage the patient to increase her incontinence. By the third week, the patient was no longer displaying this behavior. The social worker expressed her concern to the patient that now that this behavior was gone how else would the patient vent her hostility, anger and rage with regard to her illness. Through the use of a pad and pencil the patient began to send notes to staff expressing these feelings directly.

This paradoxical intervention not only caused a change in the behavior but allowed the patient to then take the nurturance from the staff. The staff was willing to nurture the patient as long as her unacceptable behavior decreased.

[101] Haley, *Problem Solving Therapy*. p. 258.
[102] *Ibid*., p. 259.

When negotiating a task with clients or giving a directive, the social worker should be as precise as possible. Reinforcement for tasks should be given by the worker. If a task is not done, the social worker should try and encourage the patient and or family to do the tasks they originally agreed to, stressing the benefit to the patient. Patients need to be held accountable for task accomplishment. If the therapist does not value the tasks and states this clearly to the patient, it is less likely that the patient will perform.

Another technique used by social workers in health care settings is the use of metaphor, that is, talking about something in action that resembles the problem of the patient. For example,

A woman who was professionally competent and also competent in her personal life found it impossible to deal effectively with the staff and the structure of the hospital when she was given a diagnosis of cancer. The social worker spoke with the patient about her previous ability to deal with and motivate people in business. The therapist made the point that the techniques and skills that she had effectively used in business and personal life might help her cope better with hospital staff. Without ever defining that specifically as a resolution of the problem, the patient understood the metaphor on some level and began to apply what she knew to the situation of being in the hospital.

An additional key area of social work skill is in using communication as a device for problem resolution and change. Haley divides communication into digital and analogic modes.[103] Digital communication consists of that class of messages where each statement has a specific referent and only that referent, that is, one stimulus-one response. When a message has multiple references, it is analogic and it relates one thing to another. In the intervention phase, it is crucial for the social worker to understand how the patient is communicating (digitally or analogically), and to make sure that the social worker uses digital or analogic communication where appropriate.

Another important aspect of communication is the notion of sequence and hierarchy.[104] Sequence is the order in which things occur. A sequence can be altered, leading to change in the client or client system. For example,

A patient calls the nurse and begins to complain about the quality of care at the hospital, thus setting a negative interactional field. The patient then makes a request that the nurse either reluctantly grants or is too busy to grant. The social worker noting the sequence suggests to the patient that the request might precede the complaint and that the complaint and request should be

[103] Haley, *Problem Solving Therapy*. p. 260.

[104] *Ibid.*, p. 261; and Salvador Minuchen, *Families and Family Therapy* (Massachusetts: Harvard University Press, 1974).

separated into two interactions. The patient learns that making a request without coupling it with a negative comment, leads to a more effective response from the staff. Thus, the patient's needs are met.

An understanding of hierarchy is best viewed through the family. For example, in a family consisting of two parents, two children, and four grandparents, there are eight people who can make 56 triangular combinations. Each person can be involved in 21 triangles setting hierarchies.[105] Grandparents are hierarchical as compared to parents, parents as compared to children. This notion is best applied in hospital organization to staff and patients. For example,

A president of a large corporation may be used to a kind of top hierarchical relationship with others in his business life within the health care system. Someone perceived to have lower class standing may have more power than the corporate president in his patient role.

Thus, hierarchy and understanding of hierarchy can help the patient and social worker resolve problems together, particularly problems regarding reactions to the system of health care.

The Family and Illness

In the case of psychiatric illness, families were seen as a key interacting variable. Lewis suggests a direct relationship with the competence of the family and the severity of individual psychopathology.[106] Genetic factors, temperamental or developmental traumas can play crucial roles in the development of psychiatric disorders in family members. Family interactional variables may also be involved in the selection of a patient. Irrespective of the genesis of psychiatric illness and the effect of the family, the family is particularly useful in the treatment of psychiatric disability. The role of concurrent family interactions should be observed and utilized but only as part of a total assessment and treatment of illness and problem-related behaviors. Families with psychiatric disability range widely on the levels of family competency. Single-parent families and families of different ethnic and cultural belief systems require special understanding and consideration.[107]

[105] Haley, *Problem-Solving Therapy*, p. 261.

[106] Jerry M. Lewis, "The Family Matrix in Health and Disease," ed. Charles K. Hoffling and Jerry M. Lewis, *The Family: Evaluation and Treatment* (New York: Bruner Mazel, 1980), pp. 5-38.

[107] Joseph Giordano, "Community Mental Health," *International Journal of Mental Health* 5, no. 2 (Summer 1976), p. 13.

The Family and Physical Illness

With an integrated biopsychosocial model, psychosomatic research has become more concerned with the susceptibility of individuals to illness rather than the earlier and narrower search for specific psychosocial variables associated with specific illness.[108] Many social workers view the family as the unit of illness. Minuchin, describes an open system model of psychosomatic illness in children and reports exceptional results with family treatment, particularly with children with diabetes, asthma, and anorexia nervosa.[109] Family therapy is the suitable treatment of choice in situations where the presenting problem appears in systems terms, that is, marital conflicts, sibling rivalry, intergenerational conflicts, and disturbances. In addition, difficulties with developmental transitions in the family also are amenable to family therapy.[110] The social worker can help the spouse of a chronically ill person by sharing and understanding the spouse's feelings. The social worker helps the family member to release anguish, grief, fear, pity, sadness, or resentment; encourages and clarifies communication in the family; assists in planning the patient's care; and helps the spouse maintain a healthy balance between serving the patient and looking after his or her own needs.[111]

Group Services

Groups are an important, yet sometimes underutilized modality for the effective care and treatment of patients in health care settings. Gitterman states

> The formed group provides members an opportunity to experience, contribute and evolve a mutual aid system in which people share relevant concerns and ideas and begin to experience others in the same boat moving through the rocky waters of life. As they confide, share and move into taboo areas, they feel less singled out and their concerns and problems become less unique, less unusual and often less pathological. By its very nature, the group mutual aid system universalized people problems, reducing isolation and stigma.[112]

He goes on to state that this process unleashes the group's inherent potential for multiplicity of helping relationships with all members. The group is an area in which members' problems in social and interpersonal responses are repeated; adaptive and maladaptive perceptions and responses can be examined; new responses rehearsed and experimented with; and feedback on subsequent events received.[113] The

[108] Minuchin, *Families and Family Therapy.*

[109] *Ibid.*

[110] Joan K. Parry and Arthur K. Young, "The Family as a System in Hospital-Based Social Work," *Health and Social Work*, 3, no. 2 (May 1978), pp. 55-64.

[111] Susan Farkas, "Impact of Chronic Illness on the Patient's Spouse," *Health and Social Work*, 5, no. 4 (November 1980), pp. 39-46.

[112] Alex Gitterman, "Development of Group Services," in *Social Work with Groups in Maternal and Child Health*, Conference Proceedings, New York: Columbia University, June 14 and June 15, 1979, pp. 15-21.

[113] *Ibid.*

group, thus, is a dual focused entity. It helps people to gain comfort from being to-gether from the collaborative constraints and power of the mutual bonds and al-liances; it assists the individual in coping and mastering both interpersonal and environmental difficulties. Gitterman suggests that groups can be organized around life's transitional stresses, crisis events, environmental stresses, and interpersonal stresses.[114] Lonnergan has reported on research where medical patients participated in group meetings which identified the following coping mechanisms supported by group services: (1) hope; (2) fight for life, that is, the will to live; (3) increasing in-terpersonal skills; (4) denial, such as, absorbing the trauma in small doses and pro-tecting self-esteem; (5) narcissistic defenses; (6) faith in religion or other powerful external forces; and (7) existential resolve.[115] Groups form support networks par-ticularly for people whose families are unable to provide such support groups. As Lonnergan suggests a small group can remind both patients and staff that they are all human.[116] Adaptative and coping mechanisms need to be recognized and en-couraged. Group intervention is one vehicle that can help further communication between patients and staff and help patients draw their own strengths to support themselves and one another. Groups can offset the destructive consequences of the dehumanization of health care settings.

Termination

Termination of the helping process between the worker and patient may oc-cur either because of a mutual decision that the work is finished through task ac-complishment and problem resolution, or through the nature of the setting—dis-charge from the hospital or other environmental or personal reasons. Discharge planning has been a crucial role and function of social work in health care both in the health and mental health subdivisions. Lindenberg and Coulton point out that a substantial number of patients discharged from hospitals do not have their needs met.[117] Although many services are recognized and planned at discharge, the pa-tient does not always receive them on his return home. An unacceptable number prove inadequate. Whether based in the hospital or community, there is no doubt that social workers must exercise greater responsibility to assure that posthospital plans are carried out. The termination phase should include exploring feelings about ending, recapitulating accomplishments, and identifying what has yet to be achieved. One metaphor for termination is separation. Clients tend to use all defense mech-anisms with regard to separating events, ranging from denial or sadness to exhilira-tion. Epstein cogently suggests

---

[114] Elaine Cooper Lonergan, "Humanizing the Hospital Experience: Report on a Group Program for Medical Patients," *Health and Social Work*, 5, no. 4 (November 1980), pp. 53-63.

[115] Elaine J. Cooper, "Beginning a Group Program in a General Hospital," *Group*, July 1976, pp. 6-9.

[116] Lonergan, "Humanizing the Hospital Experience," pp. 53-63.

[117] Ruth Ellen Lindenberg and Claudia Coulton, "Planning for Post-Hospital Care: A Followup Study," *Health and Social Work*, 5, no. 1 (February 1980), p. 48.

Practitioners tend to overestimate the value they have as persons for a client's well-being. The rewards of termination to clients are great: more money in the pocket (if the client is paying a fee), more time, more independence. A practitioner may provoke unhappiness in a client about termination if the practitioner has overvalued the relationship and if the excess valuation has been communicated to the client by word and deed.[118]

EVALUATION

Social work practice evaluation takes place through mechanisms such as single-subject design, peer review, audits, and through special research studies. Blatterbauer, Kupts, and Shulman describe a well-designed study in which medical information without personal intervention was essentially meaningless and confusing to families.[119] Social workers were effective in educating families to cope with the realities of health care systems and to become more active in physician-patient relationship. This is an excellent example of the special study with regard to specific problem-focus practice. At the very least, the practitioner should have clearly defined goals and some way of arriving at those goals. Systematic consumer evaluation is an excellent method for measuring contracting and outcome in social work practice, particularly in health care. (See Chapters Five and Six.) It is our belief that the social worker should not seek long-term involvement but rather brief intensive problem-focused interventions and rapid sensitive disengagements.

The Effects of Settings on Practice

The effects of organization and structure on practice have been described in different parts of this chapter as well as in Chapter Five. However, practice is modified and practice roles are different, depending on the purposes and functions of organizational units. Within the scope of this chapter, we cannot attempt to cover all or most practice settings. Nonetheless, a number of practice settings will be described, particularly those we believe to be innovative and harbingers of future practice organization in order to illustrate their effects on practice roles and functions of the social worker.

Primary Care

The social worker as a member of the primary health care team is affected by the purposes of primary health care. As Weiner so perceptively stated, primary health care has the quality of a social movement similar to the community mental health movement of the 1960s.[120] Its purposes are to give services to the underserved, to encourage students to practice family medicine, to contribute to cost containment,

[118] Epstein, *Helping People*, p. 257.

[119] Blatterbauer and others, "Enhancing the Relationship."

[120] Hyman J. Weiner, "Social Work Role and Function in Primary Care," Society of Hospital Social Work Directors, Denver, Audiotape, 1980.

to treat the total person or family, to contribute to a more egalitarian team effort in the delivery of care, and to change the relationships between physicians and hospitals. The principles of primary care include first contact care, responsibility for a person not an illness, longitudinal and on-going responsibility assuring easy access to the system, helping the person negotiate the health care system, coordinating care, and comprehensive care.[121] In primary health care, social workers serve the functions of intake, liaison, and referral[122] and fill the role of mental health officer.[123] Goldberg and Neal in their classic book, *Social Work in General Practice*, describe a five-year project, jointly undertaken by the Health Group Practice team and the National Institute for Social Work Training, which combined general practice and social work.[124] Their findings included the fact that social work services were more successful if the need for them was initiated by medical staff. (This is not so in all studies.) Another finding revealed that waiting lists were virtually nonexistent; social workers and physicians saw five to ten cases an hour. Other significant project results showed that patients most uncooperative in their medical treatment had the most severe psychosocial pathology and were in greatest need of social work help; elderly patients were the major case load of the social worker and twice as many women as men were referred to social work; middle and upper class persons found psychiatric help from a social worker in a general practice held less stigma than in a mental health facility; lower social class persons found social work services more acceptable in the medical practice; social work methods did not vary according to social class; emphasis was on short-term treatment lasting not more than three months, 80 percent of the patients had fewer than ten interviews.[125]

Another issue for social workers in primary health care is the base for their funding. Some examples are income from fees for service, grants, support costs and cost saving on physician time, and so on. Nason and Del Banco point out that social workers serving on a team consisting of physician, nurse, social worker, health assistant, and secretary contribute to the psychosocial diagnosis and treatment of individuals and families.[126] The team approach has proven effective and less expensive than medical treatment only, which would have treated recurring physical symptoms with an emotional base. Phillips has pointed out that the social worker in a family medicine center was seen as competent to handle a comprehensive range of problems.[127] Wolfe and Teed found the doctors, with no psychiatric training, use social

[121] *Ibid.*

[122] Joan Brockstein, George Adams, Michael Trestam, and Charles Cheney, "Social Work and Primary Care: An Integrative Approach," *Social Work in Health Care*, 5, no. 1 (Fall 1979), pp. 71-81.

[123] Jules Coleman and Donald Patrick, "Integrating Mental Health Services into Primary Medical Care," *Medical Care*, 14, no. 8 (August 1976), pp. 654-61.

[124] Matilda Goldberg and June Neal, *Social Work in General Practice* (London: George Allen and Unwin, 1972).

[125] *Ibid.*

[126] Frances Nason and Thomas Del Banco, "Soft Services: A Major Cost-Effective Component of Primary Medical Care," *Social Work in Health Care*, 1, no. 3 (Spring 1976), pp. 297-309.

[127] William Phillips, "Attitudes Towards Social Work and Family Medicine: A Before and After Survey," *Social Work in Health Care*, 3, no. 1 (Fall 1977), pp. 61-66.

work services less than those with some psychiatric training.[128] Social workers became more involved and interested in patients than some doctors did. In collaboration with community resources, they avoided duplication of services.

Social Work in the Private Office of the Physician

A more prevalent form of practice today is the social worker joining the private office practice of a physician. The social worker is supported by fees for service, by grants, or by sharing in the physician's income pool basis as part of a practice scheme.[129] Barkin describes a private practice in an Ohio medical clinic where she had been invited to join this team by physicians who saw a need for social work services. Although anecdotal, the findings of her paper include improved overall patient care and increased likelihood that patients would accept and follow through on physician referrals.[130] Korpella describes the use of social workers to provide group and family counseling in a private pediatric service. She suggests that only the most difficult and obvious problems were referred by the physicians. She particularly explains how group treatment was effective with pediatric populations.[131] Goldberg describes the use of social work students in the private office of family physicians.[132] Social workers were effective in collaborative skills with physicians and nurses, in providing appropriate referrals and helping patients accept social work services.

Social Work in the HMO

HMOs are becoming a more frequent employer of social work services. Bell and Gorman's article on social work in an HMO suggests a new social work specialty in health care—the sociomedical specialists.[133] It clearly resembles social work practice in health and mental health and demonstrates that same inherent difficulty of interprofessional collaboration as seen in other settings. Other models described by Coleman and others suggest that the primary care physicians in HMOs need to col-

[128] Samuel Wolfe and Genevieve Teed, 'A Study of the Work of a Medical Social Worker in a Group Medical Practice," *Canadian Medical Association Journal*, 96 (May 27, 1967), pp. 1407-16.

[129] Barbara S. Brockway, Judith Werking, Cathleen Fitzgibbons, and William Butterfield, "Social Work in a Doctor's Office," in *Social Work in Practice*, selected paper, 4th NASW Professional Symposium, eds. Bernard Ross and S. K. Kainduka (Washington, D.C.: National Association of Social Workers, 1976).

[130] Teresa Barkin, "Private Casework Practice in a Medical Clinic," *Social Work*, 18, no. 4 (July 1973), pp. 5-9.

[131] J. Korpela, "Social Work Assistants in Private Pediatric Practice," *Social Casework*, 54, no. 9 (November 1973), pp. 537-44.

[132] Irving Goldberg, Goldie Kranz, and Ben Lock, "Effects of a Short-Term Outpatient Psychiatric Therapy Benefit on the Utilization of Medical Services in a Prepaid Group Practice Medical Program," *Medical Care*, 8, no. 5 (September/October 1970), pp. 419-28.

[133] Cynthia Bell and Laurel Gorman, "The HMO's: New Models for Practice," *Social Work in Health Care*, 1, no. 3 (Spring 1976), pp. 325-36.

laborate daily with the social workers.[134] With such daily collaboration, patient care improves and referrals become more appropriate. HMO settings offer the opportunity for primary prevention activities and for health education efforts.

Social Work in Mental Health Settings

Ewalt identifies the roles of social work in mental health settings as preventive in nature.[135] Interventions are directed towards improving the quality of life by enhancing or maintaining interactions between people and environment. She suggests that social work practice in mental health can be both brief as well as long term and needs to be adaptive to suit ethnic, racial, and class differences.[136] Berg suggests that social workers need to provide consultation to community caretakers; to provide mental health information to the public; and to help other community-based programs developmental health resources.[137] Within the mental health framework, social workers have been active in helping to form natural support groups, special interest groups and in advocating for services that prevent disability and family breakdown.

Other Innovative Settings

Home care referrals to social workers are usually done by nurses and physical therapists. One article by Axelrod reported that even after such preparation by nurses and physical therapists, patients would not allow social workers into their homes. Social workers had to be creative with their own outreach efforts.[138]

Social work has also been involved in dentistry services by improving references to dental care through aid in emotional and social components in dental practice and education.[139] Significantly, in the future more and more social work will be community based as opposed to hospital based. Long-term care settings for medical and psychiatric patients are the major areas where social workers are now employed.[140]

[134] Jules Colman, Donald Patrick, Jeff Eagle, and Jarred Hermalin, "Collaboration Consultation and Referral in an Integrated Health Program in an HMO," *Social Work in Health Care*, 5, no. 1 (Fall 1979), pp. 83-98.

[135] Patricia Ewalt, "Clinical Social Work in Community Mental Health Programs," *Community Mental Health Issues for Social Work Practice and Education*, ed. Arthur J. Katz, New York Council on Social Work Education, pp. 28-41.

[136] *Ibid.*

[137] Lawrence Berg, "Coordination of Services: The Interdisciplinary Team and Social Work Practice in Community Mental Health," *Community Mental Health Issues for Social Work Practice and Education*, ed. Arthur J. Katz (New York: Council on Social Work Education, 1979) pp. 1-15.

[138] Terry Axelrod, "Innovative Roles for Social Workers in Home Care Programs," *Health and Social Work*, 3, no. 3 (August 1978), pp. 48-66.

[139] Roslyn Soble and Harris Chaiklin, "Social Work in Preventive Dentistry," *Social Work*, 20, no. 2 (March 1975), pp. 142-53.

[140] Robert L. Kane and Rosalie Kane, "Long Term Care: Can Our Society Meet the Needs of Its Elderly," *Annual Review of Public Health* (1980), pp. 227-53.

CONCLUSIONS

In developing the values, knowledge base, and practice roles of social work in health care, this chapter has taken a somewhat narrow view of these roles by focusing primarily on clinical social work practice. Advocacy, social planning, social development, and community organization are all key parts of enhancing delivery systems as is planning and management. Because of the need to emphasize the clinical roles of social work, these factors have been left out. They are, however, a part of other chapters in this book. Many studies illustrate the effectiveness of social work and the fact that social workers are essential professionals in the health care system. A consumer of health care summarizes those issues that the social worker must address in practice:

> The psychology of the seriously ill puts barriers between us and those who had the skill and grace to minister to us. There was first of all the feeling of helplessness—a serious disease in itself.
>
> There was the subconscious fear of never being able to function normally again—and it produced a wall of separation between us and the world of open movement, open sounds, open expectations.
>
> There was the reluctance to be thought a complainer.
>
> There was the desire not to add to the already great burden of apprehension felt by one's family; this added to the isolation.
>
> There was the conflict between the terror of loneliness and the desire to be left alone.
>
> There was the lack of self-esteem, the subconscious feeling perhaps that our illness was a manifestation of our inadequacy.
>
> There was the fear that decisions were being made behind our backs, that not everything was made known that we wanted to know, yet dreaded knowing.
>
> There was the morbid fear of intrusive technology, fear of being metabolized by a data base, never to regain our faces again. There was resentment of strangers who came at us with needles and vials—some of which put supposedly magic substances in our veins, and others which took more of our blood than we thought we could afford to lose. There was the distress of being wheeled through white corridors to laboratories for all sorts of strange encounters with compact machines and blinking lights and whirling discs.
>
> And there was the utter void created by the longing—ineradicable, unremitting, pervasive—for warmth of human contact. A warm smile and an outstretched hand were valued even above the offerings of modern science, but the latter were far more accessible than the former.
>
> I became convinced that nothing a hospital could provide in the way of technological marvels was as helpful as an atmosphere of compassion. Also, continuity of personnel. Well-to-do patients are generally in a position to protect themselves against a long procession of different faces; they can hire medical attendants according to any standards they may wish to apply. But for most people, the facts of hospital life involve discontinuity, fractioned care, and inadequate protection against surprise. People come and go; you make your adjustments as best you can.[141]

[141] Norman Cousins, *Anatomy of an Illness* (New York: W. W. Norton & Co., Inc., 1979), pp. 153-154.

The social worker in clinical practice in health care focuses on problem definition and resolution. The practice field includes the purposeful use of interaction, process, content, cognitions, affects, and the retaining of resources as areas utilized by the social worker in problem resolution. The social worker communicates through structure metaphor looking for themes and patterns to be used for problem resolution. The social worker provides for caring in the curing environment of health care as providing problem solving. Meyer identifies four principles of clinical practice that sum up the effort of the work:

1. To serve as many people as quickly and parsimoniously as possible;
2. To view individuals in their natural life situation as part of a transactional field of person-in-environment;
3. To provide for reestablishment of psychosocial balance rather than for "long term" therapeutic efforts at "cure";
4. To intervene directly to strengthen individual coping mechanisms and to reinforce social supports.[142]

Further research to correct and improve practice and innovation in practice is necessary to continue the future quality of the social work contribution to health care services. The social work practitioner specializing in health care can enter the field with a sense of pride in the past accomplishments of their colleagues and can make in the future substantial contributions to the patients and to enhancing a caring environment in health care settings.

APPENDIX: CLINICAL VIGNETTES[143]

The Case of Mrs. R.
Reframing a Problem—The Patient and Staff

Mrs. R., 48 years old, white, Jewish, married, mother of one child, and bearing a history of chronic paranoid schizophrenia with multiple psychiatric hospitalizations had been admitted to a general surgical service for repair of bleeding hemorrhoids. Diagnostic tests had been completed for this "routine" procedure when Mrs. R. unexpectedly refused a final pre-op blood test and became loudly and verbally abusive to nurses and house staff. Mrs. R.'s resident physician reacted angrily and discharged her on the basis of noncompliance and the nonemergency nature of her illness, just as the social worker arrived on the floor. Yet, three weeks later, Mrs. R. was readmitted by mutual choice to the same service to undergo surgery successfully.

This change did not happen magically! Rather, Mrs. R. offers a nice example of the delicate balance between meeting patient and staff system needs. Borrowing the technique of positive reframing from the field of family therapy enabled the

---

[142] Carol Meyer, *Social Work Practice* (New York: Free Press, 1976), p. 199.

[143] The following material has been contributed by Susan Rubenstein, Ruth Brown, Goldie Mulak, Susan Raber, Joyce Lasko, and Leslie Holland.

worker to accomplish this task. Positive reframing attempts to place a symptom or behavior in a different light, connoting it positively. Thus, it changes the cognitive and perceptual view of the symptom.

To Mrs. R., whose habitual tendency had been to view the world as hostile, the prospect of surgery with its aggressive, painful, and visible effects seemed unacceptable at first. For a person with little sense of control, losing more control risked going out of control. It can easily be forgotten just how much patient status alone implies heightened dependencies. For surgical patients undergoing general anesthesia implies total dependency. The first effort, therefore, was to learn from Mrs. R. what her primary concerns were. It was assumed that she wished for treatment whether or not she could presently tolerate the stress of receiving it (an attitude that immediately and helpfully separated the social worker from other staff and permitted the engagement of Mrs. R.). Though at first she regarded the worker with skepticism, the social part of the service won out! She agreed to talk and identified her physical pain, her mistrust of physicians and other strangers in the hospital network, the long delays in completing a diagnostic work-up, her loneliness for husband, son, home, and her clearly articulated fantasies (even convictions) of death or mutilation if surgery proceeded under general anesthesia. Most of all was her repetitive worry that she had failed to be a "good" patient as evidenced by her discharge. It was from her own perception that the worker molded her main intervention. Her "failure" to comply could be reframed; perhaps she and staff could both benefit. By the end of the first discussion (interrupted by her husband who thereafter participated in her treatment), it was agreed to try for a series of meetings over the next few weeks. These appointments would include, at times, a liaison psychiatrist attached to the service, her attending surgeon, resident surgeon, anesthesiologist, and various persons in the preadmission and admission offices who proved most cooperative re: room and floor assignment as well as date and length of readmission. These meetings allowed Mrs. R. to receive psychotropic medication under psychiatric guidance in order to diminish her anxiety, and to review again the surgical procedure planned and the type of anesthesia to be used. These issues were now discussed in a clinic setting, and, therefore, were much less threatening. It was arranged for her to be readmitted to the floor best known to her and for a deliberate less-than-usual time, that is, 48 hours.

In work with staff, the social worker helped nurses and doctors to depersonalize Mrs. R.'s earlier attacks and to understand her behavior as defensive and a regression (particularly her low frustration tolerance and mistrust of strangers). Seen in this way, Mrs. R.'s first admission and "failure" to comply was newly and usefully reframed to staff and Mrs. R. as a "rehearsal." Second admissions, routinely endorsed on a pediatric service, are less acceptable (although occasionally as necessary) for those persons who are chronologically older.

The interventions outlined were chosen primarily for the following reasons: as a more neutral staff member, the social worker's agenda for Mrs. R. differed from both the nurse's and physician's. Mrs. R.'s submission to authority was not required, only her alliance in gaining good care. The thrust was, therefore, chiefly towards heightening her self-esteen, self-control, and autonomy. Knowledge of the mechanisms of defense permitted explaining Mrs. R.'s initially belligerent and aggressive behavior as a mask for much deeper fears to staff less familiar with such a perspective.

Finally, Mrs. R. illustrates the point that there is no such thing as a "routine" surgical procedure since each patient anticipates in a unique manner based on his personality and character structure, prior experience, and a host of other internal and external variables. There are also real limitations to the expenditure of time and energy involved in helping a Mrs. R. through a surgical experience. For each success story we ought not forget the very real number of patients who are either lost to care or whose silence (unlike Mrs. R.'s roar) is mistaken for trust, but they may be hurting just the same.

The Case of Mrs. P.
The Threat of Dependency

This illustration centers on a patient who could not leave the hospital, who remained helpless and dependent and who saw legitimate and reasonable demands to participate in a rehabilitation program as a threat and a rejection. How to motivate and mobilize such a patient became the challenge.

Working on an inpatient orthopedic service includes working with arthritic patients coming into the hospital for replacement of diseased joints. Some have been wheelchair-bound for lengthy periods. Seeing these patients walk out of the hospital is exciting and gratifying for every staff member involved with them. However, before this goal is accomplished, the patient may experience some initial resistance to incorporating the gains made possible by surgery. Emotional adjustments to the necessity of having to rely on other people had been made, but are now threatened. A conscious desire for self-sufficiency may be undermined by deepseated fears of abandonment. The patient seeks to protect his psychological equilibrium. In the following illustration this conflict was paralyzing.

Mrs. P., 66 years old, suffering from rheumatoid arthritis, entered the hospital for elective surgery, to have arthritic hips replaced, in hopes of leaving the wheelchair to which she had been confined for over a year. She was severely deformed.

The social worker's attention was first drawn to her shortly after admission by nurses who experienced her as excessively demanding. The worker found her to be guarded and angry, making intervention very difficult. Because she would not permit family contact, assessment had to be limited.

Following surgery, she was completely uncooperative with the physical therapy program, a necessary follow-up to surgery. After subjecting herself to so much surgery, she remained as immobilized as when she had entered the hospital. She simply insisted that she could not walk. The doctors stated that this was medically inconsistent. Hospitals days went by without benefit to the patient.

Finally, the doctor suggested discharge; she became furious, feeling that the doctor had fooled and betrayed her. "He said I would walk out of here!" The worker, whom she associated with the doctor's plan to discharge her, became the focus of her anger as well. Mrs. P. seemed to expect that the change would come from outside, without the necessary effort on her part to bring it about. In attempting to understand Mrs. P., the worker considered the information Mrs. P. had given about herself. She had been widowed at an early age and raised a child alone. She had worked as a legal secretary, drove some distance daily from her home to her place of employment, and continued to do so after the onset of crippling arthritis. She capitulated finally when she could no longer walk. She had had to leave her home and live with her son and his family. Her history suggested a woman strongly defended against her dependency needs, as well as a rigid personality that had not allowed her to adjust to her altered condition. The ensuing frustration and anger as expressed in her interpersonal relationships resulted eventually in her leaving her son's home feeling unwanted and rejected. She had vowed never to return. She impressed the worker as an alienating and isolated woman. Part of her resistance to change was founded in fears of a new independent role, and the tasks this entailed. Another was the gratification she derived from being in a setting that legitimized the dependency needs she had repressed for so long. The success of the surgery would permit her to return to her own home and manage with part-time housekeeping assistance. But how to help her accept these changes, considering the strength of her resistance?

She had by then used a large portion of her insurance-covered days, a fact that she avoided knowing. Under ordinary circumstances, she was a financially responsible person. Seeing an appeal to her sense of reality as a means of mobilizing her, the worker asked whether she was aware of the limitations of her hospital insurance coverage, and advised her, after confirming this with the accounting department, that she had only 10 fully covered days left. Telling her this risked stirring up anxiety and exacerbating the anger. She was furious, "Nobody ever told me that Medicare was limited." Then, panic—"I can't walk—what will happen to me?" Finally, resolution—"I can't leave here like this." In the ensuing 10 days, Mrs. P. proceeded to work with diligence and determination, each day reporting the increasing number of steps she was able to take. As she regained control of her body, she felt more confident in regaining control of her life. Her anger diminished and was replaced by satisfaction in accomplishment which she shared with all the hospital staff working with her.

In order to help Mrs. P., the worker had to avoid her immobilizing conflict around independence, which cause her to deny reality and to address the better functioning portion of her personality by underlining a small portion of that reality. The threat to her that this signaled stirred up appropriate anxiety and stimulated necessary action. Eventually she was able to take 60 steps, which she demonstrated in a triumphal march towards the elevator on the day of discharge.

The Case of Mrs. X.
A Family Perspective

Mrs. A., a 72-year-old Puerto Rican widow, who was transferred from a medical service as an inpatient in the hospital to the Adult Psychiatric Service for the treatment of depression. She remained in the hospital for a five-week period. This vignette illustrates the use of family treatment as a method for dealing with some of the family and social issues within the context of the patient's illness.

Mrs. X. had been living alone since the death of her husband two years ago. She had been gradually spending most of her time alone in her apartment, making fewer visits to her two adult children as she felt they had their own children and families with which to deal. In addition, the previous spring her daughter had had back surgery and recuperated at home for a two-month period. During that time, when Mrs. X. spoke to her daughter on the phone, she began to feel herself a "burden" on her family and spoke less of her own concerns. After initial assessment, the social worker insisted on meeting with her and the two adult children. It was discovered that she was unable to tell them what her problem was, that it was not physical isolation that had been a source for her depression, but her isolation from the active grandmother role she had formerly had. Her daughter had since recuperated fully from her illness. This assessment disagreed with the doctor's point of view in that he felt Mrs. X. should not live alone and should be placed in an institutional setting. During the family meetings, the worker supported both the patient's reluctance to involve her children and the children's frustration at having felt that the patient did not want their help. They were held to express these concerns and to discuss ideas and plans for having the patient more involved in the care of her grandchildren. In addition, suggestions of resources within the patient's neighborhood, such as a local senior citizens center and volunteer job, were used to enable the patient to continue to stay independent in her own home with her children encouraging the patient's use of this plan. In time, the doctor changed his point of view about placement, and he agreed with the plans for discharge. The clinical thinking in this situation indicated the need for the family to enable the patient to feel she could be dependent on her children for emotional support without giving up her physical independence.

Mrs. X. now sees her children regularly and is also tutoring schoolchildren in her neighborhood once a week.

The Case of Mrs. B.
An Eclectic Approach

Mrs. B., a 68-year-old widow, lived alone in a run-down, rented apartment in lower Manhattan. She was admitted with a diagnosis of senile dementia, agitated and severely confused. A younger sister, living in upper Manhattan, had already looked after the patient, for many years doing the shopping, cooking, and checking in on her three to four times a week. This was difficult for the sister who was living with and was the primary caretaker to a third sister who was brain-damaged and confined to a wheelchair since birth. The patient's mental status progressively deteriorated and she was admitted for a neurological work-up.

Her mental condition did not improve, which meant that upon discharge from the hospital, the patient would require 24-hour supervision for her own safety. Her sister felt very guilty because she felt unable to care for both patient and the other sister in her home. Much of the worker's interactions with the sister were focused on relieving this guilt and helping her to look more objectively at the aftercare needs of the patient. Her feelings of upset with this complicated problem were acknowledged and validated. She took comfort in knowing someone was available to help her and her sister. The worker confirmed the reality of the tremendous difficulty for her in caring for two invalids, that she could not care for both sisters, and that the total family would disintegrate under this stress. Given the patient's need for constant supervision, after her acute needs were met, the discharge plan was for Mrs. B. to receive her care in a skilled nursing facility.

Her sister was helped to deal with ambivalent feelings about placing patient in SNF. She was relieved on the one hand and guilty on the other knowing that she could not take the patient home and feeling at the same time that she was somehow abandoning or rejecting Mrs. B. The worker helped her to see that the patient's needs would be met in a SNF, and given the family circumstances, placement was a very appropriate plan. She could visit the patient there just as she did in the hospital; the patient was not being abandoned.

The wait for a nursing home bed was prolonged (10 months) because of patient's coverage (no Medicaid, no savings) and her mental status; she was agitated, verbally abusive, and physically assaultive. This behavior was at first troublesome for staff. Even though agitated and assaultive behavior was recognized generally as part of Mrs. B.'s illness, the staff benefited from the social worker's interventions, which focused on reminding them not to personalize Mrs. B.'s attacks, emphasizing that the patient was out of control, acknowledging their normal responses of anger, frustration, and fear in dealing with "a difficult patient." Staff grew to be fond of her, responded in a more consistent way, that is, even-handedly, not becoming angry, not answering kind-in-kind. This attitude increased Mrs. B.'s feelings of safety and decreased her agitation.

Finally, patient was accepted at a small facility. The day after transfer the administrator telephoned, very distraught with patient's "unruly behavior." She was entering residents' rooms and exploring their drawers, going to the nurses' station and emptying all the medical charts onto the floor, and yelling and hollering. There followed a discussion of "the transfer trauma effect," exacerbation of symptoms, and increased disorientation associated with environmental change and/or new caretakers. The administrator's upset was somewhat assuaged. In an effort to enhance their staff's acceptance and or understanding of the patient during this transition, the worker asked the nurses to contact the hospital staff and share their perceptions and ways of managing the patient. The patient is still there, receiving the care she needs. The sister visits regularly.

The intervention and or approaches used in this case included careful family assessment, individual assessment and casework with the patient's sister, collaborative efforts with the hospital staff to enhance their coping with the patient's condition and in so doing provide milieu therapy to the patient, collaborative efforts with the facility's staff to enhance their understanding of the patient, and facilitating communication between caretakers for continuity of care. Input into the patient's discharge plan provided the social work staff with a sense of continuity and satisfaction. All of these interventions were required in addition to meeting the regulatory requirement of sending every 10 days a revised DMS-1 reflecting her nursing care needs to several long-term care facilities. Though the worker met regularly with Mrs. B., her mental condition precluded direct work with her.

The Terminally Ill Patient

Elizabeth Kubler-Ross has written extensively about working with the terminally ill patient. Her construction of the stages through which the dying patient moves—denial, anger, bargaining, depression, and acceptance—can be a useful guideline to those of us who work with the terminally ill. However, in practice, each patient is an individual and his or her particular death takes place within a context which influences the process of coming to terms with his or her mortality. In this case the patient's illness took place within the context of two separate hospitalizations with concomitant changes of staff, introduction into the complicated clinic system of the hospital, with the necessity of dealing with different physicians, differing medical opinions concerning the best course of treatment, and financial problems. The entire process involved a period of three months. The essential work in this case was twofold: (1) to engage the patient and his wife in the process of coping with terminal illness, and (2) to help them maneuver a complicated medical system so that it would be responsive to their needs. In helping them maneuver the system, they were engaged in a process whereby they both became trusting and responsive to subsequent interventions.

When the worker first met the patient, he was in the process of undergoing tests to confirm that he had lung cancer; the extent of the tumor and subsequent course of treatment was still to be determined. He was 64 years old, married, living in a town an hour's drive from the hospital, and he had income from a Social Security pension and part-time employment. He would not be eligible for Medicare coverage for eight months (when he became 65), and through his employment had limited insurance coverage for outpatient physician visits and treatment.

In the initial assessment, the patient was friendly, seemingly open, but not really so. He was in the phrase of David Reisman "other-directed"; he needed to be liked. Compliance would never be an issue with this patient. He used denial and avoidance as primary coping mechanisms and would continue to do so. There was evident underlying tension which was discharged by use of humor. He was a patient who might briefly touch on deep feelings, for example, guilt about his previous lifestyle as causing his current illness, and then quickly move to another topic when the worker tried to explore the feeling with him. The worker's job was to listen and to encourage his deepest expressions when patient permitted this. This patient, contrary to Kubler-Ross's construction, moved from the stage of denial to that of depression, often within a single session. Only once, when he was in intense pain did he ever "bargain," when he said he hoped the cancer would be contained if not cured.

His wife, on the other hand, was more self-aware, soft-spoken but questioning. She was able, as the relationship progressed, to discuss her deepest fears concerning his impending death, her hopes that he would not suffer, and that treatment would not prolong his suffering. Initially, under the shock of the diagnosis and prognosis, she had lost her sense of her own strength and sensitivity as to how best to support her husband. She asked in panic whether, and if so how, should she tell her husband his diagnosis. Assessing that she was capable of making her own decision, the worker discussed alternatives, helped her articulate her feelings, and questioned their previous relationship that she said had been open and forthright. This resulted in her being able to make her own decision, which not only enhanced her sense of mastery, but made her feel useful, not helpless, in the face of events (his illness) beyond her control. She decided that he must know his diagnosis and that she would like to be present when their physician told him and it was subsequently so arranged. Her husband was able to depend on her; the worker became her ally in the process. The cancer proved inoperable; thus, radiotherapy treatment was offered, 20 treatments, which if done as an inpatient would have required another month of hospitalization. Given his limited expected life span, it was important for them both that he go home and be treated on an outpatient basis. However, their limited insurance coverage presented a problem. With the consent of their physician, the worker helped him register as a clinic patient at a reduced fee, which was economically possible for them. He was also sent to the oncology clinic to discuss the efficacy of chemotherapy. Mrs. D. had real questions about the proposed treatment that the worker helped her formulate for the physicians. On the basis of "an informed choice" they decided to try chemotherapy. However, the patient's pain soon became so intense that he was sent to the neurology clinic in an effort to locate the source. It could not be determined without another hospital admission. This meant adjusting to a new staff and another physician. In each clinic and during each admission, the social worker individualized this patient and his wife to the staff concerning their needs, anxieties, and their wishes concerning treatment. This saved them that particular stress and sense of dislocation when they were trying to cope with the stress of terminal illness and, thereby, conserved their energies. Thus, social work with them and interventions were mutually interactive. It was important to negotiate the system for them, allowed them to experience a sense of safety instead of being overwhelmed by the complexity of the system. This, in turn, allowed them to spend their remaining time together in a mutually supportive way with as much open communication as in their previous relationship. The new situations and financial problems, which made up the context of this particular patient's terminal illness, were somewhat ameliorated by the worker's presence, rather than the overwhelming experience they might have had.

After the patient's death, the worker spoke with his wife several times and at length by telephone as she struggled with her grief and bereavement. It was agreed to do it by phone because she lived so far away and did not feel able to make the trip to the hospital. Also, it is often too painful for families to return to the hospital. She managed well with the support of family and friends. Several months later, she wrote a lovely letter expressing her gratitude for the assistance provided to them both in the last months of her husband's life.

The Case of Mrs. E.
Work With the Aging

Social work intervention with Mrs. E. illustrates use of reminiscence as a therapeutic agent to prepare patient and daughter for nursing home placement.

Mrs. E., a compliant frightened, depressed widow who appeared strikingly older than her 67 years was admitted to the hospital with arthritis and a bladder inflammation. She was seen initially for assessment due to high social risk factors related to her severe functional limitations and social isolation. It appeared that nursing home placement would be indicated. The patient emerged as a lonely, vulnerable woman, who, within the two years prior to admission, had undergone physical decline that seriously compromised her independent functioning. As her own health began to fail, she had had to secure nursing home placement for her mother, from whom she had never been able to separate, and for whom she had cared. However, she had coped with her loss through daily visits to her mother, until several months prior to admission, when she became homebound. Mrs. E. had one daughter with whom relations were strained, largely because of the daughter's feelings of guilt over not being able to care for her mother. The patient had been left completely dependent upon a part-time homemaker who she had experienced as being neglectful. Mrs. E. had learned not to assert herself for fear of rejection and retaliation from significant others. She requested placement in the same nursing home as her mother in order to assure her safety and to preserve this tie.

Loss of purpose and esteem, decline in function, disengagement from the environment, and a diminishing sense of identity represent major life crises which the elderly person seeks to resolve in order to emerge with a sense of ego integration and integrity. Reminiscing, the act through which personally significant factors shape the process of reconstructing the past, serves positive intrapsychic and intrafamilial functions toward crisis resolution. After a period of empathic outreach with the daughter, reminiscence of a more functional past, through dialogue between patient and daughter, stimulated through the use of family photographs, was employed as a therapeutic technique during this three-week hospitalization. Patient and daughter were encouraged to share recollections of patient's adaptive premorbid functioning in order to preserve the patient's sense of personal significance, esteem, and control over her destiny. This, in turn, helped to allay the daughter's guilt and perception of her mother as fragile and helpless. The social worker helped to reinforce the reality of the patient's independent decision to seek placement for herself. Mrs. E.'s recollection of the process of caring for and institutionalizing her own mother normalized the daughter's crisis, helped to bridge the intergenerational gap, and represented a step towards the resolution of the daughter's anticipatory grief. Finally, selective recollection of events intimately related to the patient, helped to reintegrate her personality, pulled her life into a healthier perspective, and prepared both for her eventual placement.

REFERENCES

ADAMS, J. & LINDEMAN, E. Coping with long-term disability. In G. Coelho, D. Hamburg, & J. Adams (Ed.) *Coping and adaptation*. New York: Basic Books, 1974.
AXELROD, TERRY. Innovative roles for social workers in home care programs. *Health and Social Work*, August 1978, *3* (3).
BARKIN, TERESA. Private casework practice in a medical clinic. *Social Work*, July 1973, *18* (4).

BARTLETT, HARRIET M. *Social work practice in the health field.* Washington, D.C.: National Association of Social Workers, 1961.

BELL, CYNTHIA & GORMAN, LAUREL. The HMO's: New models for practice. *Social Work in Health Care*, Spring 1976, *1* (3).

BELLOCH, N. B. & BRESLOW, L. The relation of physical health status and health practice. *Preventive Medicine*, August 1972, *1*.

BERG, LAWRENCE. Coordination of services: The interdisciplinary team and social practice in community mental health. In Arthur J. Katz (Ed.) *Community Mental Health Issues for Social Work Practice and Education.* New York: Council on Social Work Education, 1979.

BERGMAN, ANN. Emergency room: A role for social workers. *Health and Social Work*, February 1976, *1* (1).

BERKMAN, BARBARA. Psychosocial problems and outcome: An external validity study. *Health and Social Work*, August 1980, *5* (3).

BERKMAN, BARBARA. Innovations for social services in health care. In Francine Sobey (Ed.) *Changing Roles in Social Work Practice.* Philadelphia: Temple University Press, 1977.

BERKMAN, BARBARA & CLARK, ELEANOR. Survey offers guidelines for social work hospitals. *Hospitals*, March 16, 1980, *54*.

BERKMAN, BARBARA & REHR, HELEN. Anticipated consequences of the case-finding system in hospital social service. *Social Work*, April 1970, *15* (2).

BERKMAN, BARBARA & REHR, HELEN. Early social service casefinding for hospitalized patients: An experiment. *Social Service Review*, June 1973, *47* (2).

BERKMAN, BARBARA & REHR, HELEN. Social work undertakes its own audit. *Social Work in Health Care*, Spring 1978, *3*.

BERKMAN, BARBARA & REHR, HELEN. The sick role cycle and the timing of social work intervention. *Social Service Review*, December 1972, *46* (4).

BERNSTEIN, SAUL (Ed). *Explorations in group work.* Boston: School of Social Work of Boston University, 1965.

BLATTERBAUER, SANDRA, KUPST, MARY-JO, & SHULMAN, JEROME L. Enhancing the relationship between physician and patient. *Social Work in Health Care*, February 1976, *1* (1).

BRACHT, NEIL. Health care: Issues and trends. In Neil Bracht (Ed.) *Social work in health care: A guide to professional practice.* New York: Haworth Press, 1978.

BROCKSTEIN, JOAN, ADAMS, GEORGE; TRESTAM, MICHAEL, & CHENEY, CHARLES. Social work and primary care: An integrative approach. *Social Work in Health Care*, Fall 1979, *5* (1).

BROCKWAY, BARBARA S., WERKING, JUDITH, FITZGIBBONS, CATHLEEN, & BUTTERFIELD, WILLIAM. Social work in a doctor's office. In Bernard Ross and S. K. Kainduka (Eds.) *Social work in practice.* Selected paper, 4th NASW Professional Symposium. Washington, D.C.: National Association of Social Workers, 1976.

CALLAHAN, DANIEL. Health and societies: Some ethical imperatives. In John H. Knowles (Ed.) *Doing better and feeling worse: Health in the United States.* New York: W. W. Norton & Co., Inc., 1977.

CLARK, ELEANOR. Post-hospital care for chronically ill elderly patients. *Social Work*, 1969, *14* (1).

CARKHUFF, R. R. & BERENSON, R. *Beyond counseling and therapy.* (2nd ed.) New York: Holt, Rinehart & Winston, 1977.

COLEMAN, JULES & PATRICK, DONALD. Integrating mental health services into primary medical care. *Medical Care*, August 1976, *14* (8).

COLEMAN, JULES, EAGLE, JEFF, & HERMALIN, JARRED. Collaboration consultation and referral in an integrated health program in an HMO. *Social Work in Health Care*, Fall 1979, *5* (1).

COOPER, ELAINE J. Beginning a group program in a general hospital, *Group*. July 1976.

COULTON, CLAUDIA. A study of person environment fit among the chronically ill. *Social Work in Health Care*, Fall 1979, *5* (1).

COUSINS, NORMAN. *Anatomy of an illness*. New York: W. W. Norton & Co., Inc., 1979.

DANA, BESS. New directions in community medicine: Implications for social work education and practice. *The community medicine contribution to social work*. Delivered at the 75th Anniversary of the Mount Sinai Hospital Department of Social Work, New York, 1980.

DIAGNOSTIC AND STATISTICAL MANUAL 3. Washington, D.C.: The American Psychiatric Association, 1980.

DIES, RICHARD S. & HENRY, SUE. The therapeutic contract in work with groups: A formal analysis. *Social Service Review*, December 1976, *50* (4).

DOREMUS, BERTHA. The four R's: Social diagnosis in health care. *Health and Social Work*, November 1976, *1* (4).

DUBOS, RENEE. *Man adapting*. New Haven: Yale University Press, 1965.

EPSTEIN, LAURA. *Helping people with a task-centered approach*. St. Louis, Mo.: C. V. Mosby, 1980.

EWALT, PATRICIA. Clinical social work in community mental health programs. In Arthur J. Katz (Ed.) *Community Mental Health Issues for Social Work Practice and Education*. (New York: Council on Social Work Education, 1979).

FARKAS, SUSAN. Impact of chronic illness on the patient's spouse. *Health and Social Work*, November 1980, *5* (4).

FISHER, JOEL. *Effective casework practice: An eclectic approach*. New York: McGraw-Hill, 1978.

FOX, RENEE C. The medicalization and demedicalization of American society. In John H. Knowles (Ed.) *Doing better and feeling worse: Health in the United States*. New York: W. W. Norton & Co., Inc., 1977.

GERMAIN, CAREL. An ecological perspective on social work practice in health care. *Social Work in Health Care*, Fall 1977, *3* (1).

GERMAIN, CAREL (Ed.) *Social Work Practice: People and Environments*. New York: Columbia University Press, 1979.

GERMAIN, CAREL and GITTERMAN, ALEX. *The life model of social work practice*. New York: Columbia University Press, 1980.

GITTERMAN, ALEX. Development of group services. In *Social work with groups in maternal and child health*. Conference proceedings, New York, Columbia University, June 14 and 15, 1979.

GOLAN, NAOMI. Using situational crises to ease transitions in the life cycle. *American Journal of Orthopsychiatry*, July 1980, *50* (3).

GOLDBERG, IRVING, KRANZ, GOLDIE, & LOCK, BEN. Effects of a short-term outpatient psychiatric therapy benefit on the utilization of medical services in a pre-paid group practice medical program. *Medical Care*, September/October 1970, *8* (5).

GOLDBERG, MATILDA & NEAL, JUNE. *Social work in general practice*. London: George Allen and Unwin, 1972.

GORDON, WILLIAM E. Knowledge and value: Their distinction and relationship in clarifying social work practice. *Social Work*, July 1965, *10*.

GORDON, WILLIAM E. & SCHUTZ, MARGARET L. A natural basis for social work specializations. *Social Work*, September 1977, 22 (4).

HALEY, J. *Problem solving therapy*. San Francisco: Jossey Bass, 1976.

HALL, CALVIN S. & LINDZEY, GARDNER. *Theories of personality*. (3rd ed.) New York: John Wiley, 1979.

HARE, PAUL A. *Handbook of small group research*. New York: Free Press, 1962.

HOGERTY, GERARD E., GOLDBERG, ESSIE, & SCHOOLER, N. R. Drug and sociotherapy in the aftercare of schizophrenic patients III: Adjustment of non-relapsed patients. *Archives of General Psychiatry*, 1974, *31*.

JAYARATNE, SRINIKA & LEVY, RONA L. *Empirical clinical practice*. New York: Columbia University Press, 1979.

KANE, ROBERT L. & KANE, ROSALIE. Long term care: Can our society meet the needs of its elderly. *Annual Review of Public Health*, 1980.

KANE, ROSALIE. The interprofessional team as a small group. *Social Work in Health Care*, Fall 1975, *1* (1).

KELMAN, HERBERT C. Manipulation of human behavior: An ethical dilemma for the social scientist. *Journal of Social Issues*, 1965, *21* (2).

KIRESUK, THOMAS. Goal attainment scaling. *Evaluation*. Special monograph no. 1, 1973.

KIRESUK, THOMAS & SHERMAN, ROBERT. Goal attainment scaling: A general method for evaluating comprehensive community mental health programs. *Community Mental Health Journal*, 1968, *5* (6).

KLEIN, DONALD C. & GOLDSTON, STEVEN E. In Donald C. Klein and Steven E. Goldston (Eds.) *Preface/primary prevention: An idea whose time has come*. Rockville, Md.: NIMH, 1977.

KLEIN, DONALD F., GITTLEMAN, RACHEL, QUITKIN, FREDERICK, & RIFKIN, ARTHUR. (2nd ed.) *Diagnosis and drug treatment of psychiatric disorders: Adults and children*. Baltimore, Md.: Williams & Wilkins, 1980.

KNOWLES, JOHN H. The responsibility of the individual. In John H. Knowles (Ed.) *Doing better and feeling worse: Health in the United States*. New York: W. W. Norton & Co., Inc., 1977.

KORPELA, J. Social work assistants in private pediatric practice. *Social Casework*, November 1973, *54*.

KUMABE, KAZUYE, NISHBA, CHIKAE, O'HARA, DAVID, & WOODRUFF, CHARLOTTE. *A handbook for social work education and practice in community mental health settings*. Hawaii: University of Hawaii School of Social Work, August 1977.

LEVY, CHARLES S. The value base of social work. *Journal of Education for Social Work*, 1973, *9* (1).

LEVY, CHARLES S. *Social work ethics*. New York: Human Science Press, 1976.

LEWIS, JERRY M. The family matrix in health and disease. In Charles K. Hoffling and Jerry M. Lewis (Ed.) *The family: Evaluation and treatment*. New York: Bruner Mazel, 1980.

LINDENBERG, RUTH ELLEN & COULTON, CLAUDIA. Planning for post-hospital care: A followup study. *Health and Social Work*, February 1980, *5* (1).

LONERGAN, ELAINE COOPER. Humanizing the hospital experience: Report on a group program for medical patients. *Health and Social Work*, November 1980, *5* (4).

LOWE, JANE ISAACS & HERRANEN, MARJATTA. Conflict in teamwork: Understanding roles and relationships. *Social Work in Health Care*, Spring 1978, *3* (3).

LURIE, ABRAHAM & ROSENBERG, GARY (Eds.) *Social work in mental health: A 25 year perspective*. New York: Long Island Jewish Medical Center, 1977.

MAILICK, MILDRED M. The impact of severe illness on the individual and family:

An overview. *Social Work in Health Care*, Winter 1979, *5* (2).

MALUCCIO, ANTHONY N. & MARLOW, WILMA. The case for the contract. *Social Work*, January 1974, *19* (1).

MEYER, CAROL (Ed.) Preventive intervention: A goal in search of a method. In *Preventive intervention in social work*. Washington, D.C.: National Association of Social Workers, 1974.

MEYER, CAROL. *Social work practice*. New York: Free Press, 1976.

MINUCHIN, SALVADOR. *Families and family therapy*. Cambridge, Mass.: Harvard University Press, 1974.

MOOS, RUDOLPH & TSU, V. D. The crisis of physical illness: An overview. In Rudolph Moos (Ed.) *Coping with physical illness*. New York: Plenum, 1977.

NASON, FRANCES & DEL BANCO, THOMAS. Soft services: A major cost-effective component of primary medical care. *Social Work in Health Care*, Spring 1976, *1* (3).

NELSON, ZANE P. & MOWRY, DWIGHT P. Contracting in crisis intervention. *Community Mental Health Journal*, 1976, *12* (1).

NORTHEN, HELEN. *Social work with groups*. New York: Columbia University Press, 1969.

PANZETTA, ANTHONY F. *Community mental health: Myth and reality*. Philadelphia: Lea & Febiger, 1971.

PARRY, JOAN K. & YOUNG, ARTHUR K. The family as a system in hospital-based social work. *Health and Social Work*, May 1978, *3* (2).

PEARLIN, LEONARD I. & SCHOOLER, CARMI. The structure of coping. *Journal of Health and Social Behavior*, March 1978, *19*.

PERLMUTTER, FELICE D. Prevention and treatment: A strategy for survival. *Community Mental Health Journal*, Fall 1974, *10*.

PHILLIPS, WILLIAM. Attitudes towards social work and family medicine: A before and after survey. *Social Work in Health Care*, Fall 1977, *3* (1).

PINCUS, ALLEN & MINAHAN, ANN. *Social work practice: Model and method*. Illinois: F. E. Peacock, 1973.

REGENSBURG, JEANETTE. *Toward education for health professions*. New York: Harper & Row, 1978.

REHR, HELEN (Ed.) *Ethical dilemmas in health care: The professional search for solutions*. New York: Prodist, 1978.

REHR, HELEN (Ed.) *Medicine and social work: An exploration in interprofessionalism*. New York: Prodist, 1974.

REHR, HELEN (Ed.) *Professional accountability for social work practice: A search for concepts and guidelines*. New York: Prodist, 1979.

REID, WILLIAM J. & EPSTEIN, LAURA. *Task-Centered Casework*. New York: Columbia University Press, 1972.

RHODES, SONIA. Contract negotiation and the initial stage of casework service. *Social Service Review*, March 1977, *51* (1).

ROSENBERG, GARY. Continuing education and the self-directed worker. In Helen Rehr (Ed.) *Professional accountability for social work practice: A search for concepts and guidelines*. New York: Prodist, 1979.

ROSENBERG, GARY. *Social work and liaison psychiatry*. Presentation before the Society of Liaison Psychiatrists, March 1980, unpublished paper.

SEABURY, BRETT A. The contract: Uses and abuses of limitations. *Social Work*, January 1976, *21* (1).

SOBLE, ROSLYN & CHAIKLIN, HARRIS. Social work in preventive dentistry. *Social Work*, March 1975, *20* (2).

STRAIN, JAMES J. *Clinical social work: The theory and practice*. New York: Free Press, 1978.

STRAIN, JAMES J. & BEALLOR, GERALD. In James J. Strain (Ed.) *Psychological interventions in medical practice*. New York: Appleton-Century-Crofts, 1978.

STRAIN, JAMES J. & GROSSMAN, STANLEY. *Psychological care of the medically ill: A primer in liaison psychiatry*. New York: Appleton-Century-Crofts, 1975.

TRAVIS, GEORGE. *Chronic illness in children*. Stanford, California: Stanford University Press, 1976.

WEINER, HYMAN J. Social work role and function in primary care. Society for Hospital Social Work Directors, Denver, Audiotape, 1980.

WEISSMAN, ANDREW. *Environmental intervention referral technology*. Unpublished doctoral dissertation submitted to University of Maryland, School of Social Work and Community Planning, 1979.

WEISSMAN, MYRNA, CLURMAN, GERALD L., & PRUSOFF, B. A., and others. Treatment effects on the social adjustment of depressed outpatients. *Archives of General Psychiatry*, 1974, *30*.

WITTAKER, J. K. Models of group development. *Social Service Review*, 1970, *44*.

WOLFE, SAMUEL & TEED, GENEVIEVE. A study of the work of a medical social worker in a group medical practice. *Canadian Medical Association Journal*, May 27, 1967, *96*.

WOOD, KATHERINE M. Casework effectiveness: A new look at the research evidence. *Social Work*, November 1978, *23* (6).

WOOLEY, SUSAN C., BLACKWELL, BARRY, & WINGET, CAROLYN. A learning theory model of chronic illness behavior: Theory, treatment and research. *Psychosomatic Medicine*, August 1978, *40* (5).

YALOM, IRVING D. *The theory and practice in group psychotherapy*. (2nd ed.) New York: Basic Books, 1975.

CHAPTER FIVE
THE COLLABORATIVE PROCESS

Bess Dana

INTRODUCTION

Webster ascribes the following meanings to the verb "collaborate": "(1) to work jointly, especially with one or a limited number of others in a project involving composition or research to be jointly accredited (Beaumont and Fletcher collaborated in writing plays); (2) to cooperate with or assist usually willingly an enemy of one's country (Frenchmen who collaborated with the Nazis); (3) to cooperate usually willingly with an agency or instrumentality with which one is not immediately connected, often in some political or economic effort (attempts of the West to collaborate with Russia)."

As defined by the characteristics of social work's long association with other health and health-related professions and disciplines, collaboration represents an amalgam of all three shades of meaning that Webster attributes to it. Although social work aspires to and increasingly achieves the partnership status in health and medical care implicit in Webster's preferred (or first) definition, collaboration at times has been experienced either as surrender to inimical values and practices or as the establishment of a state of détente with an alien power.

This chapter accepts the need to work in tandem with other professions and disciplines as a basic requirement for social work's effectiveness as an instrumentality of health and medical care. At the same time, it acknowledges that there is no inherent virtue in collaboration for collaboration's sake. Rather, social work's engagement with others in the multiple activities that influence, define, and activate the delivery of health and medical services[1] to individuals and population groups derives and maintains its integrity from the relevance of social work values, knowledge, and skills to the determination of the objectives and or implementation of the particular task or responsibility at hand. A firm hold on the values as well as the knowledge and skills of social work is therefore a prerequisite for working jointly with others—and as such, the protection that the profession affords against collaboration as either capitulation or détente.

In keeping with this point of view, this chapter will explore and explicate collaboration as one means through which social work makes its values, knowledge, and skills felt in the formulation of social health policy, the governance of social health services, and the study and treatment of health and medical care problems in individuals and population groups. In pursuit of this purpose, the chapter will

1. Identify and discuss the multiple factors in the social, political, and scientific environment that constitute the rationale for collaboration as an appropriate— indeed an essential requirement for social work engagement in health and medical care.
2. Specify and discuss the behavioral demands implicit in establishing and maintaining effective working relationships with others in the various activities associated with health and medical care as social provisions.
3. Describe and discuss the issues involved in meeting the behavioral requirements of collaborative social work practice including the issue of autonomy; the issue of physician dominance; the issues of role confusion, diffusion, dissonance, gap, and overlap; the issue of communication; and the issue of consumer participation.
4. Compare and contrast the ways these issues are expressed and dealt with in health care planning; policy making; the delivery of personal health services in primary, secondary, and tertiary care; the evaluation of health care programs and services; and research and education.
5. Describe and discuss traditional, new, and emerging models of social work collaboration with particular emphasis on the influence of objectives, auspices, settings, and financing on the collaborative mode.
6. Assess the strengths and limitations of current social work collaborative activities in addressing the problems and possibilities of the collaborative process.
7. Recommend ways of dealing with the gap that still exists between the rhetoric and the reality of collaborative practice.

Throughout the chapter, a conscious effort will be made to award the collaborative process its proper place as a set of generic principles that may be stylistically adapted to the goals and objectives of the wide range of specific tasks and responsibilities encompassed under the rubric of health and medical care. Teamwork,

---

[1] The use of the phrase "health and medical services" rather than "health" services throughout this chapter is a semantic way of highlighting the differences *and* the linkages between the goals, objectives, tasks, and responsibilities associated with health promotion, health maintenance, and disease prevention and those associated with the diagnosis, treatment, and control of illness. For further explication of this point, see John S. Millis, *A Rational Public Policy for Medical Education and Its Financing*, (New York: The National Fund for Medical Education, 1971).

consultation, interprofessional practice and education, and conjoint teaching and learning are examples of such stylistic adaptations. They represent, in other words, particular behaviors through which collaboration as working with others is carried out. They *are not* synonymous with the term.

THE CASE FOR COLLABORATION

Probably no single statement makes the general case for collaboration more succinctly or more cogently that the old saw, "two heads are better than one." Collaboration, whether viewed in the positive sense of working together in common cause, or in the negative sense of "cooperating with an enemy of one's country," derives its raison d'être from the fact that each participant in the collaborative process has a particular contribution to make to the overall task—the authorship of a book or the bombing of a city.

As Chapter Four indicates, the practice of social work in the health field is based on the recognition of the particular contribution that the profession of social work can make to the various tasks and responsibilities associated with defining and meeting the health needs of individuals and population groups. These tasks and responsibilities may be classified according to the objectives of health care: (1) the promotion of health; (2) the prevention of disease and disability; (3) the diagnosis and treatment of illness; (4) the optimum social rehabilitation of the sick and disabled; and (5) the humane and compassionate care of the irreversibly and terminally ill. They may be classified according to levels of care—primary, secondary, and tertiary care. Or, they may be classified according to functional responsibilities—policy making, planning, administration, teaching, research, and service delivery.

No matter what classification system is employed, however, and each of those cited is frequently used, the critical determinants of social work's collaborative activities and action in health and medical care can be delineated. They are (1) the factors that are considered in defining the tasks and responsibilities of the health care system itself; (2) the criteria employed in deciding the relevance of social work to those tasks and responsibilities; (3) the participants in the process of task definition and criteria selection; and (4) the forces in the political, social, and intellectual environment that influence both decisions and those that make them. The case for collaboration, as the history of social work practice in health care demonstrates, is therefore a growing and changing one. A variety of factors, both within and outside the social work profession itself, have contributed to the expectations from social work as a participating member of the health care establishment and will continue to open up new opportunities and set the boundaries for such participation.

> Medical social service in its relation to medicine, to public health and to social work in general [Cannon reminded her colleagues in 1932][2] is a growing, changing movement, one that demands that we look forward, keep closely in

[2] Author's addition.

touch with growth and changes in medical practice, in the socialization of public health service, and in the changing social situation where we find ourselves and our patients.[3]

In looking at the developmental history of social work's relationship to health care as manifested in the building of the case for collaboration, it is important to keep this broader social, political, scientific, and professional frame of reference in mind.

Social work made its formal entry into the health care system via the hospital at the dawn of what is often termed the "Golden Age of Medicine." This age, a phenomenon of roughly the first sixty years of this century, has been marked by characteristics such as

1. the unprecedented growth of biomedical knowledge and technology;
2. the gradual shift of the balance of power in health affairs from a social elite to a biomedical elite, operationally expressed in the profession of medicine;
3. the disease focus of so-called "health" services, research, and education;
4. the dominance of specialization in medical practice and education;
5. the dramatic change in the status of the hospital from its humble origins as a refuge for the poor to the glittering citadel of scientific medicine;
6. the concentration of the resources of the hospital on the sick patient in the hospital bed to the neglect and downgrading of the needs of the walking sick and worried well in service, teaching, and research;
7. the consequent physical and intellectual separation of preventive services and long-term care from the mainstream of scientific medical interest and action;
8. the power and control vested in the physician as the "captain" of the euphemistically termed *health care team*.

Even at an early stage in the development of these salient features of the health care system, the need to correct for their possible threat to the humanistic goals and values of health and medical care was recognized. Indeed, the case for social work's collaboration in health and medical care was initially based on a concept of social work as the conscience of the hospital. "We came into existence," Cannon writes, "because a physician was disturbed over the fact that he could not get the kind of care he wanted for the tuberculous woman, the mother of the family. He wanted help for the young girl he found to be pregnant, and the sick child whose mother could not give him the necessary care."[4]

In the many years that have transpired since this articulation of social work's relevance to the humanistic goals of medical care, the physician's recognition of social work's capacities to heal the social and psychological wounds inflicted or exacerbated by illness and its treatment has continued to serve as a significant component in the growing and changing rationale for collaboration. As early as 1928, however, hospital social workers began to demonstrate their interest and their abil-

---

[3] Ida M. Cannon, "The Functions of Medical Social Service in the United States," *Hospital Social Service*, 27, no. 1, (January 1933), p. 2.

[4] *Ibid.*, p. 3.

ity to make their own case for their integral place in health and medical care. For example, the preparation of the 1928 Statement of Minimum Standards for hospital social service by the American Association of Social Workers and its acceptance by the American Association of Social Workers and its acceptance by the American College of Surgeons represent a "landmark decision" in the developmental history of social work's relationship to hospitals. This statement not only establishes social casework as the primary function of the medical social worker but supports the role of the social worker in case selection via her functional responsibilities in relation to hospital or clinic administration. Cannon describes these responsibilities as follows.

> The social worker may be placed at the admission desk or in the clinic where she is called the social clinic executive. She takes a brief social history of each patient, brings to the doctor's attention significant social facts and in consultation with the doctor selects those patients who should be referred to the social case worker for fuller study.[5]

Some four years later, Cannon articulates even more firmly the centrality of social work to the clinical practice of medicine.

> Whenever the making of the diagnosis is dependent on facts about the environment of the patient, such as the exposure to detrimental hazards in his work or at home; whenever successful treatment of disease depends on participation of the patient in the plan for treatment, social service may be needed. Expert medical diagnosis is not always enough. To get its full significance it should be a medical social diagnosis.[6]

The sophistication and modernity of this 1932 description of what social work brings to medical care is all the more remarkable when compared with the following account of social work practice in medical care as interpreted by Washburn from the 1906 and 1918 annual reports of the Social Service Department, Massachusetts General Hospital.

> Their report in 1906 listed their work which included hygiene teaching, infant feeding and care, vacations and country outings where it seemed a necessary part of treatment, help in finding jobs or changing jobs according to the medical need, provision for patients "dumped at the hospital," and assistance to patients needing treatment after discharge from the hospital wards. The report of 1918 added utilization of all sanitaria, convalescent homes, vacation funds, employment agencies and charitable agencies that may . . . help the patient or his family to pay for medicine, apparatus or vacation that may assure recovery.[7]

[5]Cannon, "The Functions of Medical Social Service," p. 5.

[6]*Ibid.*, p. 3.

[7]John H. Knowles, "The Teaching Hospital: Historical Perspective and a Contemporary View," *Hospitals, Doctors, and the Public Interest* (Cambridge, Mass.: Harvard University Press, 1965), p. 15.

What had happened in the intervening years to begin to transform the hand-maiden of all neglected social tasks into the professional social worker, guided by the standards of her own profession and beginning to assume responsibility for making her own case for the importance of social work as an instrumentality of clinical diagnosis and treatment?

Although Cannon attributes this difference in part to the physician's growing appreciation of the power of social and psychological factors to influence bodily function, she places major emphasis on the growing professionalization of social work itself as the significant determinant of change in social work's collaborative behavior.

As evidence of the movement within medical social work to establish and maintain its own professional identity, she describes Gordon Hamilton's publication of a classification of social problems, based on the analysis of cases under care of the Social Service Department of Presbyterian Hospital in New York City. She calls attention as well to the efforts of individual hospital social service departments to assess the effectiveness of their service and expresses hope that through such activities "we shall see our way more clearly in choosing where to put our effort, in controling the intake of cases and in training our students for a more skillful and discriminating professional service."[8] But above all, she associates the future acceptance and appropriate use of social work as an integral component of health care with (1) improvement in the initial preparation and continuing education of "the people who carry on the day's work," and (2) efforts in education and practice to avert what she identifies as beginning signs of separatism between medical and psychiatric social work and between hospital-based and community-based practice.

Thus, within thirty years of social work's entry into the health care system, many of the variables affecting the scope, nature, and quality of the collaborative process had been noted—and many of the ways for social work to influence the case for collaboration through its own behavior had been initiated. Time, far from diminishing the relevance of these beginning perceptions, has underscored their prescience.

Now as then, the case for optimum social work collaboration in health and medical care still rests on (1) the acknowledgment and support that the health care system gives to the need to keep humanism alive and well as an operant condition of health and medical care; (2) the recognition afforded by the health care establishment and public policy to the interplay of psychological, social, and biological factors in the cause as well as the course and outcome of disease; (3) the capacity of social work to contribute its own values, knowledge, and skills to the conceptualization of health problems, needs, and responsibilities; and (4) the joining of the resources of social work education, practice, and research in broadening and deepening such capacity.

It is important to reemphasize, however, that each of these general determinants of the rationale for social work's collaborative practice is highly sensitive and reactive to changes in social goals, priorities, and provisions, scientific and tech-

[8]Cannon, "The Functions of Medical Social Service," p. 7.

nological knowledge and capabilities, and political and economic realities. The years since Cannon presented her overview of the status of medical social work to her international colleagues have been marked by almost continual turbulence in all these contributory factors to the general climate for health care itself and for social work's relationship to it.

During this period, American medicine has achieved its greatest triumphs and suffered the most serious threats to its control of health affairs. Infectious disease, with its etiology in the natural environment, has been virtually conquered and or controlled only to be replaced by long-term illness, with its roots in the man-made environment; the search for understanding of the phenomena of health and illness has been illuminated by insights from the behavioral and social sciences, the search for solutions to health problems has been extended beyond the laboratory and the hospital to include the home, the community, the workplace, legislative halls, and judicial chambers. As health care costs soar and the cost-benefit ratio of health care services is more and more questioned, economists, political and managerial scientists have joined, and sometimes replaced the biomedical scientist and the physician as the new elite of the health care system. Rights to and in health care have received unprecedented attention as the focus of public policy.

Within the health care establishment, these changes are expressed in

1. the stubborn refusal of long-term problems to be contained within the boundaries of the biomedical model and the specialization of medicine that it has spawned;
2. the growing acceptance of the influence of lifestyle characteristics on the cause, course, and outcome of disease;
3. the search for systematic ways to correct for the dehumanization of health care services;
4. organized efforts to establish and maintain closer linkages with the community;
5. increasing acknowledgment of the need to reach out to the "walking sick" and the "worried well" through restoring the family physician to his former status and encouraging the development of primary care services;
6. the involvement of the consumer in decisions affecting his or her personal health and the health of the community;
7. the initiation of a variety of methods to control both the costs and quality of health care services and enhance their effectiveness.

All these manifestations of the direction of change in the health care system serve to support interdependence and collaboration as the operational directive for defining and dealing with contemporary health problems. They thus provide new sanctions, support, and opportunities for social work's collaborative engagement with a growing band of providers *and* consumers in traditional and emerging health care programs and services and in program planning, policymaking, management, and evaluation.

In recent years, the larger world of federal, state, and local government, business, industry, and social action groups has exerted a growing influence in health affairs. The involvement of these "outside forces," experienced within the health care system as shifts in the balance of power between professional and public control of health matters, offer expanding opportunities for social work to join its voice with a new set of "others" in the planning and advocacy of system change.

What of social work's capacity to influence and respond to the growing and changing case for collaboration as it is being endorsed—and shaped by forces within and outside the health care establishment? It is sobering to find relevant clues to the state of social work's readiness to deal with both the threats and the promises inherent in the collaborative possibility, in the 1980s, in the following excerpt from Cohen's assessment of the developmental status and dilemmas of social work, in 1955.

> One of the problems which will [and does][9] continue to plague social work will be that of determining what constitutes its justifiable boundaries. Thus, there are some who view social work primarily as a network of social services to supplement the work of the family, the school, the religious institution, the court and the medical institution. Others view it as a unique process for helping the individual, the group, and the community to find within themselves the resources for solving their problems. Still others regard social work primarily in terms of social policy. The emphasis of this group is less on the individual and more on improving the social institutions within which the individual functions. These varying views make definition difficult.
>
> The difficulty in definition, however, reflects a real problem. To reduce social work to method and process around which definition might be more attainable may tend to divorce us from the reality situation with which social work must deal to be effective. To abstract social services, methods and process, or social policy to the exclusion of the others tends to partialize and oversimplify the solution to complex problems. These three approaches merely reflect different emphases in the "why," the "what" and the "how" of social work and must be seen as an integral and essential aspect of a total pattern. In our determined and desirable efforts for greater professional status we must avoid achieving it at the expense of institutional rigidity. Let us never forget that what has been a source of discomfort over the years has also represented social work's greatest strengths, namely its flexibility in helping to meet new needs growing out of the changing economic, political, and social climate.[10]

In summary then, the evolving case for social work's collaborative practice in health and medical care represents the incremental growth in the strength and power of the multiple forces that support holism in what has been termed "the war of the parts against the whole."[11] That this war goes on within social work itself as well as in the others with whom social work works will become clearer as we turn now from a consideration of the multifaceted rationale for collaboration to its implications for the behavioral code that governs social work's collaborative practice.

[9] Author's addition.

[10] Nathan E. Cohen, "Professional Social Work Faces the Future," *Social Work Journal*, 36, no. 3 (July 1955), pp. 85-6.

[11] Cecil G. Sheps, "The Campaign Against Regulation and the Health of the Public," presentation at the Departmental Conference, Department of Community Medicine, New York: Mount Sinai School of Medicine, February 13, 1981.

THE BEHAVIORAL DEMANDS
OF THE COLLABORATIVE
PROCESS

Implicit in the various ways in which collaboration is defined and in the various factors which support its validity as an appropriate component of social work practice are a variety of behavioral demands, some congruent with and some antithetical to social work values and the principles of sound social work practice. As indicated earlier, collaboration as coauthorship represents the goal toward which social work strives precisely because it offers the neatest fit with and respect for the profession's values and practice principles. Collaboration as conspiracy or surrender, on the other hand, is inimical to both what social work believes and the ways in which it expresses its beliefs and knowledge in the daily acts of doing. Yet, few social workers who have worked with others in the real world of health care delivery, management, policy making, and or planning have been fortunate enough to avoid situations that pose threats to the rules of sound social work behavior or have been spared the necessity to make accommodations to the behavioral code of others. The particular case on which collaboration rests, as the preceding discussion suggests, influences the degree of the threat and the specific nature of the accommodation to be made. It does not obviate the need to deal with threat and accommodate to difference as inherent elements of the collaborative process.

The first and continuing behavioral demand for making collaboration part of practice reality is therefore to recognize and accept that neither commonality of purpose nor the soundness of the rationale that supports it can substitute for the steps required to convert collaboration from an abstract goal or an administrative fiat into a human process. For social workers, this means, first and foremost, that the basic attitudes and many of the practice principles involved in establishing and maintaining sound working relationships with the recipients of social services are applicable to working with colleagues from other professions and disciplines, even though the collaborative imperative may feel different, address different outcome objectives, and call for different skills.

As the growing social work literature on collaboration suggests, social workers and their colleagues from other professions and disciplines, like the patients they serve, hold expectations of one another. These expectations are often influenced by personal and or prior professional experiences, reflective of a lack of knowledge of each other's roles and responsibilities, and or colored by stereotypic notions of what a doctor, a nurse, a social worker is and does.[12] The need to convert this expectation fantasy, whatever its etiology, into reality is therefore as basic to effective collaboration as to effective direct service. And, as in direct service, the process

[12] H. David Banta and Renee Fox, "Role Strains of a Health Care Team in a Poverty Community," *Social Science and Medicine*, 6, no. 2 (1972), pp. 697–722; B. Dana, H. D. Banta, and K. W. Deuschle, "An Agenda for the Future of Interprofessionalism," in *Medicine and Social Work: An Exploration of Interprofessionalism*, ed. Helen Rehr (New York: Prodist, 1974), pp. 77–88; and Saad Z. Nagi, "Teamwork in Health Care in the U.S.: A Sociological Perspective," in *Health and Society. Milbank Memorial Fund Quarterly* (Winter 1975), pp. 75–91.

of reaching agreement as to the problem to be addressed often becomes the means through which the conversion from fantasy into reality begins to take place.

As in working with clients then, collaboration from its very inception calls on time-honored attributes of social work behavior. These include an acceptance of the need to begin where one's colleagues are; respect for differences in values, knowledge, and problem-solving styles and capacities; willingness to share one's own knowledge, values, and skills even when they may conflict with the knowledge, values, and skills that others hold to; the concomitant willingness to work through rather than to avoid conflict; coupled with the capacity to change or modify one's view of the problem to be addressed or the means of addressing it on the basis of new insights derived from others' perceptions and interpretations of both problem and ways of dealing with it.

Interprofessional collaboration thus bears a close resemblance to the contracting between client and worker, an essential practice ingredient well known to every practitioner, regardless of setting or field of practice. Like contracting with the individual client or family, it calls upon the social worker's ability to communicate his or her professional knowledge and values to the formulation of the problem in language understood by all the participants in the collaborative process. Furthermore, it necessitates the capacity to develop initial agreement as to the tasks and responsibilities of the individual members of the collaborating groups, and it makes an explicit demand on the willingness of the participating members to renegotiate the initial agreement in response to new insights regarding both the problem and its solution as they emerge in the course of working together. Collaboration, like contracting, is thus rescued from rigidity by flexibility, openness, and the capacity to acknowledge errors in judgment without defensiveness.

The fact that basic social work knowledge and practice skills play such a fundamental role in the collaborative process does not obviate the need for social workers to adapt both professional knowledge and skills to the particular demands of collaborative as distinguished from autonomous practice. Falck points out that "interdisciplinary practice is a form of behavior that must be specifically learned and involves persons who make mutual adaptations to each other's differences around such variables as profession, method, use of knowledge, skill and professional goal."[13] The code of effective collaborative behavior that he proposes for social work includes the following attributes.

1. Thorough commitment to the profession's values and ethics, and belief in the usefulness of one's own profession.
2. Belief in a holistic approach to client problems.
3. Recognition of the interdependency of practice.
4. Recognition of the expertise of colleagues and others.[14]

[13] Hans S. Falck, "Interdisciplinary Education and Implications for Social Work Practice," *Journal of Education for Social Work*, 13 (Spring 1977), pp. 30–7.
[14] *Ibid.*

Seen from the perspective of these criteria, collaboration to be effective makes a heavy demand on attitudinal as well as cognitive learning.

> To divide decision-making in new ways, to shift one's traditional responsibility to others, to subject one's self to peer review, to admit that less highly trained colleagues may have better insights into certain needs . . . requires professionals to re-orient their perceptions, attitudes and behavior toward their teammates.[15]

Banta and Fox, writing on their observations of a health care team in a poverty community,[16] Phillips, speaking from the perspective of collaborative practice in an urban university medical center,[17] and Hookey, addressing collaboration in a rural health setting,[18] are among the other contributors to the social work literature of collaboration who affirm Kumabe's description of the behavioral challenge of "seeing the beauty in difference."

Meeting this challenge imposes the necessity to revisit and come to professional terms with one's own feelings and attitudes toward others as a condition for establishing and maintaining sound collegial relationships. Working with professional "others," for example, frequently brings out and engenders the need to deal with competitive feelings; it often necessitates learning to share the gratification that comes from success—and what may even be more difficult, to share in responsibility for failure. It requires seemingly constant vigilance against the temptation to avoid conflict through submission or to equate the submissiveness of others with conflict resolution. In testimony to the power of the collaborative process to evoke preprofessional accommodations to authority, reawaken the dependency-independency conflict, and threaten hard-won concepts of professional worth, workers cite various examples of what they themselves term as "unprofessional" collaborative behavior. These include restoring—with dismay at their own behavior—to long-discarded techniques of cajolery and seduction to win the physician to their cause; the mustering up of old defenses of avoidance and denial to maintain the illusion of consensus in joint decision making; or the hiding behind the mantle of confidentiality as a way of holding on to a sense of their own importance in the collaborative scheme of things.

As Lowe, Lee, and others explain, much of the learning to recognize and deal with these and related feelings of inadequacy, competition, and denial comes from

---

[15] Kazuye T. Kumabe, "Team Approach to Health Care: Seeing the Beauty of Difference," *New Concepts of Human Services for Developing the Young Child* (Pittsburgh: University of Pittsburgh Press, 1978), p. 114.

[16] H. David Banta and Renee C. Fox, "Role Strains of a Health Care Team," pp. 697-722.

[17] Beatrice Phillips and others, "Social Work and Medical Practice," *Hospitals*, 45 (1971), pp. 76-9.

[18] Peter Hookey, "The Establishment of Social Work Participation in Rural Primary Care," *Social Work in Health Care*, 3, no. 1 (Fall 1977), pp. 87-99.

the actual "doing."[19] Based on their experience as members of a renal treatment team, Lowe and Herranen identify the following developmental stages in the learning-through-doing process.

1. *The becoming-acquainted stage*: This, according to the authors, is a time when "team members are primarily socializing with each other in a superficial, polite, and impersonal way." Emotions are neutralized and repressed as each member struggles to find his place on the team. This period is characterized by low group productivity and minimal conflict.

2. *The trial-and-error stage*: This is a time of "testing boundaries and seeking allies," a time when each professional feels the need to prove his or her unique contribution to other team members. The result, the authors indicate, is a "jealous guarding of turf and little team communication . . . ; the 'modus operandi' is parallel play"; the prevailing emotions are described as "suspicion, frustration, and uncertainty."

3. *The stage of collective indecision*: This stage represents an attempt to avoid direct conflict and maintain equilibrium. Characterized by the assumption of shared responsibility and pseudo-consensus, in actuality this is a period when role conflict is supressed rather than worked through. "Team morale," according to Lowe and Herranen, "is generally poor" during this phase. "The end result is covert anger among all team members."

4. *The crisis stage*: A "crisis" caused by an internal or external event is the mobilizing force for enabling the team to move to this stage of facing the issue of its "collective indecision" and to begin "to delineate more definitive roles and responsibilities. The stage is characterized by feelings of guilt, open expression of anger, depression, and recognition of conflict."

5. *The stage of resolution*: This stage represents "growth toward maximal team functioning with flexible, open communication, shared responsibility for decision making, and accountability for carrying out team tasks."[20]

Lowe and Herranen's formulation of the developmental stages of the collaborative process points to the importance of clearing the emotional air that pollutes the collaborative environment in order to be able to address and deal with the particular cognitive and skill requirements of effective collaborative practice. As the collaborative process is more frankly discussed and systematically studied, it becomes increasingly evident that the daily experience of working in tandem with others, in addition to putting self-awareness to test, also (1) calls for a reassessment of social work knowledge in the context of the knowledge and expectations of others; (2) requires learning the professional culture and cognitive style of the various actors in the collaborative arrangement; and (3) necessitates the translation of the social work message, if you will, into a language that can be heard and understood by colleagues from other professions and disciplines.

Falck places a high priority on the demand that collaboration puts on the so-

---

[19] Jane Isaacs Lowe and Marjatta Herranen, "Conflict in Teamwork: Understanding Roles and Relationships," *Social Work in Health Care*, 3, no. 3 (Spring 1978), pp. 323–30, and Stacey Lee, "Interdisciplinary Teaming in Primary Care: A Process of Evolution and Resolution," *Social Work in Health Care*, 5, no. 3 (Spring 1980), pp. 237–44.

[20] Lowe and Herranen, "Conflict in Teamwork," pp. 328–29.

cial worker's capacity "to articulate the social functioning point of view and the philosophical logic buried within it."[21] He writes

> It has been my experience that social workers who can articulate the social functioning point of view and the philosophical logic buried within it can and do make significant contributions to the interdisciplinary task at hand. Such a view, clearly stated and consistently followed, can make contributions that define social work and gain legitimate recognition from other professions.

Understanding of and the ability to engage in the group process as the vehicle for transmitting social work knowledge also presents itself as a salient demand of collaborative practice. In fact, the emphasis that social work education and practice give to the dynamics of group as well as individual behavior often serves to distinguish social workers' performance of the collaborative role from that of collaborators from the other professions and disciplines and in and of itself constitutes a significant social work contribution to the practice of others.

Inferred, rather than explicitly discussed in most of the literature, is the demand that collaborative practice makes on the social worker's capacity to keep up with and deal with change. This demand encompasses not only the updating of social work knowledge to include new understanding of human behavior and the social environment, but also shifts in social health policy and provisions and new strategies of intervention. Collaborative social work practice in the rapidly growing and changing world of health and medical care also imposes the necessity to keep up with, respond to, and anticipate the social health implications of changes in the nature and natural history of disease, new modalities of biomedical diagnosis and treatment, new and changing forms of health care delivery, and changing role definitions and territorial claims of nonsocial work health professionals. Furthermore, social work practice must take cognizance of new and changing reimbursement and payment mechanisms, new regulatory policies, and, increasingly, new economic constraints affecting consumers and providers of health services alike.

In summary then, collaborative social work practice, as what Falck terms a *variant* of disciplinary practice, calls for the adaptation of the basic knowledge, values, and skills of social work to collective social health problem definition and problem solving. The attitudinal and cognitive attributes of such practice are those associated with interdependence, rather than either independence or dependence. The effective social worker as collaborator knows who he or she is and takes pride in the values and knowledge of the profession. At the same time, the worker recognizes and accepts the fact that members of other health professions and disciplines not only have unique knowledge and skills to bring to the study and solution of health problems but also have legitimate claims to the caring and coping functions which are too often viewed as the private domain of social work. The effective social worker as collaborator is in touch with his or her own feelings about the need to share and make full use of the principles of establishing and maintaining relationships

---

[21] Falck, "Interdisciplinary Education and Implications," p. 35.

with others in the engagement with nonsocial work colleagues. Collaborative social work behavior is therefore distinguished by a sense of the appropriate time and timing of collaborative activities, the assumption of responsibility for independent as well as interdependent actions, and demonstrated capacity to learn from as well as to educate others.

CONSTRAINTS IN MEETING
THE BEHAVIORAL
REQUIREMENTS OF
COLLABORATIVE PRACTICE

Most of the growing literature devoted to the collaborative process acknowledges that the behavioral attributes of collaborative practice are easier stated than achieved. It will be no surprise to social workers engaged in collaborative activities that the twin issues of autonomy and physician dominance are the two most frequently cited impediments to the full realization of the collaborative possibility. Although role confusion and role overlap are also identified by most authors as interfering with the establishment and maintenance of effective interprofessional relationships, the general issues of territorial rights is subsumed under the broader umbrella of the autonomy-physician dominance connection as it is elucidated by nonphysician personnel in health settings.

Leininger, a prominent nursing educator, addresses the primacy of physician dominance as follows. "It is important to recognize that, in this country, our health disciplines and educational systems still function as largely uniprofessionally controlled systems with a stratified hierarchical arrangement. Several professional groups are expected to function in a subordinate way to the superordinate profes- of medicine."[22] In what she describes as "the familiar stratified pyramid model" of perceptions of health professions held by professional and nonprofessional persons, "it is clear that the physician is at the apex of the pyramid and other professionals are viewed in a subordinate role to him in rank, status, prestige, power and control."[23]

Noble, a medical educator, attributes the persistence of the physician's dominance of health affairs to

1. Ethical and legal obligations defined by present law and licensure requirements [which mandate that] physicians retain ultimate responsibility for the health care of their patients;
2. [the nature of professionalization or socialization in the training of physicians which] contributes to an assumption of team leadership;
3. provider-directed fee-for-service medical practice which perpetuates physician-centered health care delivery;

[22] Madeleine Leininger, "This I Believe . . . About Interdisciplinary Health Education for the Future," *Nursing Outlook*, 19 (December 1971), p. 788.
[23] *Ibid.*, p. 789.

4. the very nature of acute medical problems, requiring rapid decision-making and therapeutic action which are expedited by a clear, often hierarchical, ordering of authority and responsibility.[24]

Contemporary social work literature concurs with Cannon's early perception of the relationship between the attainment of professional autonomy—the establishment, maintenance, and governance of the standards of one's practice—and the ability to do away with the problems of "suboptimal utilization" or "suppression of other professional's knowledge and skills" imposed by the physician.[25] Indeed, since collaboration requires the engagement of difference in common cause, autonomy of each profession is a necessary condition for, rather than a barrier to, the successful outcome of collaborative activities.

What, however, appears to be as yet an unsolved issue, at both the organizational and individual practitioner level, is the determination of the appropriate balance between independence and interdependence in the relationship between social work and medicine. What aspects of social work intervention require, by the very nature of the problem, physician sanction? What aspects of the organization and delivery of social services in health care should be defined and governed by the profession of social work itself? What are the problems that call for joint decision making?

In reviewing the developmental history of social work in health and medical care, there can be little doubt that social work's capacity for collaboration has been markedly influenced by (and often acceded to) medicine's interpretation of its rights of self-governance to include the determination and governance of the rights and prerogatives of nonphysician health personnel. Even today, when the autonomy of social work practice is protected and promoted by (1) an accredited system of social work education; (2) a strong national practice organization; (3) state licensing and registration requirements; (4) a statement of standards for hospital social services approved by the American Hospital Association; (5) an American Hospital Association sponsored Society of Directors of Hospital Social Work Departments; and (6) a Social Work Section of the American Public Health Association, the issue of physician dominance cannot be said to have been laid to rest.

This continuing power of the physician to influence and indeed, in some instances, control social work behavior in contemporary collaborative practice is expressed in a variety of ways. Beyond the subtle influences of physician dominance on the daily working relationships between the individual social worker and the individual physician, which have already been mentioned, the unresolved issue of physician dominance is, for example, apparent in the persistent use of the term

[24] John Noble, "Comprehensive Care and the Primary Health Team," in *Primary Care and the Practice of Medicine* (Boston: Little, Brown, 1976), p. 267.

[25] Marie A. Caputi, "Social Work in Health Care: Past and Future," *Health and Social Work*, 3, no. 1 (February 1978), pp. 8–29; Sidney Hirsch and Abraham Lurie, "Social Work Dimensions in Shaping Medical Care Philosophy and Practice," *Social Work*, 14 (April 1969), pp. 75–79; and Betty Bassoff, "Interdisciplinary Education for Health Professionals: Issues and Directions," *Social Work in Health Care*, 2, no. 2 (Winter 1976–77), pp. 219–228.

ancillary or *paraprofessional* to designate the status of social work in the lexicon of health care manpower. Physician dominance may be expressed in such a crucial matter of institutional policy and practice as the physician's control of the patient's freedom of access to social services. Physician dominance may intrude into the consideration of the role of the chief of a medical service in the selection of the social worker for his or her program. It may create friction with respect to the accountability and, indeed, the allegiance of the worker to a particular medical or psychiatric service or to the social service department. The hold of the physician on the policy-making and planning activities of health care institutions and programs is often a strong factor in determining the status and involvement of the social worker as policy maker and planner. And, as a final example of the influence of physician power on social work power, it is important to note that in many instances physician authorization is required for the reimbursement of social work services by third-party payers. In fact, in still other instances, the physician is the designated payee for services actually performed by social workers.

Many of the continuing manifestations of the influence of the power of the physician on social work's ability to establish and maintain its own identity within the health and medical care system represent the unforeseen consequences of the earlier accommodations that social work made in order to gain acceptance in the "house of medicine." Giving the physician the prerogative to determine and refer patients in need of social work help, an agreement negotiated by Cannon with Cabot as the condition for social work's formal entry into Massachusetts General Hospital in 1905, represents one such early accommodation with long-range repercussions. Gordon and Rehr, speaking to the negative effects of the physician's control of the referral system as it is manifested in contemporary practice, note that ". . . by not defining its own case finding system, social work relinquishes the right to set its own priorities."[26] As this author emphasizes:

> Doing its own thing effectively in the medical center necessitates social work's finding its own way to make services available and accessible without waiting for the physician's acknowledgment of social need or his permission or prescription for social work intervention. Such a departure from traditional social work practice would affect not only the time and timing of social work intervention, the nature of the services offered, but the selection and deployment of social work personnel as well.[27]

The tenacious hold of medicine on the casefinding and referral system in health care, despite the growing professionalization of social work since 1905, may be attributed in part to the growth of the overall power of biomedical science in the first half of the twentieth century. In part, however, this hold may be related to the

[26] Barbara Gordon and Helen Rehr, "Unanticipated Consequences of the Case Finding System in Hospital Social Service," unpublished manuscript prepared for presentation at the NASW Symposium, San Francisco, May 25, 1968.

[27] Bess Dana, "Social Work in the University Medical Center," *The Johns Hopkins Medical Journal*, 124, no. 5 (May 1969), p. 279.

fact that social work, itself dazzled by the triumph of biomedicine, for many years defined it own role and function as helping people to adjust to illness and medical care and directed its collaborative efforts to "humanizing" the doctor-patient relationship, on the one hand, and attending to the unmet needs of patients, on the other. In this definition of responsibility, it was sometimes unclear as to whether the objective of social work was to serve the needs of patient, physician, or institution. Indeed, it was not unusual to hear social work in medical care described as serving all three, with little reference to the conflicts of interests that might arise from serving three masters.

Discharge planning represents a classic example of how this conflict of interest is still played out in daily hospital life. As Mailick and Jordon indicate

> Social workers are often angry when they receive a request for discharge planning just before the patient must leave the hospital. There is no time in this circumstance for a professionally adequate plan to be developed. The dilemma is that interest in providing service to the patient and the pressures from the physician, hospital administration, and third-party insurance regulators impel the social worker to step into the breach and provide some kind of solution. Frustration and erosion of professional self-worth then become obstacles to collaboration.[28]

As Mailick and Jordon suggest, the social worker's ability to withstand the pressures exerted by the physicians and or administrator, in discharge planning or in other situations, when the physician prescribes the social work contribution rather than requests the help of social work in problem definition or solving, is greatly enhanced and reinforced by institutional and departmental policies that interpret the appropriate role, functions, and responsibilities of social work and outline the procedures for making optimum use of social work as a professional resource. Such policies and procedures have grown incrementally. Although they do not obviate the need for adaptation to individual circumstances, they strengthen the social worker in the struggle to demonstrate sound principles of interprofessional behavior in working with others.

The need for such institutional attention to and reinforcement of the right of each profession to be accountable for the conditions that promote its optimum contribution to the goals and objectives of the health care program has become increasingly important with the changing social mission of the health care system, the growing complexity of the health care environment, and the changing social orientation and preparation of both physician and nonphysician personnel.

Increasingly, social workers find that they are not alone in raising questions as to the adequacy of the biomedical model as the frame of reference for defining and meeting contemporary health problems and needs. Anger and frustration at physician-dominance is slowly giving way to attempts to use the collaborative process as a means of bringing about change in the physician's perception of the problem to

[28] M. D. Mailick and P. Jordon, "A Multimodel Approach to Collaborative Practice in Health Settings," *Social Work in Health Care*, 2, no. 4 (Summer 1977), p. 451.

be addressed and to reformulate both assessment and intervention in social health rather than biomedical terms. This clinical approach to placing medical responsibility within the broader context of social responsibility is paralleled—and sometimes integrated—with collaborative activities designed to develop and promote a socially responsive and responsible health care delivery system.

It is clear that

> On the surface, the more general acceptance of a social health frame of reference for health care organization and delivery would seem to provide the common goals and the common value base often cited as the essential ingredients needed to obviate the status differentials, the communication difficulties, and the discrepancies in objectives encountered in actual work experiences as "members of the team."[29]

These authors suggest, however, that the social definition of health problems, whether expressed in clinical practice or in planning, policy making, or managerial activities, far from promoting "instant collaboration," makes new demands on interprofessional behavior.

These are the demands that arise in part from acknowledging that social work collaboration itself has not only been greatly influenced but its turf protected by the biomedical model. Today, as a growing number of physician and nonphysician health care personnel lay claim to the psychosocial domain, where social work has so long resided in solitary and often doubtful splendor, social workers must struggle with the redefinition of their unique contribution to the collaborative enterprise. Role confusion, role blurring, and indeed, both the sharing and the surrendering of some of the counseling services associated with role performance thus emerge as the current expression of the autonomy issue. The struggle related to role is compounded by the fact that the redefinition of health care in social terms requires learning to work with a new set of "significant others"—who speak the language of managerial science and face the social worker as collaborator with the hard tasks of establishing the relevance of social concerns and interventions to efficiency and economy. Having begun to extricate themselves from the constraints imposed by physician dominance, social workers now confront the necessity to test out their hold on the knowledge, values, and skills of their profession in their engagement with the emerging new power elite of the health care establishment.

Overriding the need for the adaptation of social work collaborative behavior to changes in the behavioral orientation of traditional partners in health care delivery and the demands imposed by the growing power of the "new men and women" of health care planning, policy, and management is the necessity that all health professions face to incorporate the consumer of health services within the collaborative network. Germaine identifies the "public's diminishing trust in the superior judgment of the professional expert," associated with "the growing pressure on the part

---

[29] B. Dana, H. D. Banta, K. W. Deuschle, "An Agenda for the Future of Interprofessionalism," in *Medicine and Social Work—An Exploration of Interprofessionalism*, ed. Helen Rehr, (New York: Prodist, 1974), pp. 77-88.

of people everywhere to have a greater say in matters bearing on their own lives and destinies" as a major change in the environment of social work practice today.[30] The significance of "consumerism" for social work practice in health care has been discussed in detail in Chapter Two.

Within the context of the collaborative process, however, particular mention must be made of the challenge that consumerism poses to the validity of social work's assumption that it serves as representative and advocate of the consumer in its work with other professions and disciplines. In response to this challenge, Germaine indicates, social work

> has intensified [its] traditional concern for quality assurance. Practice theory has also responded to the challenge with its emphasis on contracting, on the client's decision-making and action in his or her own behalf, and on mutuality between worker and client that emphasizes the realities of the relationship and reduces distances and discrepancies in power.[31]

If, however, the consumer is to receive full partnership in his or her own personal health care and in decisions affecting the health care of population groups, these practice efforts must be directed toward breaking down the ideological and intellectual defenses the health care establishment has built up in order to justify the limitations placed on the consumer's participation in personal health care and in planning and governance of health care services. Social work's critical role in helping its professional colleagues to catch up with the social work profession in espousing and implementing patients' rights *to* and *in* health care is still in the process of evolving.

Even at this early stage, there is empirical evidence of the new ethical, moral, and intellectual dilemmas posed for social work as well as the other health professions by the reality testing of these fundamental values. For example, social workers acknowledge their discomfort in giving unqualified support to the patient's right of access to his or her own chart without serious consideration of the possibility that (1) confrontation with the written facts of the condition may evoke rather than diminish the patient's fears and or interfere with rather than facilitate optimum recovery, and (2) the patient's right of access to the chart may be used by some physicians to substitute for the necessity for open sharing and interpretation of findings and treatment plans as essential components of the ongoing doctor-patient relationship. Furthermore, the patient's access to social work chart notes as part of the medical record may subtly or overtly influence the social worker-patient relationship as well, reinforcing for social worker as well as physician the importance of contracting as an ongoing process.

The activation of informed consent as a mandated condition for the conduct of research and the administration of invasive diagnostic and treatment procedures

---

[30] Carel B. Germaine, "Social Context of Clinical Social Work," *Social Work*, 25, no. 6 (November 1980), p. 484.

[31] *Ibid.*, p. 486.

also subject social work's belief in the patient's right to cast the decisive vote in matters affecting his or her own care to the stresses and strains associated with the translation of beliefs into the reality of everyday practice. Social workers in health care thus frankly acknowledge that their own personal moral and ethical beliefs intrude on their professional objectivity as they participate with physician and nurse colleagues in determining the circumstances under which a parent's right to withhold recommended treatment from a child can be medically sanctioned and when such refusal is a matter for court action. They indicate their awareness of how acculturated they themselves have become to the "doctor knows best" dictum as they struggle to support the patient's right of choice against their own conscious or unconscious tendency to side with the physician in his or her effort to obtain the patient's consent to recommend medical or surgical interventions.

As in the case of access to records, the weaving in of mandated patients' rights into the overall fabric of patient care represents an exciting new challenge to the collaborative process. It is increasingly engaging the attention of the members of the health professions as evidenced by the growing number of courses in the moral and ethical implications of health and medical care, the growing number of publications that deal with moral and ethical health care issues, and the increasing use of the team format for the airing and resolution of these issues on oncology services, intensive-care, dialysis, and or neonatology units, where they are so frequently and dramatically expressed.[32]

It must be emphasized that despite the difficulties that social work encounters in the activation of the principles of "consumerism" in the daily activities of patient care, social work's fundamental belief in the importance of the patient's right to participate in his or her own care remains constant. In fact, social work has, since its formal entry into the health care system, strongly supported the need for public and institutional policies and practices that acknowledge and guarantee both patients' *rights to* and *rights in* health and medical care. In the early days of social work's affiliation with health and medical care, social work often served as the consumer's representative not only in its collaboration with doctors and nurses in the daily acts of patient care but in its collaborative relationship with hospital administrator(s) and the chiefs of medical services. Today, social work strongly supports the movement initiated in the 1960s that encourages—and in some instances mandates—the health care consumers' rights and responsibilities to serve as their own representatives (see Chapter Two). In these uncertain times when all hard-won human rights are in jeopardy, the need to keep the consumer movement alive and well in health care as in all human services emerges as a top priority in social work's agenda for the present and the future.

---

[32]M. De Wachter, "Interdisciplinary Framework," *Journal of Medical Ethics*, 2 (1976), pp. 52–7; S. Sollitto, R. M. Veatch, and N. K. Taylor, *Bibliography of Society, Ethics, and Life Sciences* (New York: Hastings-on-Hudson, 1976–1977); and Thomas K. McElhinney, ed., *Human Values Teaching Programs for Health Professionals*, in Medicine, Report no. 7 (Philadelphia: Society for Health and Human Values, 1976).

VARIATIONS ON THE
COLLABORATIVE THEME

Most of the behavioral requirements of collaborative social work practice discussed thus far as well as the issues identified as affecting the collaborative process have been derived from the written and oral history of social work's long association with nonsocial work colleagues in the offering of personal health services to the identified sick person in secondary and tertiary health care programs and institutions. As indicated both in this particular chapter and throughout this text, however, from the very beginning of social work's association with health and medical care up to and including the present moment, social work has participated actively in trying to enhance the social responsibility of health care through (1) participation in policymaking at the institutional, local, state, and federal levels; (2) participation in program planning and management both within and outside its own institutional base; and (3) collaborative research and teaching.

The discussion of the distinctive characteristics of the variants of collaborative practice that follows is based for the most part on the author's own observations and experiences, supported and or supplemented by inferences from the literature of policy making, planning, and management and illuminated by innumerable formal and informal exchanges of ideas and experiences with social work and nonsocial work colleagues.[33] As such, it is more suggestive than definitive. Nonetheless, it does illustrate the importance of taking into account the differences as well as the similarities between nonclinical and clinical collaborative social work practice in order to maximize social work effectiveness in all aspects of such practice and to strengthen the linkages between clinical and nonclinical collaborative strategies.

Policy Formulation, Planning, and Management

Just as all persons who put pen to paper are writing prose, all social workers involved in problem solving more often than not are "doing" policy making, planning, and management as part of their daily practice. For example, the single action taken in a team meeting in an adolescent program to refer a teenage pregnant young woman to the social worker for counseling may result in the institutionalization of such referrals for all pregnant teenagers without the word "policy" ever having been articulated. Similarly, discussions among doctor, social worker, and nurse as to ways of dealing with the problem of an elderly patient who "overstays" his or her

---

[33] Martin Nacman, "Reflections of a Social Work Administrator on the Opportunities of Crisis," *Social Work in Health Care*, 6, no. 1 (Fall 1980), pp. 11-21; "A Systems Approach to the Provision of Social Work Services in Health Settings: Part II," *Social Work in Health Care*, 1, no. 2 (1975), pp. 133-43; John Wax, "Developing Social Work Power in a Medical Organization," *Social Work* (October 1968), pp. 62-71; "Power Theory and Institutional Change," *Social Service Review*, 1971, 45, no. 3 (1971), pp. 274-78; and H. Levinson, "Management by Whose Objectives?" *Harvard Business Review* (July-August 1970), pp. 125-34.

welcome on a hospital floor may lead to a plan for high-risk screening of all elderly patients on a particular service and, if successful, become official hospital policy. Weekly patient care-focused rounds in which social workers, nurses, and physicians meet to review the status of each patient on a service, a practice initiated in the early 1920s at both Massachusetts General Hospital and Beth Israel Hospital in Boston, represent an amalgamation of the policy formulation, planning, and management functions as a taken-for-granted component of social work responsibility.

As collaborative undertakings, historically these "over-and-above" the case load activities" represent the initiative taken by an individual social worker to help colleagues think beyond the individual case to the case load; to bring order into the delivery of personal health services; and to avoid idiosyncratic decisions born of crisis and frustration. Such doing of policy, planning, and management on the part of the individual social worker on a service, again historically, has often served to point up the need and pave the way for the formal institutional policy making, planning, and management activities carried on by administrative and supervisory social work personnel as an inherent part of their responsibilities. In turn, the policy, planning, and management actions taken by a particular institution in addressing the social health needs of the population it serves may be fed into the mainstream of policy making, planning, and management initiatives at the local, state, and national levels. Social workers who become involved in actions at these levels traditionally entered these arenas via the route of intramural experience. In other words, they have gained acceptance and credibility in the larger health care establishment through their demonstrated competency to contribute to problem definition and solving that transcends the needs of their particular practice base.

Obviously, a different level of expectation and expertise from that of the line worker is inherent in the role and function of the social worker charged with carrying defined policy making, planning, and or managerial responsibilities in health care. Thus, the behavioral requirements of collaboration for social workers carrying such responsibilities reflect not only the need for a hold on the basic knowledge, skills, and values of collaboration already discussed, and the capacity to put these principles to new and different tests, but necessitate the acquisition and articulation of knowledge, skills, and attitudes qualitatively different from those of direct practice.

First and perhaps foremost, the struggle for status, for recognition as an essential force in health and medical care services that the social case worker inevitably must work through in becoming part of the fabric of a particular "working party" on a hospital floor or clinic becomes for the director of social services a matter of translating an institutional decision into a living demonstration of the validity of institutional judgment. The definition of the director's role and responsibilities—and who defines them—the freedoms and constraints that characterize his or her decision-making power, the place afforded the director (ex-officio or voting) on the governing councils of the institution or the program are all critical determinants of the ease or difficulty that the director encounters in establishing and maintaining a working partnership with nonsocial work colleagues in institutional policy formulation, planning, and implementation. The reconciliation of autonomy with interdependence is thus a major task for those social workers charged with formal policy making, planning, and managerial responsibilities in health care institutions and programs.

In order to make the maximum contribution to the planning and achievement of the social health goals of the institution or program, the director of social work should be afforded the same rights, privileges, and responsibilities as those that accrue to the chief of any professional service (medical or nonmedical) within a health care program or institution. Specifically, these include (1) setting the standards for social work practice within the overall program or institution; (2) establishing and maintaining the working conditions and organizational arrangements that promote the staff's capacity to meet such standards; (3) serving as a full (voting) member on the policy-making and planning bodies of the institution or program; (4) having direct accountability—and accessibility—to the overall institutional or program director.

Even when these rights, privileges, and responsibilities are fully granted and observed, however, social work collaboration at the formal policy, planning, and managerial levels is neither free of conflicts between and among personal, professional, and institutional goals nor protected from assaults on personal or professional integrity. For the program director, learning to deal judiciously with the power that goes with full status as a leader among leaders becomes a major behavioral demand of collaborative practice geared toward institutional rather than individual problem identification and solving.

This capacity is nurtured by the external organizational arrangements we have already described. It is dependent as well upon such interpersonal factors as a strong sense of professional self-worth; the ability to distinguish between authority as a positive professional attribute deriving from the integration of social work knowledge, values, and skills and authoritativeness as a stylistic manifestation of personal and professional insecurity; the capacity to respect and acknowledge difference; and the concomitant capacity to risk one's difference to the judgment of others.

It is true that most social workers who achieve full status as collaborators in the various components of institutional decision making have earned their place in the institutional scheme of things precisely because of these behavioral attributes. It is also true, however, that the very exercise of the right of full partnership in institutional decision making may evoke unanticipated behavioral responses, stimulated by confrontation between expectation of self and others and reality. Thus, social workers involved in collaborative planning, policy making, and managerial activities acknowledge their disappointment to discover that stereotypic images of the social worker hover over the conference table of the administrator's office as surely as the hospital floor. It requires the same kind of patient explication and demonstration for their modification; they learn that their successes of the past do not guarantee them immunity from feelings of insecurity as they join a company of equals in which some members—usually physicians—are more equal than others. With all this regarding the need to guard against defensive (or offensive) reaction formation;

they reaffirm the necessity to examine their own attitudes as well as the attitudes of others for clues to the possible causes of strain in the development and mainten- ance of effective collaborative relationships; and they underscore the fact that, in nonclinical as in clinical collaborative practice, a true working partnership does not emerge full-blown from administrative fiat, but represents the outcome of a process of growth and change, similar in nature to that described by Lowe and Herranen[34] as the characteristic developmental pattern of interprofessional collaboration in in- dividual patient care.

Certain behavioral demands, however, appear to be more commonly associated with interprofessional collaboration at the policy-making, planning, and or manage- rial levels than with collaboration around the care of the individual patient. For ex- ample, the need to reconcile the individual with the general (population) good is an inescapable requirement of policy making, planning, and management. For social workers engaged in nonclinical activities of such a nature, this behavioral require- ment is operationally expressed in a variety of specific ways. Collaborative decision making with respect to institutional personnel policies and practices may confront the social worker with the uncomfortable need to weigh the interests of social work personnel, individually or collectively, against the interests of the larger professional and nonprofessional employee population. Policy making, planning, and manage- ment affecting patient care may force the social worker into the equally uncomfort- able position of weighing the needs and interests of a particular patient against those of a population group, the needs and interests of the clinical personnel against those of the administration, and, increasingly, the needs of health care consumers against those of health care providers. Inevitably then, nonclinical collaborative practice requires a reaffirmation of social work values and purpose in the light of the needs and demands of the many diverse constituencies whose interests must be accommodated if the institution or program is to function efficiently and effectively as an agent of optimum health and medical care. Social workers, in defense or sup- port of such values, must be prepared to risk themselves to incurring the disfavor or frank hostility of other members of the policy-making, planning, and or managerial group, consumer and provider alike. At the same time, they must remain open to the ideas of others and, above all, not assume that they represent the single voice of humanism and democracy in the orchestration of health and medical care services. Effective social work collaborative practice, whether clinical or nonclinical, thus suggests the need for social workers to reject the concept of social work as the "conscience" of the institution or program and work toward the articulation and expression of a collective institutional or program conscience.

A heavy demand is placed on knowing as well as believing if the institutional or program conscience is to be reflected in the policies and practices which govern the actual delivery of health and medical care services. To the degree that social workers are able to provide evidence to support their convictions, their particular contribution to institutional problem solving is most likely to be understood, ac-

---

[34] Lowe and Herranen, "Conflict in Teamwork," pp. 328-329.

cepted, and valued. In nonclinical or in clinical collaboration then, knowledge is a major source of social work power.

Initially, the social worker as collaborator in institutional and or program policy making, planning, and management relied mainly on anecdotal evidence as the worker's power source. This evidence was supplemented by quantitative data of a descriptive nature designed to highlight the extent of the social problems associated with illness and its care and to point up gaps in social resources. Generalization from the specific case, however, was the characteristic mode of pointing up the nature of social needs and suggesting appropriate policy, planning, and or administrative responses to these needs. Attempts to develop more systematic ways of gathering and analyzing data were, until the 1960s, limited to a very few large social service departments in major medical centers and focused on enhancing the efficiency and effectiveness of social services rather than on institutional change.

Since the mid-1960s, however, social workers in health and medical care have increasingly begun to acknowledge the importance of hard psychosocial data as variables to be honored in the collaborative policy making, planning, and managerial processes, to demonstrate their capacity for systematic investigation of psychosocial phenomena, and to use their findings to help health care programs and institutions define and address the social health problems of the populations they serve. Engagement in nonclinical collaborative activities has also pointed up the need for social workers to become conversant with the language and principles of modern management and health care economics as they apply to the organization, delivery, and financing of health care services.

Finally, it should be emphasized that the capacity of the social worker to put knowledge, old and new, to effective use in bringing about change or modification in institutional policies and practices is, in large measure, dependent upon the nature of the linkages the worker establishes and maintains with his or her clinical social work colleagues within the institution or program, on the one hand, and with representatives of community-based providers and consumers of health and health related services on the other. The social worker involved in the daily acts of patient care is in optimum position to provide useful insights on the strengths and deficiencies of the organization and delivery of health care services. For example, as they affect the ability of patients and families to deal with the social and economic costs of illness and its care; to identify particular patients at high risk for social and psychological dysfunctioning; to examine the gaps in existing community support systems; and to suggest and test out new strategies for system change, using a particular service or population subgroup for such pilot demonstrations. The wider community network of people, program, and services can provide important information as to the social health needs, wants, and resources of the population that the institution serves; anticipate the impact of change in institutional policy or practice on the population served; and become active participants in helping to define and promote the evolving social health mission of the institution vis-à-vis the community.

Whether working within their own institutions and programs or in the larger arena of local, state, and or national health affairs, the social worker as collaborator in policy making, planning, and or management, must therefore apply the principles of collaborative practice in his or her relationships with members of the social work profession. *Intra*professionalism, in the context of the behavioral demands of both clinical and nonclinical collaboration, is both the prerequisite and the continuing requirement of *inter*professionalism. Modern methods of data retrieval, data analysis, and data management can aid and abet the feed-in and feedback process through which the insights of the parts illuminate and clarify the whole. They cannot substitute, however, for the receptivity to the ideas of others, the willingness to risk oneself to the discomfort of conflict, nor the need to put professional goals ahead of personal goals that present as minimal demands of both *intra* and *inter*professionalism.

Interprofessional Teaching

Learning and teaching, as has been emphasized over and over again in this chapter, are implicit elements of the collaborative process and critical to the incorporation of the behavioral attributes of interprofessional collaboration as essential characteristics of professional practice. Health professionals customarily learn from and about each other through the course of their interaction around the daily acts of service. This learning through doing is, however, supplemented or reinforced by formal participation in the education and or training of members of other professions and disciplines. We turn now to the consideration of the distinctive behavioral demands of this expression of interprofessional collaboration.

It should be emphasized at the outset that social work participation in the education and training of members of other professions and disciplines relies for its effectiveness on the same sense of professional worth, the same hold on the knowledge and values of the social work profession, and the same capacity to understand and deal with differences that have been identified as the basic demands of social work participation in clinical and nonclinical problem identification and solving. In addition, however, successful collaboration in the teaching of other than one's own kind, if you will, requires, first of all, learning to understand, accept, and relate to the goals, objectives, and educational system of another profession which may be stylistically and substantively different from that of social work education.

Concomitant with this need is the particular need to accept, in attitudinal as well as intellectual terms, both that social work has something of value to contribute to the educational preparation of others and that others have the right and the capacity to incorporate social work's knowledge and understanding as part of their professional armamentarium.

Determining how and when social work knowledge and skills should be built into the educational program of other professions and disciplines represents still another challenge to collaborative interprofessional education. Such determination weds knowledge and acceptance of the differences in the educational system of others with knowledge and acceptance of the other profession's right to and capacity to make use of social work knowledge and understanding.

These three fundamental behavioral demands of social work collaboration in the education of the nonsocial work health professional, whether physician, nurse, and or health care administrator, are most successfully achieved if social workers are awarded the rights and responsibilities of academic status as members of the faculty of the educational program in which they participate.

At a minimum, such rights and responsibilities should involve the social worker in collaborative planning with nonsocial work colleagues for the courses or field learning experiences in which the worker serves as instructor or preceptor and in the evaluation of such experiences. Optimally, the social work faculty member of another professional school or program should also be involved in such activities as the selection of students, faculty development, and overall program planning which affect the general climate of the professional school and promote the integration and continuity of learning.

Like other forms of collaborative social work practice, social work collaboration in the education of other health professions and disciplines has grown incrementally and only in a few medical schools and schools of nursing has attained what have been described as the conditions of optimum acceptance. Again, as in other forms of collaborative practice, the attainment of the full rights and privileges of academic status does not obviate the need to recognize and work through the real or potential problems associated with bringing social work knowledge and attitudes to bear on the preparation of nonsocial work health personnel.

It is particularly important to guard against the temptation to use the collaborative educational opportunity as a means of convincing the nursing or medical student of the significance of social work in health and medical care rather than as a means of broadening and deepening their understanding of the influence of social and psychological factors in the prevention, treatment, and control of health problems. Equal caution must be exercised against the temptation to surrender the determination of the content of the social work message to the host professional school or program as a way of maintaining the illusion of interprofessional harmony. In other words, the issues of physician dominance, of autonomy versus interdependence are no less present in the professional educational system than in the health care delivery system. And the same qualities of self-awareness, openness, and willingness to work through rather than around conflict are required of the social work educator as collaborator as are required of the case worker or the policy maker if these issues are to be successfully resolved.

Finally, it should be noted that the contribution of social work to the education of others is greatly enhanced if the social worker's knowledge and understanding of the substantive content of social work is supported and supplemented by knowledge and experience in the application of learning theory and educational methods to the tasks and responsibilities of didactic and experiential teaching. Faculty development through postgraduate and continuing education is thus identified as a critical—and as yet only minimally met—requirement for the fulfillment of the potentials of social work as a vital force in the preparation of the future health professional, whether social worker or nonsocial worker.

Collaborative Research

It is no accident that collaborative social work research is discussed last in this consideration of the nonclinical aspects of social work's engagement in interprofessional collaboration. Unlike medicine, social work has placed far less emphasis on research than on direct service and teaching in its development as a profession. As Chapter Six points out, however, social workers in health and medical care have in recent years made demonstrable progress in correcting for this lack of attention to the systematic study of social work practice and the social health problems with which such practice is concerned. The growth of doctoral programs in social work since the mid-1950s both speaks to and supports this growing acknowledgement of the importance of research to the advancement of the effectiveness of the social work profession.

Social work's growing competence in basic and applied research has as yet been only minimally acknowledged by the biomedical community which, since the early 1940s, has constituted the dominent force and influence in the scientific investigation of health problems. Even with the broadening of investigative efforts to include social and psychological as well as biomedical variables, the medical research establishment has tended to turn to the social and behavioral science disciplines rather than the profession of social work as participants in collaborative studies. Social workers have sometimes been employed to gather data for such studies. Yet true collaboration as reflected in involvement in such activities as the definition of the problem to be addressed, the determination of the design and methodology to be employed, and the analysis and interpretation of findings is at an early stage of development.

In common with engagement in interprofessional teaching, effective engagement in interprofessional research requires that social work knowledge and skills be reinforced and supplemented by a command of research knowledge and methodology. The nature of that knowledge and the skills through which it is advanced are outlined in Chapter Six. It should be emphasized, however, that collaborative interprofessional research, like other collaborative interprofessional activities of a nonclinical nature relies for its vitality and relevance as an instrument of change in knowledge and its application to the solution of social health problems on the establishment and maintenance of linkages to the real world of service delivery. Clinical colleagues can contribute to the formulation of the problem to be addressed; their observations on a case-by-case basis can also provide important insights as to the variables to be included in the data to be gathered. And they can serve as vulnerable critics and real-life evaluators of research findings. Collaborative *inter*professional research then, like other forms of collaborative practice, grows and flourishes in an environment that encourages and demonstrates *intra*professional collaboration.

The invitation to cross professional lines in the pursuit of basic and applied knowledge of social health phenomena is, in fact, often the outgrowth of the respect that social work has earned from its nonsocial work colleagues through its demonstrated effectiveness in clinical problem identification and solving. In a very real sense, clinical and nonclinical social workers need each other if the full impact of the social work contribution in the study and solution of health problems is to be made.

In summary, much of the knowledge and skill that social workers in health and medical care bring to the various operational expressions of nonclinical practice, whether autonomous or collaborative, are derived from social work's long experience in identifying and meeting the social health needs of individual patients and families. Nonclinical collaborative practice confronts social workers with the challenge of applying their clinical insights to the assessment of health problems in population groups and or systems and to the identification of solutions in population or system terms.

This difference in purpose carries with it a set of behavioral demands that are consonant with but different from the behavioral demands of clinical problem identification and solving. Ideologically, collaboration in such activities as policy formulation, planning, and or management requires the capacity to reconcile the individual with the common good. Intellectually, collaboration of this kind requires a working knowledge of the principles of epidemiology as the means for assessing the social health needs of population groups, systems and organizational theory as the means for understanding the complex social health environment, and managerial principles as the means for implementing and maintaining system change. Attitudinally, such collaborative activities require the ability to foster a close working partnership with clinical social work colleagues as the means for keeping au courant with the daily life of health care delivery as it is experienced by the consumers and providers of health care service alike.

In common with colleagues engaged in policy making, planning, and management, who must demonstrate substantive knowledge of the theory and methods underlying these activities, the social worker engaged in collaborative interprofessional research must be competent in problem formulation, study design, data gathering and analysis, and the objective interpretation of findings, including the appropriate use of tests of significance. In the absence of such fundamental knowledge and skills, the social worker engaged in collaborative and interprofessional research runs the serious risk of having only an ancillary role in both the design and implementation of the research project. As a result, the social variables of health and or health system problems are likely to be minimized or overlooked as factors to be considered in determining the general scope of the inquiry, the appropriate questions to be addressed, the specific data to be gathered, and, ultimately the inferences or conclusions and recommendations to be drawn from the findings.

Finally, the complex nature of today's health problems support the importance of forging linkages between and among the various components of nonclinical and clinical collaboration. Without solid social evidence on which to base his or her policy making, planning, and or managerial activities, autonomous or collaborative, the nonclinical social worker minimizes maximum effectiveness as an agent of positive social change. Without the support of value-consonant institutional policies and practices and the infusion of new basic and applied knowledge of social health phenomena, the clinical social worker's capacities to serve as an effective agent of individual growth and change are constricted. Neither social work researcher, planner, or administrator can achieve an optimum effectiveness without the constant refreshment and stimulus that comes from those social workers charged with translating research findings and policy directives into the daily acts of service to the individual patient and family.

MODELS OF INTERPROFESSIONAL
COLLABORATION IN
DEVELOPMENTAL PERSPECTIVE

Much of our present day understanding of the collaborative process, including many of the central ideas expressed in this chapter, is influenced by either systematic studies and or empirical observations of the interprofessional health care team or by actual experience as a team member. In fact, so dominant is the team concept in the literature[35] and life of contemporary health care that it is easy to overlook other models for achieving the goals and objectives of interprofessional collaboration and or to forget that, as Millis states

> The reality is that health service is not a single ball game. Rather it is a series of quite different ball games ranging all the way from a game of tennis singles to the most complicated football offence. . . . [There is then][36] no such thing as *the* team. Rather, there is an almost limitless variety of teams, work groups, and partnerships. . . . Effective and productive interpersonal and interprofessional relations do not just happen. They are not created ipso facto by organization and institutionalization. They come into being through knowledge, understanding, and experience.[37]

The "how" of collaborating then is an evolving rather than a static phenomenon. As has been emphasized throughout this chapter, at the heart of the collaborative process, whatever form it takes, is the acknowledgement of the multifaceted nature of health care problems and the acceptance of the difference in knowledge, values, and skills needed to assess and deal with such problems.

Situation-by-Situation Collaboration

Undoubtedly the oldest, and still characteristic collaborative modus operandi for social workers in health care is the exchange of information and ideas, the determination of common goals, and the assumption of shared and individual responsibility around a given health problem, whether individually or programatically expressed. In many social service departments throughout the country, this form of

---

[35] For detailed bibliographies regarding teamwork, see Rosalie Kane, *Interprofessional Teamwork*, Manpower Monograph No. 8 (Syracuse, N.Y.: Syracuse University School of Social Work, 1975), pp. 73–86, and M. Tichy, ed., *Health Care Teams: An Annotated Bibliography* (New York: Prager, 1974).

[36] Author's addition.

[37] John S. Millis, *A Rational Public Policy for Medical Education and Its Financing* (New York: The National Fund for Medical Education, 1971), p. 125.

collaborative practice is indeed not only the prevailing but the solo mode through which the social work contribution is made to the larger fabric of patient care and or planning, organization, and governance of health care. As a way of influencing the scope and quality of health care services, this mode has the advantage of tailoring the interpretation of both social health need and social work service to the level of understanding and knowledge of the individual nonsocial work colleague. It does not, however, provide the opportunity for the institutionalization of social services as an integral component of patient care and or institutional planning and management that are described as a major advantage of the team concept. Nor does it allow for the same control of social work rights and responsibilities that the more structured models of collaborative practice make possible.

Given these caveats, it should be emphasized nonetheless that the development and implementation of more formal organizational structures for collaboration do not obviate the on-going need for seeing and seizing the collaborative opportunity in any given clinical or nonclinical encounter. Nor should we forget the significant role that situation-by-situation collaboration has played—and continues to play—in the development of more systematic and sophisticated ways of achieving the goals and objectives of interprofessional action.

Medical social ward rounds, initiated at both Massachusetts General Hospital and Beth Israel Hospital in Boston in the early years of social work's formal application with hospital care exemplify this conversion of the social work experience in working with physicians and nurses on a case-by-case basis into an organized way of dealing with the strictures imposed by limited or variable understanding of social work role and function and insensitivity to the psychosocial needs of patients. Designed to combine service with education through joint engagement in (1) assessing the biopsychosocial needs of given patient populations; (2) determining which patients among the total population were in need of social service; (3) establishing agreement as to shared and individual responsibilities for patient management; and (4) reviewing the status of on-going patient care activities, this early model for supplementing and enhancing case-by-case collaboration has been adapted to the needs and resources of a variety of health and medical care settings.

The postclinical conference in the public health department, the regularly scheduled meetings of treatment or planning and management teams, and the case review committee represent such adaptations. Whatever specific form they take, they are viewed by the participants as important vehicles, not only for improving the efficiency of interprofessional collaboration, but for expressing and dealing with the conflicts and misunderstandings that often stand in the way of effective working relationships.

The Health Care Team

Like medical social ward rounds and the other organizational arrangements described as promoting and facilitating group decision making, the interprofessional health team is the tangible expression of the fact that differences in knowledge, attitudes, skills, and experience are required for the full understanding and comprehensive solution of today's health problems. Teamwork, as differentiated from these other forms of group decision making, however, carries with it the notion of the interdependence of the parts. In other words, the "team" is looked upon as having a life and a lifestyle of its own, generated by its members' need for one another in order to get the job done.

It follows from this perception of the team that the nature of the job, or, more broadly, the problem to be addressed will determine the composition of a particular team and be instrumental in the designation of the team leader. Just as significantly, the team's plan of action will be formulated around the dimensions of the problem under consideration rather than dictated by the need to give each profession a "piece of the action."

Implicit in this description of the salient characteristics of the team concept is the support of the multimodel approach to team practice identified by Mailick and Jordon.[38] They view it as the appropriate response to the broadening and changing mission of the American health care system, the changing nature of the health problems it addresses, and the urgent need to make maximum use of finite human and material health care resources in problem identification and resolution. The daily collaborative practice of social work, whether in a university medical center, a community hospital, a free standing or hospital-based primary care program, or a community mental health clinic will thus increasingly require participation in a variety of health care teams that are likely to differ from one another with respect to such variables as team composition, team leadership, specific task allocations, and working style. The broader the scope of institutional mission and program, the greater the demand for flexibility in team arrangements will undoubtedly be.

Although the dominant model for teamwork practice and education has traditionally been that of the physician-led triad of doctor, nurse, and social worker, focused on the care of the sick patient in the hospital bed, we are already beginning to see departures from this eternal triangle in the organization and behavior of health care teams both within and outside hospital walls. Indeed, it becomes increasingly difficult to identify any patient care, research, or teaching activity within the modern university medical center, for example, whose interprofessional needs can be fully met by the doctor-nurse-social worker triad alone. Instead, scientific and technological advances on the one hand, social, economic, and political forces on the other have served to (1) expand the number and variety of interprofessional teams needed to get the job done; (2) influence the selection of the particular professions and disciplines required for particular teams; (3) encourage serious consideration of whether, and, if so, how the consumer should be incorporated as a member of the team; and, perhaps more subtly, (4) affect the objectives and working style of individual teams.

Thus, the rapid development of new life-saving and life-sustaining diagnostic and treatment modalities has resulted in the proliferation of specialist teams which

[38] Mailick and Jordon, "A Multimodel Approach," p. 447.

expand the doctor-nurse-social worker triad to include the new professional and technical experts needed for the comprehensive assessment and resolution of the problems of particular patient groups, defined by such variables as disease stage, diagnosis, and or therapeutic intervention. In some teams, such as those serving the needs of psychiatric patients, cancer patients, or patients in a cardiac intensive care unit, it is not uncommon to find patients and or families included as members of the team.

In a similar vein, in many medical centers and community-based programs, the growing medicalization of social problems is organizationally expressed through new formal interprofessional alliances among medicine, nursing, social work, psychology, education, and law which address such social medical phenomena as alcoholism, drug addiction, child abuse, and teenage pregnancy. Growing sensitivity to the moral and ethical issues associated with scientific and technical breakthroughs and the continuing pursuit of knowledge, to cite still another example of the influence of social change on teamwork modeling, has stimulated the establishment of other health team variations. These include ethics committees, research advisory groups, abortion committees to consider the policy and practice implications of science and technology in life-and-death terms and to advise on institutional policy with respect to these issues.

New or revised models of traditional health team organization and practice are, however, not limited to these examples of changes in the health team models associated with the planning and delivery of secondary and tertiary health care services. In fact, the need for variations from the traditional health care team was dramatically highlighted by the movement, initiated in the 1960s, to correct for the health care establishment's long neglect of both the health and sickness needs of the socially and economically disadvantaged. Whether expressed in the form of free-standing community mental health clinics and or neighborhood health centers, or as satellite programs of medical centers, the changes in the organization, financing, and delivery of health care services spawned by the social health initiatives of this turbulent period in the developmental history of the American health care system served to point up the limitations in a hospital-based model for dealing with sick persons in addressing the comprehensive health needs of people in the natural environment of home and community. To compensate for these limitations, a concerted effort was made to recruit and create appropriate roles for indigenous nonprofessional health care services. These new health careerists—family health workers, patient representatives, and community members—were awarded a legitimate place on the health care team. As further expression of the wish to dilute the influence of hospital-learned behaviors on the delivery of community-related services, new and greater responsibilities in the actual delivery of health care services and team decision making were also awarded to such nonphysician personnel as nurse practitioners, nurse midwives, and physician assistants.

Currently, these innovations in the employment and teamwork practices of the so-called "anti-establishment" movement of the 1960s have become incorporated as the everyday realities of team life in establishment-sanctioned and or sponsored community medicine programs, primary health services, and or mental health initiatives, whether institutionally or community-based. Indeed, even within some medical centers, the nurse midwife is no longer a stranger on the obstetrical team of the hospital, nor the nurse-practitioner and or physician assistant on the other speciality oriented secondary and tertiary care teams that have been previously discussed. The consumer's role and function as a member of the health care team has not only been recognized as an issue for primary care to address but moreover is increasingly seen as a legitimate consideration along the whole continuum of health care services.

How successful have these changes been, however, in eliminating the generic problems of physician dominance, territoriality, maintenance of autonomy, role confusion, and value conflict that have been identified as obstacles to the optimum exercise of difference in common cause? The answer, as it emerges from the growing written and oral history of social work's engagement in new and emerging programs of primary care and family medicine and or practice as members of speciality-oriented health care teams is that old behaviors do not yield easily to new goals, objectives, and organizational arrangements, even when they are motivated by a biopsychosocial rather than a biomedical frame of reference.

For example

> the fact that primary health care deals with problems that are essentially psychosocial rather than physical in nature and is itself as much a social as a medical program does not automatically guarantee social work either autonomy in determining the conditions of its own work or the rights of full membership in the primary health care team. . . . Nor is there convincing evidence to support the belief that these full rights can be assured or achieved more quickly and less painfully in primary than in secondary or tertiary care. On the contrary, at this developmental stage, the literature describing social work's collaborative practice in primary health care bears an uncomfortable resemblance to the literature of collaborative practice in traditional medical and psychiatric programs. There is sufficient indication to warrant genuine concern that the pressure to demonstrate the importance of social work as a modality of primary health care may limit the social work contribution to primary health care to those tasks and responsibilities which provide the social worker with the greatest sense of security and fit most neatly into other professionals' concept of social work's role and responsibility, however limited.[39]

This somewhat sobering commentary on the present status of social work within the primary health care team does not negate the validity of the current trend toward breaking away from the uni-model approach to teamwork practice. It does suggest, however, that changes in the organizational structure of the team to represent the persons and the working arrangements most conducive to getting a particu-

---

[39] Bess Dana, "Directions in Social Work Training for Primary Care" in *Primary Health Care: More Than Medicine*, ed. Rosalind S. Miller (Englewood Cliffs, N.J.: Prentice-Hall, 1983), pp. 153–159.

lar job done is the beginning, not the end, of a continuing investment of each team member in the growth and development of team effectiveness. "Effectiveness," according to Beckhard, "implies that the greatest part of the energy of the group is focused on the accomplishment of the tasks of the group. Minimum energy is required for 'maintaining' the group—its morale, its member satisfaction and its work processes."[40] His studies of organizational issues in the team delivery of comprehensive health care, however, support the general theme of this chapter—that teams, like other forms of collaboration, may be born but team effectiveness is made! The developmental steps involved in this process have already been described as the generic principles of collaboration.

Consultation

If teamwork can be termed the purest form of collaboration, consultation, by contrast, should probably be termed, if not the most impure, the most deviant from the definition of collaboration as "joint authorship." Within the context of this definition, the consultant's role most closely resembles that of the ghost writer. Because his or her activities are confined to giving advice or counsel, which the consultee is free to incorporate or not as part of the latter's own on-going activities, the consultant, like the ghost writer, gets little or no credit for the final product. On the other hand, the consultant is spared both the responsibility for translating advice into action and the burden of accountability for the outcome.

Given these departures from the concept of the collaborative process as involving shared action, shared responsibility, and shared accountability, what is the justification for admitting consultation to the extended family of collaborative modes included in this chapter? In the first place, consultation may be said to have earned its place as a close relative to collaboration by the right of eminent domain. From ancient times up to and including the present moment, members of the health care enterprise, whatever its size, shape, or level of sophistication have sought the advice of colleagues as a means of enhancing their own capacities for assessing and dealing with problems. The growth of specialization as a dominant characteristic of modern health care practice has served to institutionalize this time-honored way of bringing special knowledge to bear on the decision making of others. In a health care world of infinite need for specialized knowledge and finite resources, consultation can be justified as an important and useful way of spreading the wealth.

In the second place not all situations that can benefit from the thinking of other professions and disciplines require shared doing as well as shared thinking. The fields of public and mental health, which make extensive use of consultation as a major method of interprofessional collaboration, provide convincing empirical evidence of the power of the skillful consultant from such fields as psychiatry and or social work to enhance the psychosocial understanding of, for example, the public

[40] Richard Beckhard, "Organizational Issues in the Team Delivery of Comprehensive Health Care," *Milbank Memorial Fund Quarterly*, 50, no. 3 (July 1972), p. 292.

health nurse and to help the nurse as doer apply such understanding in the discharge of daily responsibilities.

Consultation may also be effectively used as either the prelude to or as a supplement for the establishment and on-going operation of health care teams. Thus, the experience of a group of physicians and nurses with a social work consultant may point up the advisability of developing a more systematic organizational collaborative model for insuring continuing social work engagement in group problem solving. Or, a particular interprofessional work group, whether engaged in research, teaching, policy making or patient care, may reach a point in their activities when consultation from a particular profession or discipline not represented on the group, an epidemiologist, an educational psychologist, an economist, or an ethicist, will be helpful in illuminating their understanding of a specific issue and enhance their capacities as a group to deal with the issue.

Whatever the specific purpose consultation is designed to serve, its effectiveness is dependent on many of the same behavioral principles that have been identified as essential to the effectiveness of collaboration as a generic process. Thus, in common with other collaborative modes employed in social work's interprofessional health care practice, consultation requires a fundamental identification with social work as a profession and a firm hold on social work knowledge, values, and skills. Like "pure" collaboration, social work consultation derives its raison d'être from the difference it brings to the assessment and solution of health problems. Consultation, however, makes a particular demand on the social worker's capacity to trust the ability of others to make use of the social work contribution in their own work. It facilitates this process of incorporation through the active engagement of the consultee(s) in defining the goals and objectives of consultation, specifying the questions to be addressed, and deciding the most efficient and effective ways in which the services of the consultant can be used. The principles of contracting (discussed in Chapter Four and touched upon in this chapter as well) are thus applicable to consultation.

Because by definition the consultant does not carry responsibility for translating his or her counsel into on-going action, however, the important opportunity to influence and be influenced by others through actual engagement in shared doing is denied the consultant. Therefore the consultant must place heavy reliance on the capacity to assess needs and attitudes quickly, the ability to learn from the doers, and the willingness to adapt his or her own message to the language and learning style of the consultee. Above all, the consultant must be able to live with the constraints imposed by the consultee's right to take or leave the advice given.Like Lot's wife, then, the consultant looks back to his or her own peril.

In concluding this overview of the various modalities available to social work in working with other professions and disciplines, it is important to reemphasize that, as in any social work activity, the selection of the appropriate interventive strategy is dependent on the assessment of the problem to be addressed, the human and material resources available to address and deal with the problem, and the active engagement of those with the problem in its assessment and resolution.

SOCIAL WORK COLLABORATIVE PRACTICE: COPING WITH UNCERTAINTY

Even if social workers in health care might at times wish it were otherwise, a commitment to dealing with health problems is a commitment to working with a variety of "significant others" whose differences in knowledge, values, skills and experience are essential to the assessment and resolution of the complex health problems which confront the providers and consumers of health care services alike. The issue to be addressed is thus not whether but how this commitment can be strengthened to sustain and expand the social health reach of health care programs and services at a time of a retreat from the vigorous pursuit of optimum health as a goal of national health policy.

Social work in health care must continue to look to the profession of social work itself as the major source for the renewal of unifying purpose, advancement of knowledge, and refinement of skills that will enable it to illuminate its collaborative practice, with a clear sense of social direction, well-documented evidence of social need and resources, and the demonstrated capacity to make optimum use of the differences represented in the fields and methods of social work in the definition and realization of social health goals. Implicit in this statement is perhaps the central theme of this chapter—that the degree to which *intra*professionalism is honored as a basic requirement for social work practice and education will strongly influence the effectiveness—and indeed, the efficiency, of interprofessional collaboration. Intra-professionalism, viewed from this perspective, thus becomes the conditioning process for interprofessional behavior.

If this perception of the intraprofessional-interprofessional connection is to become incorporated into the generic behavioral code of social work, then practice and education must join forces in assessing the factors in the educational and practice environment of social work as they promote or impede the development of such essential attributes of interprofessional behavior as the following:

1. A sense of professional self-worth, based on an acceptance of what social work stands for and a firm grasp of the knowledge and skills through which this stance is expressed.
2. A concomitant acceptance of the limitations of social work knowledge and skills and a readiness and willingness to learn from others.
3. The capacity for lateral thinking articulated through the establishment, maintenance, and promotion of linkages, such as those between the individual and society, the consumer and the provider, prevention and treatment, mental health and physical health, and so on.
4. The willingness to put social work needs and goals, whether individually, institutionally, or universally expressed, ahead of professional self-interests in the definition and implementation of social work tasks and responsibilities.

Efforts to work toward the achievement of intraprofessional synchronization do not negate the ongoing need for conjoint teaching and learning among and between members of the health professions. Without attention to the ways social workers, or physicians, or nurses are prepared to accept and deal with interdependence among their own kind however, conjoint learning experiences, both formal and informal, are destined to be remedial rather than reinforcing and expanding. As such, they may lose both optimum efficiency and effectiveness.

No specific formula as yet exists for ways of translating these general recommendations into specific curriculum designs or programs of continuing education in social work. Indeed, such premature cloture might well stifle the creative possibilities that exist among practitioners and educators whose contribution to a general understanding of the collaborative process is reflected throughout this chapter. Such learners through doing need, however, the support of the educational system so that what they have learned is fed into the professionalization process.

In an editorial in *The New York Times*, which addresses the issue of foreign affairs, Flora Lewis quotes from Lewis Thomas' essay, "On the Uncertainty of Science."

> . . . the urge to form partnerships, to link-up and collaborative arrangements, is perhaps the oldest, strongest and most fundamental force in nature. There are not solitary, free-living creatures: every form of life is dependent on other forms.
>
> Every species, however, has some special trait, at least one thing to be very good at, even superlatively skilled. . . . In humans, Thomas suggests, that special trait is "puzzlement." Rather than proceeding directly and infallibly about the essential business of our kind, as other life forms do, we have it built into our genes to veer off from the point; somehow, we have been selected in evolution for our gift of ambiguity.
>
> Our scientific probing of the universe hasn't misled us, but we must learn a less dogmatically arrogant approach, Thomas suggests. Modern science is a mobile, unsteady structure, made up of solid-enough single bits of information, but with all the bits always moving about, fitting together in different ways, adding new bits to themselves with flourishes of adornment as though consulting a mirror, giving the whole arrangement something like the unpredictability and unreliability of living flesh.
>
> So our puzzlement and capacity for error and trial are a plus and could lead us, too, to the wisdom of the enduring mitochondria, surviving by cooperation with the rest of life and nature.[41]

There is, in the author's view, no more appropriate way of summarizing both the necessity and the process of interprofessional collaboration.

REFERENCES

BANTA, H. DAVID & FOX, RENEE C.   Role strains of a health care team in a poverty community. *Social Science and Medicine*, 1972, 6.
BASSOFF, BETTY ZIPPIN.   Interdisciplinary education for health professionals:

[41] "Man and Mitochondria," *The New York Times*, February 20, 1981, p. A27.

Issues and Directions. *Social Work in Health Care*, Winter 1976–77, *2* (2).

BECKHARD, RICHARD. Organizational issues in the team delivery of comprehensive health care. *Milbank Memorial Fund Quarterly*, July 1972, 50 (3), part 1.

BERGSTROM, CHRISTINE. Concerns and challenges facing social workers in family practice. *The Journal of Family Practice*, 1979. *9* (4).

CANNON, IDA M. The functions of medical social service in the United States. *Hospital Social Service*, January 1933. 27 (1).

CAPUTI, MARIE A. Social work in health care: Past and future. *Health and Social Work*, February 1978, *3* (1).

CONFINO, R. Medical-social teamwork in the clinic. *Journal of the Royal College of General Practitioners*, April 1971, *21* (105).

COHEN, NATHAN E. Professional social work faces the future. *Social Work Journal*, July 1955, 36 (3).

DANA, B., BANTA, H. D., & DEUSCHLE, K. W. An agenda for the future of interprofessionalism. In Helen Rehr (Ed.) *Medicine and social work—An exploration of interprofessionalism*. New York: Prodist, 1974.

DANA, BESS. Social work in the university medical center. *The John Hopkins Medical Journal*, May 1969. *124* (5).

DANA, BESS. Perspectives on interprofessional education: The school of social work-school of medicine connection. American Geriatric Society, Chicago, April 18, 1980.

DANA, BESS. Directions in social work training for primary care. In Rosalind S. Miller (Ed.) *Primary health care: More than medicine*. (Englewood Cliffs, N.J.: Prentice-Hall, 1983) pp. 153–159.

DE WACHTER, M. Interdisciplinary framework. *Journal of Medical Ethics*, 1976, *2*.

FALCK, HANS S. Interdisciplinary education and implications for social work practice. *Journal of Education for Social Work*, Spring 1977, *13*.

FRANGOS, ANN S. & CHASE, DONNA. Potential partners: attitudes of family practice residents toward collaboration with social workers in their future practices. *Social Work in Health Care*, Fall 1976. *2* (1).

GERMAINE, CAREL B. Social context of clinical social work. *Social Work*, November 1980, *25* (6).

HIRSCH, SIDNEY & LURIE, ABRAHAM. Social work dimensions in shaping medical care philosophy and practice. *Social Work*, April 1969, *14*.

HOOKEY, PETER. Education for social work in health care organizations. *Social Work in Health Care*, Spring 1976, *1* (3).

HOOKEY, PETER. The establishment of social worker participation in rural primary care. *Social Work in Health Care*, Fall 1977, *3* (1).

KANE, ROSALIE A. *Interprofessional teamwork*. Manpower Monograph, No. 8, Syracuse: Syracuse University School of Social Work, 1975.

KANE, ROSALIE A. Interprofessional education and social work: A survey. *Social Work in Health Care*, Winter 1976–77, *2* (2).

KNOWLES, JOHN H. The teaching hospital: Historical perspective and a contemporary view. In John H. Knowles (Ed.) *Hospitals, doctors and the public interest*. Cambridge, Mass.: Harvard University Press, 1965.

KUMABE, KAZUYE T. Team approach to health care: Seeing the beauty of difference. *New concepts of human services for developing the young child*. Pittsburgh: The University of Pittsburgh Press, 1978.

LEE, STACEY. Interdisciplinary teaming in primary care: A process of evolution and resolution. *Social Work in Health Care*, Spring 1980, *5* (3).

LEININGER, MADELEINE. This I believe . . . About interdisciplinary health education for the future. *Nursing Outlook*, December 1971, *19*.

LEVINSON, H.   Management by whose objectives? *Harvard Business Review*, July-August 1970.

LIGHT, DONALD, JR.   Uncertainty and control in professional training. *Journal of Health and Social Behavior*, December 1979, *20*.

LOWE, JANE ISAACS & HERRANEN, MARJATTA.   Conflict in teamwork: Understanding roles and relationships. *Social Work in Health Care*, Spring 1978, *3* (3).

MAILICK, M. D. & JORDON, P.   A multimodal approach to collaborative practice in health settings. *Social Work in Health Care*, Summer 1977, *2* (4).

MC ELHINNEY, THOMAS K.   (Ed.)   *Human values teaching programs for health professionals*. Philadelphia: Institute on Human Values in Medicine, Report No. 7, Society for Health and Human Values, 1976.

MILLIS, JOHN S.   *A rational public policy for medical education and its financing*. New York: The National Fund for Medical Education, 1971.

MULVIHILL, MICHAEL & DANA, BESS.   The health team in community medicine. In Abdel Omran (Ed.) *Community medicine in developing countries*. Section IV. New York: Springer, 1974.

NACMAN, MARTIN.   Reflections of a social work administrator on the opportunities of crisis. *Social Work in Health Care*, Fall 1980, *6* (1).

NACMAN, MARTIN.   A systems approach to the provision of social work services in health settings: Part II. *Social Work in Health Care*, 1975, *1* (2).

NAGI, SAAD Z.   Teamwork in health care in the U.S.: A sociological perspective. *Health and Society. Milbank Memorial Fund Quarterly*. Winter 1975.

NOBLE, J. (Ed.)   *Primary care and the practice of medicine*. Boston: Little, Brown, 1976.

PHILLIPS, BEATRICE.   Social work and medical practice. *Hospitals*, 1971, *45*.

PHILLIPS, WILLIAM R.   Attitudes toward social work in family medicine; A before and after survey. *Social Work in Health Care*, Fall 1977, *3*, (1).

PLOVNICK, MARK.   The dynamics of health team development. Administrative Workshop, Birmingham, Ala., November 4, 1976 (mimeographed).

REHR, HELEN (Ed.), *Medicine and social work: An exploration in interprofessionalism*. New York: Prodist, 1974.

ROGERS, KENNETH D.   A general medical practice using nonphysician personnel. *Journal of the American Medical Association*, November 18, 1968, *206* (8).

RUBIN, IRWIN M. & BECKHARD, RICHARD.   Factors influencing and effectiveness of health teams. *Milbank Memorial Fund Quarterly*, July 1972, *L* (3) part 1.

SCHENK, FREDI.   A course on collaboration between social workers and general practitioners during their vocational training. *Medical Education*, January 1979, *13* (1).

STOECKLE, JOHN D. & TWADDLE, A. C.   Non-physician health workers: Some problems and prospects. *Social Science and Medicine*, 1974, *8*.

WAX, JOHN.   Developing social work power in a medical organization. *Social Work*, October 1968.

WAX, JOHN.   Power theory and institutional change. *Social Service Review*, 1971, *45* (3).

SOLLITTO, S., VEATCH, R. M., & TAYLOR, N. K.   *Bibliography of society, ethics, and life sciences*. New York: Hastings-on-Hudson, 1976–1977.

TICHY, M. (Ed.)   *Health care teams: An annotated bibliography*. New York: Prager, 1974.

CHAPTER SIX
APPLIED SOCIAL WORK RESEARCH

Barbara Berkman and
L. Andrew Weissman

RESEARCH: CENTRAL
COMPONENT OF PRACTICE

Millions of dollars are expended each year to provide social work services to people. Little is known about what has happened to these people after they receive social work services. Information is rarely gathered systemmatically about whether those who utilize social work services feel better or function better for having received them and whether they were satisfied with these services.

We view the health setting as not just a system for the delivery of social-health care but as a "living laboratory for research."[1] Social workers in health care settings are continuously impacted by the ongoing research of the medical and psychiatric departments, hospital administration, the regulatory agencies, and their own social work departments. These sources turn to social workers to help gather data for a range of studies. Our experience leads us to believe that when social workers help pose the study problems, when their interest or expertise are brought to bear on research endeavors, or when the problems studied are in direct relevance to their actual day-to-day practice, then the final products have a direct bearing on and are more useful to social work's clinical practice.

We think that social work research endeavors in health care settings are essential. They serve to potentially enhance services to patients, and more importantly, social workers find them exciting because they affect practice. We believe that social workers should be knowledgeable about research, should be able to participate

---

[1] Barbara Berkman, "The Agency—A Living Laboratory for Research," paper presented at Council on Social Work Education, 1975 Annual Program Meeting, Chicago: March 4, 1975.

in the design and data gathering of research, and help analyze the results of these studies. We hope this chapter will encourage you as a social worker in health care, to find your place in the many interesting and socially focused research endeavors that are ongoing in the health care setting, and to begin to pose your own questions to review your practice. This chapter is designed to that end.

Although the procedures we will be describing have limitations and provide only a broad outline of how we can examine patients' reactions to social work services, finding out "even if only roughly, what happens to clients is too important to wait for a perfect set of procedures to be developed."[2]

Research is a systemmatic searching for answers to precisely stated questions using empirical facts which when analyzed, result in verifiable knowledge.[3] There usually have been sharp distinctions drawn between social work practice and social work research. But as we think about it, the process of social casework is very similar to the processes of research. Research includes formulating a problem; setting hypotheses or questions about how the problem came to be; collecting and analyzing data; evaluating the outcome of intervention; and drawing conclusions that are supported by the data. Basically, "every case can and should be a research project for the practitioner."[4]

In casework practice, the social worker goes through the process of assessing the causes for a patient's problem(s) by drawing on knowledge both of psychosocial phenomena and of the patient as an individual. Keeping specific possibilities in mind, the worker listens to what the patient is saying and begins to speculate on the meaning. The social worker then formulates an assessment drawing on knowledge and experience, and finding where the patient fits. Intervention follows with varying degrees of confidence and enthusiasm. If the patient or the family member begins to improve and to handle the situation in a manner the social worker had predicted, the assessment has probably been accurate and the intervention effective, although the patient or family could also improve when the original social work assessment was incorrect. But the conscientious social worker asks the right questions, obtains answers accurately, and draws the proper conclusions both from the individual patients and family while drawing on the experience of others described in the social work literature. Subsequent social work practice is guided by the experience the worker gathers.[5]

The process of systemmatically examining one's own practice through research may help a social worker reduce the vicissitudes of providing social work services to patients. We have all come out of sessions with families excited by our interventions, and by a patient's and a family member's responses to our efforts to help them. We

[2] Alfred H. Schainblatt, "What Happens to Clients?" *Community Mental Health Journal*, 16, no. 4 (Winter 1980), p. 342.

[3] Jerry S. Turem, "Research Priorities in Social Work Education: A Communication to Colleagues," *Source Book on Research Utilization*, ed. Allen Rubin and Aaron Rosenblatt (New York: Council on Social Work Education, 1979), pp. 31-53.

[4] Katherine M. Wood, "Casework Effectiveness: A New Look at the Research Evidence," *Social Work* 23 (November 1978), pp. 437-459.

[5] Thomas C. Chalmers, *Milbank Memorial Fund Quarterly*, 59, no. 3 (1981), pp. 324-5.

have also come out of interviews with the same families feeling we have not known what we were doing, totally confused, and wondering why we chose social work as a profession. These are very familiar thoughts and feelings for clinical social workers and these experiences have helped most social workers become more aware of their abilities. However, "we believe that the best help comes from having systemmatic procedures from learning from both our failures as well as our successes."[6] The helping process in working with people is not an exact science. Because there are no definite rules for proceeding at different points in intervention, social workers need to routinely and systemmatically examine what they do. For so doing each social worker can best know, along with practice studies, how he or she is functioning as a professional.

For our purposes, social work research may be viewed as having two interrelated areas of concern: research aimed at improving the helping process and research aimed at generating knowledge. The first related primarily to current practice issues: what seems to work best, with whom, and in what situation. These are concerned with professional practice roles. On the other hand, the verification of knowledge: what is true, what is the cause of certain events, and what is the relationship between different variables, is a major social work research goal. Within the social work education curriculum, the objectives of the research courses presently taught are to prepare students to produce, to participate in or to utilize research, or combinations of these goals. This means that students should be able to use the findings from relevant research studies to inform their practice on a day-by-day basis and or they should be able to participate in or to conduct research.

These expectations have generated different models of research for social work education.[7] This chapter will present various ways for you to begin to participate in relevant research or to conduct research on your own cases. In addition, we will present specific knowledge generated by social work research in health care that will help to inform your practice and will allow you to utilize newer existing studies as they appear.

In the following section we will discuss research the practitioners can begin to do on their own cases, focusing on four areas: (1) descriptive studies, (2) process research, (3) client satisfaction studies, and (4) effectiveness and or outcome studies.

DESCRIPTIVE STUDIES

Descriptive research details the problems of patients and the activities and characteristics of social workers, including the roles they occupy in the health service delivery system. It is essential that the descriptive studies on social work service delivery

---

[6] John M. Gottman and Sandra R. Leiblum, *How to Do Psychotherapy and How to Evaluate It* (New York: Holt, Rinehart & Winston, 1974), p. 9.

[7] Aaron Rosenblatt, "Research Models for Social Work Education," in *Research Utilization and Social Work Education*, eds. Scott Briar, Harold Weissman, and Allen Rubin (New York: Council on Social Work Education, 1981), pp. 17-20.

patterns continue to be produced. "There is as yet no comprehensive data on the incidence and prevalence of patient problems or services delivered in the health care system."[8]

The main requirement for any social worker doing a descriptive study in a health care setting is (1) categorization of the problems presented by patients, and (2) some categories of the interventive services that social workers provide in relationship to these problems. The following problem list was developed in a hospital setting and has been used in many health care settings around the country as a way of categorizing the requests patients make of social workers:[9]

1. Concrete aids medically recommended (telephone, appliances, prosthesis, equipment, etc.).
2. Coping with grief reaction and bereavement.
3. Coping with interpersonal relations (e.g., marital problems; school problems; care of children).
4. Educational or vocational functioning problems.
5. Family interrelationships adversely affect patient's condition and/or response to hospital.
6. Family members need help in coping with patient's needs.
7. Financial management/assistance/applications.
8. Health education needed (e.g., family planning)
9. Home health supports needed (coordinated home care program)
10. Home supports needed (e.g., homemaker, home health aide, baby-sitter, day care).
11. Hospital service complaints.
12. Housing unsuitable for continuing needs (e.g., too many stairs, inadequate kitchen, security).
13. Legal services needed.
14. Letters or reports needed for other agencies.
15. Long term ambulatory care needed (e.g., psychiatric OPD services; other social agencies; day hospital).
16. Long-term institutional care needed.
17. Patient/family having role disorder problems as result of illness/disorder/pregnancy.
18. Patient/family problems with staff.
19. Patient/family anxiety stress or depressive reactions related to diagnosis, medical procedures, prognosis or treatment, dying, etc.
20. Patient/family anxiety stress or depression (e.g., thought and mood disturbance/psychomatization).
21. Patient has problems in self-esteem; feelings of inadequacy; or in sexual functioning.

[8] Claudia J. Coulton, "Research on Social Work in Health Care: Progress and Future Directions," in *The Future of Social Work Research*, ed. David Fanshel (Washington, D.C.: National Association of Social Workers, 1980), p. 133.

[9] Barbara Berkman, "Psychosocial Problems and Outcome: An External Validity Study," *Health and Social Work*, 5, no. 3 (August 1980), pp. 5-21.

22. Permanent placement required for child(ren) (e.g., adoption, foster home).
23. Psychosocial evaluation only for assessment of ability to use treatment, or re-admission to hospital.
24. Sheltered care needed (e.g., half-way house; foster home for adults).
25. Social isolation/withdrawal.
26. Temporary care of dependent child(ren) during patient's hospitalization.
27. Temporary institutional care away from home.
28. Transportation services needed.
29. Visiting nurses service needed.

A categorization of the services social workers provide in hospital settings has not as yet been fully developed. A beginning typology developed at Johns Hopkins Hospital follows.[10]

1. Admission planning
2. Discharge planning
3. Other health planning
4. Counseling—illness
5. Counseling—psychosocial
6. Counseling—situational
7. Provision of marital help
8. Referral to community
9. Coordinating services

A social worker conducting a descriptive study would be involved in describing the population of patients served, and reporting the kinds of problems presented by patients and the services provided in relation to those problems. Studies that have been conducted this way have shown that the average contact with the patient on the in-patient medical services usually results in social workers dealing with two areas: (1) an environmental-resource problem that affects the patient or family, and (2) a psychological problem related to either illness or to disruption of family relationships brought about by the illness. These kinds of studies result in a data base that enable us to develop interventive models that are more in tune with the social worker's experience in health care settings rather than trying to modify intervention models that have been developed in other social work settings.[11]

On a more personal level, descriptive studies allow the practicing social worker in a health care setting to look for the similarities and differences in the people they serve. These studies help social workers begin to separate the typical patients and the problems they present from the special situations that may require different types of interventions. This process then enables the social worker to gather information,

[10] Specific definitions in the use of these service categories are explained in the *Johns Hopkins Department of Social Work, Recording and Reporting Manual*.

[11] Roslyn H. Chernesky and Abraham Lurie, "Developing a Quality Assurance Program," *Health and Social Work*, 1, no. 1 (February 1976), pp. 117-30.

identify resources, and delineate interventive techniques useful for the typical kinds of patients and families workers help.

PROCESS STUDIES

Studies of the process of care do not examine the effect of social work services on the patient. The assumption is made that good practice will lead to good outcomes. It should be noted that this assumption has not as yet been tested in social work. What has been revealed in studies of medical care is that what medical practitioners prescribe as acceptable processes do not necessarily lead to acceptable outcomes; and conversely bad practice does not necessarily lead to bad outcomes.[12]

However, "process research is a key link in the building of theory for effective practice."[13] Although attempts to define and measure the actual elements of social work process are innumerable, "social workers have yet to develop a uniform language or taxonomy for defining and labeling their services."[14]

In focusing on the process of social work care, social workers help develop criteria of acceptable practice. That is, standards are established for the key ingredients of effective practice, and a judgment is made as to whether they are present in the work that is being reviewed. Either chart notes, audio tapes, or video tapes are reviewed to determine whether there is evidence that these criteria established by colleagues have been met.

In social work in health care settings, peer review is a formal mechanism by which process research is conducted. Criteria are developed for either a whole social work department, or a service area; the work on a specific case is judged as acceptable or unacceptable by the presence or absence of the specified criteria. Considerations of process criteria for formal peer review include the following: Is there a clear rationale for opening the case? Is the negotiation of a mutually agreed-upon contract between the social work practitioner and the patient evident? Is the social worker intervention presented in a clear manner? Is there evidence of appropriate collaboration with family members and other health professions? Is the outcome of the intervention detailed? It should be noted that the social work profession has made a beginning attempt to construct formal peer review processes. However, we are not quite sure how to best carry out process studies in health care settings.[15]

Such a study can also be done by an individual social worker with his colleagues serving as an informal peer review group. We all end up talking over lunch or coffee about our cases, what we are doing, and what problems our cases present. By

---

[12] Claudia J. Coulton, "Research on Social Work in Health Care."

[13] Anne E. Fortune, "Communication Processes in Social Work Practice," *Social Service Review*, 55, no. 1 (March 1981), p. 93.

[14] Claudia J. Coulton and Nathaniel Butler, "Measuring Social Work Productivity in Health Care," *Health and Social Work*, 6, no. 3 (August 1981), p. 6.

[15] Roslyn H. Chernesky and Alma T. Young, "Developing a Peer Review System," in *Professional Accountability for Social Work Practice*, ed. Helen Rehr (New York: Prodist, 1979), pp. 74-92.

providing yourself with a framework based on criteria that you and your colleagues agree upon, you can check your own work to see if important processes are present or absent. As a check you can ask your colleagues to read what you have written about cases in your chart notes and see whether they think your work is adequate or needs improvement. The systemmatic gathering of these informal observations will alert you to areas of your practice that need reinforcement, or areas that other people think are important. They will give you a systemmatic way to begin to examine and to change your practice outside the formal structure of supervisory process.

Additional kinds of process research using what social work practitioners say to clients has been developed by Florence Hollis and later expanded by William J. Reid. The typology of social work process has been used in numerous studies and consists of examining practice through the following types of intervention. Here is one interventive or treatment typology.

1. Sustainment: expressions of interest, sympathetic understanding, confidence in client, acceptance and approval of client;
2. Direct influence: suggestions, advice, enforcement of specific action, advocating for the client;
3. Exploration-description-ventilation: encouragement of exploration or ventilation of client's current or past situation;
4. Person-situation reflection: expressions intended to change perceptions of understanding of world, own behavior, outcomes of behavior, causes of own behavior, evaluation of self, confrontation, logical discussion;
5. Personality reflection: encouragement of understanding of the client's personality patterns, characteristics, dynamics;
6. Early life reflection: encouragement of understanding of aspects of early life that influence present behavior, enhancement of understanding of developmental origins of patterns of response;
7. Others: structuring the treatment relationship, explanations of treatment, topics, fees.[16]

Such a typology provides a base for studies using either process recording or taped interviews as primary data; impartial judges then classify the social worker's communications to patients in one of the listed categories. This research attempts to determine what categories of social work intervention take place. In other words, do the patterns of social work intervention differ from one setting to another? What factors seemed to influence the use of these various processes? How do clients react to different mixes of these processes? What were the relationships of these various processes to outcome?

The results of the use of these typologies show that they are adequate for analysis of social work practice in that levels of the different processes can be measured and appear to distinguish between different types of service (for example, planned short-term treatment versus open-ended treatment). These types of process

[16] Fortune, "Communication Processes in Social Work Practice," p. 98.

studies also point up that one process, direct influence, is highly related to higher levels of client satisfaction with service. Patients complain if the social worker assumes a passive role and is reticent to offer advice; those patients who receive more advice from practitioners tend to rate social work services as more beneficial. The reasons for this are still unclear. Another important finding from these studies is that certain processes, such as insight-oriented work, personality reflection, or early life reflection occur much less frequently than we would expect from our theoretical literature.[17]

By examining the typical social work processes you use in a health care setting where you practice, you may be able to pinpoint various clusters of interventive strategies or processes that are most helpful to patients needing different kinds of services. It is evident then that informal peer review studies, formal peer review, and process studies can aid workers in accurately defining what types of social work intervention they are delivering to a patient population and where they may want to change their interventions.

CLIENT SATISFACTION STUDIES

"Obtaining the views and insights of those we help is an essential means of critically examining our practice in refining our knowledge and skills. If we allow ourselves to learn from clients we may well be able to enhance our own competence as well as theirs."[18]

Follow-up studies serve a useful purpose in that the patient's point of view of social work service is examined. One of the uses of follow-up studies, soliciting patient's opinions of social work services, is that they expose areas where social workers' and patients' perspectives and points of view are incongruent and then outcomes may be problematic. For example, one follow-up study reported that a majority of social workers thought at least half the patients they served wished to discuss personal problems in the interviews, while follow-up studies show that only 8 percent of the patients expected to do this. The same study found that over 50 percent of the social workers thought that most clients would complain about delays in receiving services but only 9 percent did so; the clients seemed to have a more realistic expectation of what was possible under the present staffing conditions than the social workers. More importantly one-third of the clients and patients who had seen social workers initially had no idea of what to expect in terms of their social work contacts.[19] In these follow-up studies the basic question being asked is "Were the social work services provided helpful to you?" This type of data can be gathered from a lengthy questionnaire or it may be a short questionnaire with no more than three or four questions. What follows is a brief questionnaire used in some studies but which could be modified for an individual practitioner's own use.

[17] *Ibid.*, p. 119.

[18] Anthony N. Maluccio, *Learning from Clients* (New York: Free Press, 1979), p. xii.

[19] E. Matilda Goldberg and R. William Warburton, *Ends and Means in Social Work* (London: George Allen and Unwin, 1979), pp. 15–16.

PATIENT QUESTIONNAIRE

1. Consider the problem you most wanted the social worker to help you with. How is this problem now compared with how it was when you started receiving social work service here?

    _____ It is no longer present
    _____ It is a lot better
    _____ It is a little better
    _____ It is about the same
    _____ It is worse
    _____ Other

2. On the whole, how are you getting along now compared with when you first began receiving social work services here?

    _____ Much better
    _____ A little better
    _____ About the same
    _____ Worse
    _____ Other

3. The social worker

    _____ Helped with most of the problems that were bothering me
    _____ Helped me with some of the problems that were really bothering me but we did not get to all of them
    _____ Didn't help me much at all
    _____ Other

4. If I had a problem again that I would need help with, I would want to have

    _____ The kind of social work services I have just completed
    _____ A different kind of service
    _____ Other

5. Did the social worker seem to understand what you wanted?

    _____ Yes
    _____ No
    _____ Unsure

6. Was the social worker able to help you?

    _____ Yes
    _____ No
    _____ Unsure

Modifications in the various wordings in this type of questionnaire can be developed to suit specific health care settings. A social worker on a surgical service might prefer to include questions related to preoperative counseling for example. Or in a survey of people receiving service in a pediatric or child guidance clinic, the questions can be focused more to the family of the child rather than to the child itself.

There are different ways to do follow-up studies. The three basic choices used in social work research are (1) face-to-face interviews, using a structured questionnaire, (2) telephone interviews, or (3) mailed questionnaires.[20] An individual worker practicing in a health care setting probably does not have the time nor the energy to conduct face-to-face follow-up interviews with patients. Depending upon the size of sample required, a worker can choose to mail questionnaires to a randomly selected sample of patients or to all patients the worker has seen, for example, during a three- or four-month period. However, using mailed questionnaires either to a randomly selected sample of patients served or to all patients the social worker has served, is certainly doable. Phone follow-up surveys are obviously more time consuming than a mailed questionnaire but they have the advantage of a higher response rate.

Whatever choice is made, the data is gathered from follow-up questionnaires and tallied; the social worker then has direct evidence from the patients served how helpful the social worker's activities have been from the patient's and or family's point of view. Very often, brief contacts with patients, which social workers tend to undervalue, are perceived as extremely beneficial by patients and their families.

Follow-up studies also enable us to gather information about resources we have tried to arrange for patients and their families. One study examining what actually happened to patients during the posthospital phase found that only 60 percent of the patients reported that their needs had been adequately met one month after their discharge from the hospital.[21] As social workers do follow-up studies in health care settings, they may find that linking patients and families to community resources and making sure those connections are adequate will require more of their time.

For the practicing social worker, follow-up studies provide important information. As we continue under heavy case loads to provide service, we attempt to help our patients before they are discharged. We rarely have time to find out what they thought of what we did. Second, we rarely have time to find out for ourselves which piece of our intervention seemed to work and which did not. The point to be reinforced here is that it pays to ask the patients and families we have provided with service what they think about what we did. It gives us an added piece of information that may help us validate our work or reassess a technique we have tried. Even if a practicing social worker can only call a few patients a week or send out questionnaires to a few patients and their families, the information gathered will help assess the practitioner's work. One problem with doing any kind of follow-up research is that it takes a commitment of time on the part of the practicing social worker. By the same token, a social service department committed to research, monitors its services to constantly enhance the quality of patient care.

[20] Tony Tripodi and Irwin Epstein, *Research Techniques for Clinical Social Workers* (New York: Columbia University Press, 1980), p. 47.

[21] Ruth Ellen Lindenberg and Claudia Coulton, "Planning for Post-Hospital Care: A Followup Study," *Health and Social Work*, 5, no. 1 (February 1980), p. 49.

We hope we have made clear in this section that follow-up studies allow us to let the patients speak to us so that we may learn from them how they perceive we can provide better services, and that conducting a follow-up study and getting the patient's or family's responses to our intervention can be a fairly straightforward process.[22]

EFFECTIVENESS AND OR
OUTCOME STUDIES

Evaluation and outcome studies examine the effect of social work intervention. These studies try to determine the success or failure of social work interventions. That is, did what the social worker do make a difference and is that difference replicable, observable, and in the direction we expect? Evaluation and or outcome studies must of necessity be based on the previous types of research we have described. We must know first what is being done with whom before it is possible to find out whether it works or not. Only through evaluative and or outcome studies will we eventually be able to improve social work practice in health care settings. Unfortunately, most outcome studies in social work are based on behavioral change indicators developed from studies of the therapeutic process. However, "the majority of social work services in health facilities are not directed towards producing behavioral change in the patient. The services delivered are more likely to be geared to changing the patient's environment as an objective and the research consequently cannot rely on the counting of observable behaviors."[23] For example, if the goal of service is to arrange for a stable, suitable living situation for an elderly amputee, we need to develop the tools to determine whether or not our intervention has led to a living situation, which while stable, is also beneficial.

Numerous instruments have been developed to measure change in patients during social work intervention. For example, Hudson has developed indexes of marital satisfaction, measures of self-esteem, and scales to measure parental attitudes towards children, designed to be answered by patients in a very brief time so as to be simple and nonthreatening.[24] Coulton is developing an interview schedule designed to measure the fit of a person in his environment.[25] By using these types of instruments during the initial stages of social work intervention and then again at the termination of social work services, a social worker will be provided with a measure of any changes that occurred over the course of working with the patient.

Goal attainment scaling is another approach that measures the outcome of

[22] For a complete discussion of the methodological problems in consumer satisfaction studies see John Ware, Allyson Davies-Avery, and Anita Stewart, "The Measurement and Meaning of Patient Satisfaction," *Health and Medical Care Services Review*, 1, no. 1 (January-February 1978), pp. 2-15.

[23] Coulton, "Research on Social Work in Health Care, p. 132.

[24] For a discussion of measurement instruments, see Walter W. Hudson, *The Clinical Measurement Package: A Field Manual* (Homewood, Ill.: Dorsey Press) 1982.

[25] Claudia J. Coulton, "Developing an Instrument to Measure Person-Environment Fit," *Journal of Social Service Research*, 3, no. 2 (Winter 1979), pp. 159-74.

social work practice.[26] This approach determines whether or not the problems that cause the patient to use professional social work help have been alleviated. It depends on a very precise goal setting by the social worker with the patient. Goal attainment scales are based on individual problems and specific levels of functioning; the problems are identified by the patient and social worker and form the basis for social worker-patient contract. In general, goal attainment scales are based on observable indicators of a patient's and or family's functioning as they relate to their problems. For example, a patient, as a result of illness and subsequent disability, identifies feeling trapped because of a reduction in the patient's community activity. Using a goal attainment scaling approach, the social worker and patient will determine how much activity outside the house the person is presently engaged in and would then describe what an intermediate level of progress would be and what their expected goals together would be. For example, the patient, who now only goes out every other week would go out three times a week. Worker and patient would also pinpoint what a better than expected goal might be (going out more than three times a week) and what a less satisfactory outcome would be (going out of the house once a month). During the process of working with the patient, the social worker, patient, or family member keeps track of the number of outside activities. The social worker's interventions might include bringing together resources, such as transportation, that would enable the patient to engage in some of the previously valued activities (see Figure 6-1).

Bloom has suggested that there are ways of evaluating a very common occurrence in health care settings, that is single interventions.[27] He points out that we should be evaluating what he terms the *intermediate goals*, representing what a social worker's contribution is to resolving a patient's problem, as well as the ultimate goals which relate more specifically to a patient's request. Very often in health care settings, we find that patients are in need of resources in the community, such as, homemakers, home health care services, or visiting nurse service. What becomes important for us to evaluate is whether our interventions made it possible for the patient to receive the services provided by the resources. Whether the resource then provided quality service is something that is beyond the control of the social worker in the health care setting. Following Bloom's suggestion, this means that we would be tracking whether in fact a referral to the appropriate resource was made, whether the resource had agreed to provide the service to the patient, whether the appropriate forms were sent to the resource, whether they were received, whether the patient understood what the resource was going to provide, and whether the resource did provide the service. This is a fairly straightforward way of looking at a large number of health care interventions that social workers provide. This type of study, coupled with follow-up research to determine whether what the resource

[26] Thomas Kiresuk and Robert Sherman, "Goal Attainment Scaling: A General Method of Evaluating Comprehensive Community Health Programs," *Journal of Community Mental Health*, 4, no. 6 (1968), pp. 443-53.

[27] Martin Bloom, Patricia Butch, Doris Walker, "Evaluation of Single Interventions," *Journal of Social Service Research*, 2, no. 3 (Spring 1979), pp. 301-310.

FIGURE 6-1 Goal Attainment Scale

Social Worker: _____ *Patient Name* _____

Problem: ___ Lack of activity outside the home _____

  Worse than initial level ___ Goes out once a month _____

  Initial level ___ Every other week _____

  Expected intermediate level ___ Once a week _____

  Expected goal at termination ___ Three times a week _____

  Better than expected level ___ More than three times a week _____

  Has this been negotiated with the patient?   Yes ___X___   No ___

---

provided was adequate and met the needs of the patient, is extremely important in evaluating the practice of social work in health care settings.[28]

Single-Subject Designs

Single-subject designs enable practitioners to subjectively monitor patient progress throughout every case to obtain continuous feedback that enables workers to scientifically evaluate the outcome of their interventions. Although the results of single-subject research have proliferated and numerous examples are available, this type of research, as yet, has little applicability to most of the work being done in health care settings.[29]

Single-subject designs follow the general rigor of experimental outcome research. Generally, these types of studies have been based on a method in which some behaviors (a patient's report of feelings, thoughts, or behaviors) are measured over a period of time before the social worker intervenes (the baseline). The social worker then compares the patterns of these observable or reported behaviors during and after social work intervention. The items to be measured are selected to reflect the problems and the goals on which the social worker and patient agree.

For example, a social worker in a hospital may learn that a patient recovering from surgery is anxious and upset. The nurses have noted in the chart that the patient, recovering well from surgery, seems upset, agitated, and unmanageable. They have learned that the patient cannot get clear information on the financial liability for the hospital bill and they speculate that this might be related to the anxiety.

---

[28] For information on referral techniques, see Joel Fisher, *Effective Casework Practice: An Eclectic Approach* (New York: McGraw-Hill, 1978), pp. 24-25.

[29] Claudia J. Coulton, "Research for the Social Work Practitioner," *Social Work in a State-Based System of Child Care*, ed. Elizabeth Watkins (Washington, D.C.: Office for Maternal and Child Health, 1980), pp. 132-146. For numerous examples of single-subject design, see any issue of the *Journal of Applied Behavior Analysis* or see "Special Issue on Single-System Research Designs," ed., Martin Bloom, *Journal of Social Service Research*, 3, no. 1 (Fall 1979).

The social worker, in talking with the patient, explores the present insurance coverage and benefits, and provides accurate information to the patient and family about the deductibles as well as the entitlements. Following this intervention, the patient, less anxious, is more manageable and can begin to talk about other areas of concern such as what is going to happen to the patient and the family as he or she prepares to leave the hospital.

The systemmatic capturing of this data will provide us with tentative evidence about the outcome of social work intervention (providing needed information in an unclear confusing situation seemed to alleviate distress). It would not provide conclusive evidence of successful outcome because we have no way of knowing who else the patient talked with (a relative, physician, or other person who might have also given information of which the social worker is unaware). However, it would give us a beginning indication of the problem. The patient was upset over a period of time and expressed it openly to the nurses and physicians on the floor; an intervention was provided by the social worker who gathered needed information and conveyed it to the patient in an understandable way; and the outcome was the patient was no longer agitated and upset.

Such a model is the basic format for both single-subject designs and more rigorous kinds of outcome studies. The numerous methodological problems of this design have been detailed elsewhere. Techniques that improve on this design are described in detail in the social work literature.[30] This literature examines both the measurement problems and the statistical problems in conducting research on individual cases and on social work programs. The approaches described detail experimental designs that involve the random assignment of patients to social work intervention and to control groups, which receive no social work intervention, or more sophisticated alternatives such as experimental designs.

These designs indicate that most studies have to involve more than the individual practitioner. For example, one study examined children who viewed a film of another child undergoing a hospital experience, and hypothesized that they would show less anxiety than children who observe an unrelated film, even when both groups of children receive additional psychological preparation by hospital staff. Numerous scales of trait anxiety by observers were used, as were state anxiety measurements using the Palmer Sweat Index (which involves measurement of active sweat glands on the index finger of children). Measurements were taken before the film, immediately following the film, before the operation, and immediately prior to the postoperative examination, three to four weeks after discharge. The results support the efficacy of using a film to prepare children for the hospital experience. However, many of the measurements utilized showed random changes between the control group and the group that saw the film with another child in it.[31] In more elaborate studies, a team or multidisciplinary approach may be indicated, with each health provider assigned to a specific research function.

[30] Srinika Jayaratne and Rona L. Levy, *Empirical Clinical Practice* (New York: Columbia University Press, 1979), and Tripodi and Epstein, *Research Techniques for Clinical Social Workers.*

[31] Barbara G. Melamed and Lawrence J. Siegel, *Behavioral Medicine* (New York: Springer, 1980), pp. 307–331.

Program Evaluation

Program evaluation studies are not merely compilations of descriptive studies, satisfaction studies, process studies, and or outcome studies. Programmatic research seeks to assess the effects of an organization's operation on the direct participants and other designated groups. Program evaluation emphasizes asking if the program changes the situation in a desirable direction.

Should social work programs be evaluated? One social work administrator was asked how he knew his program was successful and he answered, "If it weren't successful I wouldn't be doing it." Such an answer reflects a tendency to confuse a belief in program objectives with evidence of program impact.

There are three general reasons why a program might wish to evaluate itself: (1) to justify its existence to some authority (usually the source of funds and or support); (2) to ascertain the extent to which it is reaching its objectives; and (3) to improve its performance.

Program justification is one reason for conducting an evaluation, but in the beginning stages of social work programs in health care, it is probably not a very good reason. Because there is no universally accepted technology for conducting social work programs, it is not sufficient to argue that just because a program has been implemented, it will necessarily be successful. Two additional questions must be asked. First, has the program in fact been implemented according to the plan (are there tasks that were to be performed and are in fact being performed in the proper or expected manner)? Second, is it achieving its objectives or should the program plan be altered to improve performance? Even if a program need not demonstrate its effectiveness to outsiders, it certainly should be concerned with finding ways to improve its effectiveness.

For example, a planned parenthood clinic set up in the early 1950s on the southside of Chicago on the edge of a black ghetto, found itself so swamped with clients drawn from students at the University of Chicago that it never saw fit to start an outreach program to reach its original target population. The individual practitioners in the clinic were indeed providing effective and useful services, but the program, as originally formulated, was not meeting its objectives.[32]

Program evaluation may be defined as the systematic accumulation of facts for providing information about the achievement of a program, relative to efforts, effectiveness, and efficiency. Using this definition, efforts refer to the description both of type and quantity of program activities; effectiveness deals with whether the intended outcomes have been obtained as the result of program efforts; and efficiency deals with determining the relative cost of achieving these outcomes.[33]

Thus while social workers are evaluating their own practice, they must be aware of the context in which their work takes place and the multidisciplinary nature of program evaluation. Program evaluation rests on the degree to which program

[32] Peter H. Rossi, "Some Issues in the Evaluation of Human Services Delivery," *The Management of Human Services*, eds. Rosemary C. Sarri and Yeheskel Hasenfeld (New York: Columbia University Press, 1978), pp. 235-61.

[33] Tony Tripodi, Phillip Fellin, and Irwin Epstein, *Differential Social Program Evaluation* (Itasca, Ill.: F. E. Peacock, 1978), pp. 9-10.

activities and outcomes are measured with regard to the program's objectives. Without clearly defined objectives, evaluation cannot proceed since it would become impossible to judge whether objectives are being met. In multidisciplinary health care settings agreement on the objectives of both the health care program and the social work program, in measurable terms, are difficult to specify. It should not be expected that all aspects of a program will be measured all of the time. In most health care settings with limited resources, it is wiser to develop a plan that would include monitoring of a few key items that will allow adjustment of the social work program depending on its stage of development, or immediate problems. From our point of view, program evaluation should begin with the planning of programs and should enable information to be fed back to the staff and administrators in a way that enables a program to modify its activities to meet its stated objectives.

This section of the chapter has provided some guidelines for practicing social workers to begin conducting descriptive studies, process studies, and patient satisfaction studies. We have also discussed the importance of outcome studies. In summary we will try to point out where we think practice-oriented researchers should put their emphases: (1) systemmatically examine the tasks to be performed by social workers in health care settings; (2) define and test the skills needed to perform those tasks; (3) gather systemmatical information about the activities of social workers and their affects on different patient groups; and (4) establish carefully controlled experimental studies to evaluate the outcome of social work using criteria meaningful to both patients and social workers. Such studies will have to be concerned with effectiveness—is the patient better off—as well as efficiency—at what cost? We emphasize that we have placed experimental studies and outcome studies last on this list of practice-oriented research emphases. Until we know what it is we are evaluating and can formulate relevant descriptive categories for types of patients, problems, and services including desired objectives, there is very little point to establish such experimental studies.

We now want to present social work research endeavors that address specific practice concerns. The research examples illustrate systematic studies; it is hoped that these studies will introduce you to the importance of research in every aspect of the delivery of social work services in health settings and begin to inform your practice on a day-to-day basis.

RESEARCH ON UTILIZATION
AND ACCESSIBILITY
OF SERVICES

Utilization research addresses services used by our identified clientele, and attempts to uncover the needs of prospective clientele. Such research has a number of objectives. The findings can be used to document actual and perceived social health needs and also document the service utilization patterns of persons in the community. Studies of this nature uncover whether the existing (or proposed) social health program adequately meets psychosocial needs; the data may also serve to determine what additional programming or restructuring of services may improve upon quality care.[34] This type of information provides health care planners, policy makers, and consumers with documented evidence.[35] For example, Marchant reported on the study of the utilization of social services to the deaf.[36] The findings reveal that while a majority of human service agencies have had some contacts with deaf clients, only those agencies that have made an effort to develop programs especially for the deaf and employ personnel skilled in sign language could deliver services effectively to this population. The study identifies gaps between the services needed by the deaf population and the services delivered by the agencies. The findings have important implications for the future development of services to deaf patients.

Another utilization study identifies all elderly patients admitted to the medical and surgical services of a large metropolitan hospital.[37] The researchers then look at what proportion of these patients were referred to social work services and what differentiated the elderly who needed social services from those who did not. Interestingly enough, the determining factor in referral to social service is extended "length of stay." This study led the way to a series of studies that explores what other psychosocial factors are linked to extended lengths of stay so that these patients can be identified early in their hospitalization. Selig believes that the type of utilization study conducted in medical settings needs to be done in psychiatric settings.[38]

As another example of utilization research, there is the comparative study of psychosocial care among residents in different types of long-term care facilities. Residents in voluntary and nonprofit homes seem to do much better than residents who live in facilities which offer services primarily to Medicaid beneficiaries.[39] The study is important in that it identifies facilities which do not meet appropriate standards of care. Monk and Dobrof emphasize that one of the major areas for policy formulation in relation to the elderly is research data to help assess the specific needs of this population, examine what services are required, specify what are the most effective interventions, and determine how the services can be delivered in the most effective and efficient way.[40] Frequently it is not known what social services

[34] Helen Rehr and Barbara Berkman, "Social Service Casefinding in the Hospital: Its Influence on the Utilization of Social Services," *The American Journal of Public Health*, 63, no. 10 (October 1973), 857-62, and Barbara Berkman and Helen Rehr, "Selectivity Biases in Delivery of Hospital Social Services," *Social Service Review*, 43, (March 1969), pp. 35-41.

[35] Terry Mizrahi Madison, "Social Workers and Consumer Health Research," *Health and Social Work*, 2, no. 1 (February 1977), 141-62.

[36] Catherine Marchant, "Are Social Workers Turning a Deaf Ear? A Study of Social Services to the Deaf," *Health and Social Work*, 4, no. 3 (August 1979), pp. 119-34.

[37] Barbara Berkman and others, "Utilization of Inpatient Services by the Elderly," *Journal of the American Geriatrics Society*, 19, no. 11 (November 1971), pp. 933-46.

[38] Andrew Selig, "Evaluating a Social Work Department in a Psychiatric Hospital," *Health and Social Work*, 3, no. 2 (May 1978), pp. 72-87.

[39] Zeb Harel and Linda Noelker, "Sector-Related Variation on Psychosocial Dimensions in Longterm Care for the Aged," *Social Work in Health Care*, 4, no. 2 (Winter 1978), pp. 199-200.

[40] Abraham Monk and Rose Dobrof, "Social Services for Older Persons: A Review of Research," *Future of Social Work Research*, ed. David Fanshel (Washington, D.C.: National Association of Social Workers, 1980), pp. 139-61.

are already available at the state and local levels, what additional services are needed, and how services may be better utilized. Social workers need to examine the particular factors determining entry into the social work system, identifying those patients who are excluded, and determine whether they, too, have needs. If so identified, then a program may be implemented to provide the necessary services. Thus utilization surveys, while requiring fairly large populations to enable appropriate survey design, can reveal the important findings necessary for planning for improved social work services.

Although documentation of service needs is a concern to all practitioners, it is a primary focus for social workers in planning, administration, and policy development within the health field. Utilization data serves as a basis for policy making, if for no other reason, to facilitate the response of legislators and community agencies to unmet social services needs.[41]

RESEARCH INTO SOCIAL EPIDEMIOLOGY AND SCREENING INSTRUMENTS

Social work research efforts in this area are stimulated by the assumption that differential responses to illness and disability are based on differential physical, social, and psychological phenomena. Concomitantly, it is assumed that the identification of these factors and modification of the underlying risks which they represent are effective ways to prevent psychosocial breakdown.[42]

Establishing a need for social services can be done with greater validity if systematic data are available on the incidence of conditions in a population and on the degree to which existing services enable recipients to solve their problems.[43] Thus, if we can validly identify those persons at risk for psychosocial breakdown, who could benefit from social work services, we could then press for services and programs to meet the established need.

In the traditional delivery of social work services in health care, social workers depend on doctors for referrals of patients who need their help. In most medical and psychiatric hospitals these referrals are usually made late in the patient's hospitalization, even though many of these cases involve need for posthospital planning. Berkman and Rehr studied whether hospital social workers, when controlling their own early casefinding, would select persons with different social needs from those referred under the traditional system.[44] One hundred elderly inpatients were ran-

[41] Lu Pearman and Jean Searles, "Unmet Social Service Needs in Skilled Nursing Facilities," *Social Work in Health Care*, 1, no. 4 (Summer 1976), pp. 457-70.

[42] Barbara Berkman and Helen Rehr, "The Search for Early Indicators of Need for Social Service Intervention in the Hospital," *Journal of the American Geriatrics Society*, 22, no. 9 (September 1974), pp. 416-21.

[43] Francis G. Caro, "Research in Social Welfare Agencies: Perspectives on Current Issues," *Perspectives on Agency Based Research*, Community Council of Greater New York (June 1979), pp. 4-11.

[44] Barbara Berkman and Helen Rehr, "Early Social Service Casefinding for Hospitalized Patients: An Experiment," *Social Service Review*, 47, no. 2 (June 1973), pp. 256-65.

domly selected at admission and referred to social workers for evaluation of need for service. The findings were compared with data on 188 elderly inpatients referred to social workers under the traditional system. It was found that with independent casefinding social workers, in addition to reaching patients with posthospital planning needs, reached significantly more patients and family members early in the course of hospitalization and reached considerably more patients in need of help related to "being ill" or "becoming hospitalized," who under the traditional referral system did not receive social work help. This was the first in a series of studies in the development of independent screening mechanisms for social work casefinding in hospitals, which are now becoming an organizational reality for many social work departments in the country.[45] Similarly, recent work of Jacobsen and Howell identified at-risk populations in the emergency rooms of four hospitals.[46] Their study revealed a large at-risk population now underserved by social service because of inadequate assignment of social workers to emergency rooms.

High social risk screening procedures attempt to identify patients and family members whose social situation, stress, or predicted social and physical problems resulting from illness and hospitalization may interfere with their ability to make an optimum plan for coping with daily life expectations. In addition to this practice benefit, early intervention may have cost benefits not yet conceived. The early screening of a patient at-risk for discharge planning and early social work intervention may lead to shortened hospitalization for those patients who may have stays extended beyond medical or psychiatric necessity due to psychosocial hindrances to discharge. In addition, early identification may give the social worker the necessary time to mobilize home care, half-way house, or day care services, which can help to prevent early readmission due to psychosocial breakdown, and thereby focusing on preventive aspects of health care, rather than meeting patient need within the traditional medical model.

By identifying predictors of vulnerability, a department is able to make a powerful statement of need for social work services.[47] The assumption underlying these efforts is that a diagnostic or simply psychosocial labeling of a person, such as "the elderly," a stereotypical response, is not a valid indicator of high risk. Rather it is necessary to look at those physical and psychosocial factors that delineate particular types of persons as high psychosocial risks such as "the elderly living alone," from those who do not need help.

Early identification of persons in need of help through screening is not a new approach to social work. In addition to risk screening in the field of public health and medicine, Jane Addams and others in the settlement house movement used high-risk screening as a mechanism to find the malnourished, the mentally ill, and a host of others with defined social problems. However, recent high-risk screening efforts

[45] Barbara Berkman, Helen Rehr, and Gary Rosenberg, "A Social Work Department Develops and Tests a Screening Mechanism to Identify High Social Risk Situations," *Social Work in Health Care*, 5, no. 4 (Summer 1980), pp. 373-85.

[46] Peggy Jacobson and Robert Howell, "Psychiatric Problems in Emergency Rooms," *Health and Social Work*, 3, no. 2 (May 1978), pp. 89-107.

[47] Monk and Dobrof, "Social Services for Older Persons," pp. 139-61.

in social work have the benefit of a more systematic and scientific direction than did the earlier approaches.

Many screening instruments are being implemented in social work departments around the country, particularly in hospitals where a large volume of cases and limited staff time require priorities for screening at-risk patients and families. Those of you who are entering the health field of practice will find that you will become increasingly involved in the assessment of cases which have come to you through a high-risk screening procedure. It is important that you understand how this mechanism was developed and the implications for its use. You may frequently be asked to retest the screening instruments as the social work profession becomes more sophisticated in developing and refining our use of research instruments.

RESEARCH IN QUALITY AND
QUANTITY ASSURANCE

Prior to the mid-1960s the quality of social work and health care was evaluated mainly through self-regulatory mechanisms. With the Medicare legislative mandate of 1965 as impetus, hospital social workers along with other health professionals began to face the many problems involved in meeting the federal government's demands for quality and quantity assurance.[48] Increased concern for rising costs in health care and a better informed consumer movement led to the passage in 1972 (as part of the amendments to the Social Security Act) of Public Law 92–603 (Professional Standards Review Organization). PSROs were projected to assure both quality and the proper utilization of health care services.[49] Federally mandated PSRO (see Chapter Three) in its first stages was directed toward inpatient care in short-stay hospitals and was promulgated with review expectations mandated as a condition for reimbursement of care under Medicare (Title 18), Medicaid (Title 19), and Maternal and Child Health (Title 5).

Audit

The review processes initiated under PSRO led to a type of monitoring of practice that had not been consistently undertaken before. There have been a proliferation of reports on audits in the quality assurance literature. An audit is a design for evaluative review on a particular problem or topic with objective criteria which have been agreed to by professional staff representatives. Data are collected and analyzed; problems in service are identified; solutions are recommended and implemented; and after a reasonable amount of time a reaudit is undertaken. It is clear that there are a number of ways to design an audit. Regardless of whether the system is called

---

[48] Claudia J. Coulton, "Developing an Instrument to Measure Person-Environment Fit," pp. 159-74, and Barbara Berkman, "Maintaining Quality Service: New Impetus for Evaluation," in *Applied Social Work Research in Maternal-Child Health*, ed. Julia Rauch (in press).

[49] Michael Goran and others, "The PSRO Hospital Review System," *Medical Care*, supplement, 13, no. 4 (April 1975), pp. 1-33.

"a patient care audit," "social health care evaluation," "performance evaluation procedure," "health services review organization process," or "medical care evaluation," there are basic common components inherent in each of the approaches. These audit mechanisms require that thought be given to problems for evaluation, followed by the development of criteria on which to base the evaluation, and then developing the appropriate design techniques. A valid method is necessary to document the objectives of service and outcomes of interventions consistent with professional accountability. Only within recent years is this type of research expertise becoming an integral part of social work practice in health.

Initial social work endeavor has been aimed at classifying the range of social, environmental, and psychologically based needs dealt with by social workers.[50] Such disciplined activity helps identify the specific contribution social work makes to patient-family care that differentiates its contributions to patient care from the claims of other professionals.

Information Systems

Information systems not only result in accountability mechanisms but further build upon accrued social work knowledge.[51] Large amounts of data continuously collected have the potential for providing base data for other research projects to enable social work to describe practice by generalizing to a multiplicity of cases. If social workers wish to find better ways to account for what they do and to account for the effectiveness of their programs, an information system which includes both qualitative and quantitative data is essential.[52]

Today health care institutions gather statistical information which is then computerized. Social workers, among others, are required to continuously fill out questionnaires on cases. These data help hospital administration not only to understand and account for the worth and capability of social work departments, but provide a profile of service which can be used to enhance departmental efficiency and performance.[53] For example, data are needed in order to plan for the allocation and expansion of personnel. In order to determine whether or not to increase social service staffing, or change patterns of staffing coverage, it is first necessary to have information about the ways staff are used.[54]

Statistical systems in some agencies are used to help define social work services and as a means to communicate the availability of these services to other health care professionals. Volland and German give an excellent example of the value of this

[50] Barbara Berkman and Helen Rehr, "Social Needs of the Hospitalized Elderly: A Classification," *Social Work*, 17, no. 4 (July 1972), pp. 80-8.

[51] LaBiana Oystein and Gerald Cubelli, "New Approach to Building Social Work Knowledge," *Social Work in Health Care*, 2, no. 2 (Winter 1976-77), pp. 139-52.

[52] Barbara Berkman and Eleanor Clark, "Survey Offers Guidelines for Social Work," *Hospitals*, 54, no. 6 (March 1980), pp. 105-12.

[53] John Simmons, "A Reporting System for Hospital Social Services Departments," *Health and Social Work*, 3, no. 4 (November 1978), pp. 102-12.

[54] Roslyn Chernesky and Abraham Lurie, "The Functional Analysis Study: A First Step in Quality Assurance," *Social Work in Health Care*, 1, no. 2 (Winter 1975-76), pp. 213-23.

type of information system.[55] Hospital administration had questioned the high cost of social work services in a particular clinic, where service to patients was focused on reducing somatic complaints symptomatic of problems of depression and social isolation. Through the department's statistical data this service could be demonstrated as being less costly than the utilization of physician time with those patients. In a statistical system as described, identified patient problems, service categories, outcome measurements, and sociodemographic information are constantly and continuously available to the social work department as well as to hospital administration. Thus, social work can state what social work services are provided, to what population, with what problems, at what cost (defined as time and money), and with what outcome. Systems like this offer information that has short-term use, providing knowledge about current patients, but is also useful in the long run, providing retrievable data for casefinding, social work planning and intervention, and for discharge planning.[56]

Reid (in his discussion of 'The Social Agency as a Research Machine") believes computerized information systems may transform conventional research approaches.[57] Although data produced in "one-time ' projects may be more rigorous, data generated through computerized large volume systems may be more up-to-date and more useful to agency personnel.

Problem Oriented Records

Recording in any health setting serves three main functions. intelligible data base, a method of communicating about patients' care, and a means to evaluate and teach patient care.[58] At the same time that you will be introduced to computerized data systems you may be introduced to the problem-oriented record. This is an accountability approach to recording based upon a classification of patient problems, outcomes, and service modalities. Social work services now have available classification systems of psychosocial problems dealt with by social workers in health settings.[59] Work is now in progress for the development of a classification of social work activities and outcomes.[60] Demands for scientific rigor through recording the

[55] Patricia Volland and Pearl German, "Development of an Information System: A Means for Improving Social Work Practice in Health Care," *Journal of the American Public Health Association*, 69, no. 4 (April 1979), pp. 335-9.

[56] Abraham Lurie, "Social Work in Health Care in the Next 10 Years," *Social Work in Health Care*, 2, no. 4 (Summer 1977), pp. 419-28.

[57] William Reid, "Research Strategies for Improving Individualized Services," *Future of Social Work Research*, ed. David Fanshel (Washington, D.C.: National Association of Social Workers, 1980), pp. 34-52.

[58] Beatrice Phillips, "Facilitating Communication: Social Work and the Problem-Oriented Record System," *Evaluation of Social Work Services in Community Health and Medical Care Programs*, eds. Robert C. Jackson and Jean Morton, (Washington, D.C.: U.S. Department of HEW, 1973), pp. 93-113.

[59] Barbara Berkman and Helen Rehr, "Social Needs of the Hospitalized Elderly," pp. 80-8; and Patricia Volland, "Social Work Information and Accountability Systems in a Hospital Setting," *Social Work in Health Care*, 1, no. 3 (Spring 1976), pp. 277-85.

[60] Barbara Berkman, "Psycho-social Problems and Outcome: An External Validity Study," *Health and Social Work*, 5, no. 3 (August 1980), pp. 5-21, and Claudia Coulton, "Research on Social Work in Health Care," pp. 119-38.

how and why of treatment decisions and services rendered is a strong argument in favor of problem-oriented recording.[61] It is an important means of communication among those working with patients as well as a means of systematically recording data for auditing purposes.[62]

Thus we have an impetus toward accountability and evaluation from both government and nongovernmental funding agencies, which have requirements for accountability built into their granting mechanisms. Those of you who will practice social work in health settings will be asked to examine the effects of your efforts on patients and to take part in evaluations of your experience with these patients. In addition to meeting reimbursement accountability mandates, evaluations will be helpful to you as professionals in terms of identifying problems, describing alternatives techniques to problem resolution, and predicting outcomes associated with specific approaches.[63]

It has been said that all efforts at determining the needs of the client population, at developing policies that respond to these needs, in providing factual evidence that programs are implemented, and in developing empirical evidence to demonstrate whether or not these programs are accomplishing their objectives, are accountability mechanisms.[64] It is clear that to meet demands of accountability in this broad conceptual framework you must have a strong research orientation.

Cost-Benefit Analysis

Program effectiveness is concerned with whether the program is in fact achieving its objectives and to what extent its objectives are realized.[65] Program efficiency is more directly concerned with how economically the program accomplishes its objectives. Questions are raised as to whether or not there is a waste of manpower or resources, or whether alternative programs could do the same job more efficiently at the same or less cost. Program efficiency is frequently assessed through cost-benefit analysis. Therefore when program efficiency research plans are designed, they are similar to program effectiveness designs but with the inclusion of cost analysis data.[66]

Given scarce funding sources particularly during an era of fiscal constraints,

[61] Ettor Biagi, "The Social Work Stake in Problem Oriented Recording," *Social Work in Health Care*, 3, no. 2 (Winter 1977), pp. 211-21.

[62] Joan McCraken, "The Problem Oriented Record: Utilization in a Community Health Program," *Evaluation of Social Work Services in Community and Medical Care Programs*, eds. Robert C. Jackson and Jean Morton (Washington, D.C.: U.S. Department of HEW, 1973), pp. 71-88.

[63] Thomas Scullion, "Personal Curiosity and Professional Compliance," Robert C. Jackson and Jean Morton, *Evaluation of Social Work Services in Community Health and Medical Care Programs*, eds. Robert C. Jackson and Jean Morton (Washington, D.C.: U.S. Department of HEW, 1973), pp. 1-12.

[64] Frank Raymond, "Social Work Education for Health Care Practice," *Social Work in Health Care*, 2, no. 4 (Summer 1977), pp. 429-38.

[65] Abraham Levine, "Evaluating Program Effectiveness and Efficiency," *Welfare in Review*, 5, no. 2 (February 1967), pp. 1-11.

[66] *Ibid.*

systematically looking at benefits in relation to costs in alternative programs is an essential activity for social work administrators, particularly if they wish to have new programs funded, or if they wish to have continued funding of existing programs. In other words, administrators need to know not only if psychosocial treatment works, but if it works is it worth the cost, and whether or not alternatives may be more desirable. Benefits and costs are evaluated from a wide variety of perspectives, including the agency, the program participants, and the community's perception.[67]

Despite the fact that we often have testimonial evidence suggesting that there is cost effectiveness for social work services in health settings, funding bodies need hard statistical data if they are to support services. Although the task of assessing cost effectiveness and cost benefits is extremely complex, social work needs to pursue these endeavors. Thus, it is important to study the impact of social service in relation to indices that can be measured for cost effectiveness.

Social work administrators are now developing frameworks for thinking about data necessary to ascertain cost and effectiveness for social work services.[68] An interesting example of an agency study of cost effectiveness was conducted at the Levendale Day Treatment Center.[69] In a project funded by the Administration on Aging (AOA) for research and demonstration, this institution studied the relative cost effectiveness of day care and traditional 24-hour institutional care. Clinical testimonial impressions of the program's effectiveness were taken, but statistical data were also available to support these clinical impressions. The three-year evaluation found day care to be a cost effective alternative to institutionalization. Program effectiveness was evaluated by measuring trends of improvement, and stabilization or regression in the functional health states of samples of day care participants compared with institutional patients over a period of one and one-half years. The measure of health included ratings of physical, mental health, and proficiency of daily living. The study is a good example of how to combine both impressionistic data and factual data to support the relative cost effectiveness of different types of service departments.

An interesting example of how research is necessary for the development of indices for cost-benefit analysis is the effort toward uniform reporting which requires that a unit of productivity be translated into a unit of cost. In order to encourage cost containment, government has been examining the relative efficiency of hospitals. Evidence of this is seen in the Medicare and Medicaid antifraud and abuse

[67] Stanley Masters, Irwin Garfinkle, and John Bishop, "Benefit-Cost Analysis in Program Evaluation," *Journal of Social Service Research*, 2, no. 1 (Fall 1978), 79-93.

[68] Gary Rosenberg, "Concepts in the Financial Management of Hospital Social Work Departments," *Social Work in Health Care*, 5, no. 3 (Spring 1980), 287-297 and 302-303; and Patricia Volland, "A Social Work Director Comments," *Social Work in Health Care*, 5, no. 3 (Spring 1980), 297-302.

[69] Elois Rathbone-McCuan, Elliott Rathbone-McCuan, and Martha Warfield, "Geriatric Daycare in Theory and Practice," *Social Work in Health Care*, 2, no. 2 (Winter 1976-77), 153-70.

amendments of 1977 (PL 95-142), wherein hospitals are directed to adopt a uniform system of reporting costs and value of services so that the patterns of different hospitals can be compared. Such comparisons required that data be collected in such a way that output in all hospitals are measured in the same terms, that is, counted in the same units as all other hospitals. Implicit in this legislation is a responsibility that social work must develop comparable data systems. Thus it is clear that skills in measuring output and productivity will be required of health care social workers in the future. There are a number of steps necessary to measure and evaluate productivity.[70] Uniform reporting requires a sound basis in social work data collection: The valid determination of the relationship among problems, services, and outcome can only be accomplished through tightly controlled research methodology.

In this tight economy with heavy scrutiny of health care costs, it is very important that social work agencies and or departments build cost-benefit studies into their assessment of programs. Therefore, as you enter agencies you will find that you will be asked more and more to contribute to statistical data that enhances this type of analysis.

POLICY RESEARCH

An area of increasing priority for research attention is that of organizational management and policy decision making. The prime issue here is whether or not a health policy has been made on the basis of scientifically derived knowledge or on the basis of unsubstantiated beliefs.[71] Research that addresses policy has been defined as the methods and findings of social research in the development and carrying out of efforts to improve the social, psychological, and physical environments of members of the community.[72] Those who are in the position to determine policy usually plan and develop, implement, and evaluate programs. Each of these tasks includes a number of different components, and each requires a research design.

If social work is to influence public policy, our research must address issues of policy. Research must provide the scientific knowledge that directs a rational course of action.[73] In order to have adequate programs, those who are involved in planning must have access to that information concerning potential target populations. Investigators need to understand what are the available interventions or services, and, equally important, what are their relative effectiveness and efficiency in

[70] Claudia J. Coulton and Nathaniel Butler, "Measuring Social Work Productivity in Health Care," paper presented at Council on Social Work Education, April, 1980 Annual Meeting, Los Angeles.

[71] Leon Robertson, "Fact and Fancy in the Formation of Public Policy," *AJPH*, 70, no. 6 (June 1980), p. 627.

[72] Howard Freeman and Clarence Sherwood, *Social Research and Social Policy* (Englewood Cliffs, N.J.: Prentice-Hall, 1970).

[73] Dorothy L. Miller, "Research and Social Welfare Policy," paper presented at National Conference on the Future of Social Work Research, San Antonio, October 15-18, 1978.

meeting the needs of the target populations.[74] These types of information are important, and continuous updating of this data are necessary to keep the program operating effectively.

Evaluation projects have important impact on policy. One such study was developed in Hawaii.[75] Legalization of abortion was intended to bring high quality care within the reach of women of all age groups. In a multiyear study, done on a statewide basis, it was found that serious inequities in care remained, particularly for women whose abortions were paid by welfare. Studies of this nature have implications for social work intervention at the program policy level. The social worker is viewed as an advocate and agent of change who by utilizing findings of this nature can make valid recommendations affecting high-risk groups.

Another interesting example of organizational research with policy implications is a study on reducing the institutional waiting list for retarded children.[76] This research found that parents had little knowledge of outpatient services, although many parents sought institutionalization for either management of behavior difficulties or self-help skill development--services that might be readily provided for in an outpatient setting. The authors believe that expansion of community services for the retarded can be important in reducing the number of candidates for admission to state institutions for the retarded.

Two additional examples of studies that focus on program planning are the work of Rosenberg and Attinson on cultural differences in attitudes towards mental illness,[77] and the work of Vadies and Hale on cultural differences in attitudes toward abortion.[78] Both of these studies drew important conclusions for development of social work community health programs. Finally, Sandra Cates-Levy presents another reason to undertake research studies for program planning.[79] She sites an example of a study that was conducted deliberately to stimulate and increase the interest in expansion of social work services in an understaffed hospital.

In planning for social work services, researchers needed to determine what social services are already available and to what population. Studies which involve a clear description of clientele and their needs are extremely important. Baseline data of this nature are necessary before any evaluation effort can be undertaken.[80]

[74] Irwin Epstein and Tony Tripodi, "Incorporating Research into Macro-Social Work Practice and Education," *Sourcebook on Research Utilization*, eds. Allen Rubin and Aaron Rosenblatt (New York: Council on Social Work Education, 1979), pp. 121-31.

[75] Roy Smith, Patrice Steinhoff, James Palmore, and Katherine Daly, "Method of Payment-Relation to Abortion Complication," *Health and Social Work*, 1, no. 2 (May 1976), pp. 5-28.

[76] Clifford Sells, Margaret West, and Albert Reichert, "Reducing the Institutional Waiting Lists for the Mentally Retarded," *Clinical Pediatrics*, 13, no. 9 (September 1974), pp. 740-5.

[77] Gary Rosenberg and Lisa Attinson, "Attitudes Toward Mental Illness in the Working Class," *Social Work in Health Care*, 3, no. 1 (Fall 1977), pp. 77-86.

[78] Eugene Vadies and Darryl Hale, "Attitudes of Adolescent Males Toward Abortion, Contraception and Sexuality," *Social Work in Health Care*, 3, no. 2 (Winter 1977), pp. 169-74.

[79] Sandra Cates-Levy, "Triggering Change: A Case Study of Innovation," *Social Work in Health Care*, 2, no. 3 (Spring 1977), pp. 319-28.

[80] Michael Austin and Jordan Kosberg, "Nursing Home Decision Makers and the Social Service Needs of Residents," *Social Work in Health Care*, 1, no. 4 (Summer 1976), pp. 447-55.

Then research, which demonstrates a program's effectiveness, can be of value in insuring the social worker's role as a health provider who addresses the phychosocial needs of patients with physical complaints, or emotional and mental illness.

CONCLUSIONS

Those of us who work in health settings encounter dietitians, nurses, occupational therapists, physicians, and physical therapists, as well as a variety of other professionals and allied health specialists who are now broadening their concept of what health care delivery should encompass, and thereby taking on roles and responsibilities increasingly resembling those traditionally attributed to social work. Social workers must clearly delineate the responsibilities they want to assume in relation to health care, and be aware of the necessity to accumulate data to justify the effectiveness of their intervention.[81] It is important, therefore, that we participate and encourage evaluation of our services to assess the effectiveness of our interventions. The norms, standards, and decision-making criteria that direct social work practice must be described in terms that are subject to measurement.

There are three dimensions described in the role of health professionals: that of clinician, that of educator, and that of researcher. If you are working in a health institution there is a financial commitment to clinical practice as well as a financial commitment to teaching. There is also a dedication to research, some of which is conducted under grant support, while other research endeavors are conducted with very limited funding resources. We have a commitment to the research role and must share this commitment with those in administration and with those professionals with whom we work.

There is still much to be learned and much to be gained by social workers who engage in research in the health field. Many questions remain to be answered. Among these are the identification of at-risk patients, the identification of those psychological and social factors deleterious to health but which can be changed or controlled and which are accessible to social work intervention; the relationship of illness and disability and its affects on family functioning; identification and specification of our interventive approaches in order to clarify which interventions are linked to specific problems and outcomes; the relationship of needs to specific interventions and outcomes; and the relationship of cost to effectiveness.

Studies undertaken must be systematically designed and reported so that they can be replicated and validated. This chapter has emphasized research efforts undertaken by social workers in health settings. Many of these studies were part of collaborative efforts among professionals. Collaboration in practice in health care settings is essential for the management of the patients' illness and recovery (see Chapter Five). Research in the health setting is frequently part of interdisciplinary endeavors as social workers and other professional providers strive to improve the health care of patients.

[81] Stanley J. Brody, "Common Ground: Social Work and Health Care," *Health and Social Work*, 1, no. 1 (February 1976), pp. 16-31.

In an effort to meet the recent challenge for "factual" data on which to base administrative decisions and to enhance direct services to patients and families, social work research in health has focused on utilization patterns (for example, the problems, needs, and strengths of clients served); service delivery patterns (organization of services, accessibility of services, and climates for care); productivity patterns; cost-benefit analyses; social epidemiology factors (for example, psychosocial cause and effects of illness on patients and family); manpower; accountability studies, and evaluation of outcome of services. Underlining all these areas is an overall driving effort to analyze the effectiveness and efficiency of social work practice in the health field. Thus, although you may not now have the intention of engaging in research as a career focus, learning the principles and techniques of research with an emphasis on understanding research methods and utilization of research findings, you will be prepared for participation in research and find it an essential part of your role in the health setting.

REFERENCES

AUSTIN, MICHAEL & KOSBERG, JORDAN. Nursing home decision makers and the social service needs of residents. *Social Work in Health Care*, Summer 1976, 1 (*4*).

BERKMAN, BARBARA. The agency—A living laboratory for research. Paper presented at Council on Social Work Education, 1975 Annual Program Meeting, Chicago, March 4, 1975.

BERKMAN, BARBARA. Maintaining quality service: New impetus for evaluation. In Julia Rauch (Ed.) *Applied social work research in maternal-child health*, in press.

BERKMAN, BARBARA. Psycho-social problems and outcome: An external validity study. *Health and Social Work*, August 1980, 5 (3).

BERKMAN, BARBARA & CLARK, ELEANOR. Survey offers guidelines for social work. *Hospitals*, March 1980, 54 (6).

BERKMAN, BARBARA & REHR, HELEN. Selectivity biases in delivery of hospital social services. *Social Service Review*, March 1969, 43 (1).

BERKMAN, BARBARA & REHR, HELEN. Social needs of the hospitalized elderly: A classification. *Social Work*, July 1972, 17 (4).

BERKMAN, BARBARA & REHR, HELEN. Early social service casefinding for hospitalized patients: An experiment. *Social Service Review*, June 1973, 47 (2).

BERKMAN, BARBARA & REHR, HELEN. The search for early indicators of need for social service intervention in the hospital. *Journal of the American Geriatrics Society*, September 1974, 22 (9).

BERKMAN, BARBARA, REHR, HELEN, & ROSENBERG, GARY. A social work department develops and tests a screening mechanism to identify high social risk situations. *Social Work in Health Care*, Summer 1980, 5 (4).

BERKMAN, BARBARA, REHR, HELEN, SIEGEL, DORIS, PANETH, JANICE & POMRINSE, S. DAVID. Utilization of inpatient services by the elderly. *Journal of the American Geriatrics Society*, November 1971, 19 (11).

BIAGI, ETTOR. The social work stake in problem oriented recording. *Social Work in Health Care*, Winter 1977, 3 (2).

BLOOM, MARTIN.   Special issue on single system research design. *Journal of Social Service Research*, Fall 1979, *3* (1).

BLOOM, MARTIN, BUTCH, PATRICIA, WALKER, DORIS.   Evaluation of single interventions, *Journal of Social Service Research* (Spring 1979), 2 (3).

BRODY, STANLEY J.   Common ground: social work and health care. *Health and Social Work*, February 1976, *1* (1).

CARO, FRANCIS G.   Research in social welfare agencies: perspectives on current issues. *Perspectives on agency based research*. Community Council of Greater New York, June 1979.

CATES-LEVY, SANDRA.   Triggering change: A case study of innovation. *Social Work in Health Care*, Spring 1977, *2* (*3*).

CHALMERS, THOMAS C.   *Milbank Memorial Fund Quarterly*, 1981, *59* (3).

CHERNESKY, ROSLYN & LURIE, ABRAHAM.   The functional analysis study: A first step in quality assurance. *Social Work in Health Care*, Winter 1975-76, *1* (2).

CHERNESKY, ROSLYN & LURIE, ABRAHAM.   Developing a quality assurance program. *Health and Social Work*, February 1976, *1* (1).

CHERNESKY, ROSLYN & YOUNG, ALMA T.   Developing a peer review system. In Helen Rehr (Ed.) *Professional accountability for social work practice*. New York: Prodist, 1979.

COULTON, CLAUDIA J.   Developing an instrument to measure person—environment fit. *Journal of Social Service Research*, Winter 1979, *3* (2).

COULTON, CLAUDIA J.   Research on social work in health care: Progress and future directions. In David Fanshel (Ed.) *The future of social work research*. Washington, D.C.: National Association of Social Workers, 1980.

COULTON, CLAUDIA J.   Research for the social work practitioner. In Elizabeth Watkins (Ed.) *Social Work in a State-Based System of Child Care*. Washington, D.C.: Office for Maternal and Child Health, 1980.

COULTON, CLAUDIA J. & BUTLER, NATHANIEL.   Measuring social work productivity in health care. Paper presented at Council on Social Work Education, 1980 Annual Meeting, Los Angeles.

COULTON, CLAUDIA J. & BUTLER, NATHANIEL.   Measuring social work productivity in health care. *Health and Social Work*, August 1981, *6* (3).

EPSTEIN, IRWIN & TRIPODI, TONY.   Incorporating research into macro-social work practice and education. In Allen Rubin and Aaron Rosenblatt (Eds.) *Sourcebook on Research Utilization*. New York: Council on Social Work Education, 1979.

FISHER, JOEL.   *Effective casework practice*. New York: McGraw-Hill, 1978.

FORTUNE, ANNE E.   Communication processes in social work practice. *Social Service Review*, March 1981.

FREEMAN, HOWARD & SHERWOOD, CLARENCE.   *Social research and social policy*, Englewood Cliffs, N.J.: Prentice-Hall, 1970.

GOLDBERG, E. MATILDA & WARBURTON, R. WILLIAM.   *Ends and means in social work*, London: George Allen and Unwin, 1979.

GORAN, MICHAEL & OTHERS.   The PSRO hospital review system. *Medical Care*, April 1975, supplement, *13* (4).

GOTTMAN, JOHN M. & LEIBLUM, SANDRA R.   *How to do psychotherapy and how to evaluate it*. New York: Holt, Rinehart & Winston, 1974.

HAREL, ZEB & NOELKER, LINDA.   Sector-related variation on psychosocial dimensions in longterm care for the aged. *Social Work in Health Care*, Winter 1978, *4* (2).

HUDSON, WALTER W.   *The Clinical Measurement Package: A Field Manual*: (Homewood, Ill.: Dorsey Press, 1982).

JACOBSON, PEGGY & HOWELL, ROBERT. Psychiatric problems in emergency rooms. *Health and Social Work*, May 1978, *3* (2).

JAYARATNE, SRINIKA & LEVY, RONA L. *Empirical clinical practice*. New York: Columbia University Press, 1979.

KIRESUK, THOMAS & SHERMAN, ROBERT. Goal attainment scaling: A general method of evaluating comprehensive community health programs. *Journal of Community Mental Health*, 1968, *4* (6).

LEVINE, ABRAHAM. Evaluating program effectiveness and efficiency. *Welfare in Review*, February 1967, *5* (2).

LINDENBERG, RUTH ELLEN & COULTON, CLAUDIA. Planning for post-hospital care: A followup study. *Health and Social Work*, February 1980, *5* (1).

LURIE, ABRAHAM. Social work in health care in the next 10 years. *Social Work in Health Care*, Summer 1977, *2* (4).

MADISON, TERRY MIZRAHI. Social workers and consumer health research. *Health and Social Work*, February 1977, *2* (1).

MALUCCIO, ANTHONY N. *Learning from clients*. New York: Free Press, 1979.

MARCHANT, CATHERINE. Are social workers turning a deaf ear? A study of social services to the deaf. *Health and Social Work*, August 1979, *4* (3).

MASTERS, STANLEY, GARFINKLE, IRWIN, & BISHOP, JOHN. Benefit-cost analysis in program evaluation. *Journal of Social Service Research*, Fall 1978, *2* (1).

McCRAKEN, JOAN. The problem oriented record: Utilization in a community health program. In Robert C. Jackson and Jean Morton (Eds.) *Evaluation of social work services in community and medical care programs*. Washington, D.C.: U.S. Department of HEW, 1973.

MELAMED, BARBARA G. & SIEGEL, LAWRENCE J. *Behavioral medicine*. New York: Springer, 1980.

MILLER, DOROTHY L. Research and social welfare policy. Paper presented at National Conference on the Future of Social Work Research, San Antonio, October 15-18, 1978.

MONK, ABRAHAM & DOBROF, ROSE. Social services for older persons: A review of research. In David Fanshel (Ed.) *Future of Social Work Research*. Washington, D.C.: National Association of Social Workers, 1980.

OYSTEIN, LaBIANA & CUBELLI, GERALD. New approach to building social work knowledge. *Social Work in Health Care*, Winter 1976-77, *2* (2).

PEARMAN, LU & SEARLES, JEAN. Unmet social service needs in skilled nursing facilities. *Social Work in Health Care*, Summer 1976, *1* (4).

PHILLIPS, BEATRICE. Facilitating communication: Social work and the problem-oriented record system. In Robert C. Jackson and Jean Morton (Eds.) *Evaluation of social work services in community health and medical care programs*, Washington, D.C.: U.S. Department of HEW, 1973.

RATHBONE-McCUAN, ELOIS; RATHBONE-McCUAN, ELLIOT & WARFIELD, MARTHA. Geriatric Daycare in Theory and Practice. *Social Work in Health Care*, Winter 1976-77, *2* (2).

RAYMOND, FRANK. Social work education for health care practice. *Social Work in Health Care*, Summer 1977, *2* (4).

REHR, HELEN & BERKMAN, BARBARA. Social service casefinding in the hospital: Its influence on the utilization of social services. *The American Journal of Public Health*, October 1973, *63* (10).

REID, WILLIAM. Research strategies for improving individualized services. In David Fanshel (Ed.) *Future of Social Work Research*. Washington, D.C.: National Association of Social Workers, 1980.

ROBERTSON, LEON. Fact and fancy in the formation of public policy. *American Journal of Public Health*, June 1980, *70* (6).

ROSENBERG, GARY. Concepts in the financial management of hospital social work departments. *Social Work in Health Care*, Spring 1980, *5* (3).

ROSENBERG, GARY & ATTINSON, LISA. Attitudes toward mental illness in the working class. *Social Work in Health Care*, Fall 1977, *3* (1).

ROSENBLATT, AARON. Research models for social work education. In Scott Briar, Harold Weissman, & Allen Rubin (Eds.) *Research utilization and social work education*. New York: Council on Social Work Education, 1981.

ROSSI, PETER H. Some issues in the evaluation of human services delivery. In Rosemary C. Sarri & Yeheskel Hasenfeld (Eds.) *The management of human services*. New York: Columbia University Press, 1978.

SCHAINBLATT, ALFRED H. What happens to clients? *Community Mental Health Journal*, Winter 1980, *16* (4).

SCULLION, THOMAS. Personal curiosity and professional compliance. In Robert C. Jackson and Jean Morton (Eds.) *Evaluation of social work services in community health and medical care programs*. Washington, D.C.: U.S. Department of HEW, 1973.

SELIG, ANDREW. Evaluating a social work department in a psychiatric hospital. *Health and Social Work*, May 1978, *3* (2).

SELLS, CLIFFORD; WEST, MARGARET & REICHERT, ALBERT. Reducing the institutional waiting lists for the mentally retarded. *Clinical Pediatrics*, September 1974, *13* (9).

SIMMONS, JOHN. A reporting system for hospital social services departments. *Health and Social Work*, November 1978, *3* (4).

SMITH, ROY; STEINHOFF, PATRICE; PALMORE, JAMES & DALY, KATHERINE. Method of payment-relation to abortion complication. *Health and Social Work*, May 1976, *1* (2).

TRIPODI, TONY & EPSTEIN, IRWIN. *Research techniques for clinical social workers*. New York: Columbia University Press, 1980.

TRIPODI, TONY; FELLIN, PHILLIP & EPSTEIN, IRWIN. *Differential social program evaluation*. Itasca, Ill.: F. E. Peacock, 1978.

TOREM, JERRY S. Research priorities in social work education: A communication to colleagues. In Allen Rubin and Aaron Rosenblatt (Eds.) *Source book on research Utilization*. New York: 1979.

VADIES, EUGENE & HALE, DARRYL. Attitudes of adolescent males toward abortion, contraception and sexuality. *Social Work in Health Care*, Winter 1977, *3* (2).

VOLLAND, PATRICIA. Social work information and accountability systems in a hospital setting. *Social Work in Health Care*, Spring 1976, *1* (3).

VOLLAND, PATRICIA. A social work director comments. *Social Work in Health Care*, Spring 1980, *5* (3).

VOLLAND, PATRICIA & GERMAN, PEARL. Development of an information system: A means for improving social work practice in health care. *Journal of the American Public Health Association*, April 1979, *69* (4).

WARE, JOHN, DAVIES-AVERY, ALLYSON & STEWART, ANITA. The measurement and meaning of patient satisfaction. *Health and Medical Care Services Review*, January-February 1978, *1* (1).

WOOD, KATHERINE M. Casework effectiveness: A new look at the research evidence, *Social Work* (November 1978), 2 (3).

CHAPTER SEVEN
MORE ISSUES FOR THE EIGHTIES

Helen Rehr and Rosalind S. Miller

We have entered the eighth decade of this century. A century which, from its begin-ning has spawned a medical care system, a public health system, and a social welfare system with ever-growing gains and problems. More developments and changes, both scientific and in the social environment, have occurred in the last eighty years than in all the years before. Yet, in spite of all the advances, there is "a growing chasm between realities and ideas."[1] Many of our social ideas tend to remain stationary while ahead of us is a changing reality and innovative technology. An illustration of a social lag is the belief we hold that our economy is predicated solely on the princi-ple of capitalistic and private enterprise with its product of profit. However, a very large service economy exists, lodged in government at all levels and in the not-for-profit sectors, and is responsible for two out of every five jobs.[2] The not-for-profit health segment of the economy plays a significant role in the service economy. Recently, we have a new development in a private for-profit health sector which is growing rapidly. At present there is controversy as to where we should expend the dollars allocated for medical care. What are the choices? What can we afford? Should we direct monies toward the support of the very sick or should we attempt to maintain as healthy a public as is possible?

In addition, there are unresolved problems from the past, many of which have already been discussed in previous chapters. What is ahead are additional issues to which the health care reader will need to bring his or her own deliberations. As we enumerate today's patterns and projections in this chapter, we will also attempt to locate social work's role in the continuing pluralism of tomorrow's health care.

[1] Eli Ginzberg, "The Pursuit of Equity: Mirage or Reality," *Columbia* (Fall 1978), p. 28.
[2] *Ibid.*, pp. 28-35.

RISK FACTORS AND
PREVENTIVE CARE

In a world of inequality it is doubtful that there can ever be an equitable distribution of health care. The "right to health" is an illusion beyond both political reality, and financial support. The goal "to be healthy" is dependent on more than money and the political process. However, to be informed about what contributes to sound health is related to politics and dollar supported programs. The "right to health care" is an American democratic ideal and one which is closer to reality today. Medicare and Medicaid are major steps in that direction, in the support of the elderly and the poor by making medical care available to them. As we have seen, there are inequities in the delivery of care, and certainly the quality of care requires constant evaluation. If we examine the effect of social programs of the 1960s, it becomes apparent that we have not eliminated our social problems. The lack of resolution does not mean we should give up on social health planning. Ethical and democratic ideals require a continued commitment to those in need as well as attempts to deal with the social environmental ills which can affect the way we live. To make health relevant to the public takes more than medicine's contribution. In addition to the genetic and biological impacts on one's health status, there are the social, environmental, and psychological factors which influence them. Nutritious foods, our eating habits, the way and where we live, income, educational, and occupational opportunities are a few significant factors which affect us. It is clear to those in the health field that improvement in any of these "risk" factors can affect lifestyle and improve health more effectively than direct medical intervention.[3] To be concerned with the health of the public requires that these elements would have to compete for the limited health resources, along with the biomedical ones.

Social work can address the health care issue at the level of preventive services. But first, we must ask ourselves what priority we will give to focusing our energies and developing our social service programs to reflect a commitment to primary prevention. A decision to deploy staff in this area is always problematic, particularly when the host agencies for whom we work require our services at secondary and tertiary levels of care. Nevertheless, of all health providers, social workers are best equipped to move in the direction of preventive services as initiators of programs, interpreters to other community institutions, educators, and advocates to at-risk populations and conduit-agents, who "network" people with health needs to health care settings.

In a free market where competition for the patient among health providers and institutions will become greater, social work has a pivotal role to identify consumers in need of services and to provide them the access to care. Children under five years of age, adolescents, the aged, and all age groups with chronic disease problems are the target groups. Initiating programs first requires planning strategies that engage clinic and hospital administrators eager for patients and fiscal return. If

---

[3]David E. Rogers, "The Challenge of Primary Care," *Doing Better and Feeling Worse: Health in the United States*, ed. John H. Knowles (New York: W. W. Norton & Co., Inc., 1977), pp. 81-103.

social work is to meet its commitment to people most in need, then we must utilize marketing techniques to attain our goals of dealing services to people in need. To reject marketing strategies on the grounds that such approaches are not congruent with social work values is, in effect, to reject current technological approaches that have high engagement potential to those in decision-making positions, with whom we must ally ourselves.[4]

We know where to find our target population groups: day care centers, housing projects, public schools, churches and synagogues, and centers for the aged. All of these settings have an investment in their respective constituencies and are eager for support systems that will enhance their programs and their memberships. Social workers in these settings with a high degree of group work skill, able to organize groups around meaningful work, are prime agents for networking activity.

By way of example, a group of second-year master's degree social work students, trainees in a five-year funded NIMH project in primary health care have done outreach work in three alternative schools in East Harlem, working with adolescents between the ages of thirteen and sixteen. The trainees have field work placements in an Adolescent Health Center (AHC) where the project has developed this primary prevention model. The schoolchildren are socially and economically deprived youngsters who attempt to cope with multiple familial and environmental stresses. Aware that attempts to attract them to groups would be extremely difficult, initial planning addressed engagement strategies. A topic of real concern for them had to be found. The student workers initially engaged the adolescents by inviting them to join a group where they could talk about the problems of "hacking it" in the community. This was a topic with which these youngsters were able to identify and anxious to address. The work was shaped with different emphasis for each group, but the topics were not dissimilar: drugs, dating, venereal diseases, familial conflict, abusive parents, and so on. As the needs were identified, health providers—nurses, nutritionists, health educators, and others—from the AHC were invited to the schools where the groups meet. In turn, each group visited the AHC for tours and discussions.

Initial research data indicate that the adolescents who participated in these groups, when compared with their classmates who did not have the group experience, were more attuned to access to health facilities; more aware of roles and functions of health providers, including social workers; and more knowledgeable about seeking help for their problems. Most important of all, several members of the group became self-referrals to AHC.

Social workers, as planners, practitioners, and researchers are important health providers, documenting as they offer services, the effectiveness of programs concerned with the right to health care and enumerating the risk factors that limit the potentials for a better life.

There are those who believe we should continue to give the largest support to scientific and technological advances so that more is learned about cancer, stroke,

---

[4] See, for example, Gary Rosenberg and Andrew Weissman, "Marketing Social Services in Health Care Facilities," *Health and Social Work*, 6, no. 3 (August 1981), pp. 13-20.

heart disease, and depression. Then, there are those who believe the enhancement of individual everyday care in rehabilitation, acute care, and primary care is what is essential. The public wants both. To an individual in need, direct services of the best of what is available is expected. In the collective sense, the public wants the new advances in the biomedical as well as in social health areas. To meet this challenge, social work must prepare practitioners who have good clinical skills. This means a practice perspective which moves us beyond the historic "medical model" to a view of practice which encompasses an understanding of the multiple systems as they are structured within the individual, biologically and psychologically, along with those systems, external to the individual, which when functional, are the "life lines" for a fulfilled life: the family, the educational system, the world of work, peer relationships, relaxational activities, and spiritual satisfactions. For the 1980s, the "medical model storm" must be long since past: Good social work practice is not myopic practice with focus only on a biological or psychological or social perspective. Client need is the only criterion for service delivery. The broader a social worker's view of a problem, the better the outcome for amelioration of the client's internal stress and or external strain.

Hence, medicine alone cannot address the individual or the collective social health needs. It is neither equipped nor oriented toward a broad perspective of social health. Physicians acknowledge that many of their patients are not "sick" in a real and physical sense, but are "ill" due to a host of factors which do not respond to a medical armamentarium. Technical skills relevant to the biomedical care system are not sufficient. A biopsychosocial framework to social health care and maintenance is what is needed. Such a focus draws on a comprehensive and multidisciplinary approach, and includes the consumer's point of view, understanding, wants, and what he or her is willing to support.

SOCIAL DISEASE,
DISORDERS, AND STRESS

What are the major social health problems today? What brings people into medical care? In the early part of the century, the ten major causes of death were largely infectious or contagious diseases. Since then, there have been great changes in medicine, and by the end of World War II, the antibacterial drugs had greatly affected all of the health indicators. By 1970, only influenza and pneumonia remained of the infectious illnesses. The major concerns of Western society today are the chronic diseases and their consequences, and what may be considered an epidemic of social diseases and disorders.

Chronic illness affects a vast number of individuals. The Commission on Chronic Illness reported that 65 percent of the public have one or more chronic conditions.[5] The elderly carry the heaviest burden of chronic disease. As a group,

[5] Commission on Chronic Illness, *Chronic Illness in the United States*, vol. IV (Cambridge, Mass.: Harvard University Press, 1957), pp. 54-55.

they are an at-risk population in regard to heart and circulatory disorders, cancer, arthritis, rheumatism, diabetes and so on. The severely retarded and developmentally disabled are also at-risk populations. The emotionally ill make another substantial impact on the medical care system, presenting symptoms which are chronic or periodically exacerbated as a result of social, personal, or environmental stress.[6]

An individual's health status is affected by four key factors: human biology, environment, lifestyle, and the health care organization which is available to serve him both therapeutically and in the prevention of illnesses. Economists believe it is erroneous to attribute changes in health status as more related to the quality of medical care than to socioeconomic factors.[7] John Knowles, Lewis Thomas, and a host of others add that it is an individual's lifestyle, including his behavior, eating habits, and the environment, which affect health more so than medical attention.[8] The premise set forth is that most of us are born healthy and become sick due to the way we live and the impact of environmental conditions. This point of view places responsibility for prevention and health maintenance in the social, health, and personal welfare sense on the way an individual conducts his life, and on socioeconomic and environmental factors.

Studies demonstrate that the majority of patient visits to doctors are for minor illnesses, short-term in duration and usually self-curing with little after-effects. Most people with minor illnesses tend not to call on medical services at all. It is for exacerbation of chronic illnesses that physicians see patients in vast numbers, for whom palliation or offering curbs to increasing disabling effects are the essential ingredients of care.[9] For most minor disorders, fear and anxiety have prompted the visit. For those who are chronically ill and suffering social and physical dysfunctioning, one can expect that family disequilibrium will be associated with the illness, as well as a range of social and emotional problems. Seventy-five percent of doctors' office visits are for those referred to as the "worried well" or the "stabilized sick" asking for help, but essentially for their anxiety, stress, fears, depression, and worries.[10] These individuals present themselves with stress, and social and familial concerns for which physicians have been little prepared to cope. Medicine is taught to deal with sickness and not with maintaining health and mental health. There are some who claim that medical care today contributes to dependency in individuals and even may be a factor in the decline of their health status.[11]

The newer models of health care, whether HMO's, prepaid group practices,

[6] Marc LaLonde, *A New Perspective on the Health of Canadians* (Ottawa: Information Canada, 1978), pp. 29-30.

[7] Victor R. Fuchs, "Economics, Health and Post-Industrial Society," *Health and Society*, 57, 2 (Spring 1979), pp. 153-82.

[8] See Knowles, *Doing Better, Feeling Worse*, or the entire issue of *Daedalus* (Winter 1977).

[9] Leon Eisenberg, "The Search for Care," *Daedalus* (Winter 1977), pp. 237-8.

[10] Lewis Thomas, "On the Science and Technology of Medicine," *Daedalus* (Winter 1977), 6, no. 1, p. 42.

[11] Renee C. Fox, "The Medicalization and Demedicalization of American Society," *Daedalus* (Winter 1977), pp. 9-22.

family medicine practitioners, or multidisciplinary approaches, are all primary health care arrangements that focus on the biopsychosocial aspects of care. More of these models will develop in the 1980s. They offer great potential because they encompass three essential ingredients: continuity, coordination, and comprehensive health care. With further study, data may indicate an important fourth factor: This model may be more cost effective than other service delivery arrangements, either hospital ambulatory care or the private physician's office.

Primary health care settings should become important entry points for social workers entering the field. Depending upon the structure and personnel arrangements, social workers—either as consultants or as practitioners—are best able to identify psychosocial stress factors among the "worried well" or among those patients with vague physical symptoms but without organic problem. As noted by Miller and Austrian, in their investigative work in a primary care setting, the social worker

> has an initial interpretive role with the vast majority of patients (who come to a Family Care Group Practice), educating many of them to an understanding of and an appreciation for a holistic or comprehensive approach to health care. The social worker's services may be of a preventive nature; or as a positive reinforcement agent, confirming that the client's perception, that no emotional problems need to be addressed, is correct; or the social worker's task may be to help the patient to recognize situational, familial, or intrapsychic problems somaticized through bodily symptoms.[12]

The questions in the decade ahead that will need to be addressed have to do with whether or not there are changes in patient utilization patterns of physician time that warrant the inclusion of social workers in primary care practices; also if the inclusion of social workers is cost effective or only "humane effective."

In addition to the "worried well" and the "stabilized sick," physicians encounter individuals with social diseases and social disorders seeking assistance with their symptoms, for whom technology is not the answer. The recurrences and the pain are lodged in an etiology of lifestyle and environmental factors. The social disorders occur as a result of a host of self-imposed risks, deriving from immoderate behavior patterns not under control. These self-destructive lifestyle tendencies show up in excesses with drugs, alcohol, smoking, overeating, and even work style, along with the total lack of exercise, appropriate recreation, and diversion. Other risk factors are in careless living as in speed driving or in promiscuity. These risks are highly associated with cirrhosis, malnutrition, obesity, bronchitis and emphysema, lung cancer, coronary and arterial diseases, dental problems, ulcers, hypertension, accidents, suicide and homicide, and with social withdrawal and anxiety attacks.[13]

---

[12] Rosalind S. Miller and Sonia Austrian, "Mental Health Services in Primary Care: The Role of the Social Worker," paper presented at the 108th annual meeting of the American Public Health Association, Detroit: October 1980. Work supported by NIMH Grant (Social Work Section) no. 1 T31 MH15560-02, p. 8.

[13] LaLonde, *A New Perspective on the Health of Canadians*, pp. 17-8.

The social diseases which bring people to physicians are lodged in social, psychological, and environmental factors, as well as in the human biology. The environmental concerns may be less in the immediate scope of the individual, requiring public and political intervention. These are the pollutions found in the air, environment, water, and work, and noise levels. The housing in which people live and what they wear can be risk factors, too. All of these can affect the mental and physical health statuses of people. There are those diseases deriving from social psychological risks which are presented in emergency services of medical institutions everyday. They are people suffering from accidents, burns, violence, as well as those abuse situations seen in a child, a parent, or a spouse. Marital and family problems are also brought to the physician's door. Although it is the physical symptomatology in the crisis for which each individual needs the attention, it is the origins in the person's social-psychological environment that need to be addressed.

Medical attention for these problems presented by such vast numbers of people will not resolve them. When people have troubles, they seek help from those institutions available to them—the private, public, and voluntary medical and psychiatric care system. Medical care may be needed, but the burden of treatment for the underlying problems is placed on the least equipped of the providers. It is doubtful that more doctors, more hospitals, more beds, and more technology will improve the health status of the majority of the public. There is an important role for well-trained social workers, equipped to deal with these complex social problems. Programs involving counseling, support services, health education leading to self-care, and to motivation to change existing lifestyle patterns will have to be developed. Such programs will mean a shift from medical dominance if we are to focus on social health problems. The skills required are many and varied, with different social and health care professions contributing to a system of social health maintenance, including studies to examine the etiology of social diseases and disorders, as well as studies to address the biopsychosocial factors in chronic illness. The question remains whether or not the public will see the need for a social health care system which has more than physicians as providers. Although they currently ask for help of a personal and individual nature, they are not yet aware that what is required is more than biomedical skill but also social psychological and environmental skills. A new approach to social health would require redefinition of roles and functions among the social health care professionals. Although the mystique of medicine is powerful, there are indications of change as in the growing development of nurse clinicians, public health social workers, social workers in primary health care settings, health educators, and more. The traditional system may see these new practitioners as competitive, but there are indications of their support by government, by the professions, and by the American Hospital Association in its recommendation to its member institutions to offer programs which are comprehensive and which include health promotion.

How large a role social work can play and how much support it receives from the administrative, policy-making arm of health agencies for the development of health promotion, primary prevention, and consumer-educative programming will depend upon substantive evaluative research designs where data indicate patient presenting problems, interventive strategies, and outcome measures convincing enough to modify the current emphasis on medicalization. Again, a tall order, but for the 1980s, an expected social work focus of work. The fact is, as illustrated in Chapter Six, the profession is already responding to the need.

CONTROLLING COSTS

Cost containment of medical and social services has been the expectation of government—at both federal and state levels—from the beginning of the 1970s and will remain a prominent goal for all of the 1980s. The slow economic growth, inflation, and economic and political uncertainties have caused a fiscal crisis. With the withdrawal by the federal government of financial support for social and health programs, the states are left to carry the burden. By contrast, the 1950s and 1960s were affluent years in which government played an ever-increasing role in social and health affairs. The national health expenditure had moved steadily upward from 5.3 percent of the GNP in 1960, to over 9 percent in 1980, and is still rising.[14]

The medical improvements in patient care have been extensive over the last 30 years. In addition to kidney dialysis and transplants, chemotherapy and radiotherapy for cancer have been introduced. Also, trauma centers including burn facilities, neonatal intensive care units, antimicrobial vaccines, and joint prostheses are just a few of the innovations. Although medical care systems have grown more complex with their advanced technology and intensive care units, they have contributed to reduction in the mortality rates in stroke, cancer, and heart disease patients, as well as in infant mortality. Life expectancy rose to 73.2 years in 1977 and for those who would reach 65 years, it is expected they would have another 16.3 years to live. Mortality rates among the poor and minorities have also been bettered.[15]

What will tomorrow bring? The primary concerns are inflation and constant rising costs. A study by the Brookings Institute concluded that "this country may never bring its medical care expenditures under control until it is willing to agree that some benefits are not worth the cost, even when health is at stake."[16] What should we forego? For what are we willing to pay? There is no question that the affluent days are behind us and constraints ahead. There is an oversupply of doctors and an oversupply of total hospital beds, but with problematic distribution of both. There are regions within the country that have too few beds and doctors. There is no democratic way to affect a better distribution except by the use of incentives. However, given the fiscal crisis, there are less dollars for current social programs.

[14] Health United States & 1980, U.S. Department of Health and Human Services, Public Health Service, DHHS Pub. no. (PHS) 81-1939, December 1980, p. 101.

[15] Leon Zucker, "A Look to the Past Offers Hope for the Future," *Hospitals*, 55, no. 14 (July 16, 1981), pp. 72-8.

[16] "Control Means Benefit Limit," *The Nation's Health* (August 1971), p. 1.

There will be few if any new programs; rather the hope is for a steady state to prevail, knowing that cuts and belt tightening will pose problems around choices.

The health care model as we know it will undergo changes. Hospitals have been traditionally the mainstay of medical care, largely, because these have been the services paid for by the third-party payment system. They will face serious crises as a result of limits on reimbursement. Already we have evidence of in-patient institutions moving toward mergers and multi-institutional arrangements in an attempt to introduce cost efficiencies. At the same time these multihospital plans are said to enhance coordination and linkage, in addition to cost savings, by offering patients what they may need through existing services without duplicating programs. There is a growing interest of large investor-owned corporations in the hospital, nursing home, laboratory, and home care services. At this time the for-profit corporation has made a claim on about $40 billion of the health care field.[17] Private corporations have come into the health field because of the reimbursement guarantees and because of maldistribution. Middle and upper income families have relocated into areas where an inadequate medical care supply created a vacuum. As stated earlier, there is a growing emphasis in ambulatory care through health maintenance organizations, group practices, and primary care programs. Hospitals have shown an interest in adopting such outpatient medical care; in other arrangements doctors have incorporated into group practices. Government and business are the two principal purchasers of health care. Each is growing more and more reluctant to support what they get in return for constantly rising costs. Each will try to reduce the costs.

There are a number of large corporations and unions, even large insurance companies evidencing interest in providing their own services to their incumbents. Employees and businesses have begun to offset the expensive "everything" package to a package that covers consumers' choice. Cost-sharing insurance either through copayments or through supplementary charges is being discussed. Labor and their unions, and industry's management are interested in better health maintenance and health education programs, as well as family-centered ambulatory and home care packages. There will be a major shift to acute care, outpatient services, and self-care programs from the inpatient diagnostic and treatment services. Where states have suffered severe fiscal crises they have already cut back what they will cover of public medical care. The major emphasis so far, is on the patient sharing some part of the costs for drugs, clinic, or emergency visits. However, all states have shown interest in affecting inpatient per diem costs for those for whom they have covered programs. Massachusetts is experimenting with a prepayment plan whereby health care providers undertake to cover selected items of care for Medicaid enrollees at fixed rates. The state of Maryland, for example, no longer pays hospital charges incurred after 20 days of hospitalization. Some states have come up with copayment plans involving the patient. Some institutions have raised their inpatient per diem rates so as to offset the inadequate Medicaid rate of return; others are contemplat-

[17]Eli Ginzberg, "Large-scale Growth in Health Dollars Attracts Attention of For-profit Sector," *Hospitals*, 55, no. 14, (July 16, 1981), pp. 90-3.

ing nonadmission of Medicaid patients, referring them to nearby institutions which may accept them.

The present cost-consciousness of medical care by the government has affected every institution. As long as hospitals enjoyed a cost-plus-reimbursement formula for bed utilization, then it was profitable to fill every bed, sometimes irrespective of need and to be unconcerned regarding a patient's length of stay. In addition, new staff and new programs could be added readily since they could be reimbursed under the formula, but this pattern was markedly changed in the early 1970s when utilization review regulations impacted every hospital. Beds began to remain vacant while patients who did not need to be hospitalized began to be seen in ambulatory care, including same day surgery programs, under private, voluntary, or public auspices. The new technology helped to reduce lengths of stay as well. Uncomplicated coronary disease was treated in under three weeks of hospitalization in contrast to earlier five- and six-week stays. Obstetrical patients delivered and were made ambulatory as quickly as possible, and discharged not in a week but in two to three days. In addition to the trend to reduce the length of hospitalization, there was pressure to cap the per diem reimbursements from the government supported programs, Medicare and Medicaid. The result was that hospitals claimed it cost more to serve these patients than they were being reimbursed. They cited Medicare beneficiaries who were making greater demands on the system in numbers and in severity of illness than their young counterparts, and who were requiring very expensive programs.

Social work programs were also being strongly affected by this older population. Studies supported the experience that more of the elderly were in need of social services to help them and their kin make stabilizing social and environmental plans to return home and to remain at home. Early social work intervention not only enhanced the nature and quality of the planning, but also tended to shorten the stays of these seriously ill elderly. The results of shortened stays, vacant beds, tightened reimbursements, spiraling labor and equipment costs, and inflation in general were growing financial ailments in all medical institutions that required methods to reduce costs.

What then is happening to hospitals? They are changing. Some are diversifying, even into nonmedical areas. Some are merging. Some have entered the for-profit field. To survive, they are seeking or will have to seek new enterprises. The new enterprises are in a range of areas many of which may appear to take on a social mission character. But all of them are predicated on income-producing services that can return monies back into the institution.

Some institutions have diversified by drawing on existing know-how and existing holdings to make a profit. For example, Los Angeles' Northridge Hospital runs a second hospital, an inpatient alcohol and drug abuse care facility, a restaurant, and a shopping center; Baylor University Medical Center in Dallas owns four other hospitals, a construction company, an office building, a hotel, a health spa, and three restaurants; Columbia Presbyterian Hospital in New York is planning to build condominium apartments; Lutheran General Hospital in Chicago draws on its institutional know-how in offering its staff a preventive health maintenance program that reduces health benefit costs while returning revenue to the institution. Other innovations are retirement-housing, hospice care for the terminally ill, home health services, health promotion services such as antismoking, weight loss and stress dealing programs, a sports medicine service, as well as medical supply and laboratory services to private physicians and other hospitals, and even management skills to other health care institutions.[18] All of these reflect some of the profit-making schemes the voluntary medical centers have entered into to offset their financial ills.

Then there is the trend toward the merger of hospitals. The multihospital merger is intended to contain costs of institutions by the sharing of resources among the many. The growth of multiinstitutional arrangements under a centralized organization is well on its way, claiming that it curbs duplication and overlapping services within a serviceable geographic area. When institutions join together, the intent is to coordinate what is available and to provide a linkage among existing resources, facilitating their use by a larger population pool than any single institution would have. The multiinstitutional arrangement has been, at the simplest level, where many join together to cost-save on purchases by quantity buying. The merger can range from the simple to the most complex set of arrangements which can involve one or more functions including management, accounting, teaching, cross-utilization of services, training of staffs, overseeing clinical services, laboratory, diagnostic and technology availability, information systems, monitoring and accountability, and even the cross-fertilization of research. The multihospital not-for-profit system has control of almost one-quarter of the acute care beds in the country, and is expanding. The single most recognized advantage is to the small medical institutions, which now have access to clinical, management, and educational supports, not previously available to them. They are on a cost-sharing basis, receive technical assistance, budget reviews, and whatever else they may require.[19]

The for-profit medical industry has grown steadily in the last fifteen years. Although the proprietary hospital, generally small in bed number, and usually owned by a physician or a group of physicians, has been in the health care field for a long time, the new investor-owned chains, many publicly held corporations have grown so that they control 11 percent of the acute care beds in the United States.[20] They also control a wide range of other health programs. The for-profit medical industry includes long-term care programs, institutional and home services, and has made a very substantial commercial penetration into the health care field. These have been in the form of conglomerates, franchising of specialized programs, contracting with a hospital in fiscal crisis for management services, and the wholesale and retail distribution of supplies and services. Kidney dialysis centers are the most recently developed private ambulatory medical service. A very substantial portion of income the for-profit complexes enjoy are comparable to those the not-for-

[18] "Some Hospitals Are Entering Diverse Businesses, Often Unrelated to Medicine, to Offset Losses," *The Wall Street Journal*, August 12, 1981, p. 46.

[19] V. Di Paolo, "Non-Profits Predict Rise in Contract Business," *Modern Health Care*, 8 (April 1978), pp. 47-50.

[20] *Ibid*.

profit receive, from government supported programs, as well as from insurance carriers. A number of the for-profit programs offer insurance coverage of their own for services they deliver. The question that is readily raised is how can they offer "quality" services and make money, while the voluntary hospitals lose. The data are not yet available on what makes the difference. However, some of the preliminary thoughts suggest a different management philosophy and style which include an industrial, profit-making orientation, the availability of efficiently produced and only needed services, the admission of less seriously ill (short-stay) patients, and less diversification of personnel. Also they are not responsible for teaching or research which are costly enterprises to the university-based hospital. The institutional arrangements take on an industrial character comparable to the private sector's profit-making corporations. They are offering services where they are needed in areas little served by the voluntary institutions, and for which the public is paying through direct or indirect reimbursement packages. In other words, there is a demand for these private medical services.

The federal government talks about a procompetition emphasis in the belief that an open market will hold down costs. However, there are many who believe that the present medical care system does not lend itself to the economic marketplace of demand and supply. Doctors and hospitals are closely affiliated so that choice of hospital is not available to patients. In addition their limited knowledge will make it difficult for them to register concern with either over- or underutilization of available care by physicians or hospitals. Profits in the health field and price competition may well have "antisocial consequences." There are no true market forces in medicine, and the costs of care for an individual in need are beyond what he has available to him without some forms of insurance. The medical-industrial complex will continue in a range of pursuits. New social controls will be needed for the for-profit, the not-for-profit, and for governmental programs, all of which make up our pluralistic health care system and also control the direction it takes in this country.[21] There are other issues that need to be raised such as waste, abuse, fraud, inadequate institutional arrangements, and the inadequate use of manpower.

Where are the social work services in health care at this time? Unfortunately they have remained relatively unfamiliar with the way services are paid. Social workers are largely a salaried group in nonprofit programs, and they tend to see their employers as the paying agent of their services. At this time social services in hospitals are a component of the per diem rate of almost all third-party payers. Unless specially contracted for with insurance carriers, the ambulatory care social services are not covered except as a portion of Medicare and Medicaid doctor visit payments. All ambulatory care programs of hospitals impose a major deficit on their institutions and thus most of the outpatient social work services are without available income, except for specially supported programs.

Social work needs to be conscious of and concerned with what it costs to give services. The private practices of social work and some experimental programs,

---

[21] Ginzberg, "Large-scale Growth in Health Dollars," p. 93.

such as the Arthur Lehman Counseling Service in New York City, have attempted to introduce fiscal soundness to service delivery.[22] Most social workers irrespective of the locus of service are unfamiliar with what their direct services per patient visit cost, and what indirect costs are incurred. The introduction of a fee-for-service in the social services requires a training program for workers. In general, an overall philosophy of the charitable giving of services still lingers on in the profession. If fee-for-service remains as the mode of payment in the health care field, then it may well need to be social work's mode as well. Understanding costs and fee collection based on actual costs or on a margin of profit will need to be as basic a component of social work education as it is of medical. Social work administrators will need to learn costs and income sources immediately, in order to have their programs survive. Even if health care were to become nationalized or if a national health insurance package were to be introduced, social work would have to relate costs-to-services-to-needs in order to make a responsible reimbursement claim.

In New York State, Governor Hugh Carey signed into effect the Third Party Payments Law, which gives recognition to qualified social workers to act as legitimate vendors of psychotherapeutic services to patients who are insured for mental health services, in the same way as psychiatrists and psychologists.[23] The provision of comprehensive social services in all social health programs will have to be guaranteed by reimbursement. Licensure and certification of social workers are most important to secure reimbursement to accredited and qualified professionals. Without them, there is no likelihood that insurance companies and other third-party payers will be willing to open the door wide for payments for social work services, even under "freedom of choice" laws. Safeguarding the public and reimbursement for services are interrelated phenomena. The National Association of Social Workers has attempted to define *competency*, at different levels of performance, producing registries of qualified professionals, along with certification. These are the essential components for state recognized standard-setting bodies in order to insure vendor status for social workers.

ACCESS TO HEALTH CARE

To address access one needs first to look at the "state of the art" and what is available. Federal program and insurance coverage has made acute hospital care available to approximately 90 percent of the public. Medical care per se is considerably less supported. In spite of the extensiveness of coverage, equitable access to care remains difficult to achieve, although there is no question that the elderly and the poor have had improved access since the passage of Medicare and Medicaid. The fact is that access is also dependent on availability of services and as earlier noted,

---

[22] Ruth Fizdale, *Social Agency Structure and Accountability*, (Fair Lawn, N.J.: R. E. Burdick, 1974).

[23] Third Party Payments signed into Law, Chapter 893, in 1977. Reported in *Currents*, Newsletter of Metropolitan Chapter, National Association of Social Workers (October 1977), pp. 3-5.

there exists a serious maldistribution of both beds and doctors in the country. The American value of freedom of choice is one which applies not only to consumers but also to practitioners as well, in where they wish to locate. To impose an enforced location on a practitioner is in conflict with the accepted value. There is no democratic way to distribute services to where the needs exist, except by financial and professional incentives to the providers. Some communities with scarce resources have offered financial bonuses in order to secure physicians in their regions. In addition, what the medical establishment has to offer by virtue of both educational and by institutional arrangements is what the public has available to it. This is usually devoted to very specialized medical skills with an emphasis on hospitalization for diagnostic and therapeutic services. Also absent are those programs that can address social ills and diseases. Although medicine has assumed responsibility for this sphere of disorders, we have noted that it is ill equipped to deal with them, particularly within its current organizational and manpower arrangements.

At the present time the predictions are that the country will face an oversupply of physicians, particularly in the subspecialties, but an undersupply in physicians prepared to work in primary care, rehabilitation, or in geriatrics where the needs are great. The federal government has attempted to effect the development of the primary care physician by introducing special grants to medical schools which offer this concentration. The power of the medical school establishment with its emphasis on specialization has offset any major gains in this area. The over-65-year old population is growing. As a group they make the greatest demand on the existing services. There is every indication the demand for primary care will be greater, with major concentration on those 75 years of age and over. Long-term and ongoing care of chronic illnesses and disabilities will require not only medical assistance, but more supportive, continuous, and comprehensive care across program lines within some network of services.

An oversupply of specialists in any area of practice tends to either manufacture a need for the service, or to extend the scope of practice for the specialist. It makes cost control extremely difficult since there are no incentives to contain them. There is something extraordinarily extravagant in the way care is delivered by every provider. Every new piece of equipment and every new testing mechanism is sought and freely utilized. In the same way there is something erroneous and badly determined in the utilization of skilled manpower. The present reimbursement system, a fee-for-service and the built-in physician responsibility for his patient encourage services to be delivered at the highest level of training rather than at a more appropriate level. The specialist may be called upon to treat common colds, minor respiratory illnesses, and the anxieties of the "stabilized sick" and the "worried well."

Everyday social health problems including those which occur as a result of chronic illness and diseases have proved less interesting to research than the more esoteric, scientific, and technological areas. Although the service demand is greatest for a host of everyday ailments, the research has concentrated on the technological improvements. These improvements have been extraordinary but by their nature have tended to be meaningful for fewer rather than the majority of people utilizing medical services. There has been little or no research in areas that touch on health promotion such as lifestyle and social habits, and the impact of the environment on people. In addition, other urgent needs are those that affect the work environment along with those that cause work absenteeism. All of these factors limit access, in a variety of ways, to the consumer.

There is the new trend toward helping individuals to manage their own health and holding them responsible for how they do. Although the movement is excellent and one very familiar to social workers, medicine has tended to approach self-care more in the sense of "blaming the victim" rather than in terms of listening to the patient and arriving at a partnership toward reaching agreed upon goals. The failure of medicine and other health care professions to deal with the many ongoing needs and with problems of daily living has resulted in a burgeoning self-help movement wherein peers help each other, for example, Alcoholics Anonymous, Reach for Recovery (mastectomy), and Ileostomy Club.

There are a number of social reform movements that bear upon the access issue. The civil rights movement has been directed at employment and education, but large-scale problems remain in the area of health services. The claim made and well documented is that blacks have been blocked from admission to certain hospitals; many physicians have refused to take Medicare and Medicaid patients; and wide gaps in access exist between minority and nonminority groups. Public hospitals rather than voluntary seem to be the institutions open to the poor and minorities. Although policies are not intended to be discriminatory, they can be. Blacks and Hispanics also claim they are denied the same access to staff privileges and promotions that the whites are able to secure. Health care rights will continue to be a major issue in the 1980s.

The women's movement, including a number of women's groups, has been an impetus to deal with problems in health services and as they specifically affect women. Women claim there are abuses and inadequacies: they cite the extent of gynecological surgery, the abuse of drug prescriptions, and the looseness in caring for pregnancy. They have organized so that they can become informed and can act on key health care issues. It has been the women's movement that has played an active role in providing alternative health care in women's programs and also by helping to organize self-help programs and advocacy groups to deal with local and female health concerns.[24] In addition, women have become activists seeking greater opportunities for themselves and for minorities within the health care system itself. As early as the 1960s, Coggeshall in his review of the medical school establishment found the absence of women at all levels, and concluded that apart from discrimination, their small numbers explained a lack of humanitarianism and empathic relationships between physicians and their patients.[25] In the 1960s the consumer movement had its impact on health care. There was a resurgence of consumer interest in health, especially in the poor communities, since provision was made for commu-

[24] National Women's Health Network, 2075 I Street NW, Washington, D.C. 20006 is one of many such women's groups set up to deal with their own health care concerns.

[25] Lowell Coggeshall, *Planning for Medical Progress Through Education*, a report submitted to the Executive Council of the Association of American Medical Colleges, April 1965.

nity action through "maximum feasible participation." In low-income communities, control or participation in health care meant the opening of the job market. In addition, a sort of militancy in the ghettos brought about better accessibility and services, including community mental health centers, substance abuse clinics, and neighborhood health centers. The legislation of the 1960s and 1970s gave consumers in local regions the belief that the health needs of the community's populations should be the primary determinants of what should be made available. The legislation offered only advisory and recommendation roles, and not the power to affect resources. However, the "veto" power over CONs (condition of need) by the Health Systems Agencies served to force a dialogue between the HSA and its local institutions. Unfortunately, the HSAs around the country became the arena where the power conflicts among federal, state, and local leaders surfaced and mitigated against their effectiveness. Even if the Health Systems Agency opportunities are removed by the lack of continued federal support, there is indication that consumers will seek a voice at the state and regional levels. Also, consumers are on boards of institutions and agencies that govern health care and there is no question that consumers will continue to have a role and will participate in health services.[26]

There is a growing tendency in today's political climate toward returning the responsibility for advocating what health care is needed to local communities and government. In a pluralistic society there are different needs and expectations from different groups and regions, and local groups wish to be represented, whether in periods of affluence or of fiscal constraint. Regional planning and services have been attempted by the federal government in the past, for example, Regional Medical Plan (RMP) and the HSA, yet except for a few regions, neither has been very successful. The power of the health establishments and that of physicians has made any planned coordination and linkage among programs very difficult to achieve. The new development of the multihospital movement, mergers among institutions for fiscal reason, and the for-profit medical industry may make linkage and coordination more attractive in the future.

What should the health care system be? A pluralistic system from which choices can be made still seems to be the general popular direction. Monolithic health care systems, where freedom of choice and of participation of consumers and providers is nonexistent, appear to be unacceptable to American opinion, in spite of the somewhat better health indicators than our own. If a democratic system is to prevail then perhaps the multiple pulls and tugs will continue.

NATIONAL HEALTH INSURANCE

The 1970s saw a Congress that produced multiple proposals for national health insurance (NHI). Each plan, in turn, from both sides of the aisle—whether sponsored by Senator Ted Kennedy (Democrat from Massachusetts) and several of his colleagues or from the executive branch, by President Nixon—had a quick demise. At

[26] Cecil G. Sheps, "The Influence of Consumer Sponsorship on Medical Services," *Milbank Memorial Fund Quarterly*, 50, no. 4 (October 1972), part 2, pp. 41-69.

this juncture, all the NHI proposals are but a footnote in the overall health care picture. They will not receive detailed attention until such time as there is public sentiment for NHI. For now the issue remains dormant, but it is not dead. In the decade ahead, the country will again review the issue and wrestle with the complexities. How should such a comprehensive plan be financed? Do we need a National Health System, universally set by government? Should a plan be patterned on Great Britain that covers all care, including health, education, and social services, free, with little freedom of choice, or a national health insurance program that covers prescribed costs of given care and permits a choice from among many programs? Given the moral and ethical responsibility to safeguard the access to services of the poor and the elderly, it is possible to address the financing under either system, while understanding the social consequences of each. A national health insurance scheme would reorder the roles of government, industry, and the consumer and would also challenge the exclusivity of medical providers. NHI would raise the basic question of what wants and how much it is willing to spend to get it. Even within these dicta, there are hard choices that will have to be made.

We need to recognize that "an effective system of health care seems to generate more illness rather than less."[27] Better health care uncovers what has not been seen, reported, or even postponed. In addition a better system than that we currently have—one which includes health education and promotion—may affect the public's life span. It is likely that life expectancy would be somewhat lengthened but with the longer life would come more complications from chronic illness and disability.

A rational social health policy will take extensive deliberations among a host of providers, consumers, and politicians, with knowledge and information that can lead to sound action.

ETHICS AND VALUES
IN HEALTH CARE

Every society makes cultural assumptions about life, relationships, human conduct, and death that are based on traditions and views that have grown from the roots of earliest civilization. These assumptions have developed over time into value systems, widely accepted by many people and reenforced theologically and judicially in most cultures.

With the advancements in biological and medical technology, patient management problems have arisen posing questions which appear to defy answers. The questions speak to issues of ethics and values of interest and concern not only to health providers, but social scientists, theologians, and philosophers. Together they have created a new discipline—bioethics. When does a fetus become a person? When

[27] Avedis Donabedian, "Models for Organizing the Delivery of Personnel Health Services and Criteria for Evaluation of Them," *Milbank Memorial Fund Quarterly*, 50, no. 4 (October 1972), part 2, p. 107.

does a woman have the right to an abortion? When does a patient have a right to die? When does anyone have the right to take his own life? For in what ways - or in no ways—can the physician, as an enabler, assist the patient in the decision-making process? Or are such determinations beyond the jurisdiction of both physician and patient, belonging only to the province of lawyers and the judicial process? Or do the ultimate answers rest with the clergy and the church?

There are no social issues to be faced by an individual or the public which are without value determinations, and which do not force ethical considerations. In the social and health care delivery system every institution, every provider, faces ethical determinants every day.[28] Medicine makes decisions about caring for pain, for the dying, and for the treatment of illness and disability. Social health value determination is operative when "someone" decides to use machines to sustain life. In New York State, that "someone" is the courts which have ruled that doctors, family members, and selected others are to testify before the court so it can arrive at a decision on a patient-by-patient basis. Pope John Paul II, among others, has rejected this legal intrusion on patient, family, and doctor determination to sustain life of the dying. Another value determinant is the transplanting of organs. "Someone" decides who is the best candidate to receive the limited supply of viable organs. Renal dialysis is now readily available due to federal support for those with kidney disorders. The availability is irrespective of age, degree of illness, severity, and complexity of disorder as illustrated in given instances by the aged, terminally ill who are given a short extension of life. Abortions are available to control the number of children a woman wants to have, or to prevent the birth of defective children. Behavior control is possible through psychotropic drugs, as well as through behavior modification techniques.

At the societal level, the values are frequently reflected by groups of individuals who are with special interests. Those interests carry through a range of processes, political and social, if they are to become law such as the legalization of abortions, albeit with much political pressure from anti-abortionists to overthrow the Supreme Court decision. Another special interest in medicine is its pursuit of new advances and new medical technology such as in transplantation or in life-sustaining machines. In these instances, the availability of the technology affects the public choice.

At the patient-practitioner level, there are values in decision making, translated into ethical behavior. "How much to tell" the terminally ill is one illustration. In individual cases, ethical behaviors are usually situationally determined. Situations are individually perceived and the ethical behaviors may differ from situation to situation, from practitioner to practitioner. One physician may practice "heroic" medicine, utilizing life-sustaining equipment and another may reject such an approach on comparable situations of terminally dying patients.

Values are subjectively perceived. The consumer's expectations derive from

---

[28] The following discussion on values and ethics derives in part from *Ethical Dilemmas in Health Care*, ed. Helen Rehr (New York: Prodist, 1978), and from Helen Rehr "Ethical Dilemmas in Health Care Delivery," *Journal of Social Process*, XIX (1981), pp. 55-63.

the values he or she holds when entering the practitioner's office. The practitioner has a set of personally held values. Both consumer and practitioner values derive from the range of external and internal factors to which each has been exposed. Some factors that influence practitioners are their perceptions of themselves as experts, and expertise is translated into a professionalism commanding their first loyalty. Where many professionals and paraprofessionals are engaged in the laying on of hands, interventions with the patient become diffuse and tend to dilute or reduce the commitment of each of the practitioners, thus lowering the ethical demand.

On the other hand, the human service practitioner has had special education in knowledge and remedies, along with special training to deal with ailment and illnesses. That knowledge is translated into an "art" of practice based on principles which include "listening," "individualizing," and "helping" skills. These are ethical behaviors which serve the practitioner in caring for the patient. The quality and character of the behaviors are personally and situationally determined in the one-on-one. The focus on the individual situation is, in itself, a value. Professional education for medical and nursing students is primarily based on the specific individual, and is diagnosis-treatment focused. For social workers the emphasis is on the broader social good, and systems of care are seen in the context of the public's social health. Although the latter concept is emphasized more or less for the three different health care professions, it tends to be less emphasized for the clinician-to-be than for the future social worker.

The conflict exists between planners and practitioners when one views the growing commitment to medical and social technology. Rashi Fein suggests there is too little cost-benefit in the enormously expensive federally supported program for kidney dialysis and transplants because it benefits too few.[29] The monies could have been more effectively allocated if the program chosen was directed to a larger portion of the population. There is the argument that the single-disease support is a response to the pressure of a powerful special interest group, and dilutes the aid to vast numbers in the population suffering from a range of chronic illnesses and disorders. In defending the research support of a single illness, the clinician argues that in the prolongation of or in the benefit to one life, there is justification of the cost. The patient, of course, agrees with this belief. Provider and consumer values are together when service is focused on the individual.

"There is no ready reconciliation of values relevant to the individual good and those relevant to the common good."[30] There are values relevant to the interaction between consumer and practitioner. "Humanistic ethics" derived from experience suited to contemporary society and not dependent on the interpretations placed on them by the professions or by society, tend to be more relevant to direct care. The primary value in the direct service arena is the autonomy of the individual served.

[29] Rashi Fein, "On Achieving Access and Equity in Health Care," *Milbank Memorial Fund Quarterly*, 50, no. 4 (October 1972), part 2, p. 157.

[30] S. Bosch, H. Rehr, and H. Lewis, "Some Suggested Remedies, Resolutions and Future Deliberations," *Ethical Dilemmas in Health Care*, p. 81.

The primary value at the level of the public good is equitable access to and availability of health care.

In their roles of helping and advocating for patients, social workers are confronted with the same moral and ethical dilemmas as are all health providers. This is to suggest that "moral righteousness" by any one professional is not the avenue for the resolution of ethical dilemmas. In practice, individual case circumstances may highlight moral and ethical issues that are perceived differently from provider to provider, from patient to patient. The physician's value system and professional code may dictate that every technological aid should be used to sustain a patient's life; the patient and or family may not agree. In these cases the social worker is an intermediary, skillfully interacting with physician, patient, and family, sharing and interpreting communications with them from all the case data at hand. The worker may need to reconcile his or her personal value system with the values of the profession. They may not be congruent in every instance. For one worker, securing an abortion for a fifteen-year-old girl may be seen as a desired case goal; another worker may "press" the client—albeit subliminally—for a different resolution to the problem. Again, filling a prescription form for the psychiatrists's signature provokes no ethical dilemmas for one social worker, while it may for another. Value systems are not packaged for the marketplace, readily available for use by the purchaser. Rather, in the years ahead, dilemmas about ethics and values will dictate a most important reason for collaborative activity among the health professions as they work toward new insights that will enhance case management predicaments.

SOCIAL WORK HEALTH
SERVICES TOMORROW

Where will social work practice? Who will be its clientele? What will clients seek; what will they need? Under what arrangements? How will client services be paid? There is much to deliberate on. Neil Bracht indicates that while illness and chronic illness and disabilities are here to stay, new organizational designs will be essential to deal with the range of social, medical, and psychiatric problems presented by different segments of the population.[31]

Social work can make its contribution to social health services because it is the single profession that brings a concentration not only to individuals and families, but also to environmental systems. Social work is oriented to an overall system of services, recognizing the need of and the means to coordination, continuity, and the comprehensiveness of health care. It can be actively involved in assuring the implementation of these functions within the single program as well as in multiinstitutional sets of arrangements. Social work's commitment to milieu and its sensitivity to uncovering program and system obstacles to care leaves it in an excellent

---

[31] Neil F. Bracht, "Policy and Practice for Tomorrow's Health Care," paper presented at the 75th Anniversary Social Work Grand Rounds, New York: Mt. Sinai Hospital, February 18, 1981.

position to serve as ombudsman or advocate within the institution and also with community service agencies.

For reasons of choice and institutional need, delivering direct services to individuals and families will continue to be the social worker s primary function. We hope this book has amply demonstrated why this is so. How valued the social worker is as an essential health provider will depend upon the priorities the profession sets for what it can do, not only for consumers but for the institutions and systems that provide health care. To dichotomize the patient from the setting, to treat and advocate for the former with little attention to the latter, will place social work in jeopardy. This is not to suggest that there are no tensions between those served and those who provide services. The resolution of tensions and obstacles as far as social work is concerned, depends—as we have frequently reenforced the point—upon how well the social worker can identify the sources of problems, many of which are structurally and organizationally determined.

Services at the micro level continue to have priority, as they have had in the past because it is at this level that the social worker as helper, enabler, and supporter meets the pain, despair, and hurts of the patient and his family. The laying on of hands during a physical or emotional crisis or an extended illness provides the patient the reassurance that the social worker will modify the sources of institutional and environmental stress as much as possible. For cases of terminal illness, the worker, acutely attuned to the needs of family as well as patient, will help them in their pregrief and will offer professional sustenance during the patient's final days.

Quality discharge planning will continue as a major function. Early casefinding and or early referral is essential so that family members are involved in seeing the hospital experience, irrespective of disorder or illness, as a therapeutic but transitory one. Social work emphasis with patient and family will be directed toward homecoming as early as possible, to identify the social supports needed and available, and to work toward securing what is needed while also encouraging a self-care point of view. Family members would be urged to make regular visits to patients, dealing with homecoming planning while "how-to" skills and supports of the patient's at-home convalescence are taught, or made available where essential. The hospital will need to bring a new perspective by adding to diagnostic and treatment phases, one of developing self-care support for the patient's return to the community replacing that of concentrating on convalescence alone.

Social workers in hospitals are seeing three main groups of patients at this time: the long stay, consisting of the elderly sick and those with on-going chronic disorders suffering severe exacerbations; the very sick for whom social and physical rehabilitation is possible and those who may be in preterminal state; and those who have been involved in social diseases, social disorders, or in major stress problems which have been somatized. All these patients require on-going social and health services, and not solely fragmented nor periodic care related to crises. Although cures are not available, care would need to be continuous and available with emphases on self-care, developing adaptations, learning to anticipate critical incidents, and to draw on the social health care system which knows the patient and family and is prepared to offer what is needed. The on-going services that are needed are best offered outside of the hospital system in a network which encompasses the social and health services of a region.

At the macro level as well, there will be multiple functions for the social worker, although at this point the nature of regionalization, mergers, or multi-institutional arrangements is worrisome to many professionals. They see it as a loss of professional and or institutional autonomy. Others believe this organizational direction is the only way to safeguard the coordination of care, reduce duplication, overlap, and even the abuse of services. They see regionalization as a programmatic approach to offering comprehensive services. Social work services would have a place in the new institutional arrangements. If services are perceived in a continuum and linked, then social work services could reach beyond the walls of the hospital into the community network of social and health services. Given what exists in the present social and health institutional arrangements, it is conceivable that one program of social work services could be contracted for by others. Continuity and on-going care would be available. Information giving would be relevant to the linked services and referrals would be transfers of individuals and families (perhaps even the same staff) within the network of social work services. Primary care could be made available within the community. Such programs require not only somatic care programs but also social, psychological, and environmental support services. It is within these programs that people present their everyday problems. Such programs could be staffed at least with physicians, nurse clinicians, and social workers. Each would carry appropriate primary caretaking roles, drawing selectively on the others as needed. A triage at first entry could be helpful as well. One would antici-pate that there would be more of the elderly using such a service, also those with chronic diseases, and perhaps even young families seeking help with child-rearing problems.

The social work services network could share operational demands such as information systems, purchasing, billing, staffing, administrative programming, and accountability mechanisms. Although safeguarding confidentiality, service profiles on recipients of services could be shared. In addition they would share in data col-lection and needed studies, which could be relevant to targeted populations, and not limited to those who are sick and use the services, but also general needs and gaps in what is available. Such studies would be regionally rather than solely institu-tionally based, so that regional and institutional needs could be addressed for over-all planning and programming. On the other hand, institutional studies could dem-onstrate their impact on delivery of care, in the personnel and service sense, and on patient and family response and outcomes. Social workers could study the effec-tiveness of their programs, not only within the single institution, but across the range of institutions with specificity to targeted populations, special problems, and by interventions available.

The principles of regionalization are in sharing and in the exchange of perti-nent information and services. It would require new organizational designs to safe-guard not only patient's rights but linkage and coordination for continuity of care. A regional social health system would mean that individuals would have to get to the appropriate service. A centralized triage system safeguarding access entry and routing would be essential. Social work can make a major contribution to triage, referral, and tracking, as well as follow-up to safeguard the entry of individuals in need, and their continuance with recommended care.

The social and health needs have been demonstrated, the traditional and some innovative programs discussed along with a social work repertoire for effective partnership in dealing with needs and in organizations. How will they be paid? Should social work find its way into the marketing of social services on an income-producing basis or should it fight for the support of social services in the political arena? Social workers can remain a salaried enterprise within institutions and perform cost effectively and beneficially with clients. However, in remaining salaried, as evidenced with all of the social and health institutions, it is subject to the consequences of fiscal constraints. Where social work can demonstrate significant benefits to institution and individuals, it is likely that funds to support it would continue to the extent that it proves cost beneficial. This is not to suggest that institutional administrators are blind to the value of social service but that from the array of essential services, they may choose those which are more immediately relevant and needed, hoping that the social components would be addressed in the larger arena of the community. In addition, it is not meant to suggest that social workers shun the responsibility for affecting the social policy of the institution and the programs for which they work. However, fiscal reimbursement policy is made at the macro level and is translated to the micro level in support of direct and indirect services. If social workers are to be effective regarding social policy at the institutional level they would need to be very knowledgeable about the setting itself, how people enter and leave the setting, what they ask for and get, the medical policies and programs, the sources of all dollars which flow in (and out), who allocates what, and how. What is needed is as complete a knowledge of the system, the power bases, chain of command, decision makers, the linkages, and its functional orientation. A knowledge of the organization is not impossible to achieve. Social workers need to know that it is essential to have if the micro level of social policy is to be affected. They will need to make their services visible by assisting providers to know who gets their services, the benefits to recipients, and the benefits to the provider system. When social work communicates with others as to what it does, it makes itself visible; it involves itself so that it creates a constituency of supporters, both clients and other health care providers. Both are needed to reinforce the need for social services. Applied research is another means by which social work can make its cost-benefit visible. Outcome studies have a here-and-now value, as well as serving to underpin program enhancement. Application benefits to practice come from participating in studies within social work or on an interdisciplinary basis. Therefore, ideas for study should come from the practitioners themselves, and the outcomes made known to anyone who is in a decision-making role.

Given the current circumstances of administrative fiscal constraints and the social climate, social work will have three options: to negotiate in the political arena for the support of social services, to demonstrate the cost-benefit to beneficiaries as well as the providers of social services, and to market social services as income producing. It is the opinion of the authors that all three must be undertaken and concurrently. We have addressed the political processes and the cost-benefit (outcomes) of social services, here and in earlier chapters. But here it is important to reenforce the importance of marketing social services. Marketing connotes that a relationship between the service given and payment for it can be established. We shall not discuss the economics of marketing a product or a service, other than to indicate that the need and value has to be perceived at a feasible cost before there is willingness to buy it. In its way, establishing the cost-benefit of social services to institutional administrators is "marketing" the product. The cost of the services is borne for its indirect benefit to the institution and its perceived benefits to consumers.

Social services can be marketed beyond the hospital arena into industry and into unions by demonstrating the cost-benefit particularly in prevention and health promotion which permit beneficiaries of such programs to continue to conduct business as usual without the effects of breakdown in their personal and social systems. In addition, as health care providers are moving to market their services in a variety of group practice models, social workers could join them or set up side-by-side with a fee-for-service program. Whether private fee-for-services are set up in a so-called medical arts enterprise, within the medical institution, or in doctor's offices, they could serve as extensions of the institution s social services which are directly income producing and which serve to offset the costs of other established social work programs. The fees could be borne by those who could afford to pay them and who see the value of the services. Private social services have succeeded in the marketplace. Also, to a certain extent insurance coverage already exists for social work visits; however, this third-party coverage would need to be considerably expanded. If social health programs are to include social and health education, self-care, health promotion, industrial and occupational health, and short-term services, it is very likely that industry and unions will continue to seek insured coverage for their employees. Social work could claim these areas. Also, if coverage is expanded to include at-home support, home care, crisis intervention, and long-term care coverage for hospice or extended or nursing home services, and family counseling, these could be claimed by social work. Employee assistance programs, in particular alcohol and drug abuse, could be social work managed. Consultations and diagnostic services in regard to individuals suffering chronic diseases which are supported by disease-specific foundations such as muscular dystrophy, could be contracted for, as could the treatment of these individuals. As the self-help group programs expand, social work could offer consultation on a fee-for-service basis. The professional associations and leaders have been working toward achieving insured coverage for social work services through its efforts in seeking credentialing, licensing, and vendor status for the profession.

Can social work offer its services within its own autonomy, separate but linked to the medical establishment? Is it possible to create a social health maintenance system under social work's direction and leadership? In a tight market and in one of fiscal constraints, a surplus of physicians and other health care providers may mean they would seek to broaden their scope of services and compete for the same clientele. The objective will be to defend the mixed practice domain by expanding the coverage to include as wide a market as possible. Social work will need to "market" in such a way as to secure constituencies for its services. However, the doctor's office or the medical group practice and certainly the Health Maintenance Organization are the likely loci for social work services for the private clientele of physicians.

Although the decade ahead will see less federal involvement in health care along with tighter fiscal controls at state and local levels, every man, woman, and child will nevertheless require health care. We have little doubt but that social work will continue to be a part of the health care scene. But it too must enter the marketplace, as well as the political arena. The social work profession will need to innovate and build upon its health-mental health curricula, set rigorous standards for training social workers at both micro and macro levels, and then identify the entry points into the health care system—some still to be tested—and thereby continue to keep its commitment to all people who need social services as they seek health care.

REFERENCES

BOSCH, S., REHR, H., & LEWIS, H. Some suggested remedies, resolutions and future deliberations. In H. Rehr (Ed.) *Ethical Dilemmas in Health Care*. New York: Prodist, 1978.

BRACHT, NEIL F. Policy and practice for tomorrow's health care. Paper presented at 75th Anniversary Social Work Grand Rounds, The Mt. Sinai Hospital, New York, February 18, 1981.

COGGESHALL, LOWELL. *Planning for medical progress through education*. A report submitted to the Executive Council of the Association of American Medical Colleges, April 1965.

COMMISSION ON CHRONIC ILLNESS. *Chronic illness in the United States*. Vol. IV. Cambridge, Mass.: Harvard University Press, 1957.

"Control Means Benefit Limit." *The nation's health*. August 1971.

DI PAOLO, V. Non-profits predict rise in contract business. *Modern Health Care*, April 1978, *8*.

DONABEDIAN, AVEDIS. Models for organizing the delivery of personal health services and criteria for evaluating them. *Milbank Memorial Fund Quarterly*, October 1972, 50 (4).

EISENBERG, LEON. The search for care. *Daedalus*, Winter 1977.

FEIN, RASHI. On achieving access and equity in health care. *Milbank Memorial Fund Quarterly*, October 1972, 50 (4).

FIZDALE, RUTH. *Social agency structure and accountability*. Fair Lawn, N.J.: R. E. Burdick, 1974.

FOX, RENEE C. The medicalization and demedicalization of American society. *Daedalus*, Winter 1977, 6 (1).

FUCHS, VICTOR R. Economics, health and post-industrial society. *Health and Society*, Spring 1979, *57* (2).

GINZBERG, ELI. Large-scale growth in health dollars attracts attention of for-profit sector. *Hospitals*, July 16, 1981, *55* (14).

GINZBERG, ELI. The pursuit of equity: Mirage or reality. *Columbia*, Fall 1978.

KNOWLES, JOHN H. (Ed.) Doing better and feeling worse: Health in the United States. New York: W. W. Norton & Co., Inc., 1977.

LaLONDE, MARC. *A new perspective on the health of Canadians.* Information Canada. Ottawa, 1978.

NATIONAL WOMEN'S HEALTH NETWORK, 2075 I Street NW, Washington, D.C. 20006.

REHR, HELEN. Ethical dilemmas in health care delivery. *Journal of Social Process*, 1981, 19.

REHR, HELEN (Ed.) *Ethical dilemmas in health care.* New York: Prodist, 1978.

ROSENBERG, GARY & WEISSMAN, ANDREW. Marketing social services in health care facilities. *Health and Social Work*, August 1981, 6 (3).

ROGERS, DAVID E. The challenge of primary care. In John H. Knowles (Ed.) *Doing better and feeling worse: Health in the United States*, New York: W. W. Norton & Co., Inc., 1977.

SHEPS, CECIL G. The influence of consumer sponsorship on medical services. *Milbank Memorial Fund Quarterly*, October 1972, 50 (4).

"Some Hospitals Are Entering Diverse Businesses, Often Unrelated to Medicine, to Offset Losses." *The Wall Street Journal*, August 12, 1981.

"Third Party Payments Signed into Law, Chapter 893, in 1977." Reported in *Currents*. Newsletter of Metropolitan Chapter, National Association of Social Workers, October 1977.

THOMAS, LEWIS. On the science and technology of medicine. *Daedalus*, Winter 1977.

ZUCKER, LEON. A look to the past offers hope for the future. *Hospitals*, July 1981.

AUTHOR INDEX

SUBJECT INDEX

DATE DUE

DEMCO 38-297